FINANCIAL CRISIS

FINANCIAL CRISIS
Causes, context and consequences

Adrian Buckley

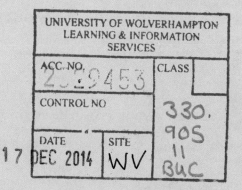
Financial Times
Prentice Hall
is an imprint of

Harlow, England • London • New York • Boston • San Francisco • Toronto
Sydney • Tokyo • Singapore • Hong Kong • Seoul • Taipei • New Delhi
Cape Town • Madrid • Mexico City • Amsterdam • Munich • Paris • Milan

Pearson Education Limited
Edinburgh Gate
Harlow
Essex CM20 2JE
England

and Associated Companies throughout the world

Visit us on the World Wide Web at:
www.pearsoned.co.uk

First published 2011

ISBN: 978-0-273-73511-3

British Library Cataloguing-in-Publication Data
A catalogue record for this book is available from the British Library

Library of Congress Cataloging-in-Publication Data
A catalog record for this book is available from the Library of Congress

10 9 8 7 6 5 4 3 2 1
15 14 13 12 11

Typeset in 9/13pt Stone Sans by 3
Printed and bound by Henry Ling Ltd, at the Dorset Press, Dorchester, Dorset

Contents

Supporting resources
Visit **www.pearsoned.co.uk/buckley**

For instructors

- Complete, downloadable Instructor's Manual
- Testbank of questions with guidelines for solutions useful for class discussion, and practice essays or examination assessments
- Additional FT articles
- Overview of the key issues in press cuttings
- Model teaching structure for financial crisis course

For more information please contact your local Pearson Education sales representative or visit **www.pearsoned.co.uk/buckley**

Preface

This book is concerned, as its title implies, with the real story of the 2007/8 financial crisis – its prelude, its unfolding and its aftermath up to June 2010, the time of writing. First of all there is a slight need for clarification of terms. The amounts of money being discussed are big bucks. So, the expression one million equals a thousand thousand: one billion equals a thousand million: one trillion equals one thousand billion.

Government, banking and regulatory elites have attempted to pass responsibility for the crisis on to others and blur the reality of the débâcle. This is because the driving forces of the collapse reside, primarily, with these establishment groups themselves. But they must be seen to be above reproach for the failure of the system. Rather than shouldering the blame, the financial élite has attempted to dodge culpability and point the finger at the subprime mortgage industry. Sure, low-quality borrowers were players on the scene of the carnage. But the reality is that the amount of subprime mortgages outstanding in 2007 might have been USD1.3 trillion, in all, whilst the destruction in terms of bank and financial institution losses totalled well over USD3 trillion. And, don't forget, not every subprime loan was a wipeout for the lending mortgage bank. Far from it. As explained in the chapters that follow, the infectious financial plague known as the credit default swap was mutating and multiplying and was the key to the meltdown. Developed by the financial industry, beloved of bankers whose bonuses blossomed in the good times, the credit default swap was an accident waiting to happen. And, unless outlawed or tamed by the time this book comes to the bookshops, it still is.

The total value of live credit default swap contracts in 2007 was a staggering USD60 trillion plus. Perhaps 70 per cent of this sum represented hedged transactions. That would leave USD18 trillion of speculative plays. In the text, we estimate that the financial annihilation may have cost USD2.4 trillion in government bailouts related to credit default swap contracts. Despite research in the area, we cannot be sure what proportion of credit default swap contracts was hedged. The above figure is merely an estimate. But it is close to that resulting from government bailouts as calculated and published by the International Monetary Fund. And there were other losses that did not require government bailout, as well as further losses unrelated to credit default swaps.

The evidence that we do have on the crash of 2007/8 indicates that guilt certainly resides with the bankers, amongst others. Their USD60 trillion monster was more destructive than Dracula and – we will argue – is as deserving of the same fate. Explanation and discussion await the diligent reader.

Coupled with the efforts of governments to court voter approval by keeping a boom in their economies going without thinking about taking the champagne away before the party became a riot, easy money and ludicrously low interest rates turned a bubble into a balloon. Rather than addressing the problem, their mantra, 'We have conquered boom and bust', plus an illusion of super-growth forever was meant to lull the electorate into comatose quiescence. And they almost succeeded.

In fact, comatose quiescence spread to the governments themselves and to the financial regulators and to the bonus-bloated bankers. Their supine indulgence of a system out of control was an amazing phenomenon surely not witnessed since Nero and the burning of the Eternal City.

It is my contention that these élite groups – banks, governments, and regulators – have attempted to pass the buck for their own irresponsibility onto the subprime business. After all, markets and bankers have to be seen to be above blame. They serve the forces of supply and demand and arrive at prices. An examination of these arguments, among other things, is contained in the chapters that follow. I hope that they constitute a good story for you: it has been fascinating for me.

I believe that capitalism, like democracy, is the least bad system. The intent here is not to point a finger at capitalism. But it is an attempt to come up with a fair view of the crash of 2007/8 in a no-stone-unturned retelling that is instructive and thought-provoking. Like all history, it cannot be objective. Edward Gibbon reckoned that history was 'the register of the crimes, follies and misfortunes of mankind'. In writing this book, I was reminded of Gibbon's words.

■ Readership

The book is aimed at the interested reader as well as students on courses in economics, finance, business studies, history, politics and ethics. They may be on MBA courses or pursuing undergraduate or postgraduate studies. But the book is also structured to tell a story that the non-specialist can readily understand. I hope that the topic is sufficiently well explained and interesting to ensure that the layperson will stick with it to the end. My intention is essentially practical. It is that this book should improve understanding and awareness in an area that is both fascinating and often misunderstood.

Should this book be adopted for use in class, there is a separate Instructors' Manual which includes teaching notes, case study suggestions with possible approaches on their use, plus further questions and guidelines towards solutions.

Acknowledgements

I am most infinitely grateful to Liz Tribe who once again deciphered my handwriting, suggested improvements, marshalled information and press cuttings and cheerfully converted untidy notes into this manuscript. Dealing with my quirky sense of humour and putting up with my ability to lose critical papers, articles and books is sincerely applauded. Thank you Liz. Of course, errors and failures of explanation should be debited to my account.

I should also like to express gratitude to my emeritus professorial colleague at Cranfield School of Management, part of Cranfield University, David Myddelton, who offered counsel and constructive criticism. May I also thank the anonymous survey respondents to a questionnaire on the appropriateness of topics covered in this book. Some of the materials comprising chapters and case studies have been used in class, seminar and tutorial sessions and I should like to express my appreciation of suggested improvements and critical input from students too numerous to mention individually.

Many thanks are also due to my five editorial contacts at FT Prentice Hall in the run-up to publication – Kate Brewin, Robin Lupton, Ellen Morgan, Mary Lince and Matthew Smith. You did a great job.

Adrian Buckley

■ Publisher's acknowledgements

We are grateful to the following for permission to reproduce copyright material:

Figures
Figure 2.1 from www.bea.gov; Figure 2.3 from http://www.statistics.gov.uk, Office of National Statistics; Figures 3.1, 3.5 from Organisation for Economic Co-operation and Development, http://www.oecd.org/; Figure 15.1 from *The Great Contraction 1929–1933*, Princeton University Press (Friedman, M. and Schwartz, AJ 1963); Figures Appendix.1, Appendix.2 from *Financial Times*, 13/09/2010, © The Financial Times Ltd; Figures Appendix.3, Appendix.4 from *The Economist*, 25/09/2010, pp. 2-3.

Text
Press cutting 10.1 from Lessons from the collapse of Bear Stearns, *Financial Times*, 15/03/2010 (Cassidy, John); Press cutting 11.1 from Alpha males must trade on more than machismo, *Financial Times*, 25/11/2009 (Coates, John); Press cutting 15.1 from Call this a recession? At least it isn't the Dark Ages, *Financial Times*, 23/12/2009 (Ward-Perkins, Bryan).

Financial Times
Press cutting 2.1 from One congressman, five finance lobbyists, *Financial Times*, 30/09/2009; Press cutting 6.1 from Tailgaters blight the markets as well as the motorways, *Financial*

Times, 20/01/2010 (Kay, John); Press cutting 8.1 from FSA under attack on regulation in boom, *Financial Times*, 17/04/2009 (Pickard, Jim); Press cutting 8.2 from Eaten alive by investment bankers, *Financial Times*, 17/04/2009 (Pickard, Jim); Press cutting 8.3 from FSA to be abolished in Osborne shake-up, *Financial Times*, 17/06/2010 (Parker, G and Masters, B); Press cutting 9.1 from The Madoff story reveals more faults, *Financial Times*, 05/04/2010 (Davis, Jonathan); Press cutting 11.2 from Beneath all the toxic acronyms lies a basic cultural issue, *Financial Times*, 26/11/2009 (MacKenzie, Donald); Press cutting 11.3 from Loss-making banks award bonuses, *Financial Times*, 31/07/2009 (Farrell, Greg); Press cutting 12.1 from Valukas report finds few heroes, *Financial Times*, 12/03/2010 (Baer, J. and Sender, H.); Press cutting 12.2 from Global harmony a distant prospect despite Lehman outrage, *Financial Times*, 16/03/2010 (Tett, Gillian); Press cutting 12.3 from Overpaid CEO award, *Financial Times*, 22/12/2008; Press cutting 13.1 from Northern Rock lacked proper financial controls, *Financial Times*, 14/04/2010 (Masters, Brooke and Goff, Sharlene); Press cutting 13.2 from Banks brought down by a new Peter Principle, *Financial Times*, 26/08/2009 (Kay, John); Press cutting 14.1 from Ireland's financial lessons, *Financial Times*, 14/06/2010; Press cutting 16.2 from An ABC of financial shocks and fiscal aftershocks, *Financial Times*, 29/05/2010 (Wolf, Martin); Press cutting 17.1 from Time to outlaw naked credit default swaps, *Financial Times*, 01/03/2010 (Munchau, Wolfgang).

In some instances we have been unable to trace the owners of copyright material, and we would appreciate any information that would enable us to do so.

Chapter 1

An overview of the financial crisis of 2007/8

■ Introduction

In presenting an overview of the crisis of 2007/8 it might seem logical to begin with a timeline of events in those two tumultuous years. Whilst we thought about beginning with just that approach, we felt that it would fail to do justice to the complicated story that preceded these two years. For the reality is that the foundations of the crisis were put in place in the years before its occurrence. With this background, we keep the timeline of relevant events in 2007 and in its aftermath until the end of this chapter.

■ The good times

The roots of the crisis were planted in the decade before 2007. In this ten-year period, real interest rates – arrived at by taking the actual quoted interest rate and deducting the actual achieved rate of inflation – were exceptionally low and public expenditure was growing rapidly. A quick look at Table 2.1 will show that real interest rates were actually negative in the USA in three of the first seven years of the 21st century – and in one other year the rate was zero. Low real rates were not just a feature of the US economy. This was an almost global phenomenon. It appeared that governments around the world were talking to each other to co-ordinate low real rates. Which is probably what occurred at all of those G6, G8 and G20 meetings at which nothing much seemed to be happening. They were bonding meetings to ensure that no single nation broke the coalition of low interest rates. And this fuelled boom times and a bubble in house prices in the USA, in the UK and elsewhere. Furthermore, banks, amongst others, were taking advantage of these low rates by increasing their debt levels as a proportion of total financing. Because debt was cheap, this could be viewed as an efficient move. But because debt interest ranks above dividends and because debt repayment ranks above shareholders' capital on liquidation it is also a source of greater risk from the standpoint of shareholders. A post-war figure for banks' debt to equity ratios of 10 to 1 moved nearer to 25 to 1, with some institutions having ratios of more than 33 to 1. At this latter figure, a drop in the worth of a bank's assets by a mere 3 per cent would wipe out the balance sheet value attributable to the ordinary shareholders. This represents risk-taking of staggering proportions. Typical businesses reckon that one part debt versus two parts equity is reasonable – and some banks were running at 33 parts debt to one part equity. Sure, every kind of business is different and every industry has different ratio standards. But our point is simple. Banks were taking on burgeoning debt. And too much debt equals too much financial risk.

Low interest rates fuelled a spend, spend, spend mentality on British high streets and on American main streets. Much of the US spending spree was on goods made in China. This had an effect on Chinese government policy. Its central bank was a buyer of US dollars from Chinese exporters. They were in receipt of US dollars from their exports to the USA. And the central bank of China recirculated these dollars by purchasing US government bonds. If the Chinese had sold the US dollars and bought their own currency, this would have weakened the dollar and strengthened the Chinese renminbi (also known as the Chinese yuan) and this would lessen, somewhat, China's competitiveness. Since China was simply investing its dollars in US government bonds, no such disadvantage for exporters accrued.

But through being a purchaser of US Treasury bonds, China's willingness to acquire trillions of dollars worth of US dollar government securities meant that the USA was getting its funds to balance its deficits more cheaply than might otherwise have been the case. All jolly convenient for the USA because it kept its interest rates low. All jolly convenient for the Chinese in terms of their trade position. All jolly convenient for the US citizen who continued to enjoy low interest rates and cheap products from China.

American and European governments were undoubtedly influenced by the pleas of lobby groups to keep the boom going. They were also a major force in hastening deregulation of the banking systems. Around the world governments were basking in the glory of booming economies with happy consumers (therefore happy voters), bingeing on borrowed money, buying properties that they could not afford and enjoying a wave of consumerism that, seemingly, would never end. Presidents and finance ministers had a new mantra – 'We have conquered boom and bust'.

Cast your eyes forward to Figure 3.1 and look at the increase of household indebtedness as a percentage of disposable income. And Figure 3.2 shows total US household debt. Figures 3.3. and 3.4 graph the explosion in UK and US average house prices respectively. Look at Figure 3.5 showing average annual house price inflation in real terms (that is, with average country inflation taken out). Clearly a bubble was being inflated. In truth though, what began as a bubble was rapidly becoming a balloon.

■ New models of lending

Since the mid-nineties, the US government had been singing the virtues of wider home-ownership and they had set up various agencies aiming to make this easier. This process was helped by the changing nature of bank lending. This involved a move away from the traditional model of originate-to-hold to the new model of originate-to-distribute. What does this mean? Under the traditional model, a mortgage bank would lend against the security of a home and the bank would hold the debt and receive interest and capital repayments. Under the originate-to-distribute model, things are different. The bank lends against the security of a home, but, instead of holding the debt, the bank sells on the debt to another bank or to a specialist financial institution where a series of similar loans, bought from various mortgage banks, are parcelled together and sold on to others as a package called an MBS (mortgage backed security). Alternatively, the financial institution which has bought the mortgages may mix them up with other debts – such as motor car loans, credit card debt, corporate loans and others – and the bundle is sold on as a CDO (collateralised debt obligation). This process is called securitisation. It should be clear that where the bank holds the mortgage debt under the traditional originate-to-hold model for, perhaps, 20 or 25 years it will be likely to be careful about its customers' abilities to repay and it will carry out a diligent appraisal in this area. However, under originate-to-distribute, one might expect that screening of borrowers to be at a lower level of care. And this was the case.

It wasn't just mortgage banks that were selling debt to be repackaged. Commercial banks (those that take customers' deposits and make lendings to their customers) were doing the same in respect of loans to companies and credit card debt. The consequence of all of this was that the exacting standards and procedures that banks had worked to in terms of credit analysis were being jettisoned. The disciplines that had been built up over generations were being dumped.

Mortgage loans were being sold on to third parties for securitisation and the model of lending had moved to originate-to-distribute. Given this background, mortgage lenders were more inclined to respond to government cajoling – and there was a lot of it, especially in the USA – to lend more to weak credit customers. After all, the banks were not holding these subprime loans on their own balance sheets but selling them on. The oil to grease the wheels of subprime lending was gushing from government goading and securitisation.

The lax nature of mortgage banks' appraisal procedures under the new model of originate-to-distribute meant that dodgy deals developed. For example, there were scams in which mortgage brokers and builders – and sometimes lawyers too – would collude to receive monies from lenders in excess of market value. This frequently involved buy-to-let properties and often involved off-plan homes where the properties had not yet been let or sold respectively. Often, houses were described to lenders as having been sold off-plan without any such deal having been made – but with a fictitious purchaser invented as part of the scam. Another dirty trick involved borrowers indicating that they would occupy a property when, in reality, purchasing it as an investment to let or, more likely, to trade on – flipping. Also, mortgage brokers were aiding borrowers to falsify their employment history and/or income level by creating false documents – the liar loan. This might involve hiding critical information. And some lenders were even accepting self-certified income figures. That is, self-certified by the borrower. This facility was on offer from a vast percentage of the lenders in the market. What sort of diligence is this?

Mortgage lending criteria which had traditionally been on the basis of the lower of three times the borrower's income or 90 to 95 per cent of the value of the property mortgaged were being stretched. Some lenders were offering loans of 100 per cent plus on homes. Northern Rock – a UK mortgage bank – was offering, via its 'Together' brand, a deal of 125 per cent based on 95 per cent of the property value plus a 30 per cent top-up unsecured loan and a lending facility based on six times income.

■ The time bomb ticks

Add to all this, a new kid on the block – the credit default swap (CDS). Imagine a contract in which one party (A) makes a series of payments, rather like insurance premiums, to a counterparty (B) and, in exchange, B would pay to A a capital sum if the credit instrument to which the CDS relates defaults. This instrument could be a bond or a loan of company C. The credit default that triggers the payment from B to A would typically be non-payment of interest or failure to make a capital repayment by company C in respect of the bond or loan to which the CDS relates.

If there were no default by company C then A would pay to B the series of payments for the life of the CDS. Figure 6.1 will make matters easier to understand. There is a secondary market in which CDSs can be traded. A secondary market is one in which second-hand shares, or other financial securities, can be sold and bought – for example, a stock exchange. CDS contracts are very much like insurance. But there are differences. The need-to-know difference at this stage is as follows. Neither party to a CDS needs to own the underlying security (the bond or loan of company C in our example) to which the CDS relates. Neither the buyer nor the seller of the CDS has to suffer a loss from the default event. This is different to insurance. With insurance, the insured has to have an insurable interest under which they can demonstrate a potential loss should the default occur. As the reader can see, insurance is available to enable one to hedge risk. With a CDS, one can hedge risk (if A held the loan or bond in company C in our example) and one can gamble.

Credit default swaps may be available on a company's debt, on a country's bonds or on a package of mortgages (MBS) or on CDOs. The CDS also differs from insurance because there is no legal limit to the number of credit default swaps that can be entered into in respect of a particular risk. So company C may have debt of USD5 billion but there could be CDS outstanding on company C debt totalling USD100 billion, or even USD1 trillion.

Now for an amazing aspect of our story. MBS and CDO securities packed full of subprime mortgages suddenly transformed from what was really junk status (really low-grade debt, as subprime mortgages are) to triple A status (the highest grade debt). Not since the frog turned into a prince thanks (most people think) to the kiss of a princess has a greater metamorphosis occurred. Actually in the original Brothers Grimm story of *The Frog Prince*, the transformation was achieved by the king's daughter throwing the frog with all her strength against the wall. We rather suspect that might have been a more appropriate fate for the MBSs, the CDOs and the CDSs. Anyway, the frog to prince transmutation was just a fairy story. Subprime mortgages to triple A was reality. How was this transmogrification achieved?

Two ways. By tranching the mortgage pool in an MBS – see Figure 5.1 – such that if the MBS produces losses, the first losses fall on the lowest tranche (maybe rated B), the next loss falls on the next lowest tranche (rated BB) and so on until the last tranche to suffer the loss would be the AAA-rated part of the MBS. For a quick review of what bond ratings imply, see Figure 5.3. The second part of the alchemy emanated from a well-reasoned and influential article written by David X Li – the details of which will have to wait until Chapter 6. Base metal was transformed to gold. That the flaws in the David X Li paper went unspotted for so long may have been helped by the fact that it fitted the ideology of Wall Street.

Credit default swaps were written on MBSs, CDOs and even bundled into debt packages. The blow-up in financial markets began with subprime debt but the major cause was the CDS. The subprime mortgage market had debt outstanding of USD1.3 trillion at its peak. The CDS market had USD60 trillion outstanding at its peak. If every subprime mortgage had defaulted, the overall loss could surely have been contained – with some pain, of course. But the CDS market was much bigger. And it has been estimated by the International Monetary Fund (IMF), in its *Global Financial Stability Report* of April 2010, that bailed out losses in this area may have totalled USD2.3 trillion, although it is too soon for us to be wholly certain of this amount. The fact is that it is big bucks. Compare it with the total income of America. The GDP of the USA was around USD14 trillion in 2009.

The transformation of frog to prince was reversed back to frog when defaults began. These had negative implications for many CDS positions. With no default or only a low probability of default, a CDS might have a positive value, say 100 based on the expected income from the stream of insurance-like premiums exceeding the expected pay-out under default. But with defaults looming and then actually happening, the worth of the CDS could alter and even move to a negative value as the chances of paying out to the protection purchaser (the insured) increased. What was an asset worth 100 in the example may become a liability worth minus 100 or minus 500. And this is what happened. It was a time bomb that exploded and wiped out Lehman Brothers and, but for government intervention, would have done the same to HBOS and RBS.

■ The time bomb explodes

The CDS market involves some banks and financial institutions as sellers and other banks and financial institutions as buyers. With so many CDSs written on MBSs and CDOs containing mortgage debt, declines in the housing market would have a massively magnified negative impact on values in the market for such securities and financial products. Remember that you could have securitised mortgages of USD10 billion with credit default swaps totalling USD500 billion or even more written on them. Hence the magnification. And this adverse effect would not be felt just in terms of values but it would impact market liquidity – which could quite easily dry up completely.

That is just what happened. The US Federal Reserve Funds rate was 1 per cent in 2005. By 2007, it had jumped to 5 per cent. When foreclosures on properties started to occur as the housing market began to head south, mortgage interest and capital repayments were not forthcoming and this was the income of the MBS and part of the income of the CDO and other similar instruments with housing debt mixed into them. Their market prices started to fall. First a trickle, then a cascade, then a storm – the metaphors gush. And they are no exaggeration. No one wanted this alphabet soup. Liquidity was at a standstill.

Over 2007, the drop in existing home sales was the steepest since 1989. In the first quarter of 2007, the S&P/Case-Shiller house price index for the USA recorded its first year-on-year fall in nationwide home prices since 1991. The subprime mortgage business was collapsing as interest rates peaked – see Figure 16.1 – and foreclosures accelerated.

In the economics textbooks, models nearly always assume that there is liquidity in markets – the price falls until buyers first nibble, then bite and this kickstarts (sorry, mixed metaphor) the upward trajectory. Reality in the latter half of 2007 was not like the textbooks.

With liquidity under pressure, it stalled when the players in the market started suspecting each other of having vast liabilities to pay out under credit default swaps – remember Figure 6.1. Banks had ceased dealing these instruments with one another. Worse, they stopped lending amongst themselves too. The inter-bank market was freezing over. This is normally an essential part of the banking business, enabling financial firms to square off positions arising from their daily cash in versus their daily cash out. Fear and panic were features of Wall Street, the City of London and elsewhere in the late summer of 2008. And, of course, stockmarkets were hit too.

■ Why, oh why, did no one see it coming?

Why didn't banks foresee this? After all, interest rates in the USA had been heading north-wards for some time. The answer to this question may lie in the risk management systems used by banks. Expectations of financial market fluctuations were substantially based upon movements in line with the normal distribution, or bell curve. The fact is that, whilst this may be almost true most of the time, it is an oversimplification because markets seem to behave according to fat tail models – see Figure 10.1 – and this means that extreme events, both positive and negative, occur more frequently than the bell curve model suggests. Bank risk management models are supposed to be augmented by 'what if?' simulation and scenario analysis. And, if one looks at Exhibit 16.1 harbingers of problems were there as interest rates climbed.

One of the remarkable things about markets is that their deviations from the bell curve are substantial. As we point out in Chapter 10, a leading pioneer in this area reported that had the Dow Jones index of industrial shares moved in accordance with the normal distribution it would have moved by 4.5 per cent or more on only six days in the period from 1996 to 2003. Whereas, in reality, it moved by at least this amount 366 times during the period.

Regulation of banks and financial institutions left something to be desired. This is an understatement. There are instances referred to in later chapters, for example, where the exploits of Bernard Madoff and his massive fraud were challenged by financial analysts but regulators failed to find anything untoward, where risk managers in banks discussed their worries with regulators who failed to react, and where the slow and possibly flawed reactions of accounting bodies who wished to maintain inflexibly their mark-to-market rules made matters worse. Regulators were widely guilty of groupthink and their common thought was that the housing boom was set to continue as interest rates seemed likely to remain low. Bankers, governments and consumers were also sucked into this naïve groupthink frame of mind.

Meanwhile, the carrot of massive bank bonuses led dealers in financial institutions to chase credit default swaps and related instruments even when markets started to look dodgy – see Figure 16.1 and Figure 6.1. The credit default swap figure (6.1) shows that as a CDS seller the bank will go on getting cash in, year after year, but will have to pay out on an eventual default. Dealers were getting big buck bonuses for selling CDSs but were incurring massive risks for their banks. A lot of these ex-dealers have moved on nowadays and own mansions and estates in the country. Bonuses were calculated individually year by year with no deductions when the day of reckoning arrived. In fact, for most bonus-bloated bankers, the day of reckoning did not arrive.

■ Escape

The economists' solution to banking crises is the mantra, 'Throw money at the problem and mop it up afterwards'. Essentially this is what governments did in order to breathe life into a banking system which was stalked by fear that counterparties might be wiped out – as some were. Some banks were nationalised, others received massive government injections of money in return for majority ownership in some cases, minority ownership in others. Some received guarantees from governments. A few were allowed to go bankrupt. Governments put money into the economy, sometimes via cheap loans to banks to encourage them to lend or at least not to sit on their hands and do nothing. Some of the impact of the money to the economy was via cuts in value added tax. All of this averted the possibility of another Great Depression. But the mopping up of this input is creating harder times for some, austerity for others.

Our discussion so far in this chapter has homed in on the key issues of the financial crisis of 2007/8. These problems will be analysed in detail in the chapters that follow. Many of the issues discussed receive academic scrutiny in the text *Restoring Financial Stability*, edited by Acharya and Richardson[1], and there is a range of books which we refer to as we progress from topic to topic. Coverage aimed at the general reader is provided in books by Paul Mason[2] and Vince Cable[3].

In Table 1.1, we present a summary of the key features of the financial crisis using just 16 bullet points. In Table 1.2, we list some of the key players who have been in office in Western countries, where the damage was done, during the build-up and in the aftermath of the crisis of 2007/8. Their office and tenure is shown. In reading the rest of this book, it may be useful to refer back to the names since some of them crop up regularly.

The timeline below presents milestones that summarise key events in the unfolding of the financial crisis. Of these events, the most critical are shown in bold.

Timeline of the financial crisis 2007/8

The prelude

- Low interest rates and housing boom in various countries, the USA and UK in particular.
- Various financial institutions take on large amounts of debt. Ratios of debt to equity rise to dangerously high levels.
- US government agencies successfully discriminate in favour of housing for the poor.
- US home ownership rising.
- Financial innovation embracing MBSs, CDOs and CDSs.
- Leading US academics warn on the housing bubble, credit default swaps and their potential effect on the financial system. They include Robert Shiller, Raghuram Rajan and Nouriel Roubini. In the UK, housing bubble warnings were frequently made by economist Roger Bootle. They received too little attention by governments.
- *Autumn 2006*: US construction is down substantially versus previous year.

2007

- *The year in general*: US home sales fall; US house prices year-on-year decline for first time since 1991; subprime mortgage business collapses; foreclosures double versus 2006; rising interest rates.
- *February–March*: Several subprime lenders announce losses, including Accredited Home Lenders Holding, New Century Financial and Countrywide Financial.
- *March 5*: HSBC announces that one portfolio of purchased subprime mortgages displayed higher delinquency than rates built in to the pricing model of these products
- *March 6*: US Federal Preserve Chairman, Ben Bernanke warns that the Government Sponsored Enterprises, Fannie Mae (Federal National Mortgage Association) and Freddie Mac (Federal Home Mortgage Corporation), were a source of systemic risk and suggests legislation to ward off a potential crisis.
- *April 2*: New Century Financial, largest US subprime lender, files for bankruptcy.
- *April 3*: CNN reports that some 13 per cent of subprime loans are delinquent, over five times the rate for home loans to top credit borrowers.
- *June 7*: Bear Stearns announces that for two of its funds it is halting redemptions.
- *July 19*: The US Dow Jones share index closes above 14,000 for the first time in its history.
- *August 9*: European bank BNP Paribas suspends calculation of asset values for three money market funds exposed to subprime mortgages and halts redemptions.
- *August 9*: European Central Bank (ECB) injects EUR95 billion overnight to improve liquidity. Other central banks inject funds too.
- *August 15*: Countrywide Financial, the largest US mortgage lender, announces that delinquencies have risen to their highest levels since early 2002. Its share price falls 13 per cent.

Timeline of the financial crisis 2007/8 *continued*

- *August 16*: Countrywide Financial narrowly avoids bankruptcy, taking an emergency loan of USD11 billion from a group of banks.

- *August 17*: US Federal Reserve cuts the discount rate by half a per cent to 5.75 per cent from 6.25 per cent in an attempt to stabilise financial markets.

- *August 31*: **Ameriquest, once the largest US subprime lender, goes out of business.**

- *September 4*: Sterling LIBOR rises to 6.7975 per cent, its highest level since December 1998 and above the Bank of England base rate of 5.75 per cent.

- *September 10*: Victoria Mortgage Funding, the UK mortgage company, fails.

- *September 14*: Bank of England announces it has provided a liquidity support facility to Northern Rock.

- *September 17*: **Following a retail deposit run, the UK Chancellor of the Exchequer announces a government guarantee for Northern Rock's existing deposits.**

- *September 18*: The Fed lowers interest rates by 0.5 per cent.

- *September 19*: Bank of England announces that it will undertake a series of three-month auctions against a broader range of collateral, including mortgage collateral.

- *October*: Citigroup, Merrill Lynch and UBS report big write-downs.

- *October 15–17*: A group of US banks backed by the US government announces a fund of USD100 billion to purchase mortgage-backed securities whose value plummeted in the subprime collapse. US Fed chairman, Ben Bernanke and US Treasury Secretary, Hank Paulson, express alarm about the dangers posed by the bursting housing bubble.

- *October 31*: Federal Reserve lowers the federal funds rate by 0.25 per cent to 4.5 per cent.

- *November 1*: **Federal Reserve injects USD41 billion for banks to borrow at a low rate, the largest single expansion by the Fed since 2001.**

- *November 20*: Freddie Mac announces 2007 third quarter losses, cuts dividend and raises new capital.

- *December 6*: President Bush announces a plan to freeze the mortgages of a limited number of mortgage debtors holding adjustable rate mortgages (ARM).

- *December 12*: **Central banks the Federal Reserve, Bank of England, ECB, Swiss National Bank (SNB) and Bank of Canada announce measures designed to deal with pressures in short-term funding markets.**

2008

- *January 2008*: Announcement of significant fourth quarter losses by Citigroup and Merrill Lynch.

- *January 11*: Bank of America confirms purchase of Countrywide, the failed subprime lender.

- *January 15*: Citigroup announces that it is to raise USD14.5 billion in new capital

- *February 11*: **AIG announces that its auditors have found a material weakness in its internal controls over the valuation of a portfolio of credit default swaps.**

→

Timeline of the financial crisis 2007/8 *continued*

- *February 17*: UK government announces temporary nationalisation of Northern Rock.
- *February 19*: Credit Suisse announces pricing errors by a small number of traders.
- *March 10*: Dow Jones Industrial Average at the lowest level since October 2006, falling more than 20 per cent from its peak just five months prior.
- *March 11*: Federal Reserve announces the introduction of a Term Securities Lending Facility and Bank of England announces it will maintain its expanded facility for high-quality collateral.
- *March 14*: J. P. Morgan Chase announces that is has agreed, in conjunction with the Federal Reserve Bank of New York, to provide secured funding to Bear Stearns for a period of up to 28 days.
- *March 16*: J. P. Morgan Chase agrees to purchase Bear Stearns. Federal Reserve provides USD30 billion of funding.
- *April 21*: Bank of England launches Special Liquidity Scheme (SLS) to allow banks to swap high-quality mortgage-backed securities and other securities for UK Treasury Bills.
- *April 22*: RBS announces GBP12 billion rights issue.
- *April 29*: HBOS announces GBP4 billion rights issue.
- *May 2*: US Federal Reserve, ECB and SNB announce further liquidity injections.
- *June 16*: Lehman Brothers confirms a net loss of USD2.8 billion in its second quarter.
- *June 18*: Morgan Stanley reports losses from mortgage trading and bad loans.
- *June 25*: Barclays announces plans to raise GBP4.5 billion in a share issue.
- *July 11*: US mortgage lender IndyMac is placed into receivership.
- *July 13*: US Treasury announces rescue plan for Fannie Mae and Freddie Mac.
- *September 7*: Fannie Mae and Freddie Mac taken into conservatorship (rather like receivership).
- *September 14*: Merrill Lynch sells out to Bank of America. Lehman Brothers collapses.
- *September 15*: Lehman Brothers files for bankruptcy.
- *September 16*: US Government provides emergency loan to AIG of USD85 billion and takes a 79.9 per cent stake and right of veto on dividend payments.
- *September 18*: US Treasury Secretary, Henry Paulson and Fed Chairman, Ben Bernanke, propose USD700 billion emergency bailout through the purchase of toxic assets.
- *September 18*: LloydsTSB/HBOS merger announced.
- *September 18*: Financial Services Authority (FSA) announces temporary regulations prohibiting short-selling of financial shares.
- *September 19*: US rescue plan is unveiled following a volatile week in stock markets.
- *September 19*: Securities and Exchange Commission (SEC) prohibits short-selling of financial companies' shares.

Timeline of the financial crisis 2007/8 *continued*

- *September 20*: US Treasury announces draft proposals to purchase up to USD700 billion of troubled assets referred to as the Troubled Asset Relief Program (TARP)
- *September 25*: J. P. Morgan Chase buys the deposits, assets and certain liabilities of the failing Washington Mutual Bank.
- *September 29*: Bradford and Bingley, the UK mortgage bank, is nationalised by UK government. Santander, the Spanish mortgage bank, buys its branches and retail deposit book.
- *September 29*: Iceland government buys stake in Glitnir Bank as part of rescue.
- *September 29*: Belgian, Dutch and Luxembourg governments to invest EUR11.2 billion in Fortis.
- *September 29*: Announcement of Citigroup's intention to acquire the banking operations of Wachovia. Transaction facilitated by the US Federal Deposit Insurance Corporation (FDIC), protecting all depositors.
- *September 30*: Irish government announces 100 per cent bank deposit guarantee. Other governments extend their deposit guarantees.
- *October 3*: US House of Representatives passes USD700 billion TARP having voted against an earlier version of the plan on 29 September 2008.
- *October 3*: Dutch government acquires Fortis Bank's Netherlands business.
- *October 6–10*: Worst week for the stockmarket for 75 years. The Dow Jones Industrial Average loses 22.1 per cent, its worst week on record. Now down 40.3 per cent since reaching a record high of 14,164.53 on October 9, 2007.
- *October 6*: German government announces package to save Hypo Real Estate.
- *October 6*: BNP Paribas announces takeover of Fortis' operations in Belgium and Luxembourg as well as the international banking division of Fortis.
- *October 6*: US Fed announces that it will provide US900 billion in short-term loans to banks.
- *October 7*: Iceland government takes control of Glitnir and Landsbanki, which owns Icesave.
- *October 7*: Fed make emergency move to lend USD1.3 trillion to companies outside the financial sector.
- *October 8*: Central banks in USA, UK, China, Canada, Sweden, Switzerland and the European Central Bank cut rates by 0.5 per cent in a co-ordinated effort to prevent collapse.
- *October 11*: The Dow Jones Industrial Average records its highest volatility day ever in its 112-year history.
- *October 13*: Eurozone announces measures to provide their banks with funding.
- *October 14*: US government announces Capital Purchase Program (CPP) of up to USD250 billion to take stakes in US banks.
- *October 19*: Dutch government injects EUR10 billion into ING.

→

Timeline of the financial crisis 2007/8 *continued*

- *October 21*: US Federal Reserve announces that it will spend USD540 billion to purchase short-term debt from money market mutual funds with the intention of unfreezing credit markets.

- *October 31*: Barclays announces plan to raise GBP7.3 billion of additional capital, including GBP5.8 billion from investors in Abu Dhabi and Qatar.

- *November 3*: UK Treasury announces that its shareholdings in banks will be managed on a commercial basis by a new arm's-length company wholly owned by the UK government called UK Financial Investments Limited.

- *November 6*: **Bank of England reduces bank rate by 1.5 per cent to 3 per cent.**

- *November 6*: International Monetary Fund (IMF) approves USD15.7 billion stand-by loan for Hungary.

- *November 12*: **US Treasury Secretary, Hank Paulson, abandons plan to buy toxic assets under the USD700 billion TARP. The remaining USD410 billion in the fund to be spent on recapitalising financial companies.**

- *November 23*: Citigroup to issue preferred shares to the US Treasury and FDIC in exchange for protection against unusually large losses on a USD306 billion pool of loans and securities. The US Treasury will invest an additional USD20 billion in Citigroup from the TARP, taking its input to USD45 billion.

- *November 24*: UK government announces temporary cut in VAT from 17.5 per cent to 15 per cent.

- *November 25*: **US Federal Reserve pledges USD800 billion more to help the financial system, USD600 billion to be used to buy mortgage bonds issued or guaranteed by Fannie Mae, Freddie Mac and Federal Home Loan Banks.**

- *November 26*: Federal Reserve announces approval of the notice of Bank of America to acquire Merrill Lynch.

- *December 4*: **Bank of England reduces bank rate by 1.0 per cent to 2.0 per cent.**

- *December 16*: **Federal Reserve establishes target range for the federal funds rate of 0 per cent to 0.25 per cent.**

- *December 23*: IMF approves USD2.35 billion loan to Latvia.

2009

- *January 8*: Bank of England reduces bank rate by 0.5 per cent to 1.5 per cent.

- *January 15*: Irish government announces that Anglo Irish Bank is to be nationalised.

- *January 19*: **UK government announces the Asset Protection Scheme (APS) to protect financial institutions against exposure to exceptional future credit losses on certain portfolios of assets.**

- *January 19*: FSA issues statement indicating that banks are expected to maintain a minimum core Tier 1 capital ratio of 4 per cent and expressing preference to incorporate countercyclical measures.

- *February 5*: Bank of England reduces bank rate by 0.5 per cent to 1.0 per cent.

Timeline of the financial crisis 2007/8 *continued*

- *February 10*: US Treasury announces a Financial Stability Plan, involving stress tests for banks, the creation of a Public–Private Investment Fund to acquire troubled loans and other assets from financial institutions, expansion of some funds and other initiatives to counter foreclosures and aid small business lending.

- *February 26*: RBS announces loss of GBP24.1 billion. UK government announces details of the APS and an agreement in principle with RBS to participate in the APS.

- *February 27*: Lloyds Banking Group, resulting from the acquisition of HBOS by LloydsTSB, announces results, including pre-tax loss of GBP10.8 billion for HBOS.

- *March 2*: US authorities announce a restructuring of their assistance to AIG. Under this programme AIG will receive up to USD30 billion of additional capital.

- *March 2*: HSBC announces plan to raise GBP12.5 billion in a rights issue.

- *March 5*: Bank of England reduces bank rate by 0.5 per cent to 0.5 per cent and announces GBP75 billion asset purchase programme.

- *March 7*: UK government announces an agreement in principle with Lloyds Banking Group to participate in the APS.

- *March 18*: US Federal Reserve maintains target range for the federal funds rate at 0 per cent to 0.25 per cent and announces an expansion of over USD1 trillion in its planned asset purchases in the year.

- *March 30*: Bank of England announces that key parts of Dunfermline Building Society, Scotland's largest mortgage bank, have been transferred to Nationwide Building Society with the Bank of England assuming control of GBP1 billion of commercial lending and poorer quality mortgages.

- *April 7*: Irish government announces plans for National Asset Management Agency to manage the worst-performing land and development loans of Irish banks.

- *April 9*: German government begins the process to take over Hypo Real Estate.

- *April 22*: UK government launches Asset-backed Securities Guarantee Scheme, under which HM Treasury will provide credit guarantees and liquidity guarantees on residual mortgage-backed securities issued by UK banks.

- *May 6*: IMP approves a USD20.6 billion loan to Poland.

- *May 7*: Federal Reserve releases the results of the stress test of the 19 largest US bank holding companies. It finds that losses at the 19 firms during 2009 and 2010 could be USD600 billion and ten firms would need to add, in total, USD185 billion to their capital to maintain adequate buffers if the economy were to record the more adverse scenario considered.

- *May 7*: ECB announces it will lower its interest rate to 1.0 per cent after reducing it by 0.5 per cent in March and by 0.25 per cent in April.

→

Timeline of the financial crisis 2007/8 *continued*

More recently

- Following injections of funds by governments into banks, some of which has been repaid, major problems have focused upon the eurozone. Its single exchange rate has prevented countries which have suffered higher than average inflation within the eurozone from devaluing their currencies. Major problems reside with Greece, Spain and Portugal. A fund has been established to aid these countries but it is not clear, at the time of writing, whether the strains on the eurozone will enable the single currency to continue life in the long term. Undoubtedly this represents a major economic problem – which could be resolved, of course, by a return to national currencies. In the shorter term, input of more EU funds may be necessary to aid governments that need to help eurozone banks.

Table 1.1 **Key features of the financial crisis 2007/8 and its prelude**

Up to 2007

- Expansion of credit availability with household debt reaching very high levels
- Emergence of dangerous debt products – credit default swaps, CDOs, MBSs and others. Being on the wrong side of these products made banks more risky
- Credit default swap bubble
- Increasing ratios of debt in bank balance sheets making them more risky
- Very low interest rates sometimes negative in real terms
- Binge in high street consumption
- Public sector spending rising fast
- Rise in real incomes
- Strong rise in subprime mortgage lending, aided and abetted by government initiatives to win popularity and votes
- Housing market boom reaching bubble proportions
- Shock to the system – house prices go into reverse

From 2007

- Subprime housing market crashes
- Crash in CDS, CDO and MBS markets, causing bank balance sheets to show financial distress and worse
- Some banks fail. Others bailed out by governments
- Governments throw money at their economies to prevent depression
- Money supply loosened to ward off deflation, recession and depression
- Unemployment increases but not on crippling scale

Table 1.2 Some key personnel in office in Western countries during the crisis, its build-up and its aftermath

Heads of State

USA – President	Bill Clinton	20 Jan 1993–20 Jan 2001
	George W. Bush	20 Jan 2001–20 Jan 2009
	Barack Obama	20 Jan 2009–
UK – Prime Minister	Tony Blair	2 May 1997–27 June 2007
	Gordon Brown	27 June 2007–11 May 2010
	David Cameron	11 May 2010–
Germany – Chancellor	Gerhard Schroder	27 Oct 1998–22 Nov 2005
	Angela Merkel	22 Nov 2005–
France – President	Jacques Chirac	17 May 1995–16 May 2007
	Nicolas Sarkozy	16 May 2007–

Ministers of Finance

USA – Secretary of the Treasury

	John W Snow	3 Feb 2003–30 Jun 2006
	Henry (Hank) Paulson	10 Jul 2006–20 Jan 2009
	Tim Geithner	26 Jan 2009–

UK – Chancellor of the Exchequer

	Gordon Brown	2 May 1997–27 Jun 2007
	Alistair Darling	27 Jun 2007–11 May 2010
	George Osborne	11 May 2010–

Germany – Minister of Finance

	Hans Eichel	1995–2005
	Peer Steinbruck	2005–2009
	Wolfgang Schauble	2009–

France – Minister of Finance

	Various	Up to 2007
	Christine Lagarde	19 Jun 2007–

Central bankers

USA – Chairman of the Federal Reserve System

	Alan Greenspan	11 Aug 1987–31 Jan 2006
	Ben Bernanke	1 Feb 2006–

UK – Governor of the Bank of England

	Sir Edward George	30 Jun 1993–30 Jun 2003
	Mervyn King	1 Jul 2003–

European Central Bank – President

	Wim Duisenberg	1 Jul 1998–30 Oct 2003
	Jean-Claude Trichet	1 Nov 2003–

Chapter 2

Governments and the financial crisis

■ Introduction

In this chapter we show that governments were major contributors to the financial crisis of 2007/8. Their later role in extricating their economies from the colossal problem that followed is the subject of Chapter 16. We begin by discussing the legitimacy of government. This is followed by a brief discussion of externalities, regulation and intervention in the economy. We follow this with a brief overview of government deficits and demand management. Short sections on two of the major tools of government economic policy follow – monetary policy and fiscal policy. In truth, these topics could fill a whole book. Indeed, for interested readers, there is a host of texts on these topics. Necessarily, our coverage here is more focused. We end this chapter with a short section on lobbying.

A government is an organisation or agency through which a political unit exercises its authority, administers public policy and directs and controls the actions of its members or subjects. Generally, the term refers to a civil government or a state but governments may be local, national or international. The nature of government can range over a broad spectrum of styles from dictatorships, monarchies, constitutional republics, oligarchies and democracies through to totalitarian regimes and, even, anarchies.

The idea of legitimacy is central to the study of government. Various attempts have been made to formalise and justify government or state control. For example, the philosopher, Thomas Hobbes[1], viewed people as rational beings who saw submission to a government as preferable to anarchy. He suggested that people in a community create and submit to government for the purpose of establishing safety and public order for their own good. Social contract theorists, such as Hobbes[2] and Jean-Jacques Rousseau[3] argued that governments reduce people's freedoms and rights in exchange for protecting them, and maintaining order. Many question whether this is an actual exchange whereby people voluntarily give up their freedom or whether they conform as a response to potential force by the ruling group. Others reject social contract theory since consent is not involved in relationships between state and individual and offer angles on legitimacy based on pragmatism and usefulness. But this is not the central theme of our discussion. The wide literature on political philosophy is available to meet the needs of those whose curiosity takes them in this direction.

An increasing part of the world can be said to operate as a market economy, based upon division of labour and where the prices of goods and services are determined in a system according to supply and demand. In reality, market economies do not exist in an utterly pure form, as governments regulate them to varying degrees rather than allowing unfettered market forces to rule supreme.

Different views are held as to how strong a role the government should play in guiding the market economy and in addressing the inequalities that the market may produce. There is no universal view on welfare nor on regulation.

Supporters of the market economy may, or may not, be economic liberalists. By and large, economic liberalism is the economic parallel of classical liberalism. It is an economic philosophy that supports and promotes laissez faire economics. Ideas of liberalism maintain that political freedom and social freedom are inseparable from economic freedom. Philosophical arguments are used to promote liberty and to justify economic liberalism and the free market. This view opposes government intervention in the free market and supports maximum free trade and competition. Whilst economic liberalism favours markets unfettered by the government, it still maintains that the state has a legitimate role in providing public goods. So what is a public good? As an example, it could be argued that the state has a role in providing roads, schools and bridges that may not be efficiently implemented by private entities. However, even these goods might be paid for proportionally to their use, for example by putting a toll on some of them – roads and bridges. But surely not schools. Children of poor parents would not receive an adequate education thus denying them the opportunity to progress, make the best of themselves, develop their talents and subsequently become socially mobile. In short, a pure market-based system of schooling would deny life chances to the poorest segment of society.

Under capitalism, the government has a substantial role in the economics of everyday life. It carries out a number of economic functions, like issuing money, supervising some industries, enforcing private contracts, ensuring that competition laws counter monopolies and prevent cartels from forming. In many countries, public utilities are allowed to operate as a monopoly under government regulation because they can achieve high economies of scale which might not be achieved because free enterprise may not provide sufficient capital to invest in such economies . Government agencies regulate the many industries, such as airlines, broadcasting and financial institutions.

■ Externalities

Externalities may be defined as consequences for welfare arising from costs not fully accounted for in the price. Welfare may be defined as the state of well-being of an individual or a society. Externalities are a bit complicated, so consider an example. Take traffic congestion or pollution created by a manufacturing plant. These cause reductions in the welfare of people living near the factory and may increase costs to adjacent factories that need to purify water from a river bordering the plant. Because these third parties receive no compensation for these externalities, there are costs of production not accounted for in the price system. These kind of externalities are termed negative externalities or external diseconomies. Negative externalities, like those exemplified above, arise in consumption (as well as production), for example where people eating take-away meals leave packaging on the pavement or cigarette smokers pollute the air.

But externalities can be positive too. They are termed external economies or positive externalities. External economies of consumption would include a well-kept garden at the front of a house that gives pleasure to passers-by as well as to the occupants and increases the value of adjoining properties. Defence and other public expenditure on research may stimulate the development of new technology that may become available to all. This is also called a spillover effect, an alternative term for an externality.

There are two ways of dealing with externalities. First, a structure of taxes or subsidies can be designed to account for the externalities and ensure that the full costs or benefits of production are reflected in the prices charged. For example, even if a factory causes pollution, it can carry on producing as long as it properly compensates society for the damage caused. Second, we might put restrictions on certain unsocial activities and/or make other beneficial activities compulsory. This is not usually as efficient as the tax or subsidy because one might restrict activity that, despite its negative external effects, still benefits the performer more than its restriction helps society. As an example of the second way of compensating for the costs of externality, consider the following. A property developer in the capital city may be required to include so many units of social housing, maybe for nurses, teachers and firefighters in return for planning permission being granted for a block of flats.

So, to summarise, a negative externality is an action that imposes a negative side effect on a third party – a social cost. Many negative externalities (aka external costs or external diseconomies) are related to the environmental consequences of production and use. Examples include the following:

- pollution by industry may poison the water, harming humans as well as animals and plants;
- when car owners use roads, they impose congestion costs on all other users;
- systemic risk of financial operations describes the risk to the overall economy arising from the risks which the banking system takes. The private costs of bank failure (for depositors) may be smaller than the social costs which impact us all (withdrawal of the service, less lending to business, potential collapse of other banks and businesses in general).

Examples of positive externalities (aka beneficial or positive externality, external benefit, external economy) include:

- a beekeeper keeps the bees for their honey. A side-effect associated with the activity is the pollination of surrounding crops by the bees. The value generated by the pollination may be more important than the value of the harvested honey;
- an individual with an attractive front garden may provide benefits to others living in the area, including financial benefits in the form of increased property values for all property owners in the road;

■ knowledge spillover of inventions and information. Once an invention or new information is made more easily accessible, other benefits may spread by exploiting the invention or information. Copyright, patents and intellectual property law are mechanisms to allow the inventor or creator to benefit from a temporary, state-protected monopoly in return for commercial production or sharing the information through publication or other means.

Clearly, if it is to be effective, pricing and policing of externalities is likely to be a governmental function.

■ Government regulation

Government regulation is said to involve the supervision and control of the economic activities of private enterprise by government in the interest of economic efficiency, fairness, health and safety. Regulation has a long history and takes many different forms. Externalities such as noise and pollution have made it necessary (among other reasons) to regulate road and air transport. The temptation for producers to collude or exploit monopoly (or oligopoly) power also requires intervention. Other forms of regulation include measures to safeguard the rights of employees, to regulate trade unions, the financial system, personal privacy (via the Data Protection Act), health and safety at work, the licensing of street traders and taxi-cabs. And the financial services are also widely regulated.

Regulation may be imposed simply by enacting laws and leaving their supervision to the normal processes of the law, by setting up special regulatory agencies, by encouraging self-regulation or delegating powers to voluntary bodies. Though regulation may be regarded as necessary to prevent the abuse of monopoly power, or to correct externalities or other instances of market failure, there may yet be a risk that the compliance costs and associated outgoings of regulation may exceed the social benefits. These associated outgoings include administration costs in government or regulatory agencies and are termed excess burdens. The growth of regulation has led to concern about its overall costs and has led to various calls for reform and even abolition of regulatory requirements, termed deregulation. Whether such calls emanate from lobbyist groups or unbiased sources is a moot point. But it is one that government has to question all of the time.

■ Economic intervention

Economic intervention is an action taken by a government in the economy – whether a market economy or a mixed economy – beyond the basic regulation of fraud and enforcement of contracts, in an effort to affect its own economy. Economic intervention may be aimed at a variety of political or economic objectives, such as promoting economic growth, increasing employment, raising wages, controlling prices, promoting equality, managing the money supply and interest rates, increasing profits, or addressing market failures. Advocates of free market and laissez-faire economics tend to see government intervention in the economy as harmful, due to the potential for regulatory growth, the law of unintended consequences, as well as ideological aversion.

■ Government deficits

Observers of government will remind us that there is a tendency for the reach of governments to grow. This is reflected in the growth of its deficit financing. Governments seem to borrow more and more each year. In almost every year since World War II the US administration has recorded a budget deficit – this means that it has received less in tax revenues than it has spent, and has had to borrow to make up the difference. It is not alone. The UK has also recorded a series of budget deficits. This is a relatively new phenomenon. For most of their history, the US and UK governments kept their budgets balanced, moving into the red only in times of war and economic slump.

There are countries that consistently operate budget surpluses. For example, Norway (because of its oil reserves) and Australia (because of its metal resources). The era of persistent government deficits began when governments started to provide extensive social security systems. This involved spending sizeable amounts on health, unemployment insurance and education, all of which tended, deep in the past, to be handled by the private sector or by charities and trusts.

A quick look at the US Federal Budget for 2008 tells us that 21 per cent of outgoings are for social security (mainly payments to the elderly) and 21 per cent for defence (salaries of service personnel, and equipment from aircraft carriers to guns). Income security gets 13 per cent (payments to poor families), medicare and other health payments gets 22 per cent (government health spending for the elderly and the poor), and interest payments on the debt that the government has taken on in previous years gets 9 per cent. Remaining amounts include spending on federal institutions such as the courts system, support for farmers and veterans and others. Very broadly, this pattern of spend is replicated in Britain and most other Western countries.

The amount that the US government spent in 2008 exceeded the amount it raised in taxes, having to make up the balance with USD410 billion worth of borrowing. On top of this, because of the Federal structure of US government, each state also has its own budget (and tax-raising abilities), most of which is spent on education and local infrastructures such as highways. Congress representatives from particular states insert additions to Federal bills to help pay for expensive local projects. This is termed 'pork barrel' politics. President George W. Bush was extremely reluctant to use his right to veto the bills.

Recurring deficits may cause a variety of economic problems for a country. It may be the case that the borrowing nation is perceived as being prone to the temptation to extricate itself from excessive indebtedness via inflation (by creating more money). Inflation at higher levels than trading partners will tend, all other things being equal, to put downward pressure on the currency and, to compensate for this risk investors would demand a higher rate of return. This results in the government having to pay more on its debt, making it more costly to borrow in the future. Of course, if its indebtedness is in its own currency, the borrowing will now be easier to repay because of the depreciation in its currency.

Most important are the long-term consequences of borrowing too heavily. Effectively, government borrowing is deferred taxation from future years, since the extra borrowed money has to be paid back at some time. This is not so much of a problem if the money is being used to enhance future growth and generations' welfare, such as investing in good new schools, but it is a real cause for concern if the money is merely being used to satisfy the public sector's voracious appetite for cash. In other words, the problem is containable if future outturns are enhanced. A recent picture of the US current account balances is shown in Figure 2.1. It indicates that the USA was importing a vastly greater amount than it was exporting and this imbalance was worsening. How could this continue for so long? It was being offset in part by China's imbalance in the opposite direction.

As we shall see in the next chapter, the USA was experiencing low interest rates, a booming housing market and strong consumer spending, especially in the period from 2002 to 2005. Much of US consumers' spending was on products made in China. From 2000 to 2005, Chinese exports to the US moved from 4 per cent to 11 per cent of non-automobile US retail sales. This impacted Chinese government policy. Its central bank was a buyer of US dollars gained by Chinese exporters. And it recirculated these US dollars by purchasing US Treasury bonds. The effect was that the exchange rate of the USD against the Chinese yuan was maintained with relatively little movement. In total, China accumulated trillions of dollars of US Treasury bonds in a remarkably short time. Because China was such a willing buyer of US bonds, this tended to keep US interest rates low. And this fed back to domestic US interest rates and helped keep US mortgage rates low.

To reiterate, the effect of all of this was to keep the exchange rate between the USD and the Chinese yuan relatively constant and to keep US interest rates low. It is worth noting that if the Chinese central bank had sold US dollars to buy yuan, rather than recirculating them into US Treasury bonds, the effect would have been a weakening of the USD and a rise in the Chinese currency. And this would, in theory, have made Chinese exports less competitive. It would also have meant that for the US to fund its imbalance, its borrowing would probably have been at a higher interest rate because China's willingness to buy US Treasury bonds would not have been there.

Apart from the practicalities of public spending, economists have been concerned with the principles justifying it, the mechanism for allocating it and the authorities responsible for it. Public spending in most parts of the Western world is running at around 40 to 50 per cent of gross domestic product with the UK and most EU countries fairly high up the list and the US at the lower end of the range. About half represents transfers to the private sector in the form of subsidies and social security benefits.

The aftermath of a financial crisis increases government debt problems. Kindleberger[4] tells us that economists think that they 'know how to handle financial crises: throw money at them, and after the crisis is over, mop the money up'. Reinhart and Rogoff[5] warn that, on the 'basis of past international banking crises, they are followed by sovereign debt crises'. As we will see in Chapter 16, this time is no different.

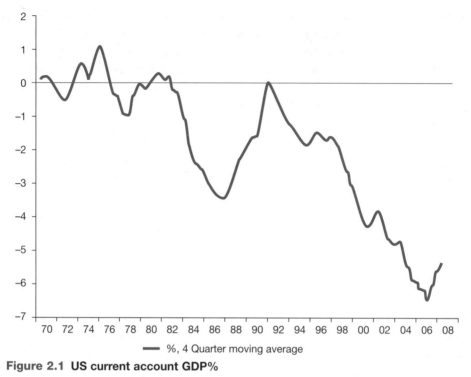

Figure 2.1 US current account GDP%

Source: Bureau of Economic Analysis.

■ Demand management

In economics, demand management is concerned with government attempts to control economic demand and to create growth and avoid recessions. The central idea is that government uses tools like interest rates, taxation, public expenditure and taxation to change key economic decisions like consumption, investment, the balance of trade and public sector borrowing. Their aim in so-doing is to smooth the business cycle. We look at the business cycle in Chapter 9.

Traditionally, governments were advised to balance the budget – not every year but over the period of the business cycle as a whole. According to this wisdom, governments run a budget surplus in the good times, in order to damp down expansion. And they run a deficit in the downturn in order to counteract the slowdown.

This cycle-smoothing approach to government budgets, whilst traditional wisdom, succumbed to the political temptation to run what looks like a permanent deficit in the US – see Figure 2.1. Some observers argue that government efforts at demand management have failed to work – whether this reflects an ideological antipathy to government or is based upon good research is a moot point. In terms of adjusting aggregate demand in the economy, government has two major kinds of tool – one is termed monetary policy and the other is fiscal policy. We now turn to the former of these.

■ Monetary policy

Monetary policy embraces government strategy and tactics with regard to the quantity of money in the economy, the rate of interest and the exchange rate. Monetary policy has the effect of either expanding the economy or contracting it. Increases in the total supply of money in the economy are likely, all other things being equal, to expand it. Decreases in the total money supply are likely to contract the economy. Lowering and raising interest rates are likely, respectively, to expand or contract the economy. Expansionary policy may be used to combat unemployment in a recession while a policy of contraction might be used to combat inflation or rid the economy of boom conditions. Monetary policy is contrasted with fiscal policy, which refers to taxation and to government spending and borrowing.

Monetary policy is often described as accommodative, neutral or tightening. Accommodative policy describes situations where the interest rate is set by the central monetary authority to create economic growth. It is neutral when it is intended neither to create growth nor to combat inflation. It is termed tight if it is intended to reduce inflation or contract the money.

In most modern nations, institutions such as the Federal Reserve Bank in the USA, the Bank of England, the European Central Bank, the Bank of Japan and so on have the task of executing government monetary policy. In general, these institutions are called central banks and also have the responsibility of managing the smooth operation of the financial system in their countries. Central banks are often referred to as being independent. But to claim that the government has no influence on them would be utterly erroneous.

The primary tool of monetary policy is open market operations. This entails managing the quantity of money in circulation through buying and selling various financial instruments, such as Treasury bills, bonds and foreign currencies. All of these purchases and sales result in more or less money entering or leaving circulation.

The short-term aim of open market operations is, usually, to achieve a short-term interest rate target. In other instances, monetary policy might entail the targeting of a specific exchange rate relative to some foreign currency. In the USA, the Federal Reserve targets the federal funds rate, the rate at which member banks lend to one another overnight. Monetary policy in China aims to target the exchange rate between the Chinese renminbi and a basket of foreign currencies. Clearly monetary policy rests on the relationship between the rates of interest in an economy and the total supply of money.

Monetary policy may involve inflation targeting and monetary aggregate targeting. Under inflation targeting approaches, the aim is to keep inflation, under a particular definition such as the Consumer Price Index, within a prescribed range. The inflation target is achieved via periodic adjustments to the central bank interest rate. The interest rate used is usually the interbank rate at which banks lend overnight to each other. The interest rate target is maintained using open market operations and it is regularly reviewed on a monthly or quarterly basis by a policy committee. Changes to the interest rate are made to various market indicators.

Turning to monetary aggregates, this approach is based on a constant (or determined) growth in the money supply. So far, we have avoided defining the money supply. What do we mean by it? Unfortunately, it has a number of definitions – there is MO, MB, M1, M2, M3, M4 and some others too. All of these have meanings to them and all define money supply. We will keep it simple and just refer to MO and M4 here. And if you, the reader, wish to pursue the matter further there is a host of economics books to accommodate your intellectual curiosity. We use the UK as our example. MO is defined as notes and coins in circulation plus banks' deposits at the Bank of England. M4 is much broader and embraces notes and coins plus the value of all sterling bank and building society accounts held by private citizens and companies.

We now return to monetary policy tools. These include adjustments to the monetary base, reserve requirements and discount window lending. Monetary policy may be implemented by altering the size of the monetary base. This directly changes the amount of money circulating in the economy. A central bank can use open market operations to change the monetary base. The central bank buys or sells bonds in exchange for money. If the central bank buys bonds it puts money into the economy. By a reverse token, if it sells bonds it takes money out of the economy.

The government exerts regulatory control over banks. Monetary policy may be observed by changing the proportion of assets that banks must deposit with the central bank. By changing the amount of total assets to be held as cash, the central bank changes the availability of loanable funds. This creates a change in the money supply. Typically, central banks do not change reserve requirements often.

Many central banks have the authority to lend funds to financial institutions within their country. By recalling existing loans or extending new loans, the monetary authority can directly lower money supply or increase it, respectively. This method of monetary policy is termed discount window lending.

We now introduce a brief and simplified overview of the quantity theory of money. This is the idea that money supply has a direct and positive relationship with the price level. Sorry about the equation, but the simplified version of the quantity theory of money is:

$$M\ V = P\ T$$

where

- M is the average total amount of money in circulation in an economy during a specified period.
- V is the transactions' velocity of money. This is the average frequency over all transactions which a unit of money is spent over a specified period. In other words, it measures how fast people turn over their money.
- P is the price level in the economy during the period.
- T is an index of the real (that is, net of inflation) value of aggregate transactions.

That's simple enough, isn't it? If V and T are constant, the inflation rate would exactly equal the growth rate of the money supply. However in booms and busts, the velocity of circulation and the value of transactions (national income) do change, meaning that changes in money supply cannot be said to immutably affect price levels. In truth, this is a fascinating area of study and we do less than scratch the surface of it here. Again, readers desiring a more detailed account have a vast literature from which to choose.

As we have stated, monetary policy may involve inflation targeting and monetary aggregate targeting. One of the most astonishing aspects of the past decade is that real interest rates, arrived at by extracting actual inflation after the event from the risk-free rate of interest quoted in the market place (Fed funds in the USA and Bank of England base rate in the UK), show extremely low rates, and in some cases negative rates – see Table 2.1. Of course this is only one way of determining real interest rates. The other is to look at index-linked government securities which guarantee a real rate of return. The statistic on this latter basis has been around 2 per cent over the last decade. This has been higher than the figures for almost all of the data shown in Table 2.1. In passing, it should be noted that there are various definitions of inflation which may give rise to slightly different figures in our exhibit compared to others.

The upshot of all of this is that, with real interest rates so low, compared with a benchmark figure of 2 to 3 per cent, it is not surprising that there has been a binge in high street consumption in the noughties and that this binge was reproduced in housing markets in the USA and in the UK and in many other countries too. Indeed with interest rates too low for too long and with easy credit available, it does not take long for a number of things to happen. These include:

- remortgaging, taking out higher mortgages, maybe via top-up mortgages or taking on higher mortgages for a bigger house;
- a consequent take-off in house prices;
- consumers deciding to go on a shopping spree using credit, which is cheap and available;
- consumer debt increases;
- corporate debt increases;
- with credit widely available the seeds of financial euphoria are sown.

Table 2.1 Real interest rates in the USA and UK

Year	USA (%)	UK (%)
2000	1½	3.1
2001	3	3.2
2002	1½	2.3
2003	minus ½	0.7
2004	minus ¾	1.5
2005	minus 1	1.7
2006	0	1.5
2007	1	1.2
2008	1	0.5
2009	½	0.5

All of the bullet-pointed eventualities came to pass. And all would be attributed, in part, to a co-ordinated policy of real interest rates being too low for too long. All of those G6, G10, G20 meetings at which nothing seems to be resolved are, in reality, get-togethers at which all parties sing from the same hymn sheet. And the song is, keep real interest rates low – very low.

For the sake of completeness, Figures 2.2 and 2.3 show the average year-on-year growth in US earnings and average UK earnings from 1993 to 2007. These figures are in nominal terms, that is gross of any inflation.

We now turn to the second key category of government economic policy namely fiscal policy.

■ Fiscal policy

The two main instruments of fiscal policy are government expenditure and taxation. Fiscal policy may be neutral or it may be expansionary or it may result in contraction in the economy. A neutral stance on fiscal policy implies a balanced budget where government spending equals tax revenues or,

$$G = T$$

Where G represents government spending and T represents sums raised from taxation. Here, government spending is funded wholly by tax revenue. The overall outcome is

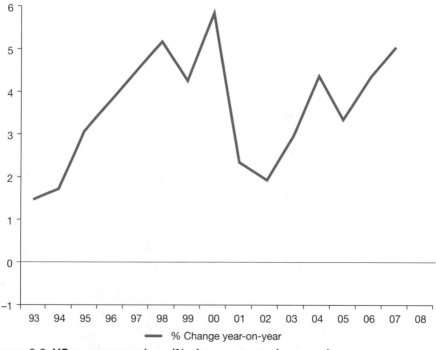

Figure 2.2 US average earnings (% change on previous year)

Source: Bureau of Labour Statistics.

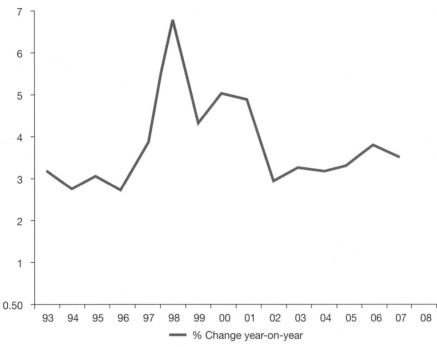

Figure 2.3 UK average earnings (% change on previous year)
Source: Office of National Statistics.

likely to be a neutral effect on economic activity. By contrast, an expansionary fiscal policy involves a situation where government spending exceeds tax returns.

$$G > T$$

Expansionary fiscal policy is usually associated with a budget deficit. Fiscal policy in which government spending falls short of tax revenues has a contracting effect on the economy. In these circumstances, fiscal policy is associated with a surplus.

Governments use fiscal policy to influence the level of aggregate demand in the economy, in an effort to achieve their objectives of price stability, full employment, and economic growth. To summarise, fiscal policy embraces decisions to lower taxation or to increase public expenditure in the interest of stimulating aggregate demand. These are referred to as loosening fiscal policy. One of the most remarkable features in the run-up to the financial crash of 2007/8 was a massive increase in public expenditure as a percentage of GDP. During the years 2000 to 2009 official statistics show an almost straight line increase in both the US and the UK from 32 per cent to 43 per cent in the former case and from 35 per cent to 45 per cent in the latter. With outgoing budget deficits, we would be surprised if the end result were anything other than an overheated boom in the economy.

■ Lobbying

Lobbying targets governments and local authorities. Lobbying in the USA aims to influence the US House of Representatives and state legislatures. In Britain, lobbyists aim to influence members of the House of Commons and the House of Lords and, at a lower level, local authorities. Lobby groups may represent client organisations in dealings with central and local governments. In 2007 there were reported to be 17,000 federal lobbyists based in Washington DC and the total lobby expenditure by sector was topped by financial, insurance and real estate interests. Their total outlay, excluding campaign contributions, totalled over USD2.5 billion over the period from 1998 to 2006. Press cutting 2.1 updates these figures and provides interesting and relevant data.

The US banks have probably been the most adept in the world in this area of influence. Johnson[6] makes the case that 'the American financial industry gained political power by amassing a kind of cultural capital – a belief system. Once, perhaps, what was good for General Motors was good for the country. Over the past decade, the attitude took hold that what was good for Wall Street was good for the country. The banking-and-securities industry has become one of the top contributors to political campaigns, but at the peak of its influence, it did not have to buy favours … Instead, it benefited from the fact that Washington insiders already believed that large financial institutions and free-flowing capital markets were crucial to America's position in the world.' Johnson's reference to the Wall Street–Washington corridor is exemplified when he observes that 'one channel of influence was, of course, the flow of individuals between Wall Street and Washington; Robert Rubin, once the co-chairman of Goldman Sachs, served in Washington as Treasury

---

Press cutting 2.1　　　　　*Financial Times*, 30 September 2009　**FT**

One congressman, five finance lobbyists

Efforts by governments and regulators to improve investor protection by curbing what big banks and the like can do will run into resistance from a financial sector whose lobbying clout is strong.

Notably in the US, that power derives primarily from its deep pockets.

Between 1998 and 2008, Wall Street investment banks, commercial banks, hedge funds, real estate companies and insurance conglomerates paid an estimated $1.7bn in political contributions and spent a further $3.4bn on lobbyists. The figure comes from a report by Essential Information and The Consumer Education Foundation, two non-profit organisations. Their research shows that in 2007 the financial sector employed nearly 3,000 lobbyists, or five for each member of Congress, to influence policymaking.

Such purchasing of political influence is widely believed to have helped secure for Wall Street the repeal of the Glass-Steagall Act, which prohibited the merger of commercial and investment banks, and the blocking by Bill Clinton's administration of a Commodity Futures Trading Commission initiative to regulate financial derivatives.

'Over the past 30 years, this sector has benefited from a process of "cultural capture", through which regulators, politicians and independent analysts became convinced this sector had great and stabilising technical expertise,' says Simon Johnson, former chief economist at the International Monetary Fund. 'Big banks are, amazingly, still presumed by officials to have the expertise necessary to manage their own risks, to prevent systematic failure and to guide public policy.'

secretary under Clinton, and later became chairman of Citigroup's executive committee. Henry Paulson, CEO of Goldman Sachs during the long boom, became Treasury secretary under George W. Bush. John Snow, Paulson's predecessor, left to become chairman of Cerberus Capital Management, a large private-equity firm that also counts Dan Quayle among its executives. Alan Greenspan, after leaving the Federal Reserve, became a consultant to Pimco, perhaps the biggest player in international bond markets. These personal connections were multiplied many times over at the lower levels of the past three presidential administrations, strengthening the ties between Washington and Wall Street.'

Johnson and Kwak[7] argue that 'Wall Street's political power was its ability to place its people in key positions in Washington. As the big banks became richer, more of their executives became top-tier fund raisers who could be tapped for administration jobs. More important, as the world of finance became more complicated and more central to the economy, the federal government became more dependent on people with modern financial expertise – which meant people from the big banks and from their most cutting-edge businesses. This constant flow of people from Wall Street to Washington and back ensured that important decisions were made by officials who had absorbed the financial sector's view of the world and its perspective on government policy, and who often saw their future careers on Wall Street, not in Washington.'

The argument is taken further in Johnson and Kwak[8]. These authors draw Wall Street as an oligarchy, a group dominated by a small number of individuals – a banking elite – that has gained political power because of its economical power and subsequently uses that political power for its own benefit. Unlike emerging economies' oligarchies, Wall Street's power group does not use bribery or blackmail. Its tools are subtler – campaign-finance contributions, the revolving door of government jobs and Wall Street directorships, and the creation of a culture that equates Wall Street's gains with America's gains. Suspicion of financial oligarchies is not a new theme in American history. Johnson[9] argues that so successful has the banking lobby been in terms of 'campaign finance, personal connections and ideology there [has] flowed, in just the past decade, a river of deregulatory policies that is, in hindsight, astonishing. It includes

- insistence on free movement of capital across borders;
- the repeal of Depression-era regulations separating commercial and investment banking;
- a congressional ban on the regulation of credit-default swaps;
- major increases in the amount of leverage allowed to investment banks;
- a light – (maybe) invisible – hand at the Securities and Exchange Commission in its regulatory enforcement;
- an international agreement to allow banks to measure their own riskiness;
- and an intentional failure to update regulations so as to keep up with the tremendous pace of financial innovation.

The mood that accompanied these measures in Washington seemed to swing between nonchalance and outright celebration: finance unleashed, it was thought, would continue to propel the economy to greater heights'.

Johnson and Kwak contend that Wall Street successfully influenced governments in minimising regulations by its persuasive and pervasive partiality for classical economics and emphasis on Adam Smith's preference for minimising government intervention – a view which was taken out of context and peddled by the banking élite. They also suggest that the same applies with respect to the osmotic spread of the efficient markets hypothesis with its focus upon unbiased market prices which can, again, be used as a thesis for non-involvement by regulators. After all, if the market arrives at fair prices, it might follow that regulation aimed to deflate bubbles is hardly necessary since prices are likely to be unbiased and approximately right anyway – at least, according to the efficient markets hypothesis. For more on efficient markets, see Chapter 10.

Indeed Johnson quotes Ben Bernanke, the Chairman of the US central bank, as saying, in 2006, that 'the management of market risk and credit risk has become increasingly sophisticated ... Banking organisations of all sizes have made substantial strides over the past two decades in their ability to measure and manage risks. Of course, this was mostly an illusion. Regulators, legislators, and academics almost all assumed that the managers of these banks knew what they were doing. In retrospect, they didn't'.

Lest it be concluded that lobbying is a heinous art, it has to be said that were politicians not so prone to accepting the gifts borne by the lobbyists there would be less of it going on. The Wall Street–Washington revolving door turns because bankers and politicians are only too happy to see it turning. It takes two to tango.

■ Summing up

Governments devolve some their decisions to regulators. We look at regulation in Chapter 8. Policy on interest rates is often delegated to the central bank – as is the case in the USA, the UK and the EU. Managing them to meet an inflation target set by the government is usually pursued. Regulation of financial markets is also devolved to various bodies which varies from country to country.

There is no doubt that the central government influences all of these issues even though central banks are often termed independent. However, final responsibility for factors such as inflation, interest rates and financial markets rests with government. If financial regulation fails, if inflation runs out of control, if interest rates are set at too low a level, if bubbles in markets occur, if public expenditure is too high, if economic growth is excessively high or excessively poor, the government is the ultimate culpable party. There is no denying this. The buck stops there.

Two major factors that emerge from this chapter are that real interest rates were truly low by every standard in the decade running up to the financial crisis and public expenditure was zooming northwards at a remarkable rate. These features fuelled a bubble in house prices in the USA, in the UK and in other places too. They were, to some extent, responsible for the deteriorating budget deficit versus GDP for each country. Both of these issues had a substantial impact on the problems of the financial crisis – as we shall see later on in this book. Governments in the USA, Britain and elsewhere were undoubtedly affected by the pleas of lobby groups to deregulate and keep the boom going. Governments basked in the glory of an economy that was working so well that consumers were bingeing on borrowed money, purchasing properties that they couldn't afford and enjoying a boom that, seemingly, wouldn't end. And consumers were being told by those at the apex of the government's finance function that 'We have conquered boom and bust'. Responsible government? We think not.

Personal finance, housing and the financial crisis

■ Introduction

Householders divide their income between consumption and saving. Saving may be regarded as a way of postponing consumption. This suggests that the issue is really one of timing – consumption now versus consumption later.

The term savings ratio refers to the proportion of household income that is saved. It is usually expressed as a percentage of total household disposable income. In arriving at disposable income, social security and income tax payments are deducted from total household income.

Savings ratios are lower in the US and the UK than in most other developed countries. In the US, the savings ratio fell from 10 per cent in the 1970s to 7 per cent in the early 1990s, and to zero in 2007. In the UK, the savings ratio fell from 10 per cent in 1997 to 3 per cent in 2007 and to 1.7 per cent in 2008. By contrast, in China, a much poorer country, ratio data show a far higher proportion of income being saved.

The advice that one should save for a rainy day suggests that when times are bad and confidence is low – in other words, when most people expect rain – they tend to save more and spend less. That implies a tendency to reduce personal consumption just when the economy as a whole may need people to maintain or even increase consumption.

Governments often seem to be happier when people consume rather than save. Their job is easier when times are good and spending is rife. Furthermore, governments always try to keep interest rates low, which favours borrowers who are more liable to spend. And it penalises savers. Small wonder that the savings ratio fell so much. Small wonder that there was a consumer boom in the run-up to the financial crisis.

After World War II and into the sixties and seventies, if one wanted something, one first saved up for it, then bought it later. The modern world is different. The attitude of 'I want it. And I want it now' is well entrenched. It results in people incurring debt on products that they cannot truly afford – and might, equally well, be able to go without in the short run (as you can see, we are oldies). Banks and other lenders encourage this attitude by readily offering to lend. Some people – perhaps like your author – do use their credit card simply as a convenient way to package their bills and pay them off in one fell swoop each month. Others choose to increase their total credit card debt each month, regardless of the relatively high interest rate payable, as long as they are allowed to do so. And if they near their credit limit they manage to increase it or obtain other credit cards. Just look at the rate of interest one pays. It really isn't clever to allow the credit card debt to balloon.

Many householders in the UK and the US have been borrowing more than they could afford. They have been putting money into houses or cars or simply living beyond their means using their credit cards. Between 1989 and 2000, UK household debt remained steady at 100 per cent of annual disposable household income, but it then rose sharply to 170 per cent by 2007. Meanwhile, US household debt rose from 100 per cent in 1997 to 140 per cent by 2007. In each case, mortgage debt in 2007 was about three-quarters of total household debt. Clearly, these are very large increases given such a short period of time. The picture of expanding household indebtedness is shown in Figure 3.1. The figure shows details of home mortgages and other household debt for Japan, Germany, Italy, Canada, the USA, France and the UK from 2001 to 2007. For each country the left-hand bar shows indebtedness as a percentage of nominal disposable income in 2001 and the right-hand bar shows similar figures for 2007. In terms of piling high debt, North America, France and Britain are doing more of it compared with Japan and Germany. And the UK's explosion of mortgage debt is really remarkable. Figure 3.2 shows outstanding household debt in the USA in billions of USD from 1975 to 2008. This shows a truly unsustainable level of borrowings. A very compliant government and indulgent bankers were to blame but the average individual is equally culpable. It is to the topic of housing that we now turn.

■ Housing

Houses last a long time. In the UK, around one in ten is over 100 years old. Compared to the stock of existing dwellings, the supply of new ones each year is relatively small currently, less than 1 per cent – and most houses that people buy are not new. The current

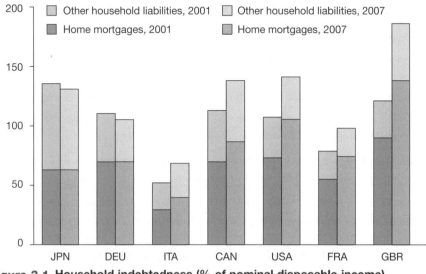

Figure 3.1 Household indebtedness (% of nominal disposable income)
Source: DataStream, OECD.

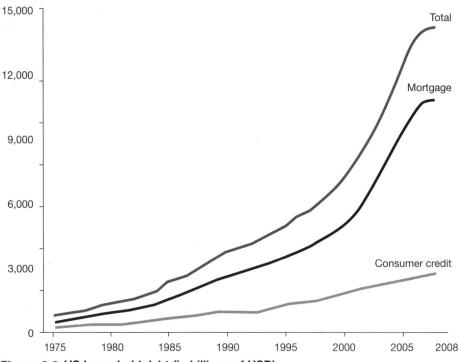

Figure 3.2 US household debt (in billions of USD)

rate of annual building is about 150,000 new homes, which compares with a stock of more than 20 million. Several factors impact the demand for houses, for example:

- the level of interest rates;
- lenders' practices in terms of loan to value and multiples of income advanced;
- changes in total population, which may be due to the difference between births and deaths as well as immigration and emigration;
- movement of people between regions, as a result of changes in income or wealth, job changes, children leaving home or retirement;
- the trend towards fewer people per house, due partly to more divorces or changing lifestyles;
- a desire, with increasing affluence, for second homes.

Since purchases and sales between existing owners offset each other, it is usual in looking at aggregate statistics to consider only the net new demand.

Few people are in a position to buy their first house outright without a mortgage loan. Important influences on demand are the level of house *prices* and the net-of-tax cost and availability of mortgage finance. Most UK mortgages bear floating interest rates, meaning that changes in interest rates have an immediate impact on the amount of regular mortgage payments. The demand for houses can change quite sharply as interest rates change. For this reason the housing market is possibly more exposed to fluctuations in the

UK than in many other countries. The reductions in post-crisis interest rates have saved people large amounts in monthly mortgage payments.

In the early 1950s Britain achieved an annual new build of 300,000 houses. Then most new houses were for local authorities in the public sector. Nowadays virtually all new houses are in the private sector. The UK has planning controls limiting the building of new houses. Green belt and NIMBY (not in my back yard) pressures restrict the location of new houses, especially in the South-east, where there is most demand. This limit on the supply of new houses puts upward pressure on prices of existing houses and makes supply slow to react to changes in house prices or in demand.

The same thing happens in other countries. In the UK and Australia, planning controls are tight, and real house prices are now between two and three times more expensive than in 1970. But Germany and Switzerland have been willing to provide land for housing new residents, and inflation-adjusted prices remain near their 1970 levels. In the US, too, some areas are strictly zoned, especially in the coastal cities. However, where inland US cities are able readily to grow outwards then increased supply helps keep prices in check.

When prices of houses go up one might expect demand will fall. In a housing bubble, increasing prices may lead to an increase in demand. In bubble times, people may assume that the future will be like the recent past and that house prices will continue to move northwards.

Between 1997 and 2007, the ratio of average house prices to average earnings in the UK rose from three and a half times to more than seven times. Average house prices tripled in this ten-year period, which probably caused both borrowers and lenders of mortgages to become over-optimistic. In the USA during this period house prices more than doubled. Data are shown in Figures 3.3 and 3.4 for the UK and the USA respectively. Many recent buyers, and first-time buyers especially, had no personal experience of house prices ever going down.

In the ten years to 2007, home prices rose by 200 per cent in the UK. They rose by 250 per cent in Ireland and by 180 per cent in Spain. In the USA, the average increase was 125 per cent, ranging from more than 200 per cent in California to less than 100 per cent in Chicago and Detroit. All of these figures are quoted in nominal terms (that is, gross of general inflation). If inflation is disaggregated from nominal terms figures, we turn our data into real terms information. In Figure 3.5, we show a comparison of average house prices in real terms for some countries. It compares average annual real increases over the decade from the end of 1996 to the end of 2006. Staggeringly, British data show a real terms advance of just short of 10 per cent per year. Comparable US data show an advance of almost 5 per cent per year over the same time. Germany and Japan recorded average annual falls in house prices.

Owner-occupiers traded up in many countries, often increasing their mortgages at the same time, and second homes became more popular than ever. In the US people of modest means were encouraged to borrow to buy houses and the government actually instituted various schemes to encourage banks to lend to them. Figure 3.6 records the considerable jump in the percentage of households owning their own home in the USA – pushing at over 69 per cent. Most people seem to have assumed that prices were certain to keep on going up. There was also a great expansion of buy-to-let (rather than to

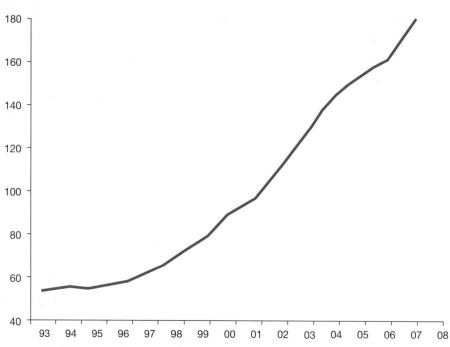

Figure 3.3 Index of UK house prices

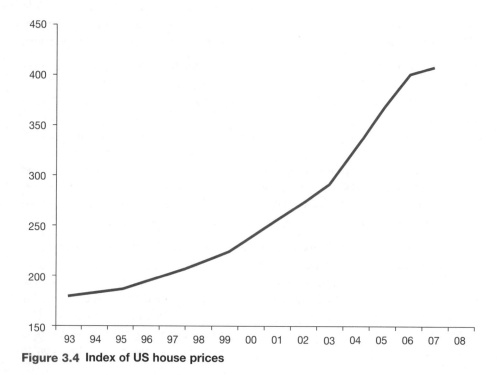

Figure 3.4 Index of US house prices

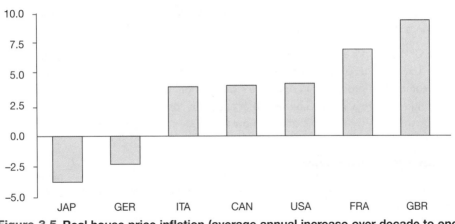

Figure 3.5 Real house price inflation (average annual increase over decade to end 2006)

Source: OECD.

occupy) which drove prices up further. Buy-to-let loans, only 2 per cent in 2000, had risen to 11 per cent of total US mortgage debts outstanding by 2008.

Some of the same causes of the boom in home ownership also led to a boom in commercial property. In particular, low interest rates and the boost the rate of economic growth made borrowing to acquire or build commercial property seem very attractive. In

Figure 3.6 US home ownership % of population

Source: Department of Commerce.

fact, since the crisis commercial property prices have fallen much more sharply than house prices in both Britain and the USA.

In the UK house prices started dropping in October 2007, about 15 months later than in the US. Average UK house prices had fallen by almost 20 per cent by April 2009, while commercial properties in April 2009 were 40 per cent below their June 2007 peak. Reverting to Figure 3.1, it can be seen that the main component of household borrowing is mortgages. It is to this topic that we now turn.

■ Mortgage borrowing

The main criteria that lenders use in terms of assessing applications for mortgage borrowing are:

- the loan as a percentage of the property's current value – loan to value or LTV. This measures the initial down-payment as a proportion of the value of the home;
- the loan versus annual income of the borrower or borrowers – that is, debt to income;
- the period of repayment – 30 years is normal in the US and 25 years is normal in Britain;
- the pattern of principal repayments over the term;
- the proportion of income needed to service the loan – payment-to-income, also known as PTI;
- the rate of interest and whether the rate of interest is fixed or floating;
- the borrower's credit rating.

Some countries have tax rules whereby mortgage interest is tax deductible – generally this is an incentive to encourage home ownership. Another relevant factor is whether the mortgage loan is in a foreign currency. If one's income is in currency X then it makes sense that one's mortgage is in currency X. This minimises foreign exchange risk on the mortgage. We would strongly discourage most individuals who are considering taking on foreign exchange risk on their loan.

We are sure that all of our readers are familiar with the term 3Rs – reading, (w)riting and (a)rithmetic. Those whose first language is not English should note that this is a typically British joke. Well, in mortgage lending it's the four Cs that are critical. This refers to collateral, capacity, character and credit. Collateral means the value of the property serving as security for the loan. Capacity means the borrower's ability to service the loan, broadly their income. Character refers to the borrower's honesty and attitude. Will they be determined to keep their side of the bargain? Finally, credit refers to a borrower's payment history, as revealed in the credit score. In the USA, credit scores range from 300 (awful) to 850 (excellent). A score between 500 and 620 would be subprime. A score below 500 is poor subprime and anything over 620 is prime.

The amount of a mortgage versus a home's value is often large – up to 100 per cent or even more. Readers who persist with this text will see, in the Northern Rock case study, that this firm was advancing 125 per cent of a home's value. Northern Rock marketed this product under the Together brand. We think that a more appropriate name would have been the Mad Mortgage. Mad from the standpoint of Northern Rock shareholders. Anyway, returning to the 100 per cent mortgage. Even this is a very high degree of borrowing – expressions of debt in a deal are termed gearing or leverage. Even a mortgage of only 90 per cent – that is, with a 10 per cent deposit – is clearly risky to both borrower and lender. A decline of only one tenth of the original value of the property can completely wipe out the owner's equity in the property.

Gearing works in both directions. Consider first this situation. Assume a house with a value of 100,000 bought by someone with an 80 per cent mortgage – hence a deposit of 20 per cent. If house prices move up by 15 per cent in the following year, then the buyer's position is set out in Table 3.1. For simplicity, the figure assumes that the capital portion of the mortgage loan remains at 80 by the year end. The borrower's position shows that with a 15 per cent advance in house prices, the owner's equity in the property has moved from 20 to 35, an equity gain of 75 per cent. Admittedly if the house owner were to wish to move home the market price of houses in general may have jumped by 15 per cent so, some would argue, that the gain is illusory. Whilst this may be true, the point that we are trying to explain is that gearing or leverage can look great when prices rise but when house prices fall it cuts the other way. So, in our example, a 15 per cent gain in house prices results in a gain of 75 per cent for the mortgagee.

Now consider the same example with a 15 per cent drop in house prices over the year – otherwise things remain as in the previous case. Note, from Table 3.2, that a 15 per cent drop in house prices has resulted in a 75 per cent drop in the house owner's equity in the property. The householder's equity has fallen from 20 to only 5.

Clearly, gearing has a substantial positive effect for borrowers when prices rise and a significant negative effect when prices fall. This argument about the effects of gearing is also true for companies and for banks. And, as we will demonstrate later in this book, the levels of gearing in banks moved stratospherically high – reaching 97 per cent debt to 3

Table 3.1 Mortgage loan on house example – prices move upwards by 15 per cent

	Start	Finish	Percentage gain
House value	100	115	15
Mortgage loan	80	80	
Householder's equity	20	35	75

Table 3.2 Mortgage loan on house example – prices move downwards by 15 per cent

	Start	Finish	Percentage gain
House value	100	85	−15
Mortgage loan	80	80	
Householder's equity	20	5	−75

per cent equity in the case of Lehman Brothers. Does this sound risky? A mere drop of 3 per cent in the value of assets wipes out the shareholders' equity in one fell swoop.

If one looks back at our statistics of UK house prices tripling on average over the period from 1997 to 2007, it is understandable that optimists were attracted by the proposition of buying property – and for some entrepreneurial types buying a portfolio of properties to let, usually with gearing galore. This is risky. For the entrant to the game in 1997, this speculator is probably sitting pretty. But for someone who entered into this business in 2007, the picture is obviously different. Having said that, many of the buy-to-let class of 1997 had gone on to buy more and more as time progressed. Perhaps, by 2007, the bulk of their portfolio was recently purchased properties. So, even the class of 1997, who expanded at high rates year by year and were still in the game in 2007, could have been wiped out. The really successful players do not stay in forever. They are prepared to enter at a propitious time but they are also prepared to sell out completely and sit on the bench for a while and wait for their next opportunity. The name of the game for them is when to get in and when to get out.

Reverting to the more domestic household finance scene of a family with only one mortgaged property, then in a rising market, they can usually expect to be able to sell their house for more than they paid for it. If the worst came to the worst, the borrower might be unable to keep up the mortgage payments. But even in this case, lenders might expect that the property which secured the loan would, usually, more than cover the amount outstanding.

An important question is whether the lender has recourse to a borrower's other assets such as a car or stocks and shares. If not, as is often the case in the US, it may be much more tempting for the borrower simply to walk away if the value of the house drops to a negative equity position. This tends not to happen in European countries, where mortgage loans are mostly made with recourse.

The mere existence of negative equity – that is, where the current value of an owner's house is less than the amount of the mortgage debt on it – need not mean the owner loses the house. As long as they keep up the mortgage payments, the property would remain theirs. If home-owners have no intention of selling any time soon, they may continue to live in the house long enough for house prices to recover.

In the 1990s a bank would grant a mortgage intending to hold it to maturity, often 25 years into the future in the UK or 30 years in the US. Every year the bank would receive interest and, normally, a partial capital repayment. If the mortgagee were to default, the bank itself might well make a loss, so it had good reason to be careful to whom it lent. A would-be subprime borrower, with too little income and poor credit history, would have had little chance of getting a loan in the first place. Where a lender grants a mortgage and holds it to maturity, we talk of the loan as being an originate-to-hold loan.

If a bank originates a mortgage intending to sell it on, an originate-to-distribute loan, that seriously weakens the bank's incentive to be so diligent about who the borrower is and its own due diligence about the borrower. In the originate-to-distribute case, it has no interest in whether the mortgage holder defaults It cares only about what it gets for selling the loan on to another party. This change in lending practice was a feature of the years running up to the financial crises – a move by banks from originate-to-hold and move to originate-to-distribute. And it did not just apply to mortgage loans. It applied to credit card debt, automobile loans, private equity debt and other lending to public companies too. It meant that lending standards by banks fell. It meant that the quality of banks' credit analysis procedures headed southwards – and fast. The process by which banks generate loans and package them to be sold on to others is an example of securitisation. It is a topic that we return to in Chapters 5 and 6.

Some of those seeking to borrow in the boom years were NINJAs – no income, no job, no assets. And for many loans – liar loans – there was often no evidence to support self-certified claims about income. If borrowers were unable to keep up with their mortgage payments, the lender might foreclose – take ownership of the property and sell it to recover some of the mortgage loan. Such forced selling would, of course, add downward pressure to house prices.

In the UK, most mortgages are at floating rates – they vary as interest rates change. The sharp reduction in interest rates in the second half of 2008 was a big help to borrowers on variable rate mortgages. But they will feel an adverse impact when interest rates increase again once the recovery is underway.

In the run-up to the financial crisis, US administrators had actually encouraged subprime lending. In 1977 President Carter introduced the Community Reinvestment Act and in 1995 President Clinton strengthened it. From 1992, Fannie Mae and Freddie Mac, government sponsored enterprises (see case study, p.191), were persuaded by government to increase their purchases of mortgages going to low-income and moderate-income borrowers. In 1996 the department of Housing and Urban Development gave Fannie Mae and Freddie Mac guideline targets: 42 per cent of mortgage financing was to go to borrowers with below-median income for their area. The target increased to 50 per cent in 2000 and to 52 per cent in 2005. In 1996, 12 per cent of mortgages dealt with by Fannie Mae and Freddie Mac were to be targeted, as special affordable loans, typically to borrowers with incomes less than 60 per cent of the median income for their area. This target increased to 20 per cent in 2000 and 22 per cent in 2005.

In the USA, about one third of securitised mortgage loans made in the first quarter of 2007 were interest-only. A further 7½ per cent were negative amortisation, also known as NegAm loans. These occur whenever the total loan repayment – interest plus capital – for any period is less than the interest charged in that period. This results in the outstanding balance of the loan increasing.

Especially in the US, the low rates of interest in the early 2000s meant that servicing mortgage loans might take a fairly small proportion of a household's income. With low interest rates and the relaxed lending environment, liar loans, NegAms and a plethora of other devices, mortgages seemed affordable – even to the weakest credits. Many US citizens were taking the first step on the elevator to the American Dream, a trip that they never believed they would take. Rajan[1] argues that the massive expansion of easy money to weak credits was a sop to the less-skilled parts of the US workforce which increasingly felt themselves being left behind in a globalised world. And, it would be a vote-winner too.

■ Credit card and other personal debt

We now turn to credit card debt. Many consumers run up large debts on their credit cards. They pay only minimum instalments each month, leaving the balance of debt to increase over time. The effect is to obscure the logical connection between buying things and paying for them. About one in ten people with credit cards in the UK only pay off the minimum amount – between 2 and 2½ per cent of the amount outstanding – each month. Average UK credit card debt has risen in real terms from GBP900 in 1999 to GBP1,250 in 2004 and to GBP2,300 in 2009, a real terms increase of 150 per cent, or nearly 10 per cent per year compound over the decade. In aggregate, the 2009 figure of credit card debt outstanding was GBP53 billion. In the USA, the rate of growth in credit card debt over the same period was much slower – at about 50 per cent – in real terms over the decade, but the total amount outstanding in 2007 was huge, at USD915 billion.

■ Pensions

The next port of call on our whistle-stop tour of personal money is pensions finance. Pensions have become a matter of great concern over the last dozen years. In 1997 the UK probably had one of the best pension positions of any country in the world. Most liabilities were funded. That meant there was enough money and investments in schemes to meet liabilities as they fell due. But problems were around the corner. In 1997, the New Labour government, in its first post-election budget, introduced an adverse tax treatment for pension schemes. Add to this the fact that companies started to take pension holidays and make no contributions when schemes had sufficient funds to meet liabilities – in other words, they were fully funded. This increased reported earnings per share and executive bonuses. But, when stock markets moved downwards, reducing the value of assets in the fund, pension schemes became unfunded – their liabilities exceeded their assets. And, usually, companies did not top up their schemes but merely reported the underfunding in their published accounts. The result is that nowadays most defined benefit schemes have been closed to new members and many have been closed altogether. The number of members of defined benefit schemes has fallen from 5½ million in 1990 to 2½ million in 2009. A defined benefit pension scheme is one under which pensioners are entitled to some percentage of their final salary or some similar formula based upon earnings prior to retirement. This contrasts with the defined contributions scheme where the actual inputs to the scheme are specified but the benefits depend upon markets at the time of retirement.

Demographics are creating problems for pensions too. Fifty years ago, people aimed to retire at 65 and, on average, lived until they were 72. This left an average seven years of pensions during retirement to be financed by contributions accumulated over a working life of 50 years – from 15 to 65. Nowadays people work only about 40 years on average

– from 18 to 58 and can expect to live until they are 80. Thus they now have to finance 22 years of pensions during retirement from only 40 years' worth of contributions. The ratio of the number of years of work to one year as a pensioner has shrunk from more than seven to less than two. If it were possible to increase the average age of retirement from 58 to 65, this ratio would increase to more than three times. An average retirement age as high as 70 would increase the ratio to more than five. But, remember, this is an average retirement age. On average, people are now retiring at only 58. To call this a problem is truly an understatement.

■ The housing market strikes back

In 2005 the US housing market peaked. Four out of ten homes being bought were not for permanent owner occupation. They were either buy-to-let or holiday homes. A building boom had produced a glut of housing, some of it of very low standard. The term McMansion was to be heard in 2005. Twenty per cent of all mortgages were subprime. House prices looked unsustainably high. The average price of a US home, which for two decades had been 3 times the average wage, was 4.6 times the average wage.

The US economy was balanced on a pillar of debt. Much of it was borrowed money against the value of homes. Much of it was credit card debt, car loans and student loans. From 1980 to 2000, US consumer debt (including mortgages) had risen from 80 per cent of disposable income to 96 per cent. By 2005 it stood at 127 per cent. On average, there were nine credit cards for every American citizen. The average amount outstanding was USD5,000 per card. The good news was that with low interest rates the cost of servicing debts had only crept upwards slowly. Furthermore, other household costs had actually fallen, helped by astonishingly cheap products from China.

In 2004 the deflationary impact of very cheap Chinese imports began to run out. Also oil prices had begun to rise. From 2003 to 2005, the price of oil moved from USD30 a barrel to USD60. This was mainly driven by China's own economic growth which, in turn, was driven by lax government in the West encouraging boom conditions in their own economies. Inflation picked up and interest rates in the US, the UK and the eurozone moved northwards. In the US, rates moved from 2½ per cent to 4½ per cent in the year 2006/7. And, as interest rates rose, the US housing market cooled. Early in 2007, a rising level of defaults in the US subprime mortgage market showed up. This was a decisive moment in our story.

Chapter 4

The business of banking

■ Introduction

This book is aimed at both general readers and specialists. It is hoped that the readership will embrace those in their own homes, reading for pleasure, as well as those in government, in the finance industry and students on courses at universities and business schools. Given this wide target readership, in this chapter we present some basic definitions and ideas that may be rather elementary for many of our readers. Nonetheless, we feel that it is worth structuring this chapter with a basic foundation and leaving it to various segments of readers to skip as they feel appropriate based on sub-headings.

We begin by presenting some basic facts about the banking business, covering commercial banks and investment banking. We move on briefly to consider the Glass-Steagall Acts of the USA and central banks. We look at asset-liability matching and mismatching before considering briefly the bank bonus culture and end this chapter with an equally brief overview of the shadow banking system.

■ Banks in general

A bank is a financial institution licensed by a government to undertake the borrowing and lending of money as its main activity. The level of government regulation of the banking industry varies widely from country to country. In the US and the UK, regulation is relatively light. Regulation is heavier (in terms of stricter rules on the level of reserves – the relationship between deposits, capital and lending) in, for example, China.

The term *bank* derives from the Italian word *banco* meaning 'desk or bench' The word can be traced back to the ancient Roman Empire. Moneylenders would set up their stalls in courtyards called *marcella* on a long bench called a *bancu* – hence the word banco.

However, money-changing activities are depicted on coins from the 4th century BC from Trapezus on the Black Sea, nowadays Trabzon. The banker's table is called trapeze, a clear reference to the name of the city. And, in Modern Greek, the word trapeza means both a table and a bank.

Under English law, a banker is defined as a person who carries on the business of banking, which is specified as:

- conducting current accounts for customers;
- paying cheques drawn on them; and
- collecting cheques for customers.

To reiterate, in most jurisdictions, banks are regulated by government and require a special bank licence to operate.

Banks borrow money by accepting funds placed in current and deposit accounts. Such deposits may be demand deposits (repayable on demand) or term deposits (repayable at a specified time in the future). Banks lend money by making advances to customers, either short term or long term.

Assume that bankers reckon, on the basis of past experience, that only ten per cent of its deposits will actually be withdrawn at any time. Then the bank may prudently lend up to 90 per cent of its deposits. As it receives more deposits, more loans are possible on a similar basis. Originally most deposits with the banker were short-term deposits. If the banker were to lend such funds for exactly similar short terms, risk would be minimised and profit would reside in charging more for loans than paying on deposits. Often, deposits on current account have attracted zero interest.

Assume that deposits from personal customers on current accounts are repayable on demand. Also, assume that the bank lends longer-term to businesses to finance longer term requirements, for example to finance working capital. In these circumstances, the bank runs a risk due to the maturity mismatch of the deposit versus the loan. In fact, mismatching of maturities like this is the essence of banking. Banks usually earn more on their longer-term lending than they pay for shorter-term deposits. This strategy is clearly dependent upon depositors not being unhappy about the mismatch. In other words, confidence in the bank, its gap between maturities and the quality of the bank's lending is of utmost importance. Without confidence, depositors' worries about maturity mismatching and the quality of the bank's loan portfolio would lead them to ask for their money back – largely demand deposits, remember. The role of confidence is the critical cornerstone of the business of banking.

Traditionally, banks generate profits from the difference between the level of interest they pay for deposits and other sources of funds and the level of interest they charge for lending. This difference is referred to as the spread between the cost of funds and the loan interest rate. Profitability from lending activities is spiky and dependent upon the susceptibility of loan customers to the business cycle. Aware of this, banks have sought more stable revenue streams and they have placed increasing emphasis on loan fees and service charges for ancillary work (international banking, foreign exchange, insurance, investments, financial advice and so on) and fees for arranging loans. However, lending activities do still provide the backbone of a commercial bank's income.

Banks are always exposed to various forms of risk. These include liquidity risk (where depositors request withdrawals in excess of available funds), credit risk (the probability that those who owe money to the bank will not repay), and interest rate risk (the chance that the bank will become unprofitable as interest rates alter, for example, if rising interest rates force it to pay more on its deposits than it receives on its loans). The actual occurrence of risks may trigger systemic crises, where a large part of the banking system is at risk because many banks become susceptible to a particular risk occurrence.

Banks' activities may be divided into:

- retail banking, dealing directly with individuals and small businesses;
- business banking, providing services to middle-sized businesses;
- corporate banking, directed at large business entities;
- private banking, providing wealth management services to high net worth individuals and families; and
- investment banking, relating to activities in the financial markets.

Most banks are profit-making, private enterprises. In some countries they are owned by governments and may be non-profit organisations. Central banks are normally government-owned and given regulatory responsibilities, such as supervising commercial banks and/or controlling interest rates. They often have custody of their country's gold and foreign exchange reserves and may, as directed by their central government, intervene in foreign exchange markets by buying or selling the home currency or the away currency, with the objective of strengthening or weakening the home currency.

We now look at the breakdown of banks into commercial banks, investment banks and central banks in more detail.

■ Commercial banks

Given the earlier list of banks' activities, commercial banking covers retail banking, business banking and corporate banking. The latter two kinds of category are sometimes clubbed together and termed wholesale banking.

After the Great Depression, US law required that banks engage either in commercial banking activities or in investment banking which was limited to capital market activities – we refer further to investment banking immediately below. This regulation was enacted in the Glass-Steagall Acts. Nowadays, and since the final repeal of Glass-Steagall in 1999, the restriction is not part of the legal requirements in the USA. Other developed countries did not implement a Glass-Steagall type law and did not maintain this separation of commercial and investment banking. Nonetheless, the terms commercial banking and investment banking – as well as wholesale banking and retail banking – are still widely used.

■ Investment banks

Top bankers are at the summit of the élite. In his poem, *Don Juan*, Byron observed that Rothschild and Baring 'are the true lords of Europe'. In Philip Auger's excellent overview of investment banking[1], he recalls a retirement party for an investment banker in which the retiree describes it as 'the best business in the world'. And John Kay[2] observes that 'if you want to understand how the City came to play such a central role in British economic and political life … you need to understand … the influence of investment banks on modern politics and policy.' So what is their business?

Investment banks are financial institutions that deal with raising capital for clients, brokering and trading in securities – on their own behalf or on behalf of clients – and advising on corporate mergers and acquisitions. Investment banks make their profit from companies and governments by raising money through issuing and selling securities in the equity market and bond markets, buying and selling financial instruments, as well as earning fees from advising on corporate finance transactions, such as mergers and acquisitions, share buybacks and flotations of companies on capital markets. Most investment banks also offer advisory services on divestments, reorganisations and other corporate finance services relating to foreign exchange, commodities and derivatives. In most countries, performance of these duties is licensed and regulated.

The final repeal of the Glass-Steagall Act in 1999 was a fillip to the investment banking business. Glass-Steagall is briefly referred to later in this chapter. Suffice to say here that the Act's provisions, instituted in the Great Depression, had restricted commercial banks from leveraging in investment banking activities.

But there were other drivers of investment bank growth in the 1990s. Information technology was a major factor. Banks had developed significant proprietary computer systems allowing each bank to act as a global information network. Flows of money, as well as information, around the system were now accelerated. The effect was to increase short-term information asymmetry in the investment bank's favour. As IT intensified and banks and exchanges became computerised, there was a move away from face-to-face relationships – not completely so, of course. Decision-making in markets became more model-based – but, again, not completely so.

Another driving force favouring the recent rise of investment banks was the wave of privatisations racing across the world. Each privatisation was managed by a team of investment banks. From zero in 1980, the total number of privatisations grew globally to 675 which had generated USD700 billion. And the 18 biggest initial public offerings (IPOs) had all been state-owned businesses privatised through IPOs. The effect was that many near-dormant stock markets were transformed, becoming bigger and more liquid. Investment bankers and their shareholders were gainers too.

Also driving growth was the expansion in foreign exchange (FX) markets. With exchange controls being pared down and computer technology on the rise, so was the size of FX markets, from USD70 billion a day in the early 1980s, to USD500 billion a day in 1988, to over USD3 trillion a day in 2007. Some of this is driven by corporations hedging but world trade and services is only some 2 per cent of the total FX market. Banks taking positions accounted for the lion's share of the rest. Bankers frequently talk of taking positions – they rarely talk about speculating (except amongst themselves). We see no difference between the two.

Finally, the emergence, on a massive scale, of derivative markets was another driver of investment banking growth. The market in derivatives grew over a century ago out of farmers using futures markets to secure prices in advance of marketing their produce. Of course, derivatives are now much more complex and the market is worth USD596 trillion or the world GDP multiplied by eight. These figures are startling. The value of the financial economy is bigger, much bigger than the value of the world economy on which it is based. This has emerged over the last 20 years.

Derivatives can be used to eliminate risk by taking on a position in the derivative market which is the opposite of the risk to be hedged. Or, they can be used to speculate by entering into a derivatives position without an underlying risk exposure. So the derivative can be used to hedge risk or to create risk. So, do derivatives make the finance system safer? Or, do they make it riskier? In this latter respect, Warren Buffet described derivatives as 'financial weapons of mass destruction, carrying dangers that are potentially lethal'.

One of the main activities of investment banks is buying and selling investment products, whether on their own account or for clients. Because they do buy and sell for their own bank's account, this part of operations has, pejoratively, been termed their casino business.

In their activities, investment banks talk about the front office, middle office and back office. The distinctions in these parts of the business are now described.

The front office is concerned with:

■ services for corporate or government clients in the raising of funds in the capital markets and advising on mergers and acquisitions;

■ investment management of clients' securities (for example, shares, bonds and real estate). Such clients may be institutions (insurance companies, pension funds) or private investors;

■ corporate finance work;

■ foreign exchange, equity and fixed interest, commodities and derivatives trading and brokering;

■ merchant banking work, which is an old term for investment banking but also embraces international trade work for clients;

■ research involving the valuation of equities or other corporate investments.

Under the last bullet point, there is a clear conflict of interest within the bank because corporate finance work for clients invariably involves inside information. The relationship between the research arm and the rest of the investment bank has become highly regulated requiring a Chinese wall between these functions.

Turning to the middle office, this is concerned with:

■ risk management, embracing the analysis and control of market and credit risk that traders in the bank are taking in conducting their daily deals. This involves setting limits on the amount of capital that traders are able to deal and monitoring them;

■ finance which, in this context, refers to the bank's capital management and risk monitoring. This embraces the bank's overall global risk exposure and profitability. The importance of this role cannot be overemphasised. It is complicated and demanding;

- compliance, which is concerned with the bank's daily operations and the personal investment activities of bank personnel to ensure that they accord with government regulations, market rules and internal regulations.

Moving to the back office, this is concerned with:

- operations involving checking trades that have been conducted and ensuring that they are accurate and involve the required paperwork. Trades have to be within written bank rules, limits and with approved counterparties. In times of buoyancy, backlogs can become massive;

- internal audit of operations, including those described immediately above;

- technology. All banks have vast amounts of in-house software and technical support and this role cannot be underestimated.

It is not difficult to guess that the back office has been massively overwhelmed by the growth referred to earlier. Moreover, in the hierarchy of the investment bank, the front office is regarded as the location of the star performers – the élite in the banks. We have been told of conversations in which back office personnel query front office deals and the dealer fobs off the enquiry with the observation that 'Yes, everything's alright. It's not a problem. The deal is exactly as stated there. Don't worry. The paperwork is fine and in line with the deal done'. End of conversation. So much for this brief overview. We will be returning to risk management in investment banking in more detail in Chapter 7.

■ Bank holding companies

The term bank holding company is applied to those banks which mix commercial and investment banking. In situations where banks only engage in investment banking, they are said to be part of the shadow banking system – see later in this chapter.

■ Glass-Steagall Act

Two separate US laws are known as the Glass-Steagall Act. The first was passed in 1932 and the second in 1933. In the Great Depression, Congress examined the mixing of commercial banks and investment banks that had occurred in the twenties. Hearings revealed conflicts of interest – and even fraud in some banking institutions' securities activities. Barriers to the mixing of these activities were established by the Glass-Steagall Act. This influence has been felt elsewhere around the globe – for example, China separates the activities of commercial banks from the securities industries. The earlier McFadden Act of 1927 had prevented commercial banks' activities from expanding across state boundaries, designed to limit a bank's geographic representation in the USA.

In tandem with successful lobbying to repeal the McFadden Act, achieved via the Riegle-Neal Interstate Banking and Branching Efficiency Act of 1994, the banking industry also sought the phasing out of the Glass-Steagall Act. In 1987, a report was tabled before Congress which explored the pros and cons of the case. In fact, in 1987, the Federal Reserve altered the Glass-Steagall rules, allowing commercial banks to undertake investment banking activities up to 5 per cent of their turnover. This dilution of the Act continued until, in 1996, it reached 25 per cent.

Just before the Act was finally repealed, the USD85 billion merger of Travelers, an insurance company which also owned investment bank Salomon Brothers, and Citicorp was approved in 1998. This created Citigroup, the biggest financial company in the world. The US Treasury Secretary, Robert Rubin, had waived the rules in advance of Glass-Steagall being repealed. Rubin himself became Co-CEO of Citigroup in October 1999. Ultimately, after continued bank lobbying, the Act was repealed under the Gramm-Leach-Bliley Act of 1999. The repeal enabled commercial banks to underwrite and trade financial instruments and various derivatives.

The reintroduction of Glass-Steagall type restrictions is one of the solutions under consideration by governments to prevent a repeat of the 2007/8 financial crash. Such a change is heartily and heavily resisted by bankers. Of course, if the mixing of investment banking and commercial banking genuinely poses a problem to the integrity and longevity of the banking system, we would support the case. The key issue here is the extent to which the mixing of bank types caused the crash and would be likely to cause another financial crisis.

■ Central banks

The central bank (sometimes called the Reserve Bank or Monetary Authority) is the body responsible for the monetary policy of a country or of a group of countries or states. Responsibilities vary but usually embrace:

- implementation of monetary policy;
- control of the nation's money supply;
- duties as the government's banker and the bankers' bank (lender of last resort – see later in this chapter);
- managing the country's foreign exchange and gold reserves and the government's bond register;
- regulating and supervising the banking industry;
- setting the official interest rate (with implications for managing both inflation and the country's exchange rate).

Nowadays, many countries have an independent central bank, designed to limit political interference. Examples include the European Central Bank (ECB), and the Bank of England. In these countries (although they are termed independent) central banks are publicly owned. In other countries they may be privately owned. Indeed, although formed in 1694 as a chartered joint stock company, the Bank of England was only taken into public ownership in 1946. In fact, nationalisation merely formalised a state of affairs that had existed for years and involved no change in the way the Bank operated.

All banks are required to hold a certain percentage of their assets as capital, a rate established by the central bank or other banking supervisor. For international banks the requirement is 8 per cent of risk-adjusted assets (some assets, such as government bonds, are considered to have lower risk than others for purposes of calculating capital adequacy – hence the risk-adjusted process).

In terms of regulating banks, central banks usually establish reserve requirements for other banks. For example, they may require that a percentage of liabilities be held as cash or deposited with the central bank. Such reserve requirements were introduced in the 19th century to reduce the risk of banks overextending themselves and suffering bank runs, which could lead to knock-on effects on other banks.

In Britain, UK banking supervision is carried out by the UK Treasury, the Bank of England and the UK's Financial Services Authority. Control and monitoring is achieved by examination of the banks' ongoing balance sheets and their behaviour and policies in the market place. Since this tripartite control mechanism failed to identify the 2007 problems and their complexity, we would conclude that the need for reorganisation is clear. Prior to 1997, regulation resided with the Bank of England.

■ Asset-liability mismatch

An asset-liability mismatch occurs when the financial terms of the assets and liabilities do not correspond. Asset-liability mismatches may occur in various ways. A bank may have substantial long-term assets, such as long-term loans to business customers, but short-term liabilities, such as demand deposits. This creates a maturity mismatch. Also, a bank could have all of its liabilities at floating interest rates but its assets in fixed rate instruments. Another example is where a bank borrows entirely in US dollars and lends in euros, creating a currency mismatch. If the value of the euro were to fall dramatically, the bank would lose out. Asset-liability mismatches like this may be controlled by hedging activities.

Controlled maturity mismatch, with average short-term deposits being less than average longer-term loans and with average higher interest rates accruing in the bank's favour, is of the essence to the business model of commercial banks.

Asset-liability mismatches may also occur in insurance and pensions management, where long-term liabilities (promises to pay the insured or pension plan participants) may not exactly correspond to the maturity and value of assets. Appropriately matching financial assets and obligations is very important in these businesses.

Business investment on plant, property and equipment generally gives rise to cash generation over a number of future years and this cash flow is usually insufficient to provide loan repayment over merely one year. So, when businesses need to borrow to finance their investments, they prefer loans with a long maturity. By contrast, individual savers, mainly households and small firms, may have somewhat unpredictable needs for cash, due to unforeseen expenditures. Consequently, they prefer liquid accounts which permit them immediate access to their deposits, namely short maturity deposit accounts. With this background, banks provide a valuable service by channelling funds from many individual depositors to corporate borrowers. Since banks provide a service to both sides, providing the long-maturity loans to businesses and liquid accounts to depositors, they are in a position to earn profit from such activities.

Under ordinary circumstances, savers' unpredictable needs for cash are unlikely to occur at the same time. In accepting demand deposits from many different sources, the bank expects only a small fraction of withdrawals in the short term, even though depositors have the right to take their deposits back at any time. Thus a bank can make loans over a long horizon, while keeping only relatively small amounts of cash on hand to pay depositors that wish to make withdrawals. Given that individuals' expenditure needs tend to be uncorrelated, banks may expect relatively few major withdrawals on any single day. We now turn to the issue of the bank bonus culture, a topic widely discussed in the wake of the financial crisis.

■ The bank bonus culture

The traditional stereotype of the banker, based on commercial banking, would probably elicit such descriptions as helpful, wise, conservative, not pushy, concerned with the bank customers' best interests, a little aloof and rather boring. The growth of investment banking, in both the USA and in Europe, and especially since the 1980s has dramatically changed the stereotype. Now, the image of the banker is one of much less conservatism, pushy, concerned with the bank's (and their own) bottom-line profit, with the interest of customers subordinated below the bank's and banker's own self-interest. And rather than the staid image, we see an elite of top banking executives with big salaries, big expense accounts, enjoying the best seats at sporting events, the opera, first nights and so on – generally on the firm. The image has morphed to a racy and a rich one (and an attitude of 'I don't care who knows it'). This picture is exemplified and reinforced in movies and in various exposés – see for example books by Frank Partnoy[3] and Geraint Anderson[4]. The changed image has been accompanied by changed banking profit outturns, from satisfactory to massive and, of course, escalating bonus payments, again from satisfactory to massive. Multi-million pound bonuses have been regular features of the banking landscape. One of the big problems of such remuneration systems is that the outcome of many of the deals underpinning the bonus may be done now but their final outturns are only revealed, maybe, five years into the future. And it is well known that many of the toxic contracts that banks were undertaking in the run up to the crash appeared to be profitable at their inception and shortly thereafter but later were revealed to be nothing more than recklessly idiotic deals with loss-making consequences for their banks. And, of course, bonuses have already been paid out on these deals. The dealers concerned may well have left the bank – retiring at the age of 35, wealthy and with little or no need to work again during their lives.

Clearly, from the standpoint of shareholders, bonuses should only be paid on finally-completed and unravelled contracts – maybe four or five years down the line. By contrast, from the viewpoint of the banker, the existing system would seem to be very much in their own self-interest. We believe that less-extravagant bonus payments would better be paid in shares which would only vest when the underlying contracts are finally complete. Even then, there should be some form of clawback for subsequently revealed poor performance. We will return to this topic in Chapter 11 where we show examples of bonuses which were dysfunctional from the shareholder standpoint but advantageous to the self-interest of the banker.

An interesting variant is the bonus/malus practice reported as being trialled at UBS. Bonuses are there for success but there are maluses for failure with an extended time horizon for adjudication on the results of deals. However, when studied in detail, the system still seems rather generous. Why? Well, consider how the system works. Under the UBS system, compensation comprises both fixed and variable components. The latter part is linked to risk-adjusted value creation over a long period and reflects sustainable profitability. The approach includes:

- a fixed base salary;
- variable cash compensation, up to one-third paid immediately with the balance held in escrow in a bonus account. This may decline and be eliminated if UBS results are poor, if there are regulatory violations, or if high risks are taken. The reduction is termed the malus;
- variable equity compensation, where awarded shares vest after three years and depend on long-term value creation. Very senior managers are locked in even beyond three years.

The above formula applies to key managers and risk-taking employees. Other employees remain under the previous compensation package.

The temptation to push for a higher fixed base salary in difficult times needs to be resisted by UBS top managers. Might there also be a temptation to switch from basic salary to bonus and back again as times change? The law of unintended consequences may suggest that the system could create an incentive to hide losses and/or reduce risk-aversion on the part of traders in boom times.

True, massive bonuses have not just been a feature of the banking business. It has become a normal part of life at the top echelons of business in general. One might argue that it is shareholders' fault for failing to check such overindulgence – after all, they vote on recommendations of corporate remuneration committees. But since the preponderance of quoted shareholdings reside in the hands of pensions funds and financial institutions, they are hardly likely to be enthusiastic about curbing executive excesses. After all, the managers of these institutions benchmark their own remuneration against banking and corporate executive salaries. Normally, they are quite happy to concur with company remuneration committee recommendations and, no doubt, feel a sense of satisfaction at the thought that it is likely to feed back into their own bank account.

The bonus culture in non-financial businesses has an asymmetric angle too. This is because when losses occur, the earlier (and already paid) bonuses are not reversed. Look at the 2008 débâcle of the banks. Look at the débâcle of UK electronics company Marconi where, despite its failure, directors' bank accounts and pension pots performed remarkably positively. Is all of this executive self-aggrandisement symptomatic of 'me generation' behaviour?

Having observed how pernicious the bonus culture at banks and other businesses has become, we are reminded of Robin Marris' theory of managerial capitalism[5]. He suggested[6] that 'top management, owning little or no equity in the firm, has three main motives (i) growth, because growth provides job satisfaction, job expansion, high salaries, high bonuses and prestige; (ii) continuity of employment which means, for the management team as a whole, avoidance of involuntary takeover; and (iii) reasonable treatment of shareholders and generally good relations with the financial world.' Do we need a new behavioural theory of managerial capitalism in which top management, owning little or no equity in the firm, has three main motives (i) massive remuneration, pensions, perks, bonuses and benefits, power, job satisfaction, prestige and rolling contracts; (ii) continuity of employment and, should that be terminated, for whatever reason, the receipt of substantial golden goodbye payments and pension enhancements and (iii) good relations with the financial community and moderately reasonable treatment of shareholders (with some more reasonably treated than others). Cynical, you might say? Well, with justification. We believe that policy makers as well as our readers should think seriously about this New Behavioural Theory of Managerial Capitalism. It is apparent to any observer and it needs to be curbed.

Before we leave the topic of the bonus culture, we think that it is worth discussing briefly the culture of the dealing room where traders buy and sell financial instruments. It is not called the jungle for nothing. Various participants have tellingly revealed the vulgarity, avarice, cheating and extravagance of the dealing room, for example Frank Partnoy's *F.I.A.S.C.O.*[7], Michael Lewis' *Liar's Poker*[8], Geraint Anderson's *Cityboy*[9], *Binge Trading* by Seth Freeman[10] and *How I Caused the Credit Crunch* by Tetsuya Ishikawa[11]. In reading these participant accounts, repeatedly one finds oneself asking, as we frequently do, how could the dealers selling some of the most toxic securities have been so unscrupulous in their peddling of these high risk, potentially destructive instruments? The answer 'greed' springs to mind. The answer that the bonus is based upon it also springs to mind. But, the same kind of question is there in respect of the purchasers. How could they have been so short-sighted as to buy them? Perhaps again the answer is greed and the bonus because they were frequently thinking that these products could be sold on to the next sucker in the financial food chain.

Of course, it is also the case that behaviour is adaptive and people conform to the culture in which they find themselves. True for the trading room, true for the schoolboys in William Golding's *Lord of the Flies*[12], and true for the rise of Nazism in Third Reich Germany.

■ The bank bonus culture and declining standards

The move away from a traditional investment banking emphasis upon corporate and investment advice towards a trading focus brought a shift in the locus of power away from traditional investment bankers towards the dealers. By the end of the last century, trading revenues in many banks were dominating traditional income. This was true for investment banks like Lehman Brothers but also for some commercial banks like Citigroup and J. P. Morgan Chase. The result was a move from building a long-term business to making the next quarter's bonus. But bonuses were massive compared to basic salary. They could be 20 or even 100 times basic salary. This inevitably distorts incentives. Wall Street and City of London bankers became fixated on end-year valuations in order to maximise their bonus payout. The corollary was a deterioration in ethical standards and an increase in accounting shenanigans. At the individual level, it became necessary to run with the bank's in-crowd. You may say, nothing new there then.

The reputation for gentlemanly capitalism in banks was being replaced by a widespread decimation of standards. Credit analysis, as we will see in Chapter 7, was being devalued. And the spread of shallow investment analysis of quoted companies leading to biased buy/hold/sell recommendations was almost fraudulent. As Das[13] relates: 'internal emails described a business as a dog; in research distributed to clients, the same business was a star.' He also observes that 'for the most part, the research distributed by investment banks to clients evolved into puffery designed to get the client to trade. Analysts were expected to build profile for the firm and for themselves.'

Similarly, Dowd and Hutchinson[14] observe that 'bankers and clients pressured analysts not to make negative or controversial claims. 'Buy' recommendations predominated – over 90 per cent of recommendations during the dotcom bubble – and 'sell' recommendations became infrequent. The catchphrase was 'pump and dump': analysis at investment banks would pump up stocks with over-optimistic reports, especially those relating to recent IPOs; insiders would then dump them as soon as they were able to, when lockup periods expired, leaving investors holding overvalued stocks.'

All of this was symptomatic of declining standards. Kotlikoff[15] lists examples. As he states '... all ... have been the subject of publicly disclosed government investigations leading to huge fines:

- Bear Stearns paid millions to settle federal charges of illegal loan collection practices.
- Bank of America deceived investors by selling risky auction-rate securities as perfectly safe.
- Ditto UBS, Merrill Lynch, Morgan Stanley, and Wachovia.
- GMAC Bank and other student loan companies engaged in deceptive advertising.
- IndyMac Bank routinely issued liar loans until it went broke.
- Countrywide engaged in deceitful lending. Its former CEO is under indictment.
- J. P. Morgan Chase, Citigroup, and CIBC paid billions to settle securities fraud charges.
- S&P, Moody's, and Fitch took billions in exchange for rating toxics triple-A.
- HSBC and Citigroup used structured investment vehicles to conceal risky mortgage holdings.
- Freddie Mac failed to fully disclose its portfolio losses.
- AIG hid huge losses on its credit default swaps.
- Lehman Brothers, Citigroup, and Merrill competed to develop abusive tax-evasion schemes.

- B of A settled with the SEC for withholding news of huge Merrill bonuses from shareholders.'

Was all of this decline in banking standards being driven by the bonus culture?

■ Risk/return implications of the bank bonus culture

Obviously, there are problems which accrue where the bonus culture is so large, widespread and asymmetric. Falling standards and dubious practices seemed to follow. But, there are other problems. If, in the long-run, greater return accrues to greater risk, then where a bonus system is operative based upon absolute money results, the tendency will be for greater risk to be taken on by the self-seeking executive coalition.

Moreover, given that it is possible to engage in dealing opaque and extremely complex financial instruments, which even baffle finance directors, it may be possible to put excess values on such instruments – which may create ongoing bonuses for their original purchasers. This was observed at some banks at the time of the crisis. And, if the executive creating the deception thinks they are likely to be found out, the alternative to move on to another bank is always there.

The whole bank bonus culture could be said to encourage greater risk taking, to encourage dealing in non-transparent financial instruments, to favour bias in valuation of such instruments, to prefer short-termism, taking on more leverage (see the section immediately below), and a desire to see the money (the cash bonus) as soon as possible rather than when the potential gain for the bank ultimately accrues or unravels. Since all bank executives are party to this culture, the chances of anyone within the organisation saying 'stop' is highly unlikely. And the shareholders too, represented by pension funds and financial institutions, are unlikely to call a halt because their remuneration is so often benchmarked against comparable businesses – namely banks.

■ Bank balance sheets

One of the ways in which banks and any other business can take on more risk is through gearing, also called leverage. This represents the proportion of debt in a company's capital structure. The main sources of capital for a business are debt and equity (that is, amounts that shareholders have subscribed plus amounts left in the business as retained profits or reserves). As mentioned earlier in this chapter, the lion's share of bank liabilities is represented by deposits that it has received from customers. This represents debt on the bank's balance sheet. The ratio of equity versus debt plus equity (debt plus equity represents total assets) has shown a long-term fall as can be seen in Table 4.1. Referring to this table, Tim Congdon[16] stresses that, whilst the average ratio of equity to total assets 'may have been about 5 per cent the effective ratio for a surprisingly high number of prominent institutions was little more than 3 per cent'.

Furthermore, the increasing risk profile of banks can be seem from two other telling figures. The first, Figure 4.1, shows the ratio of UK banks' cash reserves to deposits

Table 4.1 Equity capital to total assets of UK and US banks, 1880–1985

	UK banks*	US banks†
1880	16.8	n/a
1900	12.0	n/a
1914	8.7	18.3
1930	7.2	14.2
1940	5.2	9.1
1950	2.7	6.7
1966	5.3	7.8
1980	5.9	6.8
1985	4.6	6.9

*UK deposit banks 1880–1966, UK clearing bank groups 1980 and 1985.
†All member banks of the Federal Reserve system.
The low value of the UK ratio in 1950 reflected the high ratio of low-risk government paper in banks' assets after World War II.
Source: M. K. Lewis and K. T. Davis, *Domestic and International Banking*, Philip Allen, Oxford, 1987.

(remember, deposits are liabilities for the banks), falling from 11 per cent in the sixties to recent figures below 1 per cent. A similar trend is shown in Figure 4.2 for US banks.

Risk is often classed as being either business risk or financial risk. Business risk is concerned with the volatility of operating profit for a business through the business cycle. Financial risk is concerned with the percentage level of debt in a firm's capital structure. The presence of high financial risk is generally associated with low business risk and vice versa. Table 4.1 and Figures 4.1 and 4.2 show a colossally increasing level of financial risk. This has been occurring at the same time as banks have been taking on higher levels of risk in their operations

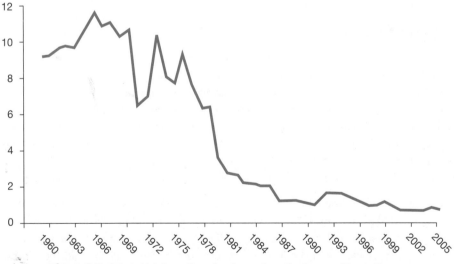

According to IMP data (which have the advantage of continuity over 45 years), the UK banks' cash/deposits ratio fell from over 9% in 1960 to under 1% in 2005.

Figure 4.1 UK bank's cash/deposit ratio, 1960–2005 (ratio of cash reserves to sight, time, savings and foreign currency deposits of UK banks)

Source: IMF.

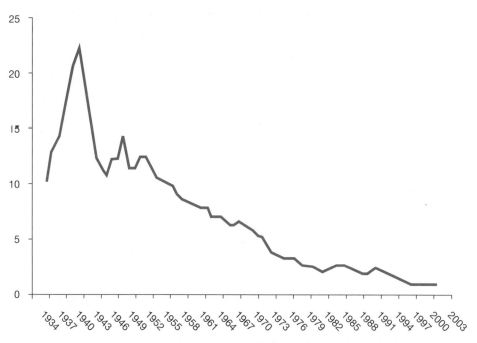

Figure 4.2 US banks' cash deposit ratios, 1934–2004 (% of deposit liabilities)
Source: Federal Deposit Insurance Corporation website.

– higher business risk. Was this cavalier financial incompetence? Was this the corollary of the asymmetric bank bonus culture? Was it propelled by the knowledge that the banks would be bailed out if they failed (moral hazard)? Or was it a combination of all of these?

■ Moral hazard

Moral hazard arises where a party insulated from risk may behave differently from the way it would behave if it were fully exposed to the risk. Moral hazard arises because an individual or institution does not take the full consequences and responsibilities of its doings, and therefore has a tendency to act less carefully than it otherwise would, leaving another party with some responsibility for the consequences of those actions. Potential financial bail-outs of lending institutions by governments and central banks may encourage risky lending if those that take the risks believe that they will not have to carry the full burden of losses. Dealing in risk-laden financial instruments with the safety net of a bail-out clearly falls into this category.

Banks take risks in making loans. Usually, the most risky loans have the potential for making the highest returns. Lending banks that are considered too big to fail may make risky loans that will pay off handsomely if the investment succeeds but will be bailed out, at the taxpayer's expense, if the investment turns out badly. It can be said that, in this instance, profit is privatised but risk is socialised.

And it does not just apply in the case of big banks. It applies to borrowers who take on unserviceable mortgages or small businesses which expand recklessly. Such borrowers, whether a business or an individual, may not act prudently when they invest or spend funds being aware that if the worst occurrence happens, they may merely seek to file for bankruptcy. Of course, the bankruptcy laws provide an example of moral hazard. The argument justifying this is that the entrepreneur may create wealth for themselves and for society. To prevent them from continuing to try to create wealth might be bad for society hence rules which enable them to try again. We bump into moral hazard again and again in business. Of course, it is there in the bank bonus schemes referred to above. And it is there in the lender of last resort concept which follows.

■ Lender of last resort

In banking parlance, the lender of last resort acts to protect depositors, prevent widespread panic-withdrawals of funds and avoid damage to the economy caused by the collapse of a financial institution. In the USA, the Federal Reserve Bank serves as the lender of last resort and in the UK this role is undertaken by the Bank of England. Borrowing from the lender of last resort is only available to deposit-taking banks and is resorted to in times of crisis. It indicates that the bank in question has taken on too much risk, or that the institution is experiencing financial difficulties. It is usually called into play when the bank is near collapse.

Critics of the lender of last resort role argue that it is a temptation for a financial institution to take on excess risk. The lender of last resort insulates the banking institution from the consequences of its own risk-taking. The essential justification of the role is that it is there to prevent widespread – or even occasional – bank failure which would result in ordinary citizens losing their deposits with less than scrupulous banking institutions.

■ The shadow banking system and non-bank financial institutions

The shadow banking system consists of non-bank financial institutions. A non-bank financial institution (NBFI) is a financial institution that does not have a full banking licence or is not supervised by a national or international banking regulatory agency. Shadow banking institutions are, amongst other things, intermediaries between investors and borrowers. A pension fund may be willing to lend money, while a company may be seeking borrowings. A shadow banking institution may channel funds from the investor to the firm, gaining from fees or from the interest rate turn between what it pays and receives on the deal. Shadow banking institutions are not usually deposit accepting and not all are subject to bank regulations.

Investment banks that are not linked with commercial banks as bank holding companies are part of the shadow banking regime. Bear Stearns and Lehman Brothers were shadow banking institutions. The system includes hedge funds, investment banks (that are not part of a mix with commercial banks) and many other non-bank financial institutions. Shadow banks have been active in most financial centres in the world. Prior to the financial crisis, lending through the shadow banking system slightly exceeded total lending via the traditional banking system.

Shadow institutions are not subject to the same safety and soundness regulations as commercial banks. Thus, they do not have to keep as much in funds relative to their lending. In short, NBFIs usually have a higher level of financial leverage, with a higher level of debt relative to their liquid assets compared with commercial banks. Shadow institutions tend to borrow from investors short term. And they lend or invest longer term in less liquid assets. Prior to the crash, many of the long-term assets purchased were the mortgage-backed securities and similar instruments, which declined significantly in value as housing prices headed south after 2007. Their reliance on short-term funding forced NBFIs to return to capital markets to refinance their businesses. With the housing market deteriorating and the value of mortgage-backed securities declining, NBFIs were unable to fund themselves. The value drop made lenders strongly question the capability of counter-parties to repay lending given the drought in the short-term funding market. This was a major factor in the failure of Bear Stearns and Lehman Brothers in 2008.

As mentioned earlier, NBFIs are not usually depository institutions and do not have central bank's lender-of-last-resort support. During periods of market illiquidity, they can easily go bankrupt if they are unable to refinance their short-term borrowings. Remember, they are usually highly leveraged and they typically lend for longer periods than their borrowings. The markets typically tapped by the shadow banking system began to close in the middle of 2007 and wholly dried up around September 2008.

The shadow banking system conducts a massive amount of trading in the over-the-counter derivatives market, which grew rapidly in the boom years prior to the 2008 financial crisis, reaching USD700 trillion dollars in terms of contract value. Credit derivatives, col-lateralised debt obligations (CDOs), bundles of mortgage securities (hedge-backed securities) and credit default swaps (CDSs) experienced the most rapid growth. Hundreds of billions of dollars of credit default swap contracts taken on by AIG, the world's largest insurance company, had a big part to play in the financial collapse. See the case study on AIG, p. 186. Much of this activity was off-balance sheet for the banks concerned. The shadow banking system has been blamed for precipitating the subprime mortgage crisis and helping it to grow into a global credit crunch. We address these issues in more detail in the next two chapters. We leave the topic of the shadow banking system with a quote often heard in financial circles – 'If it looks like a bank', regulate it like a bank. Its meaning and implications for the shadow banks is obvious.

Chapter **5**

Subprime lenders and borrowers

■ Introduction

Everyone thinks they know what subprime lending is but there is no universally-accepted definition except that it refers to lending by financial institutions in ways which do not meet prime lending standards. Subprime lending may include mortgages, motor car loans and credit card debt. Subprime loans are usually classified, at least in the USA, as those where the borrower has a FICO score, variously reported as below 620 or below 640. The acronym FICO stands for the Fair Isaac Corporation. FICO is a publicly quoted US company that developed the most widely used credit score model. FICO scores are calculated based on information from a consumer's credit files.

A credit score is a number representing the creditworthiness of a person. It indicates the likelihood that a person will pay their debts. It is predictive of bad debt risk and has made credit more widely available and helps in determining its interest cost and security requirements. Credit scores are based on statistical analysis of a person's credit report information, as provided by credit bureaux. Banks and credit card companies use credit scores to evaluate the risk posed in lending money to consumers. In short, they determine who qualifies for a loan, at what interest rate, and on what credit terms. Banks may deny credit, charge high interest rates, request security, or require full income and asset verification where the FICO credit score is low.

FICO scoring models are widely used in North America, Central and South America, the UK, Ireland, Continental Europe and Asia. Although their precise methodology is proprietorial and, therefore, not made public, FICO executives have disclosed their broad criteria as embracing:

- 35 per cent based on past payment history for bills, mortgages and credit cards;
- 30 per cent based on credit utilisation;
- 15 per cent based on types of credit used;
- 10 per cent based on recent search for credit and/or amount of credit obtained.

FICO scores range between 300 and 850 (high being a good credit). Sixty per cent of scores fall between 650 and 799. This puts the subprime score of 620 or 640 and below into context.

The lion's share of subprime lending is in respect of mortgages. The total value of USA subprime mortgages has been estimated to have peaked at USD1.3 trillion in March 2007.

At that time, the value of all outstanding US residential mortgages was around USD10 trillion. The share of new subprime mortgages relative to total new US mortgages was around 20 per cent from 2004 to 2006, up from 9 per cent a decade earlier. And there were many innovative features attaching to subprime mortgages, including:

- interest-only payments, with borrowers paying interest only for a limited period of time, maybe five to ten years. Thereafter payments would be interest plus capital;
- pay option loans, with adjustable rates, under which borrowers choose their monthly payment, ranging from full payment, interest only, or some specified minimum payment;
- hybrid mortgages with low initial fixed interest rates that subsequently alter to adjustable rates.

The last kind of mortgage became very popular during the 1990s and the first half of the following decade.

Subprime hybrids include the 2-28 loan, which allows for a low initial interest rate that stays fixed for two years but resets to a higher adjustable rate for the remaining life of the loan, 28 years. The new interest rate would be set relative to some index, for example, 5 per cent over 12 month LIBOR. Variations on the above theme would include the 3-27 and the 5-25 formula for refixing the timing of pricing changes. Clearly there is scope here for the hard-selling mortgage broker to make a pitch for business with a potential borrower, placing emphasis on the short run rate rather than the later changed rate. And there is also scope for the borrower, who wanted to get onto the property ladder at any cost, and is subsequently nursing a loss of house value, to complain that they are an innocent victim and were unaware of the actual implications of the mortgage taken on.

So, why did US subprime lending take off in the decade after the mid-nineties? There were many factors. One of the most influential was low interest rates. Interest rate levels and large inflows of foreign funds to the USA, in particular, created easy money conditions in the 1990s and in the first half of the subsequent decade. This fuelled a housing boom and drove debt-financed consumption. US home ownership increased from 64 per cent in 1994, where it had been since 1980, to a high of 69.2 per cent in 2004. From 1997 to 2006, the price of the average US home increased by 124 per cent. For the last 20 years of the last century, the median US home price was around 3 times median household income. This ratio rose to 4 times in 2004 and to 4.6 in 2006. USA household debt as a percentage of annual disposable personal income was 77 per cent in 1990 but rose to 127 per cent in 2007 and to 134 per cent in mid-2008. US household debt moved from USD705 billion in 1974, that is, 60 per cent of personal disposable income, to USD7.4 trillion in 2000, and to USD14.5 trillion by mid-2008, that is, 134 per cent of annual personal disposable income. Home mortgage debt in the USA relative to GDP moved from an average of 46 per cent in the 1990s to 73 per cent in 2008 (home mortgage debt was USD 10.5 trillion in 2008).

With housing prices bubbling, households were saving less and both borrowing and spending more. The culture of consumerism was symptomatic of an economy based on immediate gratification – the 'I want it and I want it now' syndrome. Also driving these massive trends in debt levels was the impact of the Community Reinvestment Act (CRA). Since many of our readers will be unaware of this piece of US legislation, we focus upon it below.

■ Community Reinvestment Act

Prior to the Community Reinvestment Act (CRA) being passed, there was a shortage of credit available for residents of certain low- and modest-income neighbourhoods. In its 1961 report, the US Commission on Civil Rights concluded that African-American borrowers were frequently required to make higher downpayments on loans and to adopt faster repayment schedules, presumably reflecting proven greater risk of default rather than outright discrimination. The Commission also recorded refusals to lend in particular geographical areas: this it termed redlining. This involved some withholding of mortgage monies in neighbourhoods deemed unsafe – these were lined in red on residential security maps created by the Home Owner's Loan Committee (HOLC).

The CRA was a US federal law designed to encourage commercial banks and lending associations to meet the needs of borrowers in all segments of their communities, including low-income and moderate-income neighbourhoods. The Act was passed in 1977 to reduce the discriminatory credit practice of redlining. The Act required federal supervisory agencies to encourage regulated financial institutions to meet the credit needs of the local communities in which they were mandated. It required federal regulatory agencies to examine banking institutions for CRA compliance, and the results of this information would be considered when approving applications for new bank branches and for mergers and acquisitions.

Moving on to 1993, part of the housing strategy of the new Democratic administration of Bill Clinton was focused on increased home ownership among the poor, and particularly among blacks and Hispanics. Increasing home ownership was reckoned to be correlated with less crime, better school performance and a greater sense of community. But lending practices of banks remained conservative. The Clinton administration urged banks to be more creative. In this respect, the Department of Housing and Urban Development (HUD) was delegated to pressurise mortgage banks into action.

The banks responded positively. From 1995, they began to loosen their rigorous lending criteria. Mortgages with only 3 per cent deposits, and, eventually, even less, began to appear. And banks competed hard to offer loans to low-income households and to minority customers. In five years, the number of African-American and Latin homeowners increased by two million. And the securitisation of subprime loans began, the first being launched in 1997 in collaboration with Bear Stearns. Could it be argued that the originate-to-hold model morphed into the originate-to-distribute model as a direct result of US government pressure?

Under the traditional model, a mortgage bank would lend against the security of a home and the bank would hold the debt and receive interest and capital repayments. Under the originate-to-distribute model, it is different. The bank lends against the security of a home but, instead of holding the debt, the bank sells on the debt to a specialist financial institution where a series of similar loans bought from various mortgage banks are parcelled together and sold on to others as a package called an MBS (mortgage-backed security) or mixed up with other debts and the bundle sold on as a CDO (collateralised debt obligation). This process is called securitisation.

Where the bank holds the mortgage debt under the traditional originate-to-hold model for, maybe, 20 years it will be likely to be careful about its customers' abilities to repay and it will carry out a diligent appraisal in this area. However, under originate-to-distribute, the screening of borrowers might be at a lower level of care, since the loan is being sold on. More on this topic in Chapter 7.

With house prices rising at the start of this century, with easy money, with low interest rates and with a consumer spending spree forcing credit card debt higher, the friendly mortgage brokers had a field day arranging new subprime loans and convincing customers that refinancing existing mortgage debt was a great idea – as it might have been had interest rates remained low and had house prices gone on escalating. But, all bull markets eventually run out of steam. They become bear markets before bouncing back to bull status. This has always happened and it always will. And, in 2007 this is just what happened. So much for this very brief overview of the influence of the CRA. We now move to the mechanics of subprime lending.

■ The business of subprime lending

We have seen that subprime borrowers typically have FICO scores below 620 or 640. Borrowers with scores over 620 or so are classified as conforming – that is, they conform to Fannie Mae and Freddie Mac guidelines. Conforming borrowers are prime borrowers assuming that their loan requests contain full documentation including verification of incomes and assets. Alt-A borrowers are usually prime borrowers except that their loan documentation is not of conforming standards in some way or the request may be for a holiday home or a second home. Typically, subprime borrowers have credit scores of 500 to 620. Borrowers with scores below 500 were even below subprime. But, thanks to the unethical practices of many mortgage brokers who encouraged potential borrowers to lie about job status and income levels (these loans were aptly called liar loans) many of below subprime status managed to qualify for the first rung of the American Dream ladder. It is also worth mentioning that another class of house loan is termed the jumbo mortgage. These are mortgage loans that are bigger in size than the conforming loan ceiling amount.

To explain the two companies mentioned above, Fannie Mae (the Federal National Mortgage Association) and Freddie Mac (the Federal Home Loan Mortgage Association), these are both government sponsored enterprises whose purpose is to purchase, guarantee and securitise mortgages in order to ensure that funds are consistently available to the institutions that lend money to home buyers.

The concept of mortgage lending up to the advent of securitisation was termed originate-to-hold. In other words, the loan would appear as an asset on the balance sheet of the original lender. However, following securitisation, the originate-to-distribute model evolved. Here the asset (the mortgage debt) would be sold on by the mortgage bank to another party. Securitisation is discussed in more detail in Chapter 6 but a brief look is called for here.

Securitisation of mortgages is a process whereby thousands of mortgage loans are bundled into financial products called mortgage-backed securities (MBSs). These are secured on the house mortgaged, principal payments and interest repayments made by borrowers. The process which was already in existence for conforming and Alt-A mortgages expanded to the packaging of subprime mortgages in the mid-1990s, hastened by the goading of the Clinton administration, CRA and HUD. Packaging mortgages into securities in this way turned illiquid assets, that could not be sold on their own, into liquid assets. With a secondary market to trade them, low interest rates and rising house prices, MBS prices rose and investors developed an appetite for buying these high-yield but high-risk securities. Up to the reversal in house prices, MBS investors experienced almost continual gains as did the banks packaging them and selling them on.

■ The dubious economics of subprime lending

The appetite for securitised subprime loans grew. And the volume of securitised mortgages grew. By the mid-1990s, investors were paying around 7 per cent of the face value of the loan. This meant that, for a small subprime mortgage player, the profit potential was significant. With a monthly volume of USD10 million, a gross profit of USD700,000 per month, or USD8.4 million per annum, would accrue. To fuel an increasing demand, standards of mortgage appraisal fell. Doing deals, rather than worrying about the quality of the borrower, became the driving force. As salespeople were remunerated as a percentage of the value of deals, the quality of the borrower was not part of this equation. Hardly surprising, lenders courted weaker and weaker credits.

Loans were securitised in volume. Small lenders sell mortgages to large lenders who aggregate mortgages from various sources, package them and securitise them. In the USA, if the loan is a conforming or prime loan, it may be sold to Fannie Mae or Freddie Mac, both government-sponsored entities (GSEs) although quoted on the New York Stock exchange, and this accounted for around half of all US mortgages. They may package such loans into mortgage-backed securities (MBSs).

If the mortgages fail to meet the standards established by the GSEs, lenders used investment banks to package them into non-agency MBSs. The institutions that bought MBSs from the investment banks included hedge funds, pension funds, other banks (including commercial banks and mortgage banks) and other investors. The sale of these securities is dependent upon rating agencies' judgements about whether the underpinning borrowers will pay interest on time and repay capital at maturity. Such securities are rated to indicate the level of risk associated with the investments – see later in this chapter for more on this topic.

Lending to people with a bad credit history is always a risky proposition and when the borrower is a NINJA (no income, no job, no assets) the risk to the lender is magnified.

But make no bones about it, the NINJA appeared as a frequent player on the subprime mortgage scene. Obviously, with assets like this the subprime business was an accident waiting to happen. The subprime business model will work – well, just about – when interest rates are low and house prices are on the rise. Of course, like any kind of lending, there will be bad debts. But the business model becomes highly questionable, if not downright stupid, when interest rates rise more than wages and/or when house prices move downwards. The model also has inbuilt conflicts. There are at least three key kinds of player – broker, lender and investor. They all have different agendas. Lenders receive business via brokers, whose motivation is to close the loan and obtain commission. Brokers have no financial interest in a loan's performance. They face no liability if things go wrong. Lenders need always to question the broker's motives. Investors focus upon loan performance and timely repayment. If a lender's portfolio of business performs poorly, the investor can terminate the relationship by selling on the security in the secondary market. Lenders want the performance of their loans to meet the investor's expectations. The lender is clearly caught in the middle. So, if the subprime loan can be sold on in the secondary market causing the risk to pass to another party and if a profit can be made in so doing, so much the better.

In the run-up to the financial crisis, brokers became the driving force for subprime loans. In 2003, they originated 25 per cent of all prime loans and over 50 per cent of all subprime mortgages. As Richard Bitner[1] observes in his excellent *Confessions of a Subprime Lender* (yes, he was one and therefore tells a firsthand story), 'when salespeople in any business are left to their own devices, they'll work the system to their benefit ... With few rules and minimal consumer protections, abusive behaviour flourished. The harsh reality of brokering subprime mortgages is that many loan officers are more concerned with their own paycheck than with the best interests of the borrower.'

By the new millennium, more than 250,000 mortgage brokers operated in the USA with few states having licensing requirements, which meant low barriers to entry. Where states did require licences, qualification was excessively easy – passing a multiple-choice test and not being a convicted criminal. Again, hardly surprising, the subprime lending industry attracted unethical behaviour. Briefly, this may involve any of the following devices:

- scams in which brokers, appraisers and builders (and sometimes lawyers too) collude to receive monies from lenders in excess of market value, frequently involving buy-to-let properties and frequently involving off-plan properties;
- borrowers indicating that they will occupy a property when, in reality, purchasing it as an investment to let or to trade on – flipping;
- falsifying a borrower's employment history and/or income level by creating false documents – the liar loan;
- hiding critical information;
- self-certified income figures (self-certified by the borrower). This facility was on offer (would you believe) from a vast percentage of the lenders in the market. Banks had simplified dramatically, if not eliminated, their screening processes for lending. Also, because loans were being securitised, rigorous checks had become relics of a

bygone age. The topic of bank lending criteria and screening processes is examined in Chapter 7.

Bitner distinguishes three kinds of dysfunctional broker – the pusher, the withholder and the manipulator. The first merely keeps trying to work and rework the potential mortgage, adjusting data and presenting the loan proposition again and again until a deal is done. The withholder keeps information back from either lender and/or borrower, working the system to their own advantage. Manipulators appear in various shapes and sizes using tactics such as falsifying or altering income documentation. This kind of player may place an unsuspecting borrower into an adjustable rate mortgage with no explanation of what it means or how it works. Or, the manipulator may disclose a lower rate and fee structure to a borrower but increases the figures just before closing.

Bitner tells us that 'the process of massaging loans to qualify borrowers became standard practice in the subprime industry. It was an integral part of making tough deals work.' He recalls that his sales manager referred to the process as 'making chicken salad out of chicken shit'. He adds that 'it lacks poetry but epitomises the true nature of the business.'

■ Structured Instrument Vehicles (SIV) and conduits

Readers will recall that we have mentioned that mortgage lending morphed from the traditional originate-to-hold practice to the originate-to-distribute model. The essential idea is to move the mortgage receivable off a lender's balance sheet prior to securitisation when cash would replace it. Although used for various purposes, Structured Instrument Vehicles (SIVs) and conduits were employed as intermediary links in the process of the lender transferring the mortgage receivable asset from its balance sheet and subsequently securitising it. The lender and the securitised loan are the two ends of the transaction and the SIV sits in between.

SIVs and conduits were often set up as joint ventures between banks and hedge funds and often located in off-shore tax havens. But, more relevantly, they were deemed, for accounting purposes, not to be significant because of their intermediate nature and were, therefore, not consolidated in the bank's accounts.

SIVs and conduits are very similar. The major difference is that the SIV is independent of its sponsoring bank. However, when SIVs actually went broke, as they did in the preamble to the crunch, their liabilities were absorbed by the parenting banks. In the case of the conduit, recourse was technically to the sponsoring institutions. So, the idea behind the SIV and conduit is really fairly simple even though, judging from our reading of other literature on the topic, many, commentators seem to complicate matters to make their rationale slightly less difficult than nuclear physics.

■ Repackaging mortgages

The process of securitisation of mortgages involves packaging them together so that thousands of mortgages are bundled with other kinds of debt (including some high-quality loans to make the package easier to get a good rating from the rating agencies) into financial products or bonds, termed mortgage-backed securities (MBSs). Investors in these securitised products receive principal and interest payments from the underpinning mortgages and other loans. Such investors are usually banks and hedge funds.

Assume that Wall Street firm X has a USD1 billion pool of subprime mortgages. This could be packaged, with a few high-quality loans too, into bonds. In so-doing, the services of a rating agency would be engaged. The rating agency, for example, Standard and Poor's, undertakes an analysis focusing upon the quality and performance of the entire pool of mortgages. Their rating provides the would-be purchasers with a view of the risks associated with the MBS. Figure 5.1 describes this graphically and indicates how tranches of MBS grade downwards from triple A (AAA) at the top of the mortgage pool's value to more risky levels below. Note that, as one would expect, the riskier levels attract higher returns but are exposed to first losses should the bond default. The bond is effectively sliced up according to risk and return.

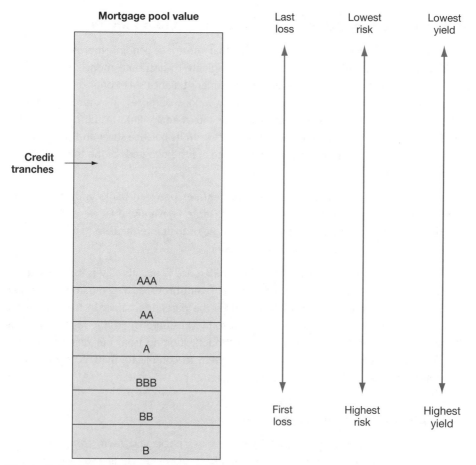

Figure 5.1 Tranche rating, risk and return

The rating agency reviews the pool of loans and, for example, rates 80 per cent of a potential security at AAA rating (the best quality investment grade), the other 20 per cent rated more lowly – see later in this chapter. Buying the AAA portion of this bond means that 20 per cent of the security pool will experience a loss before the triple A section is impacted negatively. The lower tranches protect the higher tranches by taking losses first. If the reader is wondering how a pack of subprime mortgages could be rated triple A, it's a good question. To put it simply, the argument went as follows. Even though a debt may have some risk of default on its own, a package of, say, two debts or three debts or more becomes less likely to default – especially if the AAA portion is protected by the lower layers and especially if the debt obligations are uncorrelated. So, the debt pool containing mortgages of jumbo status, alt-A and subprime together with other debts, say private equity debt and credit card debt, might, as a package, be argued to be less risky than the individual debts themselves. With bonds, one bond might default but a package of uncorrelated bonds would be unlikely to default because not many uncorrelated bonds would default at the same time. The key question about the package of subprime debt is whether its constituents are truly uncorrelated. And whether the addition of a small amount of better quality debt can create an uncorrelated package. More on this in the next chapter.

The securitised mix of mortgage debt and other debt, for example credit card debt, auto debt, private equity debt, is termed a collateralised debt obligation (CDO) and is technically different to an MBS which consists just of packaged mortgage debt. But the terms are often used loosely. As Frank Partnoy[2] observes in his memoir, called *F.I.A.S.C.O.*, 'at Morgan Stanley, we had created dozens of collateralised debt obligations, or CDOs, and we became quite skilled at persuading the rating agencies, and investors, that they should label an investment AAA, even if the underlying assets were risky'. The underpinning reasoning for this is all to do with the bottom layers protecting the top – see Figure 5.1 – and with low correlation. Individually, a collateralised debt obligation is simply a package of debts, usually with some associated security.

When a mortgage pool is sliced and diced (to coin the term used in the industry) and mixed with other debt obligations, credit card debt, credit default swaps (see next chapter) and a host of other debts, clearly the original mortgages are no longer recognisable. Judging the quality of the assets and their risk profile is a Herculean task. Investors who purchase these securities face this challenge. In reality they had no idea what they were buying. They just relied on the rating agencies' views.

By the year 2000, Lehmans and other Wall Street firms were big players in the subprime business. Merrill Lynch and Bear Stearns were acquiring subprime mortgages to feed the securitisation process. They were buying mortgages, repackaging them, and selling them on via their mortgage securitisation arm all around the globe. This was a high-margin business and the buoyant US housing market was fuelling its expansion. True, the process of mortgage securitisation was happening elsewhere, notably in Britain, but the biggest generator, by a long way, was the USA.

Many high-margin businesses are high risk too. Wall Street was focusing hard on the securitisation process and its effect on the apparent glowing bottom line profit outturns (and the impact on bonuses) without much attention to the risk profile that was being taken on. And, because mortgages and other loans were being securitised the loan screening process built up over years of good banking practice – see Chapter 7 – was being forgotten. After all, under the originate-to-distribute model, the loan asset was finding its way onto someone else's balance sheet.

So, let's simplify the process so far with the help of Figure 5.2. It shows the mortgage industry food chain from original borrower to securitised mortgage backed security. It is an interesting process packed with conflicts of interests, dubious business practices and risk creation of an inordinate scale – an accident waiting to happen. But the biggest potential for accident was created by the rating agencies. We now move on to describe rating agencies and their practices.

■ Rating agencies

Up to the 1970s, rating agencies used a business model under which an investor, wishing to be rated, bought a subscription to the agency's service. The Securities and Exchange Commission (SEC) decided, in its wisdom, that ratings served a public interest and that the subscription model should be changed. Instead, companies desirous of a rating would pay the agencies to rate their debt. This created an obvious conflict of interest since if there were no rating there was no fee – part of the problem at the heart of the financial crisis.

Apart from mortgage loans guaranteed by Fannie Mae and Freddie Mac (hence by the US government), traded mortgage backed securities were rated by one of three lending credit rating agencies – Standard and Poor's (S&P), Moody's and Fitch. These firms would evaluate loss potential relating to a pool of mortgages. They analyse the frequency and severity of defaults given the characteristics of the packaged loans. They look at a sample of loans and examine representations from the issuers. Clearly this is a tricky task and well-

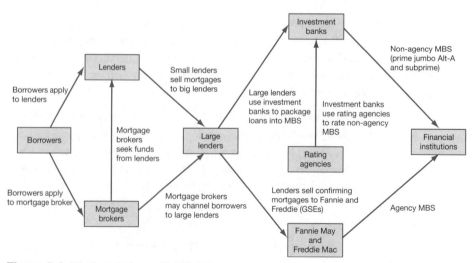

Figure 5.2 Mortgage Securitisation

trained operatives are involved. It's a pretty attractive job for MBAs specialising in finance and for qualified accountants.

Rating depends on the likelihood of payments of interest and/or capital not being paid (default) and on the extent to which the lender is protected in the event of a default (namely, the likelihood of recouping money in the event of failure or bankruptcy). Clearly, most Western government bonds have an insignificant risk of default but corporate loans have a higher risk. Well-positioned firms in stable industries with a risk averse policy should have a low risk of default: hence, all other things being equal, they should have a high credit rating. Companies with a high level of debt and a weak position in their industry, plus volatile earnings, might have a high default risk and a low credit rating.

The three main credit ratings organisations are Standard and Poor's (S&P), Moody's and Fitch. To exemplify ratings, we look first at the S&P rating method. Its long-term rating system is divided into two parts: investment grade and speculative grade. Investment grade ratings are defined as those issues that should pay principal and interest on time. These are the four highest-rating categories, namely AAA, AA, A and BBB. The higher the rating, the greater the likelihood of timely payment. A bond rated AA has a greater probability of paying principal and interest on time than one rated BBB, although both bonds should pay principal and interest on time. Investment grade bonds rated AA to B are further qualified by the addition of a plus or minus sign to indicate their standing within the category. The other half of S&P's long-term rating system relates to those bonds where there is some uncertainty as to whether they will pay principal and interest on time. These are classed as speculative grade and are assigned ratings of BB, B, CCC, CC and C. Bonds in default are rated D. Obviously, the system implies that the lower the rating of a bond, the greater the probability of default. To summarise S&P's bond rating, investment grade status is given as follows:

AAA The highest rating assigned by S&P. Capacity to pay interest and to repay principal is extremely strong

AA Debt rated AA has a very strong capacity to pay interest and to repay principal and differs from the highest-rated issues only to a small degree

A Debt rated A has a strong capacity to pay interest and to repay principal but it is somewhat more susceptible to the adverse effects of change in circumstance and economic conditions than higher-rated categories

BBB Debt rated BBB is regarded as having an adequate capacity to pay interest and to repay principal. While it normally exhibits adequate protection, adverse economic conditions or changing circumstances are more likely to lead to a weakened capacity to pay interest and to repay principal for debt in this category

Debt rated BB, B, CCC, CC and C is regarded as having predominantly speculative characteristics, with respect to capacity to pay interest and repay principal. BB indicates the least degree of speculation and C the highest. Although such debt will probably have some quality and protective characteristics, these are outweighed by large uncertainties or major exposure to adverse conditions. Debt rated D is in default. Comparable Moody's and Fitch ratings are shown, along with S&P, in Table 5.1.

Table 5.1 Standard & Poor's, Moody's and Fitch's rating scale

Standard & Poor's	Moody's	Fitch's	Grades	
AAA	Aaa	AAA	Prime, maximum safety	
AA+	Aa1	AA+	High grade, high quality	Investment grade bonds
AA	Aa2	AA		
AA-	Aa3	AA-		
A+	A1	A+	Upper medium	
A1	A2	A		
A-	A3	A-		
BBB+	Baa1	BBB+	Lower medium	
BBB	Baa2	BBB		
BBB-	Baa3	BBB-		
BB+	Ba1	BB+	Speculative	
BB	Ba2	BB-		
BB-	Ba3	BB-		
B+	B1	B+	Highly speculative	Non-investment grade, high yield or 'junk' bonds
B	B2	B		
B-	B3	B-		
CCC+	Caa1	CCC+	Substantial risk	
CCC	Caa2	CCC	In poor standing	
CCC-	Caa3	CCC-		
CC	Ca	CC	Extremely speculative	
C	C	C	May be in default	
D		D	Default	

As we know, MBSs did not perform in line with AAA ratings. They missed by a mile. What went wrong? Possibly the relationship between the sponsors and the agencies was compromised. Perhaps the sponsors provided the agencies with insufficient or incorrect information to grade the securities correctly. Or, maybe, the statistical models that the raters used to evaluate the mortgage pools were defective. These possibilities will be looked at later. But before we do, we have to consider another incendiary product in the crash. This is a product more potent than the subprime mortgage. It is the credit default swap and it is the topic of the next chapter. We will also look closer at how subprime debt got its triple A rating.

Chapter 6

Credit default swaps and toxic assets

■ Introduction

The credit default swap (CDS) played a massive role in the financial crisis. If the problem created by subprime debt is rated ten, that created by credit default swaps and related toxic assets justifies, as we will show, a rating of 100 or more. In most newspaper articles and radio and television documentaries at the time of the financial collapse the central cause of the problem was portrayed as the subprime mortgage market. The CDS was barely mentioned. It seemed to be a bit player, like Rosencrantz or Guildenstern in Shakespeare's *Hamlet*. How and why can this be so? Perhaps the commentators at the time found the CDS difficult to understand. And even if they did understand it, they couldn't explain it. Perhaps they thought that the public would find the CDS too complicated. Or, perhaps, as Galbraith[1] argues in connection with financial crashes, the banking elite is happy to perpetuate a view that the cause of the problem does not reside with them. To quote Galbraith, '… whereas it is acceptable to attribute error, gullibility, and excess to a single individual or even to a particular corporation, it is not deemed fitting to attribute them to a whole community, and certainly not to the whole financial community.' He goes on to say that 'the financial community must be assumed to be intellectually above such extravagance of error.' Galbraith continues by observing that the 'reason that the speculative mood and mania are exempted from blame is theological. In accepted free-enterprise attitudes and doctrine, the market is a neutral and accurate reflection of external influences; it is not supposed to be subject to an inherent and internal dynamic of error. This is the classical faith. So there is a need to find some cause for the crash, however farfetched, that is external to the market itself. Or some abuse of the market that has inhibited its normal performance.' For one, or more, of these reasons, the CDS failed, immediately, to take its justified place at the centre of the stage. Naturally, we give the CDS its rightful position as a star player in the history of the financial crisis of 2007/8

So what is a CDS? It is a swap contract in which one party (A) makes a series of payments to a counterparty (B) and, in exchange, B would pay to A a capital sum if the credit instrument to which the CDS relates defaults (the capital instrument could be a bond or a loan of company C). The credit default that triggers the payment from B to A would typically be non-payment of interest or failure to make a capital repayment of a loan. In our example above, if company C were to go bankrupt the same result would be achieved and B would have to pay A. It should be mentioned that even if there is no default yet, the cost of credit default swap cover for new contracts goes up as a result of the party to which the credit default relates (party C in the example) looking more likely to default. Given this situation, in the secondary market (the marker for existing credit default swaps) the value of B's position would fall and A's position becomes more valuable. There are features of CDS selling that make it akin to option writing – in particular that one can face wipeout from both. But the CDS is not an option. With a CDS contract, there is a right and an obligation. With an option, there is a right but not an obligation. A better analogy is between a CDS and an insurance contract.

Just in case it is a little difficult to understand, we suspect that Figure 6.1 might help. It is worth looking at carefully. Of course, credit default swaps have a specified contract life – they don't last for ever.

If things still seem complicated, take an example. We quote from Larry McDonald[2] who provides an inside story of the Lehman Brothers collapse. Referring to the CDS business with Lehmans as the insurer (counterparty B in the example above) he states that, '... so far as the bank (Lehmans) was concerned, that was pretty good business. For absolutely nothing, they (Lehmans) would be paid a fee of USD9 million a year. That was great – unless, of course, the corporation went down, in which case the bank (Lehmans) would hold a USD1 billion liability. More often, the bank would sell the CDS to a hedge fund, which was more willing to take the risk. The bank would pick up a fast USD200,000 fee and be rid of the hassle'. A bit clearer? We hope so.

Just in case it is still a bit hazy, we give a slightly more technical definition, quoted by John Hull[3]. 'A CDS is an instrument that provides insurance against the risk of a default by a particular company. The company is known as the reference entity and a default by the company is known as a credit event. The buyer of the insurance obtains the right to sell bonds issued by the company for their face value when a credit event occurs, and the seller of the insurance agrees to buy the bonds for their face value when a credit event occurs. The total face value of the bonds that can be sold is known as the credit default

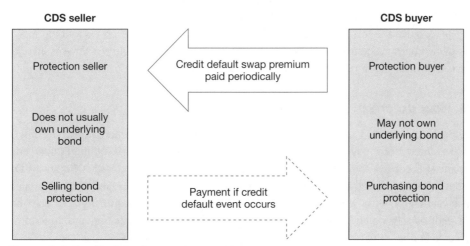

Figure 6.1 Credit default swap transaction

swap's national principal. The buyer of the CDS makes periodic payments to the seller until the end of the life of the CDS or until a credit event occurs. These payments are typically made in arrears every quarter, every half year, or every year. The settlement in the event of a default involves either physical delivery of the bonds or a cash payment.'

Note that there is a secondary market in which CDS instruments can be traded. So, in our example above, both A and B could sell their CDS positions on in the secondary market. Assume that B bought the CDS for 100 and that the CDS relates to a bond of company C. If company C suffers a credit rating downgrade following poor trading or some other unexpected event, the CDS that B holds would fall in value to, say, 85 because B is more likely to have to pay out since a default by company C is now more likely.

CDS contracts are rather like insurance but there are differences, for example:

■ Neither party to a CDS needs to own the underlying security (bond, loan or debt) to which the instrument relates. Neither the buyer nor the seller of the CDS has to suffer a loss from the default event (assuming that the CDS were not held by either party). This contrasts with insurance where the insured has to have an insurable interest under which they can demonstrate a potential loss should the default event occur.

■ Neither party to the CDS needs to be regulated.

■ The insured party in an insurance contract is bound by utmost good faith rules which require disclosure of all material facts and failure on this point can invalidate the contract. This is not so for a CDS where the maxim 'buyer beware' probably applies.

■ The party responsible to pay under default is not required to set aside any specific amounts to pay the other party were the default to occur

■ Insurers manage risk by setting loss reserves based on the law of large numbers. Dealers in CDSs may manage risk by offsetting liabilities under a CDS by hedging using a reverse transaction with another counterparty.

■ CDS contracts are subject to mark to market accounting, with income statement and balance sheet impacts. This is not the case in insurance accounting. Mark to market accounting involves revaluation of the instrument for financial statement purposes with gains, since the last reporting date, being taken into income or corresponding losses being charged against profit. Clearly, with respect to highly volatile instruments this can cause massive swings in reported profit and affect undistributed reserves.

■ How do credit default swaps work?

Evidently, a CDS is a credit derivative contract between two counterparties. The buyer makes the periodic payments to the seller and in return receives a payoff if an underlying financial event (the default) occurs. As an example, assume that investor X buys a CDS from bank Y where the underlying reference entity is company Z and the CDS has a five-year life. Investor X will make annual payments to bank Y. If company Z defaults on its debt by missing an interest payment or does not repay capital as required, investor X receives a one-off payment from bank Y and the CDS is terminated.

If investor X owns debt in company Z, the CDS would be a hedge against that risk. If investor X bought the CDS contract without owning any company Z debt, this would be a speculative transaction betting against company Z. Also, even though investor X owned no debt in company Z, the above transaction could be a hedge against debt that it does hold in companies similar to Z. In this case company Z debt would be a proxy for the debt of the similar company or companies.

The spread on a CDS is the annual amount that the protection buyer (investor X above) must pay the protection seller (bank Y) over the life of the contract. It is stated as a percentage of the nominal amount of the CDS contract. If the CDS spread for company Z is 100 basis points (that is, 1 per cent), then investor X buying USD20 million worth of protection from bank B must pay the bank USD200,000 per year. Such payments continue until the CDS contract expires, five years later in our example, or until company Z defaults.

Via the CDS, investors may speculate on changes in CDS spreads of company debt. For example, assume that hedge fund A does not rate company C highly to the extent that it feels that it will soon default on its debt. Hedge fund A buys USD20 million worth of CDS protection for three years from bank B with company C as the underlying reference entity, at a spread of, say, 400 basis points per annum. If company C does default after, say, two years, then hedge fund A would have paid USD1.6 million to bank B but would receive USD20 million, making a profit of USD14 million. Bank B will incur a USD18.4 million loss unless the bank has hedged the position by entering into a reverse deal to eliminate its exposure. Of course, if company C does not default, then the CDS contract will run for three years, and hedge fund A will have paid out USD2.4 million without any return, hence incurring a loss. There is also the possibility that before year three, hedge fund A might sell on the CDS in the secondary market. If company C looks more likely to fail than when hedge fund A bought the CDS it will make a profit on the sale and the amount of profit will depend upon the new price of the CDS which, in turn, will depend upon the increased likelihood of company C's failure.

CDS contracts took off from virtually nothing in the 1990s to around USD632 billion in 2001 and to the astounding figure of over USD60 trillion before falling back to USD55 trillion in terms of value of contracts outstanding immediately following the crash – see Figure 6.2. To put this into context, world GDP totalled USD60 trillion in 2008. Admittedly, comparing these two figures involves a stock versus a flow. Nonetheless the comparison is a telling one. Note that much of the total of USD60 trillion of CDS outstanding would involve hedging contracts. The point here is that if a bank has sold a contract to a customer, the bank itself may enter into an offsetting buy transaction to hedge, or cover, its exposure. Gillian Tett[4] describes, in colourful terms, a weekend away session for J. P. Morgan bankers in which the brainstorming topic is the understanding and development of the credit default swap – well worth reading.

The CDS market attracted considerable concern from regulators in the 2008 Crash, particularly with the collapse of bankers Bear Stearns. In the run-up to Bear Stearns' collapse, the bank's CDS spread increased dramatically. A surge of buyers were taking out protection against the bank's failure. This widening of its CDS spread had the effect of

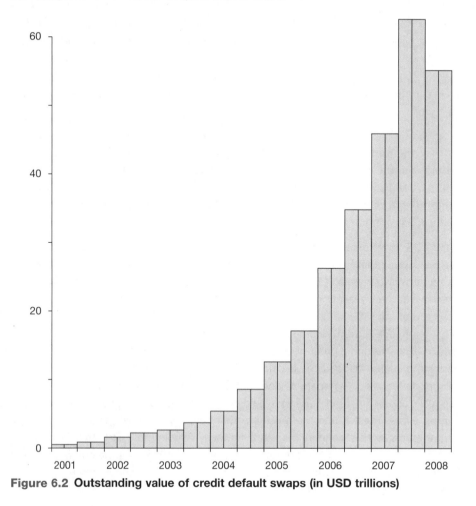

Figure 6.2 Outstanding value of credit default swaps (in USD trillions)

further increasing Bear Stearns vulnerability as it restricted Bear's own access to wholesale money markets, eventually leading to its forced sale to J. P. Morgan in March 2008. It is an open question as to whether that surge in CDS protection buyers was a symptom or a cause of Bear's collapse. Investors saw that Bear Stearns was in trouble and sought to hedge exposure to the bank – or even, speculate on its failure. In September 2008, the same kind of scenario impacted Lehman Brothers. And, in that same month, American International Group (AIG) required a government bailout because it had been selling vast amounts of CDS protection (without hedging) against the possibility that various reference entities might decline in value. This exposed AIG to potential losses over USD100 billion. In 2008 there was no clearing house for CDS transactions. They were all done over the counter (OTC). Since then, in November of 2008, a clearing facility for CDS trades has been introduced, covering a large proportion – but by no means all – of the market. Also interesting is a newly-introduced international standardisation of CDS contracts designed to prevent legal disputes in cases where it is not clear what a payout should be.

■ Drivers of the CDS market

The CDS market exploded from virtually nothing in the 1990s to USD55 trillion in 2007. So what was the prime mover of the CDS market's growth? In the early years of this century, as we have related, US investment banks were packaging subprime debt into mortgage backed securities – and they seemed to be making big profits for their banks and big bonuses for themselves in doing so. But the US market for subprime debt totalled only USD1.3 trillion in terms of outstanding debt as at 2007 – its peak. What the investment bankers were looking for was a new product that could out-do the subprime mortgage market. In short, there just wasn't enough subprime debt to go round. The bankers found the answer to their prayers in the CDS. The reader will recall that once a subprime mortgage has been packaged into an MBS or a CDO, it is used up and cannot be packaged again. There is a finite amount of subprime debt. Believe it or not, the bankers were running out of risky assets.

Enter the CDS. There is no limit to the amount of credit default swaps that can be written on company X. The company may have an equity market capitalisation of USD20 billion: company X may have USD5 billion (in market value terms) of debt all traded on stock exchanges, giving it an entity value of USD25 billion. But credit default swaps on company X are not limited to USD5 billion or to USD25 billion. They can be written for USD100 billion, or USD200 billion, or any amount you like. There is no limit. Unlike insurance where one has to have an insurable interest – that is to say, suffer a loss through the occurrence of a specified event (in this case, default on a debt) – with a CDS there is no limitation of this effect. The CDS does not require an insurable interest. So, one could, in theory, sell an infinite amount of CDS on company X debt. The bankers were hardly likely to run out of risky assets of this sort. And the bankers' efforts were rewarded as they packaged CDS assets with subprime loans into collateralised debt obligations (CDOs). And they knew that they would not run out of them. No chance. To many bankers, this was sheer alchemy – the transformation of base metal into gold.

In the last example above, the subprime loan would create inflows of interest and the CDS would involve receipt of an annual sum from the counterparty.

The reader will recall, from the previous chapter, that by adding to the mortgage pool making up a mortgage backed security (MBS) other assets that were uncorrelated in performance, the effect would be that the quality of the asset pool would be enhanced and might justify a higher credit rating. So, by adding a CDS to a mortgage asset pool, a higher rating might be obtained. Now, we would have an asset pool rather like the mortgage pool in Figure 5.1 but with the added presence of CDS inputs to create a collateralised debt obligation (CDO) pool.

During the Crash, these acquired the epithet 'toxic asset'. The toxicity is best illustrated by an example. With no default, or only a low probability of default, a CDS might have a positive value of, say, 100 based on the expected income stream from insurance-like premiums exceeding the expected outflow under default. But with defaults looming, the worth of the CDS could alter and acquire a negative value as the probability of having to pay out under the CDS exceeds the probability of receiving inflows (the insurance premiums). What was an asset, worth 100 in our example, may become a liability worth minus 100 or minus 500. The description toxic asset, also known as toxic debt, is truly justified. When defaults began to look more and more likely, these toxic assets were changing shape into infectious liabilities on bank balance sheets and, like a contagious plague, undermining their very health and existence. The disease was terminal for Lehman Brothers and would have been equally final for some other banks and financial institutions were it not for government rescues.

But we are advancing the story too fast. The creation of the CDO did not stop with the injection of CDSs. It involved more than subprime debt and credit default swaps. As we show in Figure 6.3, the addition of higher quality debt from prime mortgages was mixed in to give some credibility but so was low-grade debt which ranged from credit card debt to emerging market debt to lowly-rated corporate debt to private equity debt. Leveraged buyout debt often carries debt to equity ratios for the bought out firm of 80 per cent to 90 per cent versus typical corporate debt standards of 30 per cent to 40 per cent. Also, leveraged buyout debt might have an interest cover ratio – profit before interest and tax versus total interest – of 1.5 times versus a normal debt standard of 4 times or so. Lower quality debt invariably carries higher interest rates than normal debt. This seemed great to the investment bankers who were cobbling together the CDOs. As we will see, having somehow managed to get a triple A rating on swathes of CDOs, the interest rate that would be paid to holders would be lower than that received from the debt and credit default swap assets. Magic? Sleight of hand? We shall see.

With the constituent crew on board the CDO, the trick was that the investment banks had to convince the rating agencies that the lack of correlation between the portfolio created by the various crew members would justify an enhanced credit rating compared to the

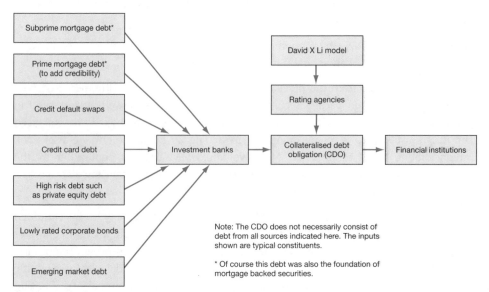

Figure 6.3 The collateralised debt obligation food chain

individual credit ratings for the constituent members on their own and then aggregated together.

Correlations are not as simple as they might at first sight appear. In illustrating this point, we draw on an example quoted in Salmon[5]. Assume a schoolgirl, A. The probability that her parents will get divorced this year is, say, five per cent. The risk of her getting head lice is five per cent. The chance of her seeing her teacher slip on a banana skin is five per cent. The likelihood of her winning the class spelling bee is also five per cent. If the market were trading securities based on these chances, they should all trade at the same price.

But, now, assume two schoolgirls, A and B, who sit next to each other and are great friends. If B's parents get divorced, what is the likelihood of A's parents getting divorced? Still about five per cent. The correlation is clearly low. If B gets head lice, the chance that A will also get head lice is high, maybe 50 per cent – the correlation is of the order of 0.5. If B sees her teacher slip on a banana skin, what is the chance that A will see it also? High, since they sit next to each other in class and are great friends, the chances are that they will both see the event. It could be 95 per cent, a correlation close to 1. If B wins the spelling bee, the chance of A winning it is zero, a correlation of minus 1. Now, if the market were trading securities based on the chances of these things happening to both A and B, the prices would be difficult to predict because the correlations vary a lot.

Clearly, getting the probabilities on the individual events for the schoolgirls A and B would be tricky enough. And getting the conditional probabilities would be more difficult. Looking at past data might help but these things get really fraught when it comes to conditional probability inputs and estimating errors.

With mortgages, correlations are tricky – as are conditional probabilities. What is the chance that a particular home in state X will decline in value? One can look at the past history to obtain some idea. And what is the chance that another particular house in state Y will fall in value? Again, historical data might help. Then there is the problem of conditional probability. And it's not just a problem about two homes but all of the houses in the mortgage backed security. An intractable problem? Maybe. Maybe not.

■ Correlations and credit ratings

We now introduce a new player to the CDS scene. Remember that the name of the game for the investment banks marketing the CDO is to enhance the credit rating, thereby increasing the price of the CDO, creating greater profit potential and greater bonus potential. The actor entering the stage is David X Li. Armed with an MBA and a PhD in statistics, his banking experience was at Canadian Bank of Commerce and Citibank where he was head of credit derivatives research. He was the sort of bright, young 'rocket scientist' that Wall Street loves to recruit. Li had moved from China where he was born (Xing Lin Li) in the 1960s. Writing in the *Financial Times* (24 April 2009), Sam Jones described Li as 'the world's most influential actuary'. Why? How did Li earn this epithet? Basically by making the CDS a more marketable security. Basically by helping to justify the triple A rating. Basically by helping to create the USD55 trillion market for toxic debt that would boomerang back to the innovating financiers.

Whilst working as a banker, Li[6] wrote and published a paper in the peer-reviewed *Journal of Fixed Income*. It was called 'On Default Correlation: A Copula Function Approach'. A copula, in statistics, is a way of formulating a multivariate distribution given various types of dependence. Referring to our earlier example of the schoolgirls, we have a number of variables – the divorce, the head lice, the banana skin and the spelling bee – and a number of dependences. There are various copula functions, the Archimedean copula, the Clayton copula, the Frank copula, the Gaussian copula, the Gumbel copula, and a number of others too. In short, the copula is used to couple the behaviours of two or more variables.

In Li's paper, he did not model default correlation but he used market data about the prices of CDSs. These prices change as default risk rises and falls. Rather than waiting to assemble historical data on actual defaults, which are rare in the real world, Li used historical prices from the CDS market. The critic might point out that the CDS market had a relatively short life up to the year 2000, when Li's paper was published, and had not experienced any big failures. So, his data were based on non-turbulent times and assumptions of the market pricing CDS products efficiently. Li developed a model that used price rather than real-world default data, making the assumption that financial markets in general, and CDS markets in particular, price default risk correctly. Li's pricing model used the Gaussian copula, based upon the normal distribution or bell curve. Another target for the critic of the normal distribution.

According to the Li paper, huge amounts of risk diminished when risky assets were pooled in a CDO. And a large share of the pooled investment can be rated AAA. Word spread. Mathematicians and other quants in banks explained the model of derivatives structures. The bankers got the rating agency analysts interested. Wall Street derivatives arrangers started to pool risky assets using the new methodology of David X Li's formula. Banks created swathes of new CDOs backed by low-rated corporate bonds, emerging markets debt, and subprime mortgage loans. They split the CDOs into tranches, based on the seniority of claims, as in Figure 5.1. The rating agencies were willing to rate many CDO tranches AAA, even though the underlying assets carried much lower ratings. The bankers loved David X Li. And the bankers paid the rating agencies over and above their normal fee. Remarkably, as pointed out by Johnson and Kwak[7], in 2005 only eight US companies had triple A ratings. They were AIG, Automatic Data Processing, Berkshire Hathaway, Exxon/Mobil, General Electric, Johnson & Johnson, Pfizer and United Parcel Service.

According to Frank Partnoy[8], '... the driving force behind the explosion of subprime mortgage lending in the US was neither lenders nor borrowers. It was the arrangers of CDOs. They were the ones supplying the cocaine. The lenders and borrowers were just mice pushing the button.' We would add that was even more true for the CDS market.

Wall Street banks now knew that they could use credit default swaps to create spiralling amounts of CDOs. They developed new repackaging transactions, using credit default swaps instead of subprime mortgages that, when pooled, could generate high ratings. These CDOs are technically known as synthesised collateralised debt obligations because of their artificial nature.

By 2006, there were more synthetic CDOs backed by credit default swaps than there were CDOs backed by real mortgage loans. And there were credit default swaps written on packages on subprime debt (CDS on MBS). Insurance companies like AIG had joined the banks as players in the CDS market.

All of these derivatives were unregulated. None of the financial institutions disclosed details about their CDS derivatives. Most just grouped credit default swaps with other derivatives in their published accounts. No one could assess the exposure to the CDS market. Banks bought large amounts of AAA tranches of synthetic CDOs but precise details – or even half precise details – were not apparent in published figures.

And here was the problem. Essentially, the banks dealing CDS products or CDOs based upon the CDSs would receive an annual payment but have to pay out on default. However, even without default, they would suffer a reduction in value in the secondary market if the credit rating of the underlying company bond or mortgages upon which the CDS was written were to fall. If there were a default, one party to the CDS (counterparty B in our earlier example) would lose out, having to pay the full nominal amount of the CDS. This looks rather like writing options. The seller gets an annual fee, rather than an up-front option premium, and has unlimited downside risk – counterparty B could lose the whole amount of the CDS. So, rather than bear the potential downside if default were to occur the bank packages the CDS into the CDO.

So, for a CDS based on subprime loans, banks selling them were essentially writing put options – see Glossary – on the value of the underpinning subprime loans. They received periodic payments from their CDS counterparties but carried exposure to pay out in the case of the default. But, of course, the package was rated AAA. Had the counterparties of the 'so-called' swap entered into a swap or an option? It has a lot of the look of an option even if it does not have the feature of 'a right but not an obligation' which is what options are all about. Or, again, is the CDS an insurance contract? As we pointed out earlier, it is not subject to insurance law. But it looks like insurance. In which case, should the insurable interest requirement discussed in the Introduction to this chapter be a requirement? We rather think so. Of course, for bankers creating the CDS market, calling the CDS a swap was a great marketing ploy. And the bank packaging the CDS liability into a CDO where it sits as a swap is satisfied. It sounds less risky. And, getting the AAA rating was a massive marketing ploy too.

Directors of financial institutions dealing CDOs based on subprime mortgages did not inform their shareholders of the massive risks they were carrying in respect of US house prices declining and defaults on subprime mortgage loans increasing and becoming highly correlated with other assets in the CDO. They did not inform their shareholders that they were, effectively, dealing options on housing prices. A decline in the price of subprime homes would put the homeowners in negative equity, with little incentive or ability to repay their debts. Many would default at the same time. Bank directors either hid, or did not understand, this risk. If either is the truth they are unfit to be directors of a public corporation – let alone a bank.

Whilst housing prices remained high, or flat, the banks and their employees would earn large profits from the subprime CDOs. And large bonuses too. But if housing prices collapsed, many banks would be wiped out. Awareness of this led several hedge funds and others to place big bets against the subprime mortgage markets and the banks. This involved them either in credit default swaps written on the bank so that in the case of default the hedge fund would gain in a big way or via short-selling of stock in the at-risk banks.

■ The unwinding

As we have pointed out, the unwinding started in the subprime housing market. Defaults increased in late 2006. Initially, the banks were not worried. Their models assumed that there would be minor defaults all over the US and these were not correlated. The defaults kept coming. By early 2007, it was clear that the US subprime market had a problem. By the summer, subprime homeowners all over the US were defaulting on their mortgages. The cheap debt made available by subprime lenders had looked like an accident waiting to happen – and now it was happening. The subprime loans should never have been made – least of all at low interest rates. The Li model failed to predict the correlated defaults which most thinking people would have said was very likely, if not inevitable. Credit default swaps that had previously been worth considerable positive dollar amounts were now beginning to register negative value for reasons that we explained earlier. The banks began taking staggering losses on their holdings of CDOs. Institutions grew fearful about one another's solvency. They stopped lending to each other and liquidity dried up. The problem spread from asset class to asset class. In a globalised financial market with international linkages, the problem of disappearing liquidity spread like a disease across frontiers. Every bank was suspicious of every other bank. Inter-bank lending, an essential part of any capitalist economy, dried up. This was the credit crunch. The banks' pain spread to the real economy. Suddenly, everything was highly correlated.

Why had Li's formula not anticipated this? It assumed events tended to cluster around an average – as in the normal distribution. The whole model was bell curve based. The range of possible outcomes was more complicated. The mortgage market was far more prone to extreme correlation scenarios than most. At crisis times, security prices move away from their bell curve behaviour. Why did no one notice such an obvious fault in the Li formula?

There had long been warnings against reliance upon Gaussian bell curve behaviour in financial markets; Benoit Mandelbrot[9], Nassim Nicholas Taleb[10], and Pablo Triana[11] remind us that stock prices do not follow a Gaussian bell shaped distribution. Mandelbrot made this clear as long ago as the 1960s. Taleb makes the point that 'if the world of finance were Gaussian, an episode such as the crash [19th October 1987] (more than twenty standard deviations) would take place every several billion lifetimes of the universe ... According to the circumstances of 1987, people accepted that rare events take place and are the main source of uncertainty. They were just unwilling to give up on the Gaussian as a central measurement tool.' Taleb goes on to remind us that '1987 was not the first time the idea of the Gaussain was shown to be lunacy. Mandelbrot proposed the scalable to the economics establishment around 1960, and showed them how the Gaussian curve did not fit prices then.'

Taleb's venom is there again when he observes that he 'only realised later that Gaussian-trained finance professors were taking over business schools, and therefore MBA programs, and producing close to a hundred thousand students a year in the United States alone, all brainwashed by a phony portfolio theory. No empirical observations could halt the epidemic. It seemed better to teach students a theory based on the Gaussian than to teach them no theory at all.'

Maybe some would defend the use of the Gaussian normal distribution because it works well most of the time. If so, they must stress 'most of the time'. It is utterly not the immutable describer of market behaviour that is often taught. And theorems based upon it must be recognised as only right most of the time. For example, Black and Scholes option pricing theory derives the well-known formula which is based upon log-normal stock returns. Gaussian again.

Returning from our important digression, in April 2008, New Century, the second largest subprime lender in the US, filed for bankruptcy. Shortly afterwards, Countrywide, the largest subprime lender, went into free fall. Hedge funds increased their short positions and the value of subprime mortgage loans dropped like a stone. And the same thing happened to CDOs and to bank stocks.

In June 2008, Moody's downgraded the ratings of USD5 billion of subprime mortgage backed securities and put 184 CDO investments on review for downgrade. S&P placed USD7.3 billion on negative watch. Banks began announcing massive losses from investments backed by CDS and subprime mortgage derivatives.

Bear Stearns imploded and was bought by J. .P Morgan; Lehman Brothers filed for bankruptcy; Merrill Lynch sold out to Bank of America, which also bought Countrywide; the US government rescued AIG, the world's leading insurance company. In the UK, Northern Rock, the mortgage bank, had failed: as had Bradford and Bingley, a similar bank; the UK government rescued HBOS and Royal Bank of Scotland following idiotic investments in CDSs. In late 2008, alarm focused upon domino effects. Banks that were liable to pay out under CDS contracts could not meet their obligations. This led to chaos in CDS markets and resulted in prices of CDS contracts dropping sharply amidst a lack of liquidity for CDS transactions. If the above banks had all been allowed to fail without government intervention, they could, through their indebtedness to other banks, have pulled down the good banks too. The whole system could have been facing the abyss. And, the impact of this for commerce could have been utterly catastrophic because business after business could have failed as bank loans would be called in. This could have been worse than the Great Depression – much worse. With co-ordinated action by governments, the doomsday scenario was averted. Nonetheless, it remains the biggest financial crisis since the Great Depression.

Without derivatives, including CDSs, CDOs and MBSs, the total losses from subprime mortgage defaults would probably have been relatively small and containable. Without derivatives, the defaults would have hurt some, but not that much. The total of US subprime mortgage loans outstanding was around USD1.3trillion. The decline in the value of these subprime loans on their own during 2008 was a couple of hundred billion USD topside. It represents less than 10 per cent of the estimated bailout losses by the International Monetary Fund[12] as at April 2010. Where did the other 90 per cent come from? Credit default swaps is the answer. The CDS market is a zero-sum game. This means that the sum of gains by winning players is equal to the sum of losses by losing players. The amount outstanding in the CDS market in 2007 was USD60 trillion. Now, let us look at the following situation. It is an example but it may bear some resemblance to reality. Assume that, of the USD60 trillion outstanding, 70 per cent represents hedge contracts. This leaves 30 per cent unhedged CDS position – that is USD18 trillion worth. If half of these were not caught up in the CDS squall, that would leave 50 per cent that were. And this would involve USD9 trillion. If half of these were winners and half were losers, this would mean USD4.5 trillion of loss-making contracts. Assume that, on average, these contracts incurred losses of 65 per cent. That would mean losses of USD2.925 trillion. Not all of these would have required bailouts. Some would be borne directly by the banks concerned. Some may have been made good from the proceeds of bank recapitalisations – rights issues and injections from sovereign wealth funds (funds owned by oil exporting states with surplus monies). However, because some banks would have had a concentration of positions resulting in losses and because these losses would have been so large that, without a government bailout, the bank would have failed, monies were forthcoming from government sources. If around USD0.5 trillion came from bank sources themselves, this would leave government bailouts of USD2.4 trillion. This is within a whisker of the IMF's April 2010 estimate of USD2.3 trillion. In truth, we cannot be sure of the amount at this stage. The figures are just what we say – estimates. And, there may be losses unrelated to CDSs and these could be worth over USD0.5 trillion. But whilst the problem first manifested itself in the subprime market squall, it multiplied into a toxic debt tsunami that might have become a second Great Depression.

We feel that it is worth mentioning a quote from John Cassidy[13]. He observes that in May 2005 Alan Greenspan sang the praises of credit derivatives, saying their development 'has contributed to the stability of the banking system by allowing banks, especially the largest, systemically important banks, to measure and manage their credit risks more effectively'. Cassidy goes on to say that 'in the case of derivatives such as CDSs, Greenspan was merely stating the official view of the Fed and other international banking regulators. After he retired in January 2006, his successor, Ben Bernanke, made no effort to reverse the Fed's hands-off stance. The idea that CDSs facilitated the spreading and management of risk had attained the status of official dogma, and so had faith in VaR-based risk management. Unless something disastrous happened, none of the regulatory authorities would seriously question the Wall Street line.'

But clearly derivatives, CDSs, CDOs and MBSs, multiplied the losses from subprime mortgage loans and took the world staggeringly close to complete meltdown. The chief culprit was the credit default swap. Specifically, credit default swaps, based on defaults of banks and insurance companies, magnified losses. As investors learned about these side bets, they lost confidence in the system. Without government intervention, the system would have crashed completely. Governments managed to prop up the tumbling dominos – just.

Finally in this chapter we refer to Press cutting 6.1 in which John Kay likens the game of selling credit default swaps to tailgating – it's a brilliant analogy. And if the reader refers back to Figure 6.1, it should be apparent how CDS tailgaiting would work. The CDS seller picks up an annual income from the protection buyer and banks were taking this to profit in the income statement. But when tailgating turns to crash, the bank has to pay out to the protection buyer – a charge to the income statement. Whilst the tailgaiting was working, the dealers were being lauded, the bankers were being praised by their non-executive directors. Everyone was looking at the income statement and saying that this is great: that this is a money machine. Where you see money machines, ask questions, ask more questions and keep asking questions – because money machines are illusions. Was there a single non-executive bank director or regulator questioning this? And was anyone within the banks suggesting that provisions should be made against potential future payments under CDSs if the credit default events were to occur? Or would this adversely affect the bankers' bonuses? The fact is that we need a new breed of non-executive director. And fast.

We cannot leave this chapter without mentioning the account (humorous in places) by Michael Lewis[14] on how big bucks were made on credit default swaps and other toxic instruments in the run-up to the financial crisis.

Press cutting 6.1   *Financial Times*, 20 January 2010 **FT**

Tailgaters blight the markets as well as the motorways

John Kay

Some people have described the process as picking up dimes in front of a steamroller. A more vulgar account refers to a creature that 'eats like a bird and shits like an elephant'. There is a more academic description: a strategy based on writing options that are substantially out of the money. But the analogy I prefer is tailgating, the practice of driving close to the bumper of the car in front at high speed.

However described, it is the same thing: a distribution of returns that produces frequent small profits punctuated by occasional very large losses. A high proportion of trading – and business – strategies in financial markets have this tailgating characteristic. I call it the Taleb distribution, after the author of *Fooled by Randomness* (an earlier, and better, book than the more widely read *Black Swan*), which gives numerous instances.

The distribution has been central to recent financial crises. Buying emerging market debt was a seemingly profitable activity with a remote possibility, eventually realised, of large losses. So was holding internet stocks of no fundamental value in the (usually correct, but

→

ultimately false) belief that they could be sold on at a profit to a greater fool. The creation of bogus synthetic securities of investment grade, which offered a higher yield than genuinely good credits because their inherent risk was underestimated, led to the credit crunch. The issue was not just that these distributions displayed Taleb characteristics: these market activities were devised with Taleb characteristics in mind.

The power of the tailgating metaphor is that it captures other essential aspects of the process – above all, the self-satisfaction of the tailgaters, a self-satisfaction that is mirrored in financial markets. These guys have talent, or so they believe. They get to their destination faster than other people because of their driving skill and finely judged risk control. Such self-delusion is possible because cognitive dissonance separates the occasional accident from the frequent success. When an incident occurs, it is someone else's fault. The driver in front made an unexpected move, there was an obstruction on the road ahead that no one could have anticipated.

There is always an element of truth in these accounts of disaster. Most tailgating drivers will never be involved in an accident. A few will end their journey at the mortuary. This means the pool of people who have learnt by experience that tailgating is dumb is therefore small. Tailgaters think the view that their behaviour is dumb is based on a purely theoretical analysis, which is refuted by the tailgater's practical experience.

And so the culture of self-confident, self-congratulatory tailgaters perpetuates itself.

You might think that the sight of the worst highway pile-up in half a century would be followed by safer driving, but you would be wrong. The sight of an accident does lead drivers to be more careful for a short time, but it is often observed that this effect wears off very quickly. And so it is in financial markets.

The investment banks currently reporting their profits and bonuses are able to reassure us that tailgating still pays. In fact tailgating has become even more rewarding, because governments are making special efforts to keep the roads clear, and the traffic police are all at conferences on safer driving.

Governments themselves have become infected by tailgating behaviour. Some officials think that government guarantees of private sector liabilities don't cost anything, because they probably won't be called on. Others tell you that governments will make a profit on their injections of emergency funds into financial institutions. These are precise analogues of the tailgater who congratulates himself on his skilful driving. The nature of guarantees and capital injections is that they often cost you nothing, but when they do cost you they cost you loads. The taxpayers who are paying for Icelandic banks and Fannie Mae have discovered that, but the wider lesson has not been grasped. Tailgating gets you to your destination faster – except when it doesn't.

Chapter 7

Bank lending and control systems

■ Introduction

Bankers have traditionally used a set of criteria in evaluating and arriving at a judgement on loan requests. These embrace a number of obvious features such as an assessment of the character of the potential borrower (or, in the case of a corporate loan, the character of the key personnel), understanding the would-be borrower's industry, position within the industry, business strategy, looking at past financial performance and trying to estimate future outturns, assessing risk, the logical maturity of the loan which would articulate with cash generation from running the business, what that cash generation might look like in recession conditions, the rate of interest to charge, whether to request security and so on. All of these issues are concerned with the big question for the banker, 'Will we get our money back, when and how?' All of this was highly germane to the banker under the originate-to-hold lending model. Unfortunately, with the advent of originate-to-distribute lending, it seems that bankers decided, because they were likely to sell on the loan to a third party, that the need to undertake good credit analysis was no longer necessary. Having said this, we summarise the precepts of good credit analysis and lending in order to show what principles lenders used and decided to discard with the arrival of originate-to-distribute banking.

■ Normal commercial bank lending criteria

Of course, no loan is without risk. No bank would have a business if it said no to every proposition that had risk attached to it. In his excellent text on bank lending Hale[1] offers 18 principles of credit analysis. These are summarised below and they indicate the banker's basic lending problem. The first seven relate to the lender and the latter eleven relate to the borrower. They are:

1. Quality of credit is more important than exploiting new opportunities.

2. Every loan should have two ways out that are not related and exist from the beginning – that is, through operational cash generation or realisation of assets. Guarantees from an utterly sound guarantor would be another possibility, but the former two are normally expected to provide the way out with the third a back-up in weaker cases.

3. The character of the borrower – or in the case of corporations, the principal management and shareholders – must be free of any doubt as to their integrity.

4. If the banker does not understand the business, there should be no lending deal.

5. Lending and its structuring is the banker's decision, and they must feel comfortable with it according to their judgement.

6. The purpose of a loan should contain the basis of its repayment.

7. If the banker has all the facts, they do not need to be a genius to make the right decision.

8. The business cycle is inevitable. In other words, the loan should be evaluated assuming good and bad times.

9. Although it is harder than evaluating financial statements, assessing a company's management quality is vital.

10. Collateral security is not a substitute for repayment.

11. Where security is taken, a professional and impartial view of its value and marketability must be obtained.

12. Lending to smaller borrowers is riskier than lending to larger ones.

13. The banker should not let poor attention to detail and credit administration spoil an otherwise sound loan.

14. Local banks should be participants in lending to local borrowers.

15. If a borrower wants a quick answer, it is 'No'.

16. If the loan is to be guaranteed, the banker must be sure that the guarantor's interest is served as well as the borrower's.

17. The banker must be clear as to where the bank's money is going to be spent and the banker needs continued assurance and confirmation through the life of the loan that this is where the money has gone.

18. The banker must think first for the bank. Risk increases when credit principles are violated.

Naturally, bankers ask to see, and study in detail, forecasts of income, cash flow and balance sheets and, to the extent that they do not agree with them, the bank would produce its own forecasts. The essential thing that the banker is looking for is sufficient cash generation to repay the prospective loan. Financial ratio analysis is part of the banker's routine in the assessment of whether the forecast is reasonable, believable and does not breach financial covenants that the bank may impose. Failure to comply with bank covenants would technically trigger immediate repayment of the loan. Operational cash generation provides the banker with the first way out of the loan – see criterion #2 above. If it should transpire that this seems to be so weak that the loan is not likely to be repayable on time, the second way out is through business asset realisations (hence the emphasis on the shape of the balance sheet) or through personal loan security or guarantees. Without a reasonable view of two ways out, the banker should say no. Or, maybe, offer a smaller loan and/or adjust repayment dates.

One of the most valuable forecasts that traditional bankers make is the recession cash flow forecast – which is exactly what it says on the tin. The conservative banker would like to see, even in recession, sufficient cash generation, year by year (or quarter to quarter) to cover loan interest and loan repayments. As a result of looking at these forecasts, the loan's repayment schedule and maturity may alter. Or more security may be sought. Or, the loan may be refused. Figure 7.1 shows one format of such a cash flow forecast which may be used for normal forecast cash flows and recession cash flows. In conjunction with normal and recession forecasts of income statements and balance sheets plus ratio analysis, the banker stands a good chance of assessing the virtue of a lending proposition together with its potential risk and return.

The most suitable loan structure is also a key question for the banker. Maybe it is a short-term loan to cover an export contract, maybe an overdraft to cover a short-term seasonal and self-liquidating working capital requirement. Maybe it is a long-term loan.

Also, banks tend to limit and quantify their exposure to any single customer or customer type, such as housebuilders and property developers. These rules are normally written into the bank control system manual. Presentation and review of data on these scores at regular and fairly short intervals is of essence in bank financial control. Unfortunately, in the boom conditions of 2000 to 2007, the standards of credit analysis and control listed above were widely diluted or ignored – as is frequently the case in boom times.

Mortgage lending is another core part of the banker's business. The traditional mortgage lender has a set of lending criteria, rather like those for businesses, but concerned with more domestic financial questions. Residential mortgage decisions involve evaluating the character and quality of the borrower (job, length of time in the job, its probability of continuing, income, prospects, wealth and so on, how the potential borrower rates on credit scoring criteria) in the context of certain require-ments. These key issues are:

Forecast year†	2012	2013	2014	2015	etc.
Enter figures for normal or recession forecasts (GBP)					
Sales					
Forecast profit before tax and interest					
+ Depreciation and amortisation* charged in arriving at profit above					
− Additional working capital (inventory, trade receivables less trade payables)					
− New fixed capital investment					
− Tax expected to be paid					
Net cash flow before debt repayment					
− Interest and loan repayments					
Net cash flow before dividends					
− Dividends expected to be paid					
Net cash flow after dividends					

* More correctly, depreciation, amortisation and impairments (if any) charged in arriving at forecast profit above.
† Or quarter by quarter. Preferably quarter by quarter for early years.

Figure 7.1 Format for cash flow forecast and recession cash flow forecast

- loan to value ratio (against the lender's maximum criterion);
- interest and capital payments versus income;
- interest and capital payments versus risk;
- maximum loan size;
- minimum down-payment.

Traditionally, the loan to value ratio was around 75 per cent to 80 per cent with a loan set at 3 to 4 times income. In the 'originate to hold' model of mortgage lending, the lender would advance money secured on the property itself and show the loan as a secured asset on its balance sheet. With the development of securitisation, in which mortgage loans and their security (and other loans too) are bundled together and sold on to third parties – the 'originate-to-distribute' model – bankers argued that since the loan was being sold on to third parties, the bank could cut costs by reducing credit analysis for mortgages and corporate loans. Massive indiscipline in evaluating loans to firms and in issuing mortgages followed. In fact, we are aware of banks where new chief executives with a non-banking, non-financial background were appointed and they proceeded to push well-tried disciplines onto the back burner. This applied in terms of loan evaluation and control systems. But rather than just saying that credit analysis was to be watered down, it was frequently disguised with business process re-engineering consultants coming in and being given terms of reference to apply their investigations to the credit analysis discipline.

Business process re-engineering (BPR) was a hot idea in the run-up to the turn of the century. Although enthusiasm for BPR has waned since, it was popular with consultants and boards of directors. What does it involve? Its champions, Hammer and Champy[2], define BPR as 'the fundamental rethinking and radical redesign of business processes to achieve dramatic improvements in critical, contemporary measures of performance, such as cost, quality, service and speed.'

The US Federal Government took to BPR in a big way. It informed government agencies that the following transitions had to take place in any re-engineering approach:

From	To
From ▶	*To*
Paper-driven ▶	Electronic-based
Hierarchical ▶	Networked
Power by hoarding information ▶	Power by sharing information
Stand-alone ▶	Virtual and digital
Control-orientated ▶	Performance-orientated
Compliance-orientated ▶	Benchmark-orientated
Sole resident experts ▶	Teams by talent
Stovepipe organisations ▶	Honeycombed organisations
Oversight agencies ▶	Coaching agencies
Slow response ▶	Prompt response
Data entered more than once ▶	Data entered once
Technology-fearful ▶	Technology-savvy
Decisions pushed to top of agency ▶	Decisions pushed to customer transaction

Note that it advocates a move from control-orientation and compliance-orientation. Unfortunately it is very much in these areas that banks have to excel.

Hammer and Champy suggested the following BPR principles:

- organise around outcomes, not tasks;
- integrate information processing work into the real work that produces the information;
- treat geographically dispersed resources as though they were centralised with IT playing its part;
- link parallel workflow activities instead of just integrating their results;
- put the decision-making point where the work is performed and build control into the process;
- capture information once – at the source.

All very well, but for banks this obviously means dilution of loan appraisal and control systems. And this is just what happened at a number of banks. But the directors and top executives in the banks themselves were cavalier on this point. After all, the loans were being sold on to third parties under the originate-to-distribute model (as opposed to the originate-to-hold model where the loan would remain on the bank's books). Thus the securitised packages of loans were to become collateralised debt obligations and if they were to become triple A rated and these were being sold on outside the bank, spending time and money on credit analysis would not add value. The flaw in the argument was that the banks themselves became both creators of CDOs and purchasers too. In this latter role they were buyers of debt which had not been subject to the credit analysis discipline.

Worse still, some banks, notably new arrivals on the scene and those in less-sophisticated banking markets, decided to follow suit – even though they remained committed to the originate-to-hold model. They spurned credit analysis and serious control of their loan books basing their decisions on qualitative assessment only. Such a friendly and amateur-style of banking has attracted the description of crony banking and it always ends in tears.

■ Lending control systems

Managing credit risk begins with a clear credit philosophy in order to set management priorities. Banks' credit philosophies may range from emphasis on the highest quality loan portfolio, based on highly conservative low-risk standards, to an emphasis on aggressive loan growth and market share with highly flexible risk standards. A bank's lending philosophy is frequently articulated in a formal loan policy. The credit philosophy and loan policy should be consistent with the credit culture. This is reflected in the organisation's loan systems and procedures.

Figures 7.2 and 7.3 show expected returns and risk profiles for a possible range of credit philosophies. Figure 7.2 is straightforward and merely suggests a linear (in truth, it may not be a straight line trade-off) relationship between risk and return. The implication that a business (banks included) can increase return by carrying greater risk is clear. Figure 7.3 reinforces the idea that expected returns increase when banks emphasise growth with more risky and flexible standards. But, most importantly, note that the volatility of returns increases as bank style shifts from a conservative, asset quality, low-risk profile through to a growth orientation with a sales-driven aim at increased market share. A priority that emphasises loan quality is low risk and produces stable earnings. The growth and marketing orientated choice is a high-risk strategy and is associated with relaxed loan quality, a risky portfolio of loan assets and unstable earnings, albeit with higher peaks in the good times but with lower outturns in bad times. This kind of bank is clearly courting operational leverage (profit volatility with high ups and downs through the cycle) and, in our opinion, should be balanced with lower financial leverage – its ratio of debt to equity within its capital structure should be lower than competitors. Unfortunately this was not always so in the run-up to the financial crisis of 2007/8 – a lesson here for the whole banking industry.

To some extent, loan authorisation in banks is devolved. Most bank control systems involve some level of decentralisation – but with loan committee approval required for larger loans. Traditionally, there are committees such as an officers' loan committee, a directors' loan committee and, for banks with a number of troubled loans, a special assets committee. These committees are authorised to approve only those loans that conform to loan policy. Loans above certain minimum sizes are proposed by individual loan officers before the officer's loan committee, usually consisting of the most experienced loan officers.

Again, traditionally the directors' loan committee reviews major loans approved by the officers' committee. It is often composed of the bank's chief executive, the most senior loan officers, and two or more external members of the board of directors. This committee makes final judgement on the officers' loan committee decisions, giving particular attention to the largest credits. It is particularly concerned with congruence with bank loan policy and law and policies that control insider loans. This committee also reviews significant overdue loans and other credit problems.

The special assets committee is usually concerned with troubled loans. This committee monitors the progress of such problem loans and tries to determine how to achieve repayment through creative co-operation with distressed borrowers and use of other collection possibilities.

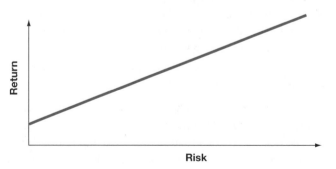

Figure 7.2 The risk and return trade-off

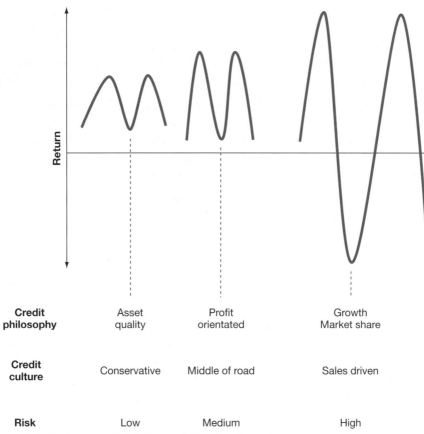

Credit philosophy	Asset quality	Profit orientated	Growth Market share
Credit culture	Conservative	Middle of road	Sales driven
Risk	Low	Medium	High

Figure 7.3 Returns and risk through the credit cycle

The scope for cost cutting in the traditional system of loan controls would have been mouth-watering under the move from the originate-to-hold style to the originate-to-distribute style. Having said this, of course, not all loans were securitised and therefore cost cutting was not at a 100 per cent level in this area.

One of the biggest control problems in banking is keeping tabs on positions that the bank dealers may have entered into. Although all bank dealing personnel have levels of maximum transaction authority, the problem remains a massive one because dealers are entering into positions all of the time all around the world. Of course, electronic reporting has improved this but the task can be seen to be gigantic. Not only is the task of bank control and monitoring vast, so is its complexity. This is a very important point. It has ramifications far more extensive than many realise. If successful, the bank treasurer really earns their weight in gold.

■ Value at risk and risk management

One of the many tools available and one of the most-used prior to the crisis was value at risk (VaR). Value at risk is a single number estimate of how much a firm can lose due to the price volatility of the instruments it holds – for example, a fixed-rate bond or an unhedged currency payable/receivable or a credit default swap or subprime mortgage. It indicates the likelihood of potential loss not exceeding a particular level, given certain assumptions. These assumptions may involve time horizon, holding period, confidence limits, distribution of probabilities, correlation and the potential for shocks to the system.

VaR has been widely used by financial institutions and features strongly in the rules contained in the Capital Adequacy Directives for banks. Its development owes much to bankers J. P. Morgan whose past chairman demanded a one-page report at the end of business each day summarising the bank's exposures to losses because of possible market movements in the coming day. J. P. Morgan's 'Riskmetrics' (a system of measuring VaR) evolved from this request.

VaR's popularity with banks lay in the fact that it holds out the prospect of aggregating risks across a range of diverse activities and articulated well with the banking industry's interest in installing group risk management systems.

VaR is conceptually and practically a powerful tool and its workings and shortcomings need to be understood by bankers and treasurers alike. It falls far short of providing a complete panacea for group risk measurement, particularly for banks. It does, however, provide a moderately useful estimate of possible losses over a short period under normal market conditions for investments and other instruments which are liquid; in other words, assets and liabilities that can be marked-to-market (valued at objective market prices) and traded freely, not therefore in respect of credit default swaps and subprime mortgages.

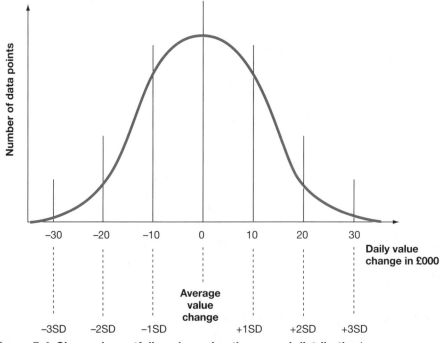

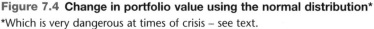

Figure 7.4 Change in portfolio value using the normal distribution*
*Which is very dangerous at times of crisis – see text.

To explain the concept, assume that a financial institution holds a portfolio of fixed interest bonds. The portfolio is unhedged and its value today is therefore based on the current term structure of interest rates – the yield curve today. If we have comparable historic yield data, then we can calculate the value of the portfolio under a wide range of past interest rate scenarios in order to get a distribution of values and of potential changes in value. Most VaR models assume that changes in the value of the portfolio are, on average, random and that their frequency distribution can be estimated using a normal curve – see Figure 7.4. For the normal curve, the standard deviation (σ) is the measure of volatility and data points will be distributed as follows

    68.3% within $\pm 1\sigma$
    95.5% within $\pm 2\sigma$
    99.7% within $\pm 3\sigma$

If one believes in the applicability of the normal distribution to such situations (which is highly dangerous – see later in this section) this means that if one standard deviation in Figure 7.4 is USD100,000, then 95.5 per cent of the time the change in value of the portfolio value will be within $\pm$USD200,000. So, the VaR at a 95.5 per cent confidence level is USD200,000. Note that in excess of one day per year the value will be outside $\pm$USD300,000. If the data are at daily intervals, then this would give the 24-hour VaR. Note the word 'if' as the first in this paragraph. The fact is that at times of financial crisis or stress the real world does not behave in accordance with the normal distribution. We return to this topic again in Chapter 10. Its importance cannot be overemphasised. The fact is that banks were using an inappropriate model for control when the need for risk management was at its highest.

It is easy to see how the concept can be applied to exchange rate exposure or interest rate exposures that banks may hold. And, bank capital adequacy regulations require measurement of market risk on bank open currency positions via the VaR at 95 per cent confidence limits based on five years' daily data or at 99 per cent confidence limits based on three years' daily data. The bank is then obliged by regulations to support that VaR by a specific amount of capital – equity and subordinated debt. If the bank's view of risk differs from the regulators, then the bank is left with a dilemma. It would need to alter its portfolio and select a portfolio of activities such that, in aggregate, the economic capital requirements and the regulatory capital requirements coincide.

As mentioned above, like most management techniques, there are problems with VaR. The following are some of the caveats concerning VaR.

- Empirically, at times of financial crisis, changes in value do not follow the normal distribution. This is true for options, credit default swaps and subprime mortgage values, to say nothing of equity shares. Outturns display fat tails rather than the 4.5 per cent tails in the normal distribution. In other words, in the real world of financial markets, unlikely events occur far more frequently than implied by the normal distribution. Although we take the topic further in Chapter 10, the key iconoclasts in this area have been Mandelbrot[3], Taleb[4], and Triana[5]. Their message has taken a long time to filter through but, at last, it has – but that is not to say that there won't be other financial meltdowns.

- As mentioned above, shocks to the system may occur with greater frequency than the normal curve implies. Because of this, VaR may be used for normal market conditions and supplemented by stress testing and scenario analysis as modelling devices to quantify the potential impact of large future shocks.

- For portfolios of risks, some may be correlated, for example, exposures to the housing market and to bond markets. Thus, for other than very simple portfolios, other methods must be used. These include:

  (i)   Methods involving statistically adjusting data for such correlations.

  (ii) Computer simulations using past historic portfolio returns including past crisis inputs.

  (iii) Monte Carlo analysis, which involves a large run of scenarios, say 10,000, to generate a distribution, using assumptions about volatility and correlation and stressed for crisis conditions.

  (iv) Stress testing for crisis shocks to the system

- An appropriate holding period for each type of risk needs to be established and corresponding data captured. One key factor is the degree of liquidity for selling on an exposure – that is, how fast can the position be liquidated? The assumption in many parts of finance theory is that markets are continuous – in other words (well almost) one can sell as much as one wishes into the market. This was patently not the case in September 2008 when the financial crisis was at one of its worst points as far as market liquidity was concerned.

- The first two of these bullet points cannot be overemphasised. It is a fact that VaR performance, as well as stress testing and other risk measurement techniques, failed to indicate magnitudes of loss in the 2007/8 crisis. To reiterate, VaR is calculated using the normal distribution of outturns and the standard deviation of past results. This is often inadequate. When? Well, when there are crises. In other words, just when VaR is needed most, it seems to fail. Financial market behaviour exhibits fat tails. It may appear to conform to the normal Gaussian distribution a lot of the time but those fat tails can only be ignored at one's peril. For massive critiques of the inappropriate use of the normal distribution, the three books mentioned in the first bullet point cannot be recommended too highly.

We now turn to some of the practical problems which make risk management so difficult to implement. Risk management involves the measurement and management of exposure to risk. Financial risk management requires identification of its sources, measuring it, and devising and implementing plans to address it. Risk management may be qualitative and/or quantitative. Financial risk management focuses upon when and how to hedge exposures to risk. Worldwide, the Basel Accords (see Glossary) are adopted by banks for tracking, reporting and managing operational credit and market risks.

One of the big problems at regulators and in banks is that, according to Smith[6], they 'have weak risk management discipline. Even if they could assess the dangers accurately, risk managers typically have insufficient authority to rein in producers'. Referring to the faults in models specified above, Smith continues to offer us an example drawn from the blog of Richard Bookstaber, who had previously been head of risk management at a major investment bank. The imagined conversation involves Bookstaber (Me) and one of the CDO traders at the bank (Them). It goes as follows.

Session 1

Me: Hey, guys ... our CDO-related inventory has been growing ... we had just a few billion and then it went up to $20 billion, and now nearly $40 billion. That seems worrisome to me.

Them: Maybe that's because you aren't sitting here on the desk watching these things all day ... Look, you can't make money in this business without ending up holding some inventory from time to time. At least if you can, be sure to let us know how. And in this case a lot of this inventory is rated AAA. You wouldn't have a problem if we had a bunch of AAA corporate bonds, would you? I mean, that stuff is a better bet than our company is. ...

Session 4

Me: I'm sorry to bother you again. But, maybe we have been focusing on the wrong thing here ... not if these are really AAA or not; our concern is not just with defaults ... The issue is whether these could trade substantially lower for any reason ... The instruments in our inventory are not very liquid ... So what if someone suddenly is forced to liquidate ... it wouldn't take much of a price drop to hit us hard. When you have $40 billion of this stuff, a ten per cent drop will lead to a mark to market loss that will out all the profits you guys have made over the last few years.

Them: Good to see you are cranking out the scenarios. But if we worried about every little 'what if' that you can cook up, we wouldn't be doing anything. We are risk takers. That's how we make money. So, if you want us to stop making money – or if you have a better idea on how to do it without taking risk – then let us know. Otherwise, do you mind if we get back to work here.

Clearly, traders have the advantage when risk managers try to pursue problems. The trader knows their markets better than the risk manager. Furthermore, aspiring junior risk managers may wish to become traders. It's better paid and more exciting. So, junior risk police may not be politically advised to follow up sufficiently on every problem. And, if the head of risk management takes an issue to the CEO of the bank, they may receive the same sort of rebuff that 'they' gave in Session 4 above. Risk management needs the committed authority of the CEO. The head of risk management needs to know that they can rely on this backing. But it is not always forthcoming. The practical problems of risk management are self-evident.

■ Bank capital adequacy

At this point, bank capital adequacy requirements are worth mentioning. These are a framework of rules on how banks and depositor-taking institutions must capitalise themselves. It involves asset risk-weighting. In other words, bank assets are weighted according to a formula devised to reflect their riskiness. Internationally, the Basel Committee on Banking Supervisions at the Bank of International Settlements sets banking capital requirements. In 1988, the Committee introduced a capital measurement system commonly referred to as the Basel Accord. This framework is now replaced by a new and more complex set of capital adequacy rules known, at the time of writing, as Basel II. The rules specify risk weights. The capital ratio is the percentage of a bank's capital to its risk-weighted assets. Weights are defined according to perceived risk-sensitivities. As we write, a new version, Basel III is being worked upon.

Basically, the guidelines are used to evaluate capital adequacy based primarily on the credit risk of balance sheet assets, as well as certain off-balance sheet exposures such as unfunded loan commitments, letters of credit and various derivatives. The risk-based capital guidelines include an equity to debt ratio (the leverage ratio) requirement.

Tier 1 capital consists largely of shareholders' funds. It is made up of the amount paid originally to purchase the shares of the bank (not their market value) plus retained profits minus accumulated losses. Regulators have since allowed instruments, other than ordinary shares, to count in Tier 1 capital. These instruments are unique to each national regulator, but are always close in nature to common stock. These are referred to as upper Tier 1 capital.

There are several classifications of Tier 2 capital, which comprises supplementary capital and includes undisclosed reserves, revaluation reserves, general provisions, hybrid instruments and subordinated term debt.

To be adequately capitalised under US Federal Bank regulatory agency definitions, a bank holding company must have a Tier 1 capital ratio of at least 4 per cent, a combined Tier 1 and Tier 2 capital ratio of at least 8 per cent, and a leverage ratio (equity to debt) of at least 4 per cent. To be well capitalised, a bank must have a Tier 1 capital ratio of at least 6 per cent, a combined Tier 1 and Tier 2 capital ratio of at least 10 per cent, and a leverage ratio of at least 5 per cent. The absolute minimum for the Tier 1 ratio under the Basel Accord was only 2 per cent. This is to be increased under Basel III. These new scales are briefly discussed in the Afterword to this book.

In effect, the ratios, in the well-capitalised case, may be summarised as:

$$\text{Tier 1 capital ratio} = \frac{\text{Tier 1 capital}}{\text{Risk-adjusted assets}} \geq 6\%$$

$$\text{Total capital ratio} = \frac{\text{Tier 1 capital and Tier 2 capital}}{\text{Risk-adjusted assets}} \geq 10\%$$

$$\text{Leverage ratio} = \frac{\text{Tier 1 capital}}{\text{Average total consolidated assets}} \geq 5\%$$

A text of this kind can hardly do justice to the full intricacies of these requirements nor to the complexities of bank treasury control. Suffice to say that the task is of such monumental proportions that in cases where bank failures result from a lack of efficient and effective control, we are not surprised in the least. The successful bank treasurer certainly earns their bonus.

Chapter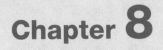

Regulation

■ Introduction

Regulation involves the control of human or societal behaviour by rules and/or restrictions. It can take many forms. It embraces legal restrictions set by a government or similar authorities. It may involve self-regulation by an industry, for example via a trade association. It could involve social regulation via norms of behaviour which may vary from group to group. And it may involve market regulation. Regulation imposes sanctions against deviation.

Government regulation aims to produce outcomes which might not otherwise occur. Examples include patents, property development approvals, controls on prices, wages and pollution and so on. A whole field of economics is devoted to the study of regulation of markets and it is termed regulatory economics.

Regulation, like most forms of conforming behaviour, has costs for some and benefits for others. Efficient regulation has been said to occur where the total benefits to some exceed the total costs to others. Regulation may result from a number of drivers, broadly categorised as:

- **Market failures**. Here intervention may be justified on various grounds, such as
  - risk that monopoly may distort prices, wages and availability of a good or service;
  - risk that public goods, like policing, enforcement of law, schools may not be provided in a purely market system;
  - asymmetry of information, where one party to a contract may have knowledge of a situation that another may not;
  - externalities, which were briefly discussed in Chapter 2.
- **Interest group transfers**. Here regulation results from self-interest groups' attempts to redistribute wealth in their own favour.
- **Collective desires**. Here regulation many concern societal preferences or considered judgements on the part of a significant segment of society, for example the establishment and maintenance of national parks, museums, art galleries and so on.
- **Irreversibility**. Here regulation is concerned with types of conduct from current generations which may result in outcomes that future generations regret.
- **Social subordination**. Here regulation aims to alter the subordination of various social groups.

- **Diversity**. Here regulation attempts to eliminate or enhance opportunities for diverse preferences and beliefs.
- **Endogenous preferences**. Here regulators attempt to ensure the maintenance and/or development of certain preferences.

Regulation of businesses was present in the ancient civilisations of Egypt, India, China, Greece and Rome and has usually been present wherever people have traded. Social regulation has, probably, always existed in terms of norms, customs, and privileges, with sanctions against those who do not conform.

Whilst governments impost regulation, business tends to seek to minimise it. We are not talking about legal regulations which ensure that contract law, for example, works but we refer to regulation that business views as adversely affecting their welfare. Indeed, the last 60 years or so has seen the growth of attempts to modify some regulatory structures and replace them with new regulations or, even, self-regulation. This movement is termed deregulation. The basic concept of deregulation is not necessarily a bad idea. As time goes on, the need for regulation changes, ideas change, ongoing cost-benefit analysis may reveal that regulation in certain areas is no longer justified. Some commentators have expressed concern at the growth of the lobbying industry. We touched upon this in Chapter 2 where we pointed out that the biggest expenditure on lobbying in the USA comes from financial institutions, broadly defined.

■ The need to regulate financial services

Retail purchasers of financial services possess much less knowledge than the providers and they may find it hard to tell which providers are both honest and competent. The same asymmetry of information applies elsewhere, for example for doctors and garages. Mistakes on large financial transactions may easily cause serious loss. Moreover, with few repeat purchases – most people buy only one pension – the normal market safeguard of reputation may not be so clear: Hence the need for regulation. The question is: what sort and how much? As we will show, the financial crisis has revealed that regulators are fallible, very fallible.

■ Capital adequacy and liquidity

The quest for profits in privately-owned banks has influenced the industry's structure. Banks have to pay debts as they fall due and maintain sufficient funds to meet normal withdrawal levels. Beyond that, lending banks' basic aims are to maximise funds loaned out and to minimise non-interest-earning cash as a proportion of total assets. There must be general rules against fraud, to which financial services are especially prone. But letting large financial institutions collapse carries systemic risk. This is the risk in which problems in one financial institution or market may spread and endanger other institutions and, even, the whole system. This risk is a preoccupation of central banks and is the rationale for prudential regulation. Consequently, financial services rules tend to require that banks hold a minimum amount of capital, a minimum level of liquidity, and regularly report both to their regulator.

Retail banks take and repay cash deposits over the counter. They need to maintain a cushion of equity capital against possible loan losses. Retail banks' main assets are their loan portfolios, on which annual losses normally amount to under 1 per cent. Bankers favour ways of financing themselves which enable them to lower their ratio of cash to deposits – the liquidity ratio – or their ratio of capital to assets – the solvency ratio – without undue risk. Readers are referred to Table 4.1 and Figures 4.1 and 4.2. A bank's liquidity ratio is given by the proportion of the total assets of a bank which are held in the form of cash and liquid assets. These assets consist, in general, of money lent out to the money market, at call and short notice, short-term bonds issued by the government and other borrowers and balances held at the central bank. There is no longer a mandatory liquidity ratio in most advanced economies. It is worth mentioning that in the past, in Britain, large banks were required to deposit a small percentage of liabilities with the Bank of England. This deposit earned no interest and was effectively a tax to provide income for the Bank. This is what is meant by reserve asset requirements and it is still an operational requirement in banking in many countries. The solvency ratio is simply the ratio of a bank's own assets to its liabilities. Also a bank's cash ratio is defined as its cash holdings to its total deposit liabilities – almost the same as its liquidity ratio. Central banks monitor the adequacy of liquidity and its composition for each bank but do not make public what they regard as satisfactory liquidity ratios. Over the years, there has been almost nonstop pressure from banks to be allowed to increase debt and reduce both liquidity and equity capital.

In the USA and the UK, banks have adopted more aggressive financial stances. Dating back to Victorian times, banks' ratios of equity to total assets was well in excess of 10 per cent. US banks had ratios of 14 per cent in 1930. By then, the comparable UK figure had fallen to 7 per cent – see Table 4.1. By 1985, UK and US figures were 4.6 per cent and 6.9 per cent respectively.

In terms of ratios of cash to deposits, UK banks moved downwards from over 10 per cent in the 1960s to less than 1 per cent in 2005. US banks also moved down from 7 per cent to less than 1 per cent over a similar period – see Figures 4.1 and 4.2. The same was true in continental Europe. But Japanese banks, with even lower ratios, were able to undercut their rivals. Banks were clearly playing a risky game. They might claim that it was more efficient from a balance sheet point of view. Of course, that is so often the story with financial leverage.

To create a level international playing field, and to prevent fraud and better ensure that risk taking in banks was contained, the Basel Accord – see Chapter 7 – was created. The Basel Committee consists of representatives from central banks and regulatory authorities. The Committee does not have the authority to enforce its recommendations although most countries have adopted them.

■ Lender of last resort

Fears that means of payment to meet bank liabilities will be unavailable at any price can ignite a financial crisis. In a fractional reserve banking system, this may lead to a desperate scramble for funds. A fractional reserve banking system is one in which banks hold minimum reserves of cash or highly liquid assets equal to a fixed percentage of their deposit liabilities. The minimum percentage of reserves may be adopted voluntarily as a matter of commercial prudence, or as required by law or convention. In either case the intention of minimum reserve requirements is to safeguard the ability of banks to meet their obligations. In trying to restore reserves, banks may restrict new lending, call in loans or sell assets, even at knockdown prices. All of these things happened in the recent financial crisis. This can lead to a credit crunch as banks become reluctant to lend to their weaker brethren. And this may lead to bank failures. Of course, this can also cause a sharp contraction in the money stock and lead to economic recession.

Where a bank with a liquidity problem has adequate collateral, the central bank stands available to help by acting as lender of last resort – see Chapter 4. It provides enough cash, usually at a penalty rate of interest, to solvent but illiquid banks to meet the sudden panic-driven demand. Walter Bagehot, the commentator and editor of *The Economist* until his death in 1877, observed that it was important to leave some ambiguity – by design – about whether the Bank would provide support in any and every case. Having said this, we are not sure that Lehman bankers should blame Walter Bagehot.

Another unofficial function of the central bank is to act as crisis manager. It may seek a private sector firm willing to take over a troubled bank, inject new capital and supply competent management. Or the central bank may arrange for a public sector purchaser to manage the bank while it gradually runs it down or even breathes new life into it again.

■ Deposit insurance

A large bank's failure, due to a bank run, could lead to a costly collapse of the whole fractional reserve banking system. Such runs are less significant for the ordinary person in the street if there is adequate deposit insurance. Almost all modern governments guarantee some or all retail deposits in one way or another – even where there is not a formal insurance scheme in place. Not all depositors may be confident enough of this before the event and, in any case, the guarantee may be capped.

The trouble here is the effect on incentives. If there is no deposit insurance, then savers have an incentive to be careful and place deposits only with banks that they consider to be safe. This gives banks themselves a big incentive to follow prudent policies – and to be seen to do so. They need to ensure confidence that they have adequate liquidity and ample reserves of capital, otherwise they might be risking a run. As a result, depositors accept low rates of interest on their deposits with safer banks.

■ Tight versus loose regulation

Compulsory rules are likely to be more complex than voluntary guidelines and have higher compliance costs. Those setting rules from the top down may not fully understand what is happening in the real world, especially if they have little recent practical experience. Do they listen to what those in the business say? In which case the wool may be pulled over their eyes. In truth, they must develop independent, informed, unbiased views of what is going on in their area of regulation.

A highly prescriptive regime of rules may be subject to problems, for example:

- risks may be too complex for simple rules to cover;
- it may be slow to respond to changing market conditions;
- balance sheets reflect data at a particular point in time and markets may change rapidly after the balance sheet date;
- it tends to add more rules over time while few are withdrawn;
- there needs to be a distinction between wholesale and retail business, otherwise there is a danger of over-regulating wholesale markets;
- regulation may become over-focused upon inputs rather than outcomes. This can lead to box-ticking with inadequate attention being paid to what the data imply.

Any system of rules needs to evolve and be open to revision. This may be hard to achieve. Under a voluntary system, people usually have some ability to influence changes and, even, make them whenever they choose. But voluntary regimes of regulation are excessively prone to being fixed by the very group which is supposed to be regulated.

Self-regulation may be cheap and flexible. But it will likely be written by the elite of the industry for the benefit of the industry itself rather than for the protection of Joe Public. Self-regulation has all of the likelihood of quickly becoming no regulation at all. And given the damage caused by the regime of weak regulation prior to the financial crisis we see nothing but a tightening of oversight. Furthermore, the fact that many economic historians – Kindlebeger[1], Reinhart and Rogoff[2] and a lot of others – have concluded that banking crises are not only inevitable but recurrent, the need for adequate, serious, competent, unbiased and independent oversight of the system is a must. Given the pathetic attempts of the banks at control of their own bonus culture and their own risk-taking, bank self-regulation is an utter and very bad joke.

■ The US system of financial regulation

There are several different financial regulators in the US system. They are set out below in the chronological order in which they were set up. President Barack Obama and his Democratic administration are thinking of rationalising some of these regulatory bodies.

The US regulatory authorities comprise:

- **The US Department of the Treasury** was established by an Act of Congress in 1789 specifically to manage government revenues – whereas the Federal Reserve manages payments – and has now evolved to encompass several different duties. It recommends and influences fiscal policy, regulates US imports and exports, collects US revenues, including taxes, and designs and mints all US currency. In terms of financial regulation, the Treasury Department functions primarily through the operations of two of the agencies it oversees, the Office of the Comptroller of the Currency and the Office of

Thrift Supervision – see below. The 74th Secretary of the Treasury was Henry (Hank) Paulson who occupied the office until 2009. The 75th Secretary of the Treasury, who took office on 26 January 2009 is Tim Geithner.

- **The Office of the Comptroller of the Currency (OCC)** is a federal agency established in 1863. It charters, regulates and supervises all national banks and the federal branches and agencies of foreign banks in the US. It is an independent bureau of the US Department of the Treasury.

- **The Federal Reserve System (FRS)**, established in 1913, is the central bank of the US. It comprises 12 regional banks, with a chairman appointed by the US President. From 1987, Alan Greenspan was chairman of the Federal Reserve System (often shortened to the Fed) until Ben Bernanke took over on 1 February 2006 as the 14th chairman. The Fed supervises commercial banks (but not investment banks) and the banking system. Its mandate, broadly, is to promote stable prices and economic growth. It is obviously a very important part of financial regulation in the USA. Because of that, we look at the Fed further in the next paragraph.

- **The Federal Deposit Insurance Corporation (FDIC)** was created as part of the Glass-Steagall reforms of 1933. It protects the first USD250,000 per depositor per bank (due to reduce to USD100,000 from 2014).

- **The Securities and Exchange Commission (SEC)** is a government agency, established in 1933 as part of the reforms arising out of the Great Depression. It supervises the stock exchange (NYSE and NASDAQ) and the Financial Accounting Standards Board (FASB).

- **The Commodities Futures Trading Commission (CFTC)** was set up in 1974. It aims to protect market users and the public from fraud, manipulation and abusive practices related to the sale of commodity futures and financial futures and options, and to foster open, competitive and financially sound futures and options markets.

- **The Office of Thrift Supervision (OTS)**, established in 1989, is the primary regulator of all federal and many state-chartered thrift institutions, including savings banks and savings and loan associations.

In addition there are separate state regulators for banking, insurance and securities. These are:

- **The Federal Housing Finance Board (FHFB)** was established in 1989 to supervise federal home loan banks.

- **The Office of Federal Housing Enterprise Oversight (OFHEO)** was an agency within the Department of Housing and Urban Development (HUD) charged with ensuring the capital adequacy and financial safety of Fannie Mae and Freddie Mac. It was established by the Federal Housing Enterprises Financial Safety and Soundness Act of 1992.

- In 2008 the Housing and Economic Recovery Act combined OFHEO and the Federal Housing Finance Board (FHFB) to form the new **Federal Housing Finance Agency (FHFA)**.

The Federal Reserve System (the Fed) is the central banking system of the USA. It is organised on a regional basis given the large area involved and the multiplicity of small- and medium-sized US banks. The Federal Reserve System comprises 12 regional Reserve banks, 25 branches and 11 offices under the control of a board of governors located in Washington DC. The board approves the discount rate and other rates of interest of the system, supervises and generally regulates the operations of the banking system. The regional Reserve banks supervise banking practice and management, act as lenders of last resort, provide common services in cheque clearing, statistics and research, and apply monetary policy. Monetary control is exercised through open market operations.

The nucleus of US financial regulation is the Federal Reserve System. Roubini and Mihm[3] are seething about the role of Alan Greenspan in the genesis of the financial crisis. Greenspan was appointed chairman of the Fed in 1987. In their words, four months after his appointment, the stock market crashed, and Greenspan immediately rode to the rescue ... If Greenspan could acknowledge that the central bank had a role to play in mitigating the effects of a financial crisis, he declined to do anything to prevent such crises from developing. He seems to have had little interest in a long-standing central banking philosophy that ... powerful institutions should prevent bubbles from forming in the first place.' An earlier Federal Reserve chairman, William McChesney Martin, Jr., once said that the job of the central banker was to 'take away the punch bowl just as the party gets going'.

Roubini and Mihm continue thus: 'Greenspan revealed himself to be unwilling to take [the punch bowl] away. In 1996, as the stock market spiralled into a giddy bubble focused on tech and internet stocks, he warned of irrational exuberance, then did next to nothing to stop the bubble from inflating ... When the dot.com bubble finally popped in 2000, Greenspan poured more alcohol into the proverbial punch bowl. In the wake of the attacks on September 11, he kept cutting the funds rate, even after signs of a recovery started to appear ... This policy kept rates too low for too long and normalised them too late and too slowly. The result was the housing and mortgage bubble. By pumping vast quantities of easy money into the economy and keeping it there for too long, Greenspan muted the effects of one bubble's collapse by inflating an entirely new one ... It created a Greenspan put ... the markets believed that the Fed would always ride to the rescue of reckless traders after a bubble collapsed. It created moral hazard on a grand scale, and Greenspan deserves blame for it.' Our sentiments precisely.

■ The UK system of financial regulation

The Bank of England is the central bank of the UK. It was founded in 1694 as a private bank, chiefly to lend money to the state and to deal with the national debt. In succeeding centuries its royal charter gave it responsibility for the circulation of its own bank notes and it became a banker to other banks. The Bank Charter Act 1844 recognised it as the central note-issuing authority and the lender of last resort. By 1870, it was responsible for the general level of interest rates and for the general state credit in the country. By the early 20th century the bank was recognised as being responsible for the execution of national financial and monetary policy, under the overall direction of the government. In 1946, the bank was nationalised.

The Bank of England Act 1998 gave sole responsibility to the Bank for determining UK interest rates, a function which it achieves through its Monetary Policy Committee. Previously, interest rate policy was exercised by the UK Treasury. Since 1997, the bank has had statutory responsibility for the effectiveness and stability of the financial system as a whole, while the Financial Services Authority supervises the individual banks and building societies for prudential risk capital and ensuring capital adequacy. As mentioned above, in the mid-1980s the UK government set up a new super-regulator with extensive powers, the Financial Services Authority – also known by its acronym, FSA. Its aim was to promote efficient orderly and fair markets in financial services. It brought together an alphabet soup of regulators under a single umbrella – see Figure 8.1.

It was the new Labour government, in 1997, that decided to severely restrict the previous part played by the Bank of England in its traditional role as overall supervisor of the banking system. The Bank of England was given the responsibility of setting interest rates independently of the Treasury and to achieve an inflation target, set by the UK government. As a result, after 1997, no single body oversaw the system as a whole. Instead there were gaps between the so-called Tripartite Authorities – the Bank of England, the FSA and the Treasury. These gaps became apparent in the major financial crisis of 2007. Figure 8.2 shows the system prevailing from 1997 and Press Cuttings 8.1 and 8.2 detail criticisms of the workings of the FSA.

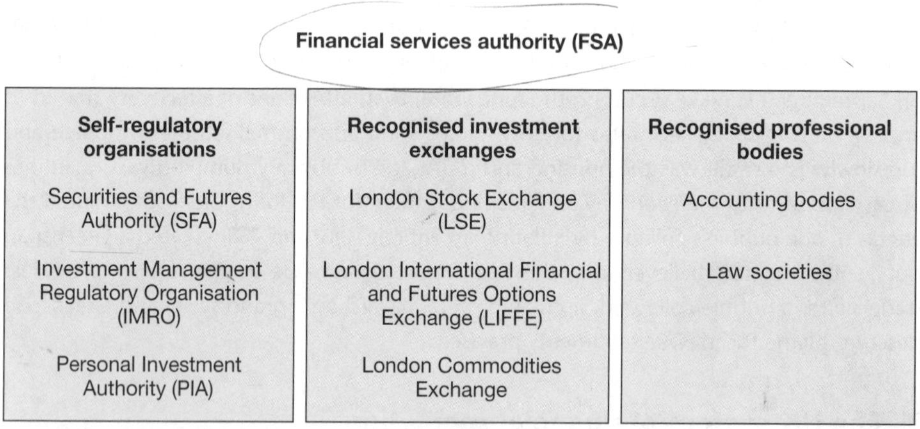

Financial services authority (FSA)

Self-regulatory organisations	Recognised investment exchanges	Recognised professional bodies
Securities and Futures Authority (SFA)	London Stock Exchange (LSE)	Accounting bodies
Investment Management Regulatory Organisation (IMRO)	London International Financial and Futures Options Exchange (LIFFE)	Law societies
Personal Investment Authority (PIA)	London Commodities Exchange	

Figure 8.1 The component parts of the FSA

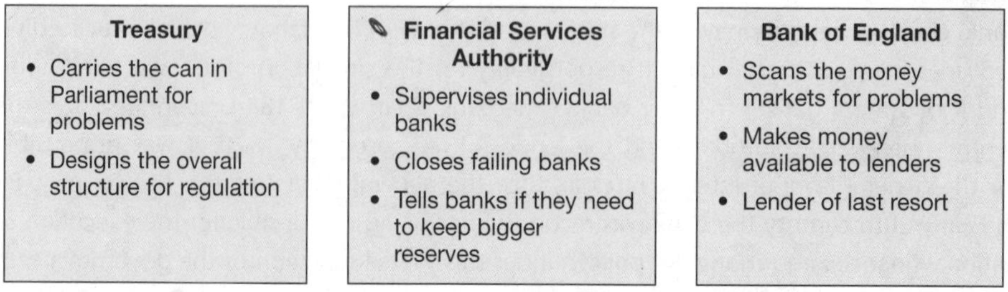

Treasury	Financial Services Authority	Bank of England
• Carries the can in Parliament for problems • Designs the overall structure for regulation	• Supervises individual banks • Closes failing banks • Tells banks if they need to keep bigger reserves	• Scans the money markets for problems • Makes money available to lenders • Lender of last resort

Figure 8.2 UK system of tripartite financial regulation introduced in 1997

Press cutting 8.1   *Financial Times*, 17 April 2009   **FT**

FSA under attack on regulation in boom

Jim Pickard, Political Correspondent

The City watchdog has been accused of 'apathy and complacency' in its regulation of building societies during the boom, by one of its former supervisors.

Vince Cable, Treasury spokesman for the Liberal Democrats, has written to Lord Turner, Financial Services Authority chairman, asking him to investigate the claims which he called a 'scathing indictment' of regulatory failure.

The MP was contacted by the whistle-blower just days before Moody's, the credit ratings agency, cut its ratings for nine building societies on Wednesday.

The former supervisor claimed that FSA management ignored a warning three years ago that risky self-certified loans had been bundled up and sold to building societies that thought they were buying conventional mortgages.

The whistleblower worked as a supervisor at the FSA's retail firms division, which has a remit over smaller building societies. The man – who now works in the City – has refused to disclose his identity because he fears legal action by the regulator.

He warned that building societies were now 'highly vulnerable' because they had moved away from their traditional business of taking deposits to fund mortgages. Instead, many have moved up the risk curve into specialised lending such as commercial property, subprime, self-certified and buy-to-let lending. Many had been 'eaten alive' by bankers who had sold them low-quality loan books. The Dunfermline recently collapsed after it emerged that the 140-year-old society had acquired portfolios of subprime loans and ramped up its commercial property lending even after the bubble had burst.

The former FSA supervisor said that in late 2005 and early 2006 he had taken part in 'thematic reviews' of mortgage books bought by building societies from wholesale lenders.

One book of tens of millions of pounds of loans was classified as 'full status', defined as mortgages with full evidence of borrowers' incomes. But it emerged that none of the loan files had any proof of the borrowers' income from payslips, P60s, tax returns or bank statements.

After being told about this, the FSA management 'turned a blind eye', merely sending a general letter to chief executives of building societies, reminding them to carry out thorough due diligence before buying such loan books, the supervisor said.

This was typical of the body's 'apathy and complacency' and refusal to deviate from an official light-touch policy, said the former supervisor.

The FSA said on Friday morning that the allegations were 'half-truths and distortions' and did not accurately reflect the body's supervision of building societies in recent years.

The regulator admitted that it had failed to focus in the past on lenders' business models or commercial judgments of firms 'with the intensity we do now'.

However, all of the building societies rated by Moody's had passed stress tests last autumn, with the exception of Dunfermline.

The Building Societies Association said on Thursday it would be unfair to presume that every building society that bought loan books from elsewhere was now in trouble.

Press cutting 8.2   *Financial Times*, 17 April 2009   FT

'Eaten alive by investment bankers'

Jim Pickard, Political Correspondent

A withering critique of both the City watchdog and some of Britain's building societies is contained in information sent by an FSA whistleblower to Vince Cable, the Liberal Democrat Treasury spokesman.

The former FSA employee, who had previously worked in banking, said some building societies had embarked on a foolish voyage into products that were not always fully understood.

'I witnessed trusting and naive provincial building society executives and non-executives, who had no real understanding of securitisation or structured finance or any other aspect of the workings of global capital markets, being eaten alive by cynical, rapacious and short-termist investment bankers,' he said.

Not only did building societies increase their lending to commercial property, self-certified borrowers and buy-to-let investors – all of which were more risky than their traditional loans – but they also bought books of loans originated by other lenders.

They pursued these activities because such loans offered a slightly higher yield and appeared on the surface to be safe.

In the recent past, half a dozen weak building societies have been saved through friendly mergers with bigger rivals.

But in the case of Dunfermline this month, it was two British loan books created by GMAC and Lehman Brothers, two subprime lenders, that helped precipitate its collapse.

No one was prepared to step in without massive public subsidy, because of the horrors lurking on its balance sheet.

Dunfermline was the subject of a convoluted rescue with Nationwide – the largest operator in the sector – taking on its savings accounts and the state acquiring its more toxic commercial loans.

This scenario could soon be followed by other building societies, according to the former FSA supervisor.

'No other society will swallow other bad balance sheets whole, so in future there will be no mergers entailing lock, stock and barrel assumption of assets and liabilities,' he told the *FT* in an interview this week. 'Taxpayers will take the strain of ensuring the survival of the building society movement.'

It was not clear from Dunfermline's annual report that it had exposure to subprime loans or £650m of commercial property. That was true of other building societies, the individual said. 'Many of these public accounts are sketchy and didn't cover any of the real risks,' he said. This view is contested by the Building Societies Association, which says that its members all meet their legal obligations in terms of financial disclosure.

Adrian Coles, director general of the BSA, said last night that it was ridiculous to claim that building societies had bought loans from originators without any independent advice. 'I do not believe another institution is in the same position as Dunfermline,' he said.

The whistleblower criticised the failure of the FSA to prevent building societies venturing into more exotic fields during the boom. The regulator had been determined not to 'regulate business models', he said.

Central to the criticism is that in 2005 and 2006 there were thematic reviews of mortgage books sold by wholesale lenders to building societies.

One such book contained several thousand loans categorised as 'full status' – with evidence of borrowers' income – but not a single loan file contained any proof of borrower's income from payslips, P60s or bank statements.

'We had unearthed incontrovertible proof that societies had been paying big prices for what were ostensibly the safest residential mortgages but were in fact risky self-certification loans,' he said. 'FSA management turned a blind eye.'

He alleges that the bank which originated the loans was not sanctioned. And that the building societies which bought the loans were not contacted.

'The FSA's only action following the thematic review was to send a general "Dear CEO" letter to all building societies reminding them of the need to conduct thorough due diligence,' said the individual.

The criticism echoes a recent internal report by the FSA into its failings over the collapse of Northern Rock. Regulators had failed to engage properly with the management of the failed bank or carry out adequate oversight, it found.

Yesterday the FSA refused to comment on the criticism other than to say it would reply in due course.

Following the UK general election in 2010, the new Conservative/Liberal Democrat government immediately altered the system to its preferred choice with the Bank of England as overall supervisor of British financial regulation. Given that the previous tripartite system failed to deal adequately with the state of affairs that occurred in 2007, this change seemed inevitable. The new regulative system is designed to:

- Abolish the tripartite system and transfer the FSA's responsibilities for supervising individual firms to a subsidiary of the Bank of England, the so-called Prudential Regulator – the name may change – which is to be chaired by the Governor of the Bank of England.

- Create an independent Financial Policy Committee at the Bank of England with the tools and the responsibility to look across the economy at the macro issues that may threaten economic and financial stability and the tools to take effective action in response. The Committee, which will do for financial stability what the Monetary Policy Committee does for monetary policy, will be chaired by the Governor of the Bank of England. Like the Monetary Policy Committee, it will publish minutes of meetings and quarterly reports and will be scrutinised by the Treasury Select Committee.

- Establish a new Consumer Protection and Markets Authority that will regulate the conduct of every authorised financial firm providing services to consumers.

- Unite the crime-busting powers of the FSA, the Serious Fraud Office and the Office of Fair Trading into a new single agency responsible for tackling serious economic crime.

Figure 8.3 summarises the new system of UK regulation and Press Cutting 8.3 details some of the shortcomings of the tripartite system of regulation previously in operation.

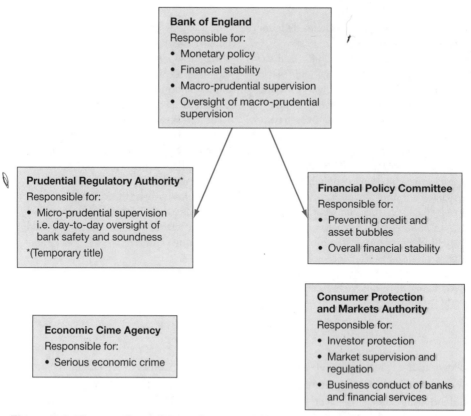

Figure 8.3 The new financial regulatory architecture of the UK

Press cutting 8.3   *Financial Times*, 17 June 2010   FT

FSA to be abolished in Osborne shake-up

George Parker and Brooke Masters

George Osborne last night moved to redress what he described as the spectacular regulatory failure of the City, announcing the abolition of the Financial Services Authority and a sweeping increase in the Bank of England's powers.

Mervyn King, Bank governor, will become one of the most powerful central bankers in the world, with a new remit to prevent the build-up of risk in the financial system in addition to his monetary policy role.

Mr King told a City audience at the Mansion House last night that his new role in enforcing financial stability was to 'turn down the music when the dancing gets a little too wild'.

Mr Osborne confirmed his plan to split up the FSA – a creation of Gordon Brown in 1997 – which the chancellor largely blames for failing to spot the approaching financial hurricane and the weakness of banks like Northern Rock.

'The FSA became a narrow regulator, almost entirely focused on rules-based regulation,' Mr Osborne said. 'No one was controlling levels of debt and when the crunch came no one knew who was in charge.'

The FSA will lose much of its role to a new Consumer Protection and Markets Authority, charged with regulating every bank and policing the City.

The rump of the organisation will be refocused as a prudential regulator – as yet unnamed – in charge of ensuring individual banks, building societies and insurance groups operate safely.

It will become a subsidiary of the Bank of England, feeding intelligence back to a new Financial Policy Committee, chaired by Mr King, which will be given unspecified tools to stop a dangerous build-up of credit or asset bubbles.

Hector Sants, the FSA chief who had announced his intention to quit, has agreed to stay on for a further three years after pleading from Mr Osborne. The announcement prompted loud applause from the Mansion House audience.

'The chancellor sees it as a real coup,' said one aide to Mr Osborne. 'Hector will ensure a smooth transition and he will hopefully allay concerns that there will be a big upheaval.'

Adair Turner, FSA chairman, said he welcomed the changes.

Mr Osborne insisted the reforms would end uncertainty but some City figures believe the upheaval is highly undesirable and will not compensate for the fact that regulators had simply fallen down on the job.

Banks face further uncertainty after Mr Osborne confirmed that an independent commission, headed by Sir John Vickers, would review the banking system, focusing on competition issues and the possible splitting of retail and investment banking operations.

■ Eurozone regulation

The eurozone splits financial regulation between the European Central Bank (ECB) and the national bodies of the euro member states. It is the organisation responsible for conducting monetary policy in the eurozone at the supra-national level. It was established in Frankfurt in 1998 and became fully operational on 1 January 1999, when it became responsible for monetary policy in the euro area. It is independent of national governments and it works with the national central banks of the member states that have adopted the euro. The ECB has the sole right to authorise the issue of euro banknotes. The objectives of the ECB are laid down in the Maastricht Treaty and are stated to be the maintenance of price stability – implying less than 2 per cent annual increase in the harmonised index of consumer prices – and, subject to price stability, support of the general economic policies in the European Community. Clearly, the ECB itself plays no part in regulating European banks. Its role in setting interest rates applies only to member states in the eurozone European Union. Member states remaining outside the eurozone continue to maintain their own national currencies and their own central banks. Of the first 15 EU member states, the UK, Denmark and Sweden have not adopted the euro. Norway and Switzerland are not members of the European Union though they have arrangements with the EU in many areas.

■ International regulation

In an attempt to impose international banking regulations, the Bank of International Settlements in Basel in Switzerland arranged meetings to agree measures by which all banks would limit risk. The Basel Accords agreed global banking rules. Basically the guidelines measure capital adequacy based upon financial ratios and the credit risk of balance sheet assets – as well as off-balance sheet exposures including unfunded loan commitments, letters of credit and various derivatives.

In 1988 the original Basel I specified minimum capital adequacy requirements and set up a system of measuring credit risk. This has been replaced by Basel II which was briefly discussed in Chapter 7. The Basel ratios are complicated and we can hardly do justice to their complexities in a text like this. Interested readers are referred to the actual Basel Accord rules. In any case, we believe that Basel II will probably be succeeded by Basel III very shortly.

Regulators also recommend the adoption of Value at Risk methodologies and stress testing of bank ratios and exposures. These methods have problems associated with them, as discussed in Chapter 7. Also it is fair to say that the whole capital adequacy approach is pro-cyclical. As stock markets rise, the capital of banks increases, creating a tendency for ratios to move above those required. This frees up capital which enables banks to buy more assets. This itself may bid up prices. It is the same idea in reverse on the way down. If stock market prices fall, the capital of banks may fall below the required minimum, requiring them to sell some assets to restore their capital adequacy requirements. Such asset sales may depress prices further, forcing the banks sell more assets, and so on.

■ Too big to fail

Many global banks seem to be too big to be allowed to fail. The failure of one very large bank could mean that a domino effect would be set off involving indebtedness between this bank, that bank and almost every other bank. This is what is meant by systemic risk. Formally, systemic risk can be defined as a situation in which problems in any one financial institution or financial market spread and thereby endanger the whole system. As mentioned earlier, this risk is a preoccupation of central bankers and is the concern of prudential regulation. The failure of a minor bank may not create systemic risk but failure of a large one certainly would.

Furthermore, big banks are difficult to regulate and to manage. One simple solution is to break up the largest banks into smaller units, in theory reducing systemic risk. Another solution might be to prevent them from growing so big in the first place. Strengthening anti-merger regulations for banks might achieve this but might have ruled out some large recent rescue deals. Restoring Glass-Steagall in the USA and, perhaps, bringing its main rules in elsewhere, might have a similar effect.

We now turn to one of the big issues in the financial crisis. How big a problem were the relatively new mark-to-market accounting rules?

■ Mark-to-market accounting

Accounting is regulated by various bodies in various countries. Traditionally, accounts were presented recording assets at historic cost which were depreciated each year. In recent years, rules have changed and the new regulations probably had a big impact on the financial crisis. The new accounting standards required certain assets to be shown at current market value on balance sheets. This system of using market values is termed mark-to-market accounting.

Mark-to-market accounting, also called fair value accounting, involves showing the value of an asset or liability based on the current market price of the asset or liability. Fair value accounting has been a part of US accounting principles since the early 1990s. Mark-to-market accounting can make values on the balance sheet change frequently, especially where a large proportion of assets involve items traded on financial markets.

The accounting standard that introduced mark-to-market accounting distinguished certain assets and set rules for their valuation as below:

■ Debt securities that the enterprise has the intent and ability to hold to maturity are classified as held-to-maturity securities and reported at amortised cost less impairment.

■ Debt and equity securities that are bought and held principally for the purpose of selling them in the near term are classified as trading securities and reported at fair value, with unrealised gains and losses included in earnings shown in the income statement.

■ Debt and equity securities not classified as either held-to-maturity securities or trading securities are categorised as available-for-sale securities and reported at fair value, with unrealised gains and losses excluded from earnings and the income statement and reported in a separate component of shareholders' equity.

These accounting rules came in first in the USA in 1993. As marking to market caught on, some companies saw the opportunity of using it as a source of accounting fraud, especially when the market price could not be objectively determined. The fraud involved assets being marked to a mathematical model using estimates of future results – the estimate would be generous of course.

Garbage in, garbage out. And one of the biggest offenders? Enron. It became the first non-financial company to use the method to account for complex long-term contracts. In the Enron brand of mark-to-market accounting, long-term contracts were shown on the balance sheet as the present value of estimated future net cash flows from the contract. The increase in value passed through the income statement. Of course, these anticipated profits were impossible to judge and investors were typically given false or misleading reports. The expected income from these projects was recorded up front. So, in future years, even if the firm achieved these profits, they could not then be included in the income statement because they had already been taken to credit. Remarkably, these mark-to-make-believe figures were accepted by the auditors. This was only one of the devious accounting tricks that Enron dreamt up. Mark-to-make-believe accounting could be a fraudulent finance director's favourite fantasy. The word fantasy is not chosen for its onomatopoeic qualities. Fantasy is just what Enron accounting was all about.

Hardly surprising, the use of this accounting device was outlawed. Mark-to-market accounting remains but the extravagant use of present value of future cash flows as a means of recording assets is out of bounds.

A new accounting standard was introduced in the USA in 2006 that clarified the definition of fair value, expanded disclosure requirements for assets and liabilities measured at fair value and introduced a fair value hierarchy. This hierarchy uses three levels to rank the quality and reliability of information used to determine fair values. Level 1 inputs are the most reliable and Level 3 inputs are least reliable. The way it works is as follows:

1. Level 1 are assets that can be priced in active markets, like shares traded on an exchange

2. Level 2 applies to positions where there is not a quoted price, but where prices can be extrapolated using observable inputs. For example, a corporate bond that did not trade often could be valued using credit ratings, maturity, and interest rate along with other data to estimate a price based on how other traded bonds are priced. These inputs derive from market data for similar bonds. This is sometimes called mark-to-model, but the key point is that factors going into the estimate are verifiable.

3. Level 3 assets are based on unobservable inputs. Here, there may be no market trading upon which to base estimates. Infrequently traded stocks and private company shares are two examples. This method of valuation has also been termed mark-to-make believe.

Problems arise when the market-based measurement does not accurately reflect the asset's true value. This can occur when a company is forced to calculate the selling price of an asset during crisis conditions or volatile times or when liquidity has dried up. If trading is low or investors are fearful, the selling price of a bank's assets could be much lower than their value under normal conditions. The result would be lower assets on one side of the balance sheet and lower shareholders' equity on the other. This occurred during the financial crisis of 2007/8 when many securities on banks' balance sheets could not be valued because the market for them had disappeared.

In short, in boom conditions there were exaggerated profits and valuations for bank assets and in bust conditions asset values appeared at exaggeratedly low values. Of course, bankers were only too happy to cream off their unjustified bonuses in the boom based on unrealised and extremely dubious profit figures. But did they pay them back when the market went into reverse? Of course they didn't. Accounting rules changed again in 2009 to allow valuation to be based on a price that would be received in an orderly market rather than a forced sale.

Many observers have placed much of the blame for the financial crisis of 2007/8 on the accounting profession and, in particular, on the US Securities and Exchange Commission for the mess surrounding fair-value accounting rules requiring banks to mark their assets to market especially in respect of CDSs and CDOs.

So, how did mark-to-market accounting rules turn out to be such a big factor in the financial crisis? The new accounting rules required companies to adjust the value of marketable securities, for example CDOs and CDSs, to their market value. The intent was to help investors understand the value of these assets at a particular point in time. When the market is distressed, it is difficult to sell CDSs and CDOs. As originally interpreted by banks and their auditors, the lower firesale value was used as the market value. Many large financial institutions recognised significant losses during 2007 and 2008 as a result of marking down CDSs and CDOs to this firesale value.

Problems were multiplied for two reasons. First, for some banks, this triggered a margin call. Banks that had borrowed funds using CDSs and CDOs as collateral were required to put up more cash. This occurred because prices had fallen below certain levels. This resulted in further forced sales of CDSs and CDOs. This further depressed their prices and led to other emergency efforts to obtain cash to pay the amount required by the margin call. The second problem arose because many banks had looming liabilities to pay out under CDS instruments and these liabilities were getting bigger day by day. These two factors morphed into a third, namely that the losses being recorded in respect of the first two items above were affecting bank regulatory capital ratios adversely. This naturally created worries about the health of the bank – with justification. Widespread rights issues were arranged to bail out the banks. Government rescues were made available to keep the ailing banks afloat. Of course, in case after case bonus payments continued unabated. Remarkable.

As a corollary of all this, the USA enacted the Emerging Economic Stabilisation Act of 2008 in which Section 132 subhead Authority to Suspend Mark-to-Market Accounting, formalised the Securities and Exchange Commission's authority to suspend the application of FAS 157, the accounting standard on fair value accounting, if the SEC determines that it is in the public interest to do so and if it protects investors. The Emergency Economic Stabilisation Act of 2008 was passed and became law in October 2008.

In April 2009, the US accounting standard board (FASB) issued an official update on fair value accounting that eases the mark-to-market rules when the market is unsteady or inactive. These changes have significantly boosted banks' earnings. The changes are applicable to a broad range of derivatives, including CDSs and CDOs.

Like ourselves, Adair Turner, the chairman of the FSA in Britain, concluded that marking to market had been a cause of inflated bankers' bonuses. We return to this topic in Chapter 11.

Chapter 9

The business cycle, booms, busts, bubbles and frauds

■ Introduction

The term business cycle refers to fluctuations in the level of economic activity moving from depression to recovery to boom to recession, with aggregate demand falling short of its potential during depression and recession and in excess of its potential in the boom phase. Assuming a general upward path in the level of economic activity, Figure 9.1 shows how the business cycle pans out. The boom is a phase of the cycle in which full employment and maximum levels of output are achieved. Boom conditions are associated with expansionary fiscal and monetary policy creating high aggregate demand.

The business cycle is a widely-observed economic phenomenon. Western government policy has aimed to dampen the ups and downs of the cycle. Indeed, it is possible to argue that the decade of the 1990s and the first half of the following decade experienced boom conditions and this boom was a major contributing factor in the subsequent bust. Governments run boom conditions for too long at their peril.

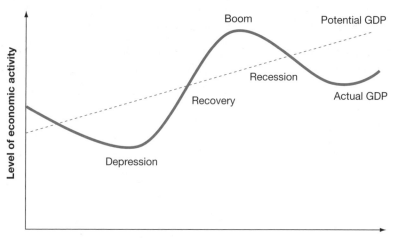

Figure 9.1 The business cycle showing fluctuations in the level of economic activity

Possible major drivers of the business cycle have been postulated to include:

- interest rate levels;
- money supply growth;
- inventory levels;
- capital spending;
- asset prices;
- building construction;
- animal spirits;

We look at each of these in turn.

A stimulus is usually given to economic activity when interest rates are low. By this, we refer to real interest rates – that is, interest rates with anticipated inflation deducted. In looking at interest rates, it is real rates that are critical. Over the very long term, real interest rates on government bonds[1] have averaged around 1 to 2 per cent although they have varied considerably over time. The real interest rate[2] is given by:

$$\frac{1 + \textbf{nominal (or quoted) interest rate}}{1 + \textbf{inflation}} - 1$$

The nominal interest rate is the rate which is quoted in the market place and is sometimes called the money terms interest rate. When inflation is eliminated via the above equation, the real rate is obtained. An approximation of the above equation is that the real interest rate equals the nominal rate minus inflation.

Likewise, a stimulus to the economy generally follows relatively high levels of money supply growth, although there is ongoing discussion as to whether this makes a long-term difference or only a short-term positive boost. So, when real interest rates fall below their natural, long-term levels and money supply growth exceeds trend, two of the conditions for subsequent growth in GDP are in place. The next few factors are major, non-monetary phenomena that can drive economies forward and create cyclical movements dependent upon demand.

Low levels of inventory induce companies to replace stock levels. If growth follows, which means more sales, which further depletes inventory leading to further building of stocks. Next there is the capital spending driver. Bottlenecks in existing facilities force companies to build more capacity. Again, this creates more growth, which means more capacity is installed. There is also the collateral accelerator. Rising asset prices create added collateral value. This enables more borrowing, which stimulates business, driving asset prices higher. This has the largest impact when it happens in property markets, whether commercial or personal, but is also true for equities. In property markets, asset price rises frequently feed on themselves, inducing new investors in before prices rise too much. This, in turn, drives building and construction. Rising asset prices also capture the imagination of ordinary unsophisticated investors, which leads to momentum investing (driving prices higher) and to bubbles.

The next factor which is highly significant in cyclical movements in the economy is what Keynes[3] termed animal spirits which is really rather similar to the confidence of businesspeople. Keynes suggested that knowledge of future outturns of projects are uncertain, so much so that 'our basis of knowledge for estimating the yield ten years hence of a railway, a copper mine, a textile factor, the goodwill of a patent medicine, an Atlantic liner, a building in the City of London amounts to little and sometimes to nothing'. Of course, those familiar with net present value calculations will see that Keynes is saying that we just don't have even a fair idea of medium-term net cash flows. And perhaps the cash outflows on investment decisions are pretty cloudy too – see Myddelton's case studies[4] of government projects, although it is possible to argue that these were frequently deliberately biased on the low side in order to get the project done. Having said this, the same observation can be made about private sector projects. With this background, Keynes goes on to ask whether if projects' futures are so uncertain, how are projects chosen? And he concludes that they 'can only be taken on as a result of animal spirits', which he defines as 'a spontaneous urge to action rather than inaction'. This contrasts with what rational decision-making might suggest, namely reference for 'the outcome of a weighted average of quantitative benefits multiplied by quantitative probabilities'. As Akerlof and Shiller[5] observe, the term animal spirits is now an economic term referring to a restless and inconsistent element in the economy implying an ambiguity with uncertainty – 'sometimes we are paralysed by it. Yet at other times it refreshes and energises us, overcoming our fears and indecisions'. These two authors go on to think in terms of positive animal spirits as implying confidence and they suggest a confidence multiplier rather like the Keynesian multiplier. According to this idea, an input of confidence creates further confidence. Tests of confidence (via confidence indexes) feeding into future GDP[6] do indicate such a multiplier. One interesting piece of work in this area used credit quantity spreads, that is, the difference between interest rates on risky debt versus those on less risky debt, as indicators of confidence and tested whether they feed into GDP.

Naturally, animal spirits can turn negative and take a lot of reviving. This is associated with the state of the economy at cyclical turning points. It is, in truth, an exhaustion phenomenon. The boom creates bottlenecks in labour, physical resources and credit, which put pressure on further growth in private spending and tend to make new business less profitable. At this time, with credit being cut back, the economy slows and can easily go into reverse. Significant contractions may lead to debt deflation and credit crunches. Of course, this is a very simplified model and cannot be expected immutably to occur.

Different drivers of the economy ebb and flow cyclically at their own rate, giving rise to various identified cycles. These cycles and their drivers are:

- **The Kitchin cycle** (3 to 5 years). This refers to the rate at which businesses build up inventories of goods which, as mentioned above, can affect a country's economy rate of growth or decline
- **The Juglar cycle** (7 to 11 years). This refers to companies' property, plant and capital equipment spending. Investment in fixed capital is typically twice the length of period of the Kitchin cycle.
- **Kuznets cycle** (15 to 25 years). This refers to the time between government spending on infrastructural investment – roads and railways.

- **Kondratiev wave or cycle** (45 to 60 years). This refers to phases of capitalism. Maybe, every 45 to 60 years there is a crisis of capitalism.

■ Booms, busts and bubbles

Discussing booms and busts, Kindleberger[7] interprets Minsky[8] in the following words 'according to Minsky, events leading up to a crisis start with a "displacement", some exogenous, outside shock to the macroeconomic system. The nature of this displacement varies from one speculative boom to another. It may be the outbreak or end of a war, a bumper harvest or crop failure, the widespread adoption of an invention with pervasive effects – canals, railways, the automobile – some political event or surprising financial success, or a debt conversion that precipitously lowers interest rates.' He goes on to say: 'but whatever the source of the displacement, if it is sufficiently large and pervasive, it will alter the economic outlook by changing profit opportunities in at least one important sector of the economy. Displacement brings opportunities for profit in some new or existing lines, and closes out others. As a result, business firms and individuals with savings or credit seek to take advantage of the former and retreat from the latter. If the new opportunities dominate those that lose, investment and production pick up. A boom is underway.'

Vines[9] interprets the Minsky-Kindleberger stages of the cycle with his own 11 stages, which we summarise below.

- The cycle begins with some kind of shock to the system. This creates important opportunities for at least one sector of the economy, for example the rise of the internet at the beginning of this century.
- This driving event fuels a boom, aided by the expansion of bank credit, enlarging the money supply.
- With more cash around, the seeds of financial euphoria are well and truly sown. This can lead to speculative activity, increasing gearing and then buying of assets on margin.
- News spreads of the profit opportunities and the average person suddenly wants to get rich and a bubble forms. New investors with no previous experience arrive in the market place.
- Real dangers become manifest as the media focus in the non-financial pages upon market movements and television programmes on property development and/or stocks and shares proliferate.
- The market becomes populated with more small, inexperienced players who may be preyed upon by disreputable dealers. Derivatives issues grow and small players may be drawn in using highly geared positions.
- The bubble grows and market prices move ahead of underlying fundamental value (that is, value based upon the net present value of future cash flows).
- Scams, swindles and dubious investments become apparent. So often, these tragically unravel in the bust.

- By now, more savvy investors are heading for the exit. Newer players tend to stay put. The fact that some players are getting out puts a brake on the upward movement of prices. There is an increasing movement away from assets into cash, depressing prices and causing banks to call in loans as collateral values fall.

- The market is in retreat. The peak has passed. The exit of players is often accompanied by dramatic events such as the unravelling of a significant fraud or scam.

- This acceleration to the exit leads to Kindleberger's revulsion phase with revelations that the very assets which were once so highly valued are now of no interest whatsoever.

A good warning signal that the bubble is about to bust is when phrases such as 'this time is different' (often described as the four most dangerous words in investment strategy) and 'the new paradigm' are echoed around the corridors of finance and in the media.

Calverley[10] neatly summarises the characteristics of bubble conditions and these are reproduced in Table 9.1. We have added the last two items in the list – namely that animal spirits are positive and that real interest rates are relatively low. Of course, we would stress that all of the characteristics listed in the exhibit do not have to be present to drive a bubble but most would likely be there.

Vines[11] neatly summarises causes of stock market booms and lists potential drivers of crashes and panics and these appear, respectively, in Tables 9.2 and 9.3.

Table 9.1 Typical characteristics of a bubble

- Rapidly rising prices
- High expectation for continuing rapid rises
- Overvaluation compared to historical averages
- Overvaluation compared to reasonable levels
- Several years into an economic upswing
- Some underlying reason or reasons for higher prices
- A new element, e.g. technology for stocks or immigration for housing
- Subjective 'paradigm shift'
- New investors drawn in
- New entrepreneurs in the area
- Considerable popular and media interest
- Major rise in lending
- Increase in indebtedness
- New lenders or lending policies
- Consumer price inflation often subdued (so central banks relaxed)
- Relaxed monetary policy
- Falling household savings rate
- A strong exchange rate
- Positive animal spirits
- Relatively low real interest rates

Source: Calverley.

Table 9.2 Causes of stock market booms

- Fads emerge encouraging investment
- Rising share prices encourage optimism and expectations of continuing boom
- A benign background of economic circumstances and growth encourages corporate profitability
- Deregulation may create new opportunities, either in developed markets or in emerging markets
- Buying is fuelled by plentiful easy credit
- Equity issues are a market feature
- New derivatives appear and margin trading increases
- Share price rises overtake bond price rises
- A tendency towards talking up the market is common whether from governments or small investors
- Buoyed by strong performance, fund managers and the financial community feel like and behave like 'Masters of the Universe'
- Stories of spectacular profits draw in novice share buyers in great numbers
- Fund managers, professional investors and others in the financial community try to gear higher profit by taking bigger and bigger risks

Source: Vines.

Table 9.3 Causes of crashes and panics

- Signs of doubt over the frailty of rising markets emerge
- News stories cast doubt on profit potential of the fads which fuelled the investment boom
- Corporate failures emerge
- Prices edge downwards, accelerating later
- Pressure builds on margin traders and similar players forcing more selling pressure
- Search for good news or good stories in the light of negative pressures
- Scandals and scams unravel. Jitters accelerate.
- Negative news about the local economy, or world economy plus corporate profits under pressure
- Panic sets in and feeds on itself, causing a downward spiral in prices

Source: Vines.

How do we know that the bubble is about to burst? Well, we don't. But there are tell-tale signs. Again, drawing from Vines[12] and adapted by ourselves, such harbingers are listed below:

- relatively high levels of corporate and bank debt;
- upward movements in interest rates from previous low levels;
- past rises in lending by banks moving into reverse;
- relatively high price/earnings ratios;
- increases in merger and acquisition activity;

- rush of new stock issues;
- stock price news is elevated from the business pages to the front pages of newspapers;
- much talk of new eras and/or new paradigms;
- stockbrokers and investment banks on recruitment drives;
- conspicuous spending and lavish behaviour by corporations and financial institutions;
- capitalisation of stock markets in excess of gross domestic product. Banks in country X with debt in excess of reserves of country X.

It is worth mentioning at this point that Mishkin[13] distinguishes two kinds of bubble. For him, the first is the dangerous category called the 'credit boom bubble', in which exuberant expectations about economic prospects or lax credit, or changes in financial markets lead to a credit boom. Increased demand for some assets raises their price and this encourages further lending against these assets, again increasing demand, and hence their prices, thereby creating a positive feedback loop. This loop involves increasing leverage, further easing of credit standards, again increasing leverage, and the cycle continues.

Subsequently, the bubble bursts and asset prices collapse, leading to a reversal of the feedback loop. Loans go bad and deleveraging begins, demand for the assets declines further and prices drop more. Resultant loan losses and declines in asset prices erode the balance sheet values at financial institutions, further diminishing credit and investment across a range of assets. This deleveraging depresses business and household spending, weakens economic activity and increases risk in credit markets. Of course, this description contains many of the features of the 2007/8 crisis.

The second kind of bubble, the irrational exuberance bubble, is – according to Mishkin – less dangerous. It does not involve the cycle of leveraging against higher asset values. Without a credit boom, the bursting of the bubble does not cause the financial system to seize up and therefore does far less damage. Mishkin claims that the bubble in technology stocks in the late 1990s was not fuelled by a feedback loop between bank lending and rising equity values. And the bursting of that bubble was not accompanied by a marked impact on bank balance sheets. Because of this the bursting of the tech stock bubble was followed by only a mild recession. Also, the bubble that burst in the stock market in 1987 did not put the financial system under great stress and the economy fared relatively well in its aftermath. It is worth mentioning that Mishkin's distinction on bubble damage is not universally accepted.

Your author, who is of the opinion that a bursting credit default swap bubble was the cause of the financial crisis of 2007/8, takes the view that this does not fit neatly into either category but is certainly as dangerous as a pure credit boom bubble.

Accounts of various bubbles through history are related in Mackay[14]. His stories include many other tales of gullibility from witchcraft to alchemy and a few more to boot.

In Chapter 15, we look at the Wall Street Crash and we show how the bubble then, driven by a boom in credit, deflated at an astonishing rate.

■ Frauds and swindles

Frauds, swindles, white collar crime and financial shenanigans are always with us. But the volume of such felonies increases in the boom times. Kindleberger[15] puts it succinctly. 'The propensities to swindle and be swindled run parallel to the propensity to speculate during a boom. Crash and panic … induce still more to cheat in order to save themselves. And the signal for panic is often the revelation of some swindle, theft, embezzlement, or fraud.'

In 2008, the US Securities and Exchange Commission (SEC) launched a record number of actions against market manipulation and investigated the biggest number of cases of insider trading allegations in its history. High-profile scandals were revealed after the crash of 2008, but none as great as that perpetrated by Bernard Madoff – more of this later in this chapter. Under the subheading 'Dubious Practices', Kindleberger[16] shows his mastery of understatement by listing, and we quote, 'the forms of financial felony are legion. In addition to outright stealing, misrepresentation, and lying, there are many practices close to the line: diversion of funds from the stated use to another, paying dividends out of capital or [out of] borrowing, dealing in company stock on inside knowledge, selling securities without full disclosure of new knowledge, using company funds for non-competitive purchases from or loans to insider interests, taking orders but not executing them, altering the company's books … one could go on'.

Booms encourage skulduggery and fraud of every variety. Standards fall as the scramble to become rich overcomes scruples. Well worth a visit because of their close-ups of fraud at work are such films as the classics *Wall Street* and *Glengarry Glen Ross* and *Rogue Trader* and *Boiler Room*. Also *Enron: The Smartest Guys in the Room* can be recommended as can the book upon which it is based, by McLean and Elkind[17]. And the inside story of Enron from Swartz and Watkins[18] is also a must in this area. There is a wide range of other frauds including falsification of company legal documents, cold calling names from company share registers with news of a hot new issue or an offer of shares with a name similar to an existing company (the boiler room scam – you get a worthless share certificate and, if you try to telephone the so-called broker, the bird has flown), internet offers of something for nothing (beware: the term no free lunch is well chosen) and there is a legion of financial shenanigans – try Schilit and Perler's[19] book of the same name. The term financial shenanigans is a euphemism for cooking the books.

It is a fact that as markets enter the panic stage, they lead to the revelation of a host of crooked practices that were nurtured as the bubble grew. Indeed, the revelation of frauds adds fuel to the bonfire of the markets.

We would have liked to focus upon the Enron fraud but it was blown before the 2007/8 crash. Instead we look next at Ponzi schemes. We jump back in time to relate the tale of Charles Ponzi and then focus upon the biggest Ponzi scheme to date. It is, of course, the now-famous Ponzi game that has ensured Bernard Madoff a position in the financial chamber of horrors. But we look at Charles Ponzi's financial history first.

■ Charles Ponzi

Ponzi did not invent financial fraud. Indeed he followed a list dating from the 17th century which includes such stories as the South Sea bubble and John Law's Mississippi bubble – see Chancellor[20] and Ferguson[21] for good summaries and especially Chancellor for others too.

Charles Ponzi (1882–1949) was one of the great swindlers in American financial history. The term Ponzi scheme describes a scam that pays early investors returns from the incoming investments of later investors. Ponzi offered clients a 50 per cent profit within 45 days, or 100 per cent profit within 90 days. How? By buying discounted postal reply coupons in other countries and redeeming them at face value in the US. In theory, the scheme might have worked but Ponzi turned it into a big scam aiming to make him rich by stealing from investors.

In November 1903, Ponzi, an Italian, arrived in Boston, Massachusetts. He learned English and spent a few years doing odd jobs from being a dishwasher in a restaurant, where he advanced to become a waiter, before being fired for short-changing customers and theft.

By 1907, he had moved to Montreal and had become an assistant cashier in a bank started by Luigi Zarossi to service the needs of Italian immigrants. Zarossi paid double the going rate of interest at the time and the bank was growing rapidly as a result. Ponzi rose to become bank manager. Maybe Ponzi learnt a lot here. Zarossi was funding the interest payments not through profit but by deposits in newly opened accounts. The bank failed and Zarossi fled to Mexico armed with a pile of other people's money.

Shortly afterwards, Ponzi walked into the offices of a former Zarossi customer and, finding the office deserted, wrote himself a cheque for USD423.58 from a cheque book he found there. He forged the signature of a director of the company. Quickly confronted by police, Ponzi admitted guilt and spent three years in prison.

After his release in 1911 he returned to the USA and became involved in smuggling illegal Italian immigrants. After being caught, he spent two years in prison in Atlanta. On release Ponzi moved back to Boston. The seeds of his great scheme followed receipt of a mail shot from a company in Spain. Inside the envelope was an international reply coupon (IRC). He saw a great opportunity. The purpose of the IRC was to allow someone in one country to send it to a correspondent in another country, who could use it to pay the postage for a reply. The IRC was priced at the cost of postage in the country of purchase. However it could be exchanged for stamps to cover the cost of postage in the country of redemption. However, if these values were different, there was a potential profit. The cost of postage in Italy expressed in USD differed from that in the USA. An IRC could be bought cheaply in Italy and exchanged for US stamps of higher value, which could then be sold. Ponzi reckoned that the net profit on such transactions, after expenses and exchange rates, was in excess of 400 per cent. This was a form of arbitrage, buying an asset in one market and selling it in another where the price is higher – all perfectly legal, so far.

Ponzi contacted friends in Boston and promised that he would double their investment in 90 days. He explained the arbitrage opportunity and attracted takers. Further investors appeared by word of mouth and even more joined. Ponzi hired agents and paid good commission rates for business brought in. By February 1920, Ponzi's total takings were USD5,000 (approximately USD55,000 in 2010 terms). By March, he had made USD30,000 (USD330,000 in 2010 terms). Ponzi hired more agents and by May 1920, he had taken USD420,000, the equivalent of USD4.62 million in 2010 terms.

Ponzi lived extravagantly. And his rapid rise made people suspicious. A Boston financial journalist suggested there was no way Ponzi could legally achieve such high returns in such a short period of time. Ponzi sued for libel and won. Shortly after that, the Barron's financial journal observed that to explain the apparent inflows of cash in the scheme, 160 million IRCs would have to be in circulation. In fact, no more than 27,000 actually were. Whilst the profit margin on buying and selling each IRC appeared to be very high, the overhead to handle the purchase and redemption of these low value items would have exceeded the profit. The stories caused a panic run on Ponzi's scheme but he managed to sweet-talk customers and dealt with redemptions. Furthermore, Ponzi hired a publicity agent, William McMasters. Unfortunately for Ponzi, McMasters became suspicious of Ponzi's postal reply coupon business. In July 1920, McMasters found clear evidence that Ponzi was robbing Peter to pay Paul. He went to his former employer, the *Post* newspaper with this story. On 2 August, McMasters wrote an article declaring Ponzi technically insolvent. The story sparked a massive run which, again, Ponzi managed to finance.

But, on 11 August 1920, things came to a new head. The *Post* ran a front page story about Ponzi's activities in Montreal including his forgery conviction and his role at the Zarossi fraudulent bank. At the same time investigators of Ponzi's books of account found a pack of irregularities. Ponzi admitted guilt to police authorities on 12 August 1920. He was sentenced to five years in prison.

On release, Ponzi headed for Florida where, in 1925, he offered investors tracts of land, some under water, promising 200 per cent returns in 60 days. Obviously a scam, Ponzi was found guilty in February 1926 and sentenced to a year in prison. Ponzi appealed and was freed after paying a USD1,500 bond. Ponzi shaved his head, grew a moustache and tried to flee the country on a ship bound for Italy. Docking at a further US port, Ponzi was caught in New Orleans and sent back to Massachusetts to serve a prison term for an earlier indictment there. Ponzi served seven more years in prison. He was eventually released in 1934. His previous charm and confidence had gone.

Back in Italy, Ponzi could not make good. He went from scheme to scheme, with no positive result. He eventually moved to Brazil where he spent the last years of his life in poverty, working occasionally as a translator. He suffered a heart attack in 1941. He became almost blind by 1948. A brain haemorrhage paralysed his right leg and arm and he died in a charity hospital in Rio de Janeiro in 1949. Just prior to death, he gave a last interview to an American journalist. Ponzi is reported as saying, 'I had given them the best show that was ever staged in their territory since the landing of the Pilgrims.'

In truth, to describe the rob Peter to pay Paul scam as a Ponzi scheme is a bit of a fraud itself. In New York in 1899 William Miller (aka William 520 per cent Miller) promised 10 per cent per week and defrauded investors before paying for his crimes with a ten-year jail sentence. His methods were very similar to the scam of Charles Ponzi. But maybe the scam is older still. In Charles Dickens' novel *Little Dorrit* (1857) a remarkably similar fraud appears to be perpetrated.

■ Bernard Madoff

Madoff was born in 1938 in New York City, in the borough of Queens. He was raised in the Jewish tradition. His father was a stockbroker. After obtaining a degree in political science from Hofstra College, Madoff set up a Wall Street stockbroking firm, Bernard L. Madoff Investment Securities LLC in 1960. He was its chairman until his arrest in December 2008. Initially, the business grew quickly with the assistance of his father-in-law, who introduced a circle of friends and their families.

At one time, Madoff Securities was the largest market maker at the NASDAQ. In 2008 it was the sixth biggest market maker on Wall Street. The firm also had an investment management division that was the focus of the Ponzi scheme. The stockbroking arm occupied the 18th and 19th floors of Manhattan's Lipstick Building. Madoff's investment management Ponzi business was on the 17th floor. The 18th and 19th floor offices were immaculate – a typical trading floor, vibrant and money-making. The firm traded stocks, bonds and other securities for clients and on its own behalf. Its net profit in 2006 was around USD40 million. This brokerage business was regulated by the Securities and Exchange Commission (SEC) with books and records to verify transactions, compliance, financial records and so on. But the 18th and 19th floor operations were a smokescreen for the Ponzi operations on the 17th floor. Here the office was chaotic – paper untidily all over the place. Higgledy piggledy would flatter the 17th floor. Visitors did not see the 17th floor shambles. Nor did the employees on the 18th and 19th floor. The 17th floor was the home to the Madoff hedge fund (which, it transpired, wasn't a hedge fund).

Different cultures divided the 18th and 19th floors – this was the typical Wall Street divide. On the 19th floor were the traders, aspirant masters of the universe, whilst those on the 18th were the back office group. The 17th floor was 'Bernie's world'. Here there was a group of insiders to the fraud and also a lower level group who were reconciling the bogus trades that the hedge fund was supposed to be making.

When asked about Madoff's secret of investment success, the standard answer was that he did not want to give away his formula for achievement of good returns but that it was essentially a split-strike conversion strategy. The technique appears in options trading manuals. So, what is it? In essence it is an index options strategy, in which the hedge fund manager buys listed stocks in, say, the Standard and Poor's 100 index but also deals in options that give the right (but not the obligation) to buy the stocks at an agreed future price – the strike price. The dealer then buys and sells options against those same stocks. In more detail, the original purchase of stocks would be, say, 30 to 50 or so out of the S&P 100. The chosen stocks would likely be those most closely correlated with the S&P 100 index. Then there's the buy and sell options strategy (usually termed a collar). This would involve buying out-of-the-money S&P 100 put options and selling out-of-the-money S&P 100 call options. As markets move, readjustment of the out-of-the-money positions is necessary to ensure a desirable profit strategy. If it sounds complicated, that's because it is. And that was just what Madoff wanted so that his reference to split-strike conversion would draw acquiescent nods and smiles from his questioner.

With this background, Madoff's 17th floor henchmen would use past data to create apparently profitable trades. So, if a 0.8 per cent return for the month was required, one could work backwards to choose which Blue Chip stocks would have yielded the desired payoff. Madoff, or his insider henchmen (of which there were relatively few), would then enter trades that never happened, with actual market prices, into an old IBM computer and a fictitious track record was forged. Then an Excel spreadsheet of client accounts was updated to show the desired 0.8 per cent gain that month.

Then came a phoney paper trail. This involved false contract notes, confirmations and settlements – a completely fictitious set of books. Madoff sent out an array of confirmations justifying trades that never happened. In fact there were no trades for 20 years or so. Clients got their statements, were probably happy about their fictitious returns, mentally congratulating themselves on their choice of investment advisor, Bernard Madoff. And they might think about upping their investments with such a proficient hedge fund.

In 1983, Madoff set up his London office to enable employees in the US to make trades when US markets were closed. However, in 1989, the NASDAQ extended its hours to enable out-of-hours trading. This made the London office less essential. But Madoff found a use for it. Whilst it continued to trade, Bernie used it as a conduit through which to launder clients' money which he was spending on real estate, yachts, high living and every conceivable luxury. It became his source of money laundering. And, as you would expect of a proper (not a fraudulent) outstandingly successful businessperson he became a donor to Jewish charities – and on a colossal scale.

Madoff's marketing strategy was interesting. Rather than offer very high returns, he offered modest and steady returns to an exclusive clientele. Madoff first concentrated on well-off Jews he met at country clubs on Long Island and in Palm Beach. His investment funds were perceived as exclusive. One potential investor begged Madoff to take her money. But he refused. And, as word disseminated, Madoff drew in international banks, charities, hedge funds, the wealthy and the famous, Hollywood stars, sports starts, celebrities – just about anyone with money thought about putting some capital the way of Bernard Madoff.

Madoff annual returns were consistent at around 10 per cent or more. Ponzi schemes often advertise returns of 20 per cent or higher – and they disappear quickly. One Madoff fund had reported a 10.5 per cent annual return over the previous 17 years. At the end of November 2008, with a general stock market collapse, the same fund showed that it was up 5.6 per cent, while the total return on the S&P 500 stock index was negative 38 per cent.

Not everyone believed Madoff's claims. Harry Markopolos complained to the SEC in 1999 that it was impossible to make the profits Madoff reported using the investment strategies that he claimed to use and that he should be investigated. The SEC investigated Madoff in 1999 and 2000 but concluded that there was no violation or any major issues of concern.

In 2005, Markopolos sent a 17-page memo to the SEC, titled *The World's Largest Hedge Fund is a Fraud*. He also approached the *Wall Street Journal* about the existence of the

Ponzi scheme in 2005, but its editors decided not to pursue the story. The memo listed 30 red flags and concluded that Bernie Madoff was either running a Ponzi scheme or front running, that is placing the hedge fund's orders before his brokerage clients. Markopolos concluded that it was most likely a Ponzi scheme. The list of red flags appears in a book by Markopolos[22] which makes interesting reading. His book is called *No One Would Listen*. They should have listened. His arguments seemed utterly convincing.

In 2001, finance journalist, Erin Arvedlund, published an article for Barron's questioning Madoff's consistent returns. In 2004, after published articles appeared accusing the firm of front running, the SEC's Washington office cleared Madoff. In 2005, SEC inspectors examined Madoff's brokerage operation and found only technical violations – nothing fraudulent. In 2006 to 2007, the SEC completed an investigation into a Ponzi scheme allegation. It resulted in neither a finding of fraud, nor a referral for legal action. Markopolos claimed that to deliver 12 per cent returns to the investor, Madoff had to earn 16 per cent gross and distribute 4 per cent as a fee to the feeder fund managers, who were introducing new business. Erin Arvedlund[23] has written a fascinating book on the whole Madoff affair.

Madoff's fraudulent scheme began to implode in December 2008, as stock markets plunged. As the market downturn accelerated, investors tried to withdraw USD7 billion from the firm. To pay off these withdrawals, Madoff needed new money – and fast. In November 2008, the London office had sent USD164 million to Madoff's New York headquarters. On 1 December, Madoff received USD250 million from Carl J. Shapiro, a 95-year-old Boston philanthropist and one of Madoff's oldest friends and financial backers. He also managed to raise close to USD50 million elsewhere. But it wasn't enough. On 10 December 2008, Madoff and his two sons met. They worked in the business. Madoff told them that the firm would pay several million dollars in bonuses two months ahead of schedule out of USD200 million in assets that the firm still had. The sons, allegedly unaware of the firm's pending insolvency, questioned this and the whole story came out with confessions of guilt by Madoff following.

The amounts missing from client accounts, inclusive of fictitious gains, amounted to USD65 billion. The trustee appointed by the Court put actual losses at USD18 billion. In June 2009, following charges of securities fraud, investment advisor fraud, mail fraud, wire fraud, money laundering, false statements, perjury, making false filings with the SEC and theft, Bernard Madoff received the maximum sentence of 150 years imprisonment suggesting release in 2160, By then, he will be 220. With good behaviour, perhaps his sentence could be cut by 20 years.

Press Cutting 9.1, on the Madoff affair, makes interesting reading. Madoff is the tip of a Ponzi iceberg and many other similar fraudulent investment schemes have been revealed. Some have already gone through the courts and their protagonists are in jail. At the time of writing, some await trial and some have vanished accompanied by a fistful of dollars. We could go on. We could add names and comment. But we won't. The laws of libel restrict us. But do remember: when the promised return looks too good to be true, that's for one simple reason. It isn't true.

Press cutting 9.1   *Financial Times*, 5 April 2010 **FT**

The Madoff story reveals more faults

Jonathan Davis

What are the lessons of the Madoff scandal? The more that comes out about this incredible story, the more complex and intriguing it becomes. Harry Markopolos, the whistle-blower who tried unavailingly to get the Securities and Exchange Commission to investigate Bernie Madoff over more than 15 years, sub-titles his book about the affair 'a true financial thriller'. And so it is, with the twist that the book is a story not of triumph, but of heroic failure to persuade anyone to take seriously his well-founded allegations that Mr Madoff was a fraudster on a grand scale.

Taken together with the SEC inspector general's damning report into the SEC's failings published last year, it provides more disturbing evidence that the real world can often be crazier than the way it is portrayed in drama or fiction.

Small wonder that the first people to queue up to watch *Enron*, the play, or *Wall Street*, the movie, are professionals, or that the books *Liar's Poker* and *Barbarians At The Gate* remain essential reading for anyone wanting to understand the extremes to which unfettered capitalism can be taken.

Some of the details in *No One Would Listen*, Mr Markopolos' highly readable book, are beyond invention. For example, having failed to get the SEC interested in his original allegations, he turns to the media for help and eventually prompts MARHedge, a specialist hedge fund publication, to run a story raising questions about Mr Madoff's performance.

A similar story appears shortly afterwards in Barron's. He and the informal team of former colleagues who pursue their futile crusade against Mr Madoff wait triumphantly for the SEC to take action, convinced that it cannot ignore such public exposure.

But what happens? Nothing. According to Mr Markopolos, the SEC does not even subscribe to specialist industry publications. Staff members have to pay for their own media subscriptions, even for the *Wall Street Journal*. A specialist publication such as MARHedge costing more than $1,000 (£657, €741) is simply not on anyone's reading list.

Why was the SEC so reluctant to investigate the allegations that the split strike options strategy Mr Madoff claimed to be running was too implausible to be genuine? Too many lawyers is the first item on Mr Markopolos' lengthy charge list.

All the key people in charge of the potential investigation, he points out, were lawyers rather than financial experts. Ignorance, turf wars and lack of resources also played a part. When staff needed to research what derivatives were, in the absence of an investment library they had to rely on Google and Wikipedia.

The agency was also too quick, it appears, to dismiss Mr Markopolos as a bounty hunter with a grievance rather than as a serious investigator. Mr Madoff himself had few fears of the SEC, which he derided as useless. As the owner of one of the largest broker-dealers in New York, he was already such a big fish in the securities industry that only the bravest of regulators would be willing to take him on. (Since the crisis, as always happens, the incentives for regulators to seek big scalps have dramatically changed, as recent events have demonstrated.)

→

The MARHedge article on Mr Madoff appeared in 2001, by which time he was already running what was effectively the largest hedge fund in the world, with more assets than George Soros or any other much better known names. Yet because of the secrecy requirements that Madoff imposed on anyone who put money into his bogus strategy, and his refusal to charge fees, his name did not even feature in the MARHedge database at the time.

Mr Markopolos is right to say that the scale and durability of Mr Madoff's scam raises troubling issues for the financial services industry. By the time he turned himself in, Mr Madoff was taking money from more than 330 feeder funds of funds in over 40 countries; yet many of them continued to believe they had exclusive or preferential access to his impressive but non-existent winning strategy. Their claims to have carried out exhaustive due diligence were risible.

At the same time there were many on Wall Street who knew there was something not right about what Mr Madoff was doing, and steered well clear. Some invested anyway, believing that whether it was front-running or some other improper activity, they would rather not know as long as the returns kept racking up. The irony is that Mr Markopolos himself only first took an interest in Madoff because his employer kept badgering him to try to replicate what Mr Madoff was doing. Yet nobody else felt it worth their while to expose him.

The Madoff story is ultimately a story about breach of trust. Investors were naïve to trust Mr Madoff, naïve to trust the intermediaries who channelled money to him in such prodigious amounts, and naïve to believe that regulators could or would stop such an accomplished liar and conman.

In Mr Markopolos' view, although the majority of individuals in the financial services industry are honest, incentives to cut corners and breach both client trust and regulations are hard-wired into the system they work in.

■ What makes Ponzi schemes crash?

Ponzi schemes usually crash. The sponsor may, of course, die before the ultimate implosion. When and why do they implode? Possibly the following list answers these questions.

- the promoter vanishes, taking the remaining investment with them;
- investigations by regulatory authorities find the scheme to be fraudulent;
- the scheme may collapse under its own weight as new investment slows and there are problems paying out promised returns. Such a crisis triggers panic, as more people start asking for their money;
- whistleblowers emerge. They may be disgruntled insider employees or previously-compliant professionals, like auditors or lawyers;
- the scheme is exposed because the promoter fails to validate the claims when asked to do so by legal authorities;
- the scheme becomes so large (e.g. Madoff) that, in a market downturn, the reported returns appear to be too large given the size of the market segment. This causes alert financial analysts, regulators and journalists to question the whole scheme. Further official investigation and publicity can throw the whole scheme into meltdown, cause the promoter to file or bring out whistleblowers;
- market forces, such as a sharp decline in markets or in the economy, cause many investors to withdraw their funds (not due to loss of confidence in the investment, but simply due to market fundamentals). Incoming funds are insufficient to meet the need for cash to pay out existing investors.

Chapter **10**

Finance theories

■ Introduction

According to the foundations of financial economics, the objective of corporate finance is to maximise shareholder wealth. Generally speaking, this translates into making financing and investment decisions that add as much value as possible to the firm. And this, in its turn, translates into corporate executives managing the assets under their control efficiently and effectively. Since all actions in the company affect the value of the firm, understanding how value is created, preserved and destroyed is vital to all executives, not just financial managers.

Individuals attempt to maximise well-being. A person's well-being is, in part, a function of consumption of goods and services. Thus, people generally prefer more wealth to less since wealth represents the ability to consume. People may acquire wealth by deferring consumption now and investing the cash so released. If one is relatively risk averse one may become a bondholder, lending money to a company in return for an agreed interest rate and repayment of the loan at some specified future date. If one is willing to bear more risk, one might become a shareholder, providing equity capital in return for partial ownership of the firm. As partial owners, shareholders receive a share of the firm's profits and losses. Shareholders only have a residual interest in a company's earnings. Bondholders and lenders must be paid their interest before shareholders have a claim on any of the company's earnings. And, if the directors see fit, some of these earnings may be declared as dividend. If the firm fails to meet its interest and principal payments to lenders and bondholders on time, it is said to be in default and the bondholders may sue the firm to recover such money as is due. The shareholders are the legal owners of the firm and management has an obligation of trust to act in shareholders' best interests.

The importance of this discussion is to make clear that, in financial economics, the primary objective of the financial function in a company is to maximise the shareholders' well-being. As shareholders have invested their money with this expectation it translates into the goal of maximising shareholder wealth and this is, by and large, reflected in share price plus future dividends, in terms of today's money (or present value). Although modern companies do not have wills of their own, the principle of shareholder wealth maximisation provides a logical guide to decision making.

■ Earnings versus cash flow

The emphasis on money so far has not been misplaced. In most economies of the world, all other things being equal, the more resources one has, the more one may consume. Companies benefit their shareholders by providing them with cash, either by paying dividends now or by reinvesting cash to pay future dividends. And the value in the stock market should reflect such potential dividend streams. This simple statement has a profound implication. Accounting profits not reflected by cash flows, or future cash flows, should have no value to investors. If cash flow and accounting profits are not in line, it is theoretically the case that it is cash flow that matters. It is not for nothing that the expression 'cash is king' has evolved and continues to be frequently-quoted in financial circles. The implication of this is that, for valuation purposes, debates as to which accounting method to use should be irrelevant – except in so far as they impact tax payments. It is cash flow that matters.

However, even casual observers of the financial pages will have noticed how investors have been hoodwinked by bogus accounting in such high-profile cases as Enron, WorldCom and Tyco International, to name but three. The Enron case is succinctly described in Ferguson[1] and written up in detail in McLean and Elkind[2] and in Swartz and Watkins[3]. All of the above companies managed to bolster their share prices for a number of years helped by dubious accounting (to say the least) before their corporate judgement day. If one really wants to probe further into how the real world seems to become befuddled by accounting results rather than cash flow one can spend an interesting time reading of the financial shenanigans described by Schilit and Perler[4]. The fact is that despite the best efforts of the accounting profession to evolve and police reporting standards, the perpetrators of accounting sleight of hand and, indeed, outright fraud seem to have managed to deceive financial markets with remarkable consistency before their comeuppance. Because of the plethora of cases in which dubious accounting has won out over cash flow (at least in the short term), we suspect that the next generation of Enrons, WorldComs and Tycos are waiting in the wings.

■ Market efficiency

Various theorems in financial economics have proved valuable in developing the study and practice of corporate finance – arbitrage, market efficiency and the capital asset pricing model amongst them. We now briefly examine these.

Arbitrage has been defined as the purchase of securities or commodities in one market for instantaneous resale in another to profit from a price discrepancy. Under this definition, arbitrage is close to riskless. More recently, the term arbitrage has been used in relation to a broader range of financial activities. Risk arbitrage involves buying one asset and selling an almost-similar asset and this ensures that, in equilibrium, risk-adjusted returns on similar assets are equal. For example, in a takeover bid with payment in shares, risk arbitrage may involve buying or selling the shares in the company in receipt of the bid and dealing in the reverse direction in respect of the shares of the bidder. Or it may involve buying shares in a company being bid for in the expectation of an increased offer.

Risk arbitrage may also involve identifying similar companies, assessing whether one is overvalued relative to the other and selling the overvalued stock and buying the under-valued one. This is in fact, one of the techniques used by hedge funds. The fund may buy HSBC shares and sell Standard Chartered Bank shares. Both are banks which have a large part of their operations in the Far East. But the truth is that they are different – one is hardly a perfect substitute for the other. In reality, unless one is buying and selling assets which are perfect substitutes for each other, there is likely to be an element of risk involved. Hence the term risk arbitrage. According to this definition, risk arbitrage is certainly not risk-free. Through true arbitrage, markets arrive at fair prices. And fair and unbiased prices are what market efficiency is all about. We now define this term more carefully.

Market efficiency suggests that if a market is composed of numerous well-informed players, with easy and cheap access to information, their trading activities cause prices to adjust to reflect all relevant and available information. Hence price changes at any moment must be due solely to the arrival of new information. Because new information useful for profitable trading activities arrives randomly, so the arguments goes, price changes must follow a random walk, often called a drunkard's walk for obvious reasons. (In truth asset prices are assumed to follow a submartingale, which is a random walk with a drift. The drift equals the expected return of the asset.) In other words, in an efficient market, price changes from one period to the next are independent of past price changes and are no more predictable than is the content of the next piece of new information.

The basic idea of market efficiency can be exemplified thus. When Shell announces that it has just discovered a large, new oil field in the North Sea, investors who had reckoned that Shell shares were worth GBP18 will go back to their computer models and, maybe, decide that they are now worth GBP20. Should we buy the stock and attempt to profit from this recently-announced knowledge? The chances are that by the time we place an order with our broker, the price would have risen to GBP20, already reflecting this new information.

Investors adjust security prices rapidly to reflect new information. While the price adjustments made are not always perfect, they are unbiased – sometimes there is an overadjustment; sometimes there is an underadjustment. But one does not know which it will be. Adjustment of security prices takes place rapidly because the market is dominated by profit-maximising investors. The combined effect of new information being obtained by market participants in a random, independent fashion plus the presence of numerous investors who adjust stock prices rapidly to reflect this new information means, according to efficient market theorists, that price changes are likely to be independent and random. For investors who use charts of past movements to predict future prices (often called chartists), price changes are not independent – they are to some extent a function of past price movements. It is evident why market efficiency proponents utterly reject the claims of chartists.

Also, in our brief overview of market efficiency, it should be mentioned that, because security prices adjust to all new information and, therefore, supposedly reflect all public information at any point in time, the security prices that prevail at any point in time should be an unbiased reflection of all currently available information.

■ The efficient markets hypothesis

Based on this brief description, an efficient market is evidently one in which security prices adjust rapidly to the infusion of new information, and current stock prices fully reflect all available information, including the risk involved. Therefore, the returns implicit in a security's price reflect merely the risk involved, so the expected return on a security should be consistent with its risk – nothing more. There are three gradations of efficient market: the weak form, the semi-strong form and the strong form.

The weak form of the efficient market hypothesis assumes that current stock prices fully reflect all stock market data, including the historical sequence of prices, price changes and any volume information. Because current prices already reflect all past price changes and any other stock market information, this implies that there should be no relationship between past price changes and future price changes. That is, price changes are independent. In other words, past market data cannot be of any use in predicting future prices.

The semi-strong efficient markets hypothesis asserts that security prices adjust rapidly to the release of all new public information. In short, stock prices fully reflect all publicly available data. Obviously the semi-strong hypothesis encompasses the weak form hypothesis because all public information includes all market information such as past stock prices, trends and so on, plus all non-market information such as earnings, stock splits, economic news and political news. A direct implication of this form of the hypothesis is that investors acting on important new information after it is public cannot consistently derive above-average profits from their transactions, allowing for the cost of trading, because security prices already reflect the input of new public information.

The strong form of the efficient markets hypothesis contends that stock prices fully reflect all information, whether public or otherwise. Hence, it implies that no group of investors has a monopolistic access to information relevant to the formation of prices. Therefore, no group of investors should be able to derive above-average profits consistently. The strong form hypothesis encompasses both the weak and the semi-strong forms. And it also includes effects of insider information. The strong form hypothesis requires not only efficient markets, where prices adjust rapidly to the release of new public information, but also perfect markets in which all information is available to everyone at the same time. Brief reflection on this point will suggest that this is hardly possible. Company directors and top executives in the firm are likely to be aware of information before it is released into the public domain. Continuing scandals of insider trading are evidence that information is not automatically and evenly distributed between all players.

The notion that shares and other assets are fairly priced given their expected risks and returns is appealing. In a world where thousands of investors, including professional fund managers and risk arbitrageurs, are continuously searching for marginally better returns, it would be difficult to see how overvalued or undervalued securities could exist for more than a few seconds. Furthermore, it should be the case that new information would be required to move markets – especially if movements are really dramatic. Evidence of big market movements without accompanying new information, together with other anomalies that are referred to later in this chapter, has cast doubts upon market efficiency. The date 19 October 1987 has acquired the moniker 'Black Monday' because leading stocks fell 23 per cent in one day. When one asked oneself what new information caused such a setback, it was not clear that there were any substantive new things happening since Friday's close. No new information but a massive market movement. This is clearly not what efficient market theory suggests. And this is not the only occasion that dramatic falls have taken place without apparent new information. Such happenings are nails in the coffin of the efficient markets hypothesis. Events subsequent to 1987 have added so many more nails to make us think that the theory is less than alive and kicking. Paraphrasing the television show *Monty Python's Flying Circus*, it's pretty much a dead parrot.

■ The capital asset pricing model

Investors require higher returns on riskier investment. In financial markets, return can come in the form of a cash payment, such as dividends or interest, or via appreciation in the value of the investment, a higher share price or bond price. The difficulty lies in quantifying the riskiness of an investment and establishing the trade-off between risk and expected return. More effort has probably been devoted by financial economists to this issue than to any other. The outcome is a relationship between diversification, risk, and required return. This is formalised in the capital asset pricing model (CAPM). Risk itself is assumed to depend on the variability of returns – the more highly variable the return, the riskier the asset.

The CAPM is based on the idea that the variability of an asset's returns are attributed to two sources; first there are market-wide influences, like the level of interest rates or growth in GNP that affect all assets and, second, there are other risks specific to a given firm, for example, a strike at a factory or a new patent. The first type of risk is termed systematic or market risk. The latter is called unsystematic or diversifiable risk. According to financial theory, unsystematic risk is largely irrelevant to an investor holding a well-diversified portfolio, because the impact of such disturbances can be expected to cancel out, on average, in the investor's portfolio. However, no matter how well diversified the portfolio, systematic risk cannot be eliminated.

The distinction is paramount to the pricing of risk in the CAPM. Only the systematic risk will be rewarded with a risk premium. In financial theory investors will not be rewarded for unsystematic risk, because they can avoid it, at no cost, by diversifying their portfolio. Thus, the CAPM assumes that people will follow the rule 'Don't put all your eggs in one basket' as investors will be compensated only for bearing market risk. This illustrates an important rule in finance, namely that one does not get paid for doing something that is unnecessary. It is the economist's idea that there is no such thing as a free lunch.

The CAPM suggests that investors can diversify away unsystematic risk. It also suggests that equity returns provide compensation for systematic risk. And CAPM suggests the required return (return here means dividends plus capital gains versus the amount invested) on any equity share bears a definite relationship (via its systematic risk, called beta) to the return on the whole equity market. A firm's beta factor is based upon the firm's past share price returns (dividends and capital gains versus investment value) compared to the equity market return over the same past period (again dividends plus capital gains for the whole market versus the market's value). A beta of 1.0 implies that the firm's return is in line with the market. A beta of more than 1.0 implies that the firm's return beats the market and beta of less than 1.0 implies that the firm's return falls short of the market. According to CAPM, the reason that returns are in excess of or below the market is that the firm's risk is above or beneath that of the market respectively.

To estimate the required return for an investment that a firm may undertake, one must add a risk premium to the risk-free return. In CAPM theory, this risk premium is the whole market's risk premium multiplied by the investment's beta. The CAPM formula for the company's cost of equity capital, and hence its required equity return, is given by: $R_f + \beta(R_m - R_f)$. In words, the cost of equity capital is the risk-free rate of interest plus the market's equity risk premium ($R_m - R_f$) multiplied by the investment's beta.

The market risk premium term ($R_m - R_f$) may be in real terms (with inflation cut out) or in money terms (that is, including inflation). The expression money terms is sometimes referred to as nominal terms. If we use a money terms return on capital, we use a money terms risk-free rate, based on the current yield on a suitable government security. This figure should, of course, include inflation. To obtain a real risk-free rate, we would take the yield on a suitable index-linked government security.

But a number of questions arise in using the CAPM formula, of which the following are a few:

■ What time period should we use:
  – for the risk-free rate of return (R_f)? Very short term, such as 90-day Treasury Bills? Or should we match the term with the typical life of a project, say 10 to 15 years, that we are reviewing? It makes a big difference. We suggest the latter.
  – for betas? These are usually based on the past 60 months of data. But why five years rather than five months or any other period? After all, the firm may have changed its risk profile over five years due to increased borrowing or taking over other companies. On this argument, perhaps five months could be said to provide a better period because it is more contemporary.
  – for the equity market risk premium? Long-term data are generally used for this estimate because they even out short-term blips. Data are derived from returns from investing in the equity market in excess of returns from risk-free investment in government securities. But, should short term investors and speculators demand a higher rate than long-term investors? After all, they are exposed to the blips.
■ Should we use a leveraged equity beta (which the published figures usually are), relating to the cost of equity capital in a leveraged (that is, with borrowings) company? Or should we use an ungeared asset beta, which is what the beta would be if the company had no borrowings? We favour a beta based upon the amount of debt that the investment can bear. But this is clearly somewhat subjective. Different individuals use slightly different approaches but usually end up with similar valuations.

- How stable are company betas over time? Clearly if a utility business were to make a significant takeover of a toy business, one would expect its beta (reflecting its business risk) to rise. After all, as a utility one would expect low risk. Following the takeover of a rapid-change type business one would expect higher risk. There is a danger that betas based on longer data periods could become out of date due to the changing business risk of the firm.

- Is it correct simply to use the domestic stock market in order to calculate the required market risk premium and the beta? Or should we aim to cover global stock markets? Or, indeed, a much wider set of assets than just listed equity shares? Most analysts use domestic equities.

In theory, given the CAPM formula, where the required return is equal to $R_f + \beta(R_m - R_f)$, investments with higher betas should yield higher returns compared with lower beta investments.

But the test of a theory is how well it stands up in the real world. And there has been a challenge to CAPM emanating from research work originally carried out in the USA by Fama and French[5] which has been well and accessibly summarised by Haugen[6]. So what are the findings of Fama and French? CAPM uses a single factor, beta, to estimate the return on a stock with the returns of the market as a whole. It was found to over-simplify the situation. Fama and French observed that two classes of stocks have tended to do better than the market as a whole. These are small companies' stocks and those with a high book value to market value ratio – often termed value stocks. They are different from growth stocks which have a low book value to market value ratio. Fama and French added these two factors to CAPM better to reflect potential returns. With this three factor model Fama and French found that greater precision in forecasting returns was achieved.

The CAPM is widely used in the world of business as part of the apparatus to value new capital investment projects and to value stock market equities. Its key role is in calculating a firm's cost of equity capital and thence its weighted average cost of capital. This is usually the key input (maybe adjusted to allow for perceived risk) in specifying a discount rate in the discounted cash flow model used for valuing assets. The other key ingredient in the valuing process, whether in relation to investment projects or share valuation, is forecasts of future cash flows and their expected timing. This horizon of time might stretch out to 10, or 15 years, for purposes of calculating value. Forecasts, as underpinnings of value, have long been advocated by such investment gurus as Ben Graham[7] and Warren Buffet (one of Ben Graham's pupils in the thirties).

■ Risk and uncertainty

The distinction between risk and uncertainty was clarified by Frank Knight[8]. For example, risk can be priced by markets because it depends upon a known distribution of events to which investors assign probabilities and thence estimate price. But, uncertainty cannot be priced because it relates to events and possibilities that cannot be predicted or measured or modelled. Roubini and Mihm[9] give an excellent example. 'To understand this distinction, imagine two men playing a game of Russian roulette. They take a standard revolver with room for six bullets, put a bullet in the chamber, and spin it. Whoever pulls the trigger first has one-in-six chance of blowing his brains out. That's risk. While the men playing this game may be suicidal idiots, they know the odds. Now imagine that the two men are handed a mystery gun prepared by someone else. The gun could have one bullet; it could have six; or it could have none. It may not even be a real gun; it could fire blanks instead of bullets. The players don't know. That's uncertainty: they have no idea how to assess the risk. The odds of dying are impossible to quantify.'

The distinction is important in the context of the 2007/8 financial crisis. Before the crises, risks of CDSs and CDOs could be related to the ratings given by the rating agencies. With the fall of the housing market and the implosion of financial markets, adverse outturns seemed to be lurking around every corner. Triple A was turning into junk. Financial markets were becoming illiquid. There was a credit crunch because banks did not trust the credit-worthiness of each other. This looks like Roubini and Mihm's mystery gun. This looks like uncertainty. And in these circumstances, how does the stock market assess an appropriate discount rate, and how does it assess future cash flows? This is uncertainty and, therefore, unquantifiable. In these conditions, prices fall. Do markets add in a massive guesstimate to their discount rate as a premium for uncertainty? Do markets slash forecasts of future outturns? Maybe a bit of both. Hardly surprising, security prices bomb.

■ Risk management models and the normal distribution

In Chapter 7, we presented a brief section on Value at Risk and Risk Management. We now develop further some of that earlier material. One of the great questions in the theory and practice of financial economics is whether the widespread use of the normal distribution is justified. Its elegance has been accepted and applied in terms of securities movements and in terms of options pricing, to name but two important cases.

In the normal distribution, often called the bell curve, the first and second standard deviations together cover 95.4 per cent of outturns. The two ends of a normal distribution curve are called the tails – see Figure 10.1. The two tails cover the remaining 4.6 per cent. They may include really disastrous outcomes with very low probabilities. Terrorist attacks may only have a 2 per cent chance of occurrence, but the results may be awful in the extreme.

In truth, most of us tend to underestimate the likelihood of occurrence of events in the financial markets. Benoit Mandelbrot[10] showed that if the Dow Jones industrial average moved in accordance with a normal distribution, it would have moved by 4.5 per cent or more on only six days between 1996 and 2003. In reality, it moved by at least that amount 366 times during the period.

Clearly, the normal curve may not be entirely applicable to many financial situations. The probability of future financial events may be better captured by a distribution with fat tails. Figure 10.1 shows both the normal distribution and one with fat tails. In the former, the two tails cover 4.6 per cent of possible outturns. In the latter, they cover 10 per cent. With other fat tail shapes, it could be more.

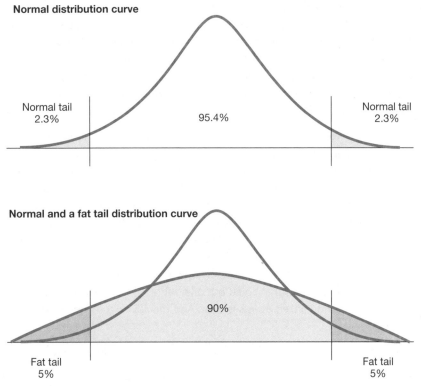

Normal distribution curve

Normal tail
2.3%

95.4%

Normal tail
2.3%

Normal and a fat tail distribution curve

90%

Fat tail
5%

Fat tail
5%

Figure 10.1 Normal distribution versus fat tails

In support of the fat tails description, Triana[11] says that 'events in the credit, equity, and interest markets implacably bear witness, but there is also plenty of historical precedent. During the European Exchange Rate Mechanism débâcle in 1992 (whereby Europe's system of officially managed currency rates collapsed), 50-standard deviation moves in interest rates were witnessed, while 1987's Black Monday was a 20-standard deviation (or 20-sigma) event. During the summer 1998 convolutions that eventually brought down Long Term Capital Management, 15-plus sigma deviations were occurring. Plenty of smaller (yet still sensationally non-normal) similar gyrations have been observed in finance. So-called "one in a million years" events have been experienced, several times, by people whose age is way below one million years. Which one is wrong, the real world or the model?'

And to reproduce the quotable quote by Lanchester[12], 'the last decades have seen numerous five-, six- and seven-sigma events. Those are supposed to happen, respectively, one day in every 13,932 years, one day in every 4,039,906 years, and one day in every 3,105,395,365 years. And yet no one concluded from this that the statistical models in use were wrong. The mathematical models simply didn't work in a crisis. They worked when they worked, which was most of the time; but then the whole point of them was to assess risks, and some risks by definition happen at the edge of known likelihoods.' Precisely.

At the time of the financial crisis, large banks and financial firms were using a computerised system of risk measurement called Value at Risk (VaR). Developed at the J. P. Morgan bank, it is designed to measure the aggregate risk of a portfolio over short time periods. For example, if a firm has USD20 million of weekly VaR in its USD1 billion bond portfolio, then this implies that there is a 96 per cent chance that its maximum loss in that portfolio over the next week will not exceed USD20 million. VaR is based upon a normal distribution of outcomes. It is a useful tool but it may provide too much comfort since it does not cover fat tail events. In fact, it is just these events that can bring down a financial firm in crisis times. And it is, in the main, to quantify the risk of big bad events that VaR is designed for.

Generally, in the world of earthquakes and hurricanes, the low probability events in the fat tails are independent of each other. In the financial world, by contrast, apparently independent events may be linked, multiplying their likelihood of occurrence. For example, assume that there is a 2 per cent chance of the housing market falling by over 20 per cent sometime during next year in the absence of problems in the bond market. However, housing prices could also fall if the market for bonds froze up for reasons unrelated to the housing market. If this problem spread to the mortgage-backed bond market and reduced the financing available for houses, then the chances of housing prices falling by over 20 per cent would surely be far higher than 2 per cent. The need to identify low probability events that could put one out of business over the next five years, especially those involving linked events is clear. And the advice to hedge or insure against them then follows.

Many risk management models are based upon the following dubious assumptions:

■ that financial returns and risks follow Gaussian (normal) distributions, ignoring the fat tails which on some occasions can be so destructive;

■ that a single statistic, the standard deviation (which tells us so much about normal distributions), captures potential outturns in capital markets;

■ that correlations are constant, although they tend to change in crises and therefore make perfect diversification and hedging nigh on impossible;

■ that liquid funds will always be available, even though in extreme conditions they may not be.

It is possible to argue that, at the time of the financial crisis, all of the above bullet point problems were impacting markets for CDSs and CDOs – and all at the same instant.

Risk management models often focus too much on routine market conditions and tend to ignore the abnormal conditions typical of a crisis. As a result they may give managers a false sense of security. As an example using the latter two bullet points, CDOs and CDSs became hard to value because their prices were so sensitive to changing correlations and to illiquidity in their volatile markets. Clearly, reliance upon risk management models based on the normal distribution is utterly unjustified.

■ Options

We now move on to look at option contracts and their valuation. Their theoretical pricing is also based upon the normal distribution. Options are contractual arrangements giving the owner the right to buy or sell an asset at a fixed price anytime on or before a given date. Share options are options to buy and sell shares. Share options are traded on stock exchanges. In this section, we identify and discuss factors that determine option values.

As we have explained, an option is a contract giving its owner the right to buy or sell an asset at a fixed price on or before a given date. For example, an option on a building might give the buyer of the option the right to buy the building for GBP1m on or at any time before the Saturday prior to the third Wednesday in January 2013. Options are a singular type of financial contract because they give the buyer the right, but not the obligation, to do something. The buyer uses the option only if it is a sensible thing to do so. Otherwise, the option can be simply discarded. To obtain this advantageous position, the buyer of an option must pay an up-front price called the option premium.

There is a vocabulary associated with options. Some of the most important definitions are as follows:

- **Exercising the option**. The act of buying or selling the underlying asset via the option contract is referred to as exercising the option.
- **Strike or exercise price**. The fixed price in the option contract at which the holder of the option can buy or sell the underlying asset is called the strike price or exercise price.
- **Expiration date**. The maturity date of the option is termed the expiration date. After this date, the option is dead.
- **American and European options**. An American option may be exercised at any time up to the expiration date. A European option differs from an American option in that it can only be exercised on the expiration date. Both types of options are traded in America and Europe. Sorry, it's confusing.

The most frequently encountered option is a call option. It gives the owner the right to buy an asset at a fixed price during a particular time period. The most common options traded on exchanges are options on shares and bonds. Usually the assets involved are ordinary shares (also known as common stock).

Assume that call options on XYZ plc shares can be purchased on the London Stock Exchange. XYZ itself does not issue call options on its ordinary shares. In fact, banks and wealthy individual investors are the original creators, sellers and buyers of call options on XYZ ordinary shares. A call option on XYZ enables an investor to buy, say 1,000, shares of XYZ on or before, say, 15 July 2013, at an exercise price of GBP12. This is a valuable option if there is some probability that the price of XYZ ordinary shares will exceed GBP12 on or before 15 July 2013.

Virtually all option contracts on shares specify that the exercise price and the number of shares are adjusted for stock splits – see below – and stock dividends. Suppose that XYZ shares were selling for GBP18 on the day the option was purchased. Suppose that the next day it split 6 for 1. Each share would drop in price to GBP3, and the probability that the share would rise over GBP12 per share in the near future becomes very remote. To protect the option holder from such an occurrence, call options are typically adjusted for stock splits and stock dividends. In the case of a 6-for-1 split, the exercise price would become GBP2 (GBP12 divided by 6). Furthermore, the option contract would now cover 6,000 shares, rather than the original 1,000 shares. Note that no adjustment is made for the payment by XYZ of cash dividends to shareholders. This failure to adjust clearly hurts holders of call options, though, of course, they should know the terms of option contracts and the proximity of dividends before buying.

Three US economists were developers of the famous Black and Scholes formula for valuing European call options. Besides Fischer Black and Myron Scholes, Robert C Merton is credited with the specification of the theory and formulation for pricing options. Fischer Black's death in 1995 meant that when the Nobel Prize in Economics was awarded in 1997, it was given to Myron Scholes and Robert C Merton for their work in option pricing. The Nobel Prize has rules which prevent awards to deceased individuals. Many of our readers need not bother about the formulation that follows but just jump to the next paragraph having accepted that there is an option pricing formula. For more adventurous readers, the Black and Scholes[13] formula can be quoted as:

$$C = SN(d_1) - X \, e^{-rt}N(d_2)$$

where

$$d_1 = \frac{\ln(S/X) + (r + \frac{1}{2}\sigma^2)t}{\sqrt{\sigma^2 t}}$$

$$d_2 = d_1 - \sqrt{\sigma^2 t}$$

The derivation of the formula for the call option premium (that is, the amount of the non-returnable, up-front payment one has to make to deal a call), C, is one of the most complex in finance. However, it involves only five inputs:

S = current share price;

X = exercise price of the option (some instructors and some textbooks use the notation E, not X);

r = continuous risk-free rate of return (annualised);

σ^2 = variance (per year) of the continuous return on the stock;

t = time (in years) to expiration date;

In addition, there is the statistical concept:

$N(d)$ = probability that a standardised, normally distributed, random variable will be less than or equal to d.

Then there is the mathematical constant e (also known as Euler's constant) and it is equal to 2.71828. It's a bit like π, also a mathematical constant, but e is much less well-known.

In the real world, an option trader would know S and X exactly. Traders generally view government bills as riskless, so a current online quote would be obtainable for the interest rate. The trader would also know (or could count) the number of days to expiration exactly. Thus, the fraction of a year to expiration, t, could be calculated quickly. The problem comes in determining the variance of the share's return. The formula calls for the variance in operation between the date of doing the valuation and the expiration date.

Unfortunately, this represents the future. And the future value for variance is not available. Instead, traders frequently estimate variance from past data. In addition, some traders may use intuition to adjust their estimate. For example, if anticipation of an upcoming event is currently increasing the volatility of the share, the trader might adjust their estimate of variance upward to reflect this. This problem was really severe immediately after the stock market crash of 19 October 1987. The stock market was viewed as risky in the immediate aftermath. Consequently, estimates using pre-crash data were reckoned to be too low.

The formula allows one to calculate the value of an option given a few inputs. The attraction of the formula is that four of the inputs are observable – the current price of the stock, S, the exercise price, X, the interest rate, r, and the time the option has to run to expiration, t. Only one of the inputs must be estimated: the variance of return, σ^2 and we discussed this briefly in the previous paragraph.

Think of option valuation another way. Note what inputs are not needed. First, the investor's risk aversion does not affect value. The formula can be used by anyone, regardless of willingness to bear risk. Second, it does not depend on the expected return on the share, an area in which different investors may disagree.

The assumptions of the Black and Scholes model are worth mentioning as they are very important – especially the last listed bullet point below.

- there are no penalties for or restrictions on short selling;
- transaction costs and taxes are zero;
- the option is European;
- the share pays no dividends – but, if needed, an appropriate adjustment to allow for dividends is readily available;
- there are no jumps in share price. Prices move continuously;
- the market operates continuously;
- the short-term interest rate is known and constant;.
- the share price is log-normally distributed.

The Black and Scholes formula is widely reckoned to be among the most important contributions in finance, although it has its critics – some of them vehement adversaries. Why? Well, note the last of the above bullet points. Note the presence of the normal distribution. We have already explained that the normal distribution falls perilously short of the reality of how financial markets behave. The formula works brilliantly in a theoretical world. It works well in financial markets most of the time but in stressed markets its performance becomes equally stressed. In truth, in times of crisis it's about as useful as a chocolate kettle. Two notable and scathing critics of the formulation are Taleb[14] and Triana[15]. Both are well worth reading. Both make the point that the normal distribution fails abysmally to describe market movements in crisis or panic times.

So much for our brief overview of options. We now turn to some of the anomalies of financial theory – more places where theory and the actuality of the real world diverge.

■ Behavioural finance

We now turn to the emerging topic of behaviourism in the field of financial economics. Behavioural aspects of finance and economics use social, cognitive and emotional factors to understand economic decisions of investors and borrowers and their impacts on prices, returns and resource allocation. Behavioural models integrate insights from psychology into financial theory.

Behavioural finance focuses upon a series of market inefficiencies and their effects on market price overreactions and underreactions with possible impacts for bubbles and crashes. These effects may be attributed to limited attention, overconfidence, over-optimism and herding (following the market). Critics of behavioural finance often argue that it has evolved from and reflects a collection of anomalies which may eventually be priced away.

For example, value stocks (those with lower P/E ratios or higher dividend yields or higher book to market ratios – defined in the Glossary) have consistently outperformed growth stocks (higher P/E ratios, lower dividend yield or lower book to market ratios). If the market were to price stocks efficiency, this tendency would not exist. In the real world, value stocks and growth stocks would achieve similar returns when measured after the event. Supporters of efficient markets attribute the superior return to value stocks as a reflection of greater risk. This line of thinking is not reinforced by Haugen and Baker[16].

There are other widely observed oddities too. Stock returns appear to be consistently – but not immutably – higher in January than in other months. And they seem to be lower on Mondays compared to other days of the week. Other anomalies concern equity investor behaviour in reaction to new information from a company in terms of its results. The tendency is for the share price to underreact to unexpected new information – whether good or bad. In other words, investors wait for subsequent confirmatory evidence before fully incorporating the information into the share price. Likewise, there is the new issue anomaly by which investors bid up the prices of new shares in an initial public offering only to find that they tend, on average – but not always – to fall back in much later trading.

Psychologists have observed that, when making financial decisions, investors are loath to take losses. Investors seem not to focus solely upon the current value of their holdings, but glance back to check whether their investments are showing a profit or a loss. Logically, a rational investor would look at today's share price and future prospects when considering the decision to sell or buy. Past prices should be irrelevant. The investor's cognitive error is the basis for prospect theory, which states first that the value investors place on a particular outcome is determined by the gains or losses that they have already incurred since the asset was acquired and, secondly, that investors are averse to taking even small losses.

Psychologists have found that, in assessing future outcomes, investors tend to look back at past occurrences and they tend to place excess weight on a small number of apparently representative happenings. Another investor bias is overconfidence. Most believe that they are better-than-average car drivers. Most investors also think that they are better-than-average in the stock market. Speculators who trade with each other cannot all make money from a deal. But investors seem to be prepared to continue trading because they are confident of their skills. Overconfidence shows up in the certainty that people express in making judgements. Perhaps this leads investors to feel so confident of their views and skills as to trade excessively.

To précis findings of psychologists in respect of investor behaviour, a series of bullet point summaries follows.

- **Anchoring**. In making assessments, especially quantitative ones, investors' views are influenced by past events. Investors valuing shares are swayed by past prices. They anchor valuation on prices in the past. This could affect their underestimation of new information following an announcement. Anchoring is consistent with prospect theory – see above.

- **Conservatism**. Investors are resistant to changing their opinion, even when relevant new information becomes available. When profits are unexpectedly high they initially underreact. They tend to need further positive earnings surprises to revisit their views. The same kind of argument is said to apply on the downside.

- **Narrow framing**. Investors tend to have, and hold on to, a framework of evaluation. Such investors narrow frame rather than look at the broader picture. Thus Benartzi and Thaler[17] showed that framing errors cause investors to avoid equities in favour of risk-free government securities, missing out on potentially better returns on equities.

- **Overconfidence**. Overconfidence may be caused by self-attribution bias. Investors ascribe success to their own brilliance, but failures to bad luck. Overconfidence may be a cause of excessive trading because investors believe they can beat the market – see Barber and Odean[18]. It even seems that inexperienced investors are more confident that they can beat the market than experienced investors.

- **Confirmation bias and cognitive dissonance**. People search for information that agrees with their existing view. Information that conflicts is often ignored. This is linked to cognitive dissonance, where people experience conflict when presented with evidence that their beliefs may not be 100 per cent correct; thus they seek out confirmatory stories and disregard conflicting stories. In 2007 many continued to ignore arguments that property prices could fall big time.

- **Regret**. Psychologists believe that investors forgo benefits within reach in order to avoid the small chance of feeling they have failed. Thus, they are overly influenced by the fear of feeling regret.

- **Availability bias**. Investors, and people in general, may focus on a particular fact or event because it is visible, or fresh in the mind, at the expense of perceiving the bigger picture. Thus, following a big train crash, people tend to avoid trains and use their cars more. The bigger statistical picture is that train travel is safer than road transport. Likewise, in financial markets, investors tend to place excess weight on recent big news stories.

- **Representativeness**. Representativeness is the making of judgements based on apparent stereotypes. It is the tendency to perceive identical situations where none exist. With the sharp declines in the stock market in 1987, 2001 and 2008, articles appeared asking whether this was 1929 all over again, backed up by charts showing the index movement then and now. Although the similarities may be there, this does not mean that the Great Depression is about to be re-enacted. But investors tend to give too much weight to such observations and not enough to other very different features.

■ **Positive feedback and extrapolative expectations**. Market bubbles may, partially, be explained by positive-feedback traders who buy shares after prices have risen and sell after prices fall. They have extrapolative expectations about prices. This tendency seems to have occurred in house prices in the run-up to the financial crisis.

■ **Ambiguity aversion**. Investors are excessively fearful when they feel that they do not have much information. But when they think that they have good information they tend to gamble.

■ **Miscalculation of probabilities**. Psychologists show that people consistently fail to evaluate the probability of both likely outcomes and quite unlikely ones.

Work in this interesting area has been pioneered by Kahneman and Tversky[19] and Thaler[20], amongst others. It is well-summarised in books by Shefrin[21], Shleifer[22] and Montier[23].

Whilst focusing upon the psychology of investment, it is worth paying attention to the behaviour of crowds. Why? Well, in crowds, people behave differently. They do things that they would not do on their own or with a small group of friends. Crowds are all about emotions not about logic. Go to an association football match – watch the crowd. Result? Emotion 15, Logic nil.

Economic decision-making is assumed to be based upon individuals acting rationally. So, total market movements would, according to this idea, be based upon the sum of the buying and selling decisions of rational individuals. However, if we watch some markets, they seem to behave, on occasion, like a crowd. When this is the case, rationality may not be so obvious. It would probably be wrong to say that markets always exhibit crowd behaviour. Sometimes they are quiet. Sometimes they are frantic. In this latter case, we would be more likely to see evidence of the crowd instinct.

In terms of making money, dealers are extraordinarily good at spotting the best game in town. And they join in. They buy or sell in common with the crowd and this forces prices up or down depending upon how the herd is thundering. Crowd behaviour may magnify movements in markets. This may create momentum upwards or downwards as the case may be.

Of course, the dealers in banks may be following the crowd but they may also be aiming to improve their own bonuses. From their personal points of view, this may be rational. It may also be precisely what John Kay describes in Press Cutting 6.1 as tail-gating with all of its inherent risks. And these risks may be such that when the risk turns to a crash, the bank may be wiped out. This looks like another example of self-interest not working to anyone's advantage except the dealer who gains because the bank's bonus system gives reward for short-term profit but fails to claw back for losses.

It is worth noting that the findings of the proponents of behavioural finance would seem to advance ideas which hardly conform to rational economic man. In economic theory, the assumption is that individuals act rationally in specifying their objective and then take decisions that are consistent with those objectives – this is what economic man is all about.

Conclusion

Finance theory needs to be taught with the caveat, handle with care. Despite abundant empirical evidence of the frailties of deductive finance theory, too many academics have continued to teach students, in an uncritical way, that markets value cash flows above earnings, that stock markets in Western countries are semi-strong efficient markets, that the capital asset pricing model works fine, that valuation models based on normal distributions reflect the way markets work and that other prescriptions based on rational economic man hold. Normative theory (how things should be) certainly has its place high in the study of any subject, but so does the positive viewpoint (the way things are in reality). Finance is often taught without sufficient reference to the realities of markets, without reference to a plethora of empirical deviations from deductive theory. Why? Perhaps some are simply unaware of the empirical findings. Perhaps business schools are excessively orientated towards producing students who sing from the hymn book of banks and industry. And perhaps, as Posner[24] observes, 'the entwinement of finance professors with the financial industry has a dark side. If they criticize the industry and suggest tighter regulation, they may become black sheep and lose lucrative consultantships. This conflict of interest may have caused some economists to pull their punches.' Posner continues by observing that 'one does not expect economists employed by real estate companies or by banks to be talking about housing and credit bubbles.' On this darker side, it is possible that conventional teaching, for example of efficient market theory, meets the requirements of the right-wing ideology that, since the market arrives at unbiased prices, the need for a central banker to deflate bubbles is not an issue because price levels are unbiased responses to corporate, economic and political news. And, since market prices in an efficient market are unbiased, the need for regulation is hardly likely to add any improvement. It is certainly a point worthy of discussion. On this issue and one or two others, we found Press Cutting 10.1 fascinating.

Press cutting 10.1	Financial Times, 15 March 2010 **FT**

Lessons from the collapse of Bear Stearns

John Cassidy

Two years ago on Sunday, Treasury Secretary Hank Paulson called up Alan Schwartz, the chief executive of Bear Stearns, and told him the jig was up. 'Alan, you're in the government's hands now,' he said. 'Bankruptcy is the only other option.' Thus began the epic stage of the credit crunch and 24 months on, many costly lessons have been learned.

→

Leverage kills. In March 2008, Bear had tangible equity capital of about $11bn supporting total assets of $395bn – a leverage ratio of 36. For several years, this reckless financing enabled the company to achieve a profit margin of about a third and a return on equity of 20 per cent; when the market turned, it left Bear bereft of capital and willing creditors. During the ensuing months, the same story was to be played out at scores of other banks and non-banks.

Last year, the group of 20 leading economies agreed to impose higher capital ratios. So far, no figures have been published. Officially, the gnomes of Basel – the Basel Committee on Banking Supervision – are at work. Unofficially, Tim Geithner, the US Treasury secretary, has a maximum leverage ratio in mind. What that figure turns out to be will indicate how serious the authorities are about preventing future blow-ups.

It if quacks, it is a duck. If it borrows short and lends (or invests) long, it is a bank. Officially, Bear Stearns and Lehman Brothers were investment companies; Washington Mutual was a savings & loan; AIG was an insurance company, GMAC and GE Capital were subsidiaries of industrial corporations; the Reserve Fund was a money market mutual fund. In reality, all of them were handing out money, or near money, and accumulating illiquid assets. Any such institution is vulnerable to a run by creditors and regulators should treat them alike – as banks. Failure to adhere to this principle will result in regulatory arbitrage and more blow-ups.

Markets are not always efficient. Does this lesson need restating? I fear it does. Over the years, free market ideology has displayed an uncanny ability to resurrect itself. And there will always be powerful interests eager to cloak their selfish ends in the invigorating language of Adam Smith and Friedrich Hayek.

Big banks are like nuclear power stations. They provide valuable services, such as channelling capital from savers to entrepreneurs. Occasionally, they blow up, causing damage to the rest of the economy and necessitating spending vast sums of taxpayers' money on clean-up operations.

In retrospect, the solutions to this problem are obvious: stricter supervision to reduce the probability of blow-ups and institution-specific 'pollution taxes' to cover their cost. President Barack Obama recently proposed such a tax, and Gordon Brown has taken it upon himself to transform this proposal into a global initiative. For once, a good idea appears to be making progress. Somewhere in the heavens, Arthur Cecil Pigou, the economist who invented the concept of negative externalities, must be smiling.

Statistical models are like bikinis: what they reveal is suggestive, but what they conceal is vital. So said Aaron Levenstein, a late (and politically incorrect) professor at New York's Baruch College. On Wall Street and in the City, the bikinis came in the form of 'Value-at-Risk' models that assumed investors (and mortgage holders) were like so many molecules bouncing around randomly in a heated jar. These mathematical contraptions had the charming feature that when they were not needed they worked perfectly, and when they were needed they did not work at all.

Bagehot and Keynes were both right. During a financial crisis, the role of the central bank is to lend money where nobody else will. During an economic slump, the government has to boost demand. In applying these truths, authorities from Washington to Frankfurt to Beijing prevented the Great Recession from turning into another Great Depression.

Rent-seeking is not wealth creation. Some of the money that financial companies make consists of economic rents diverted from other groups, such as investors in actively managed funds, workers in companies taken over by private equity groups, and taxpayers who eventually bear the costs of excessive risk-taking. The losses that UK banks suffered in 2008–2009 wiped out roughly half of the economic valued added – wages, salaries, and gross profits – that the banking sector generated between 2001 and 2007.

A century ago, progressive English thinkers such as J. A. Hobson and L. T. Hobhouse argued that much wealth is, in part, socially created, providing a justification for the state redistributing some of it to old age pensions and health programmes. As far as modern finance goes, the New Liberals had it doubly right. Not only are some of the 'profits' that bankers generate contingent on implicit state guarantees: much of the capital they put at risk belongs to others.

Given its lobbying power, the financial industry may yet head off some of the restrictions on its activities. But never again will bankers be able to argue that what is good for Citigroup is good for America, or what is good for Royal Bank of Scotland is good for the UK. Not with a straight face anyway.

Chapter 11

Other academic theories

◼ Introduction

In this chapter, we now introduce one or two theories from various disciplines including social anthropology and economics. An excellent overview of the range of economic theories and how they influenced the financial crisis and how the crisis has affected the theories is provided in Cassidy[1]. We attempt to introduce some new angles derived from occurrences in the financial crisis relating to the social sciences above. Our chapter begins with a section relating, largely, to social anthropology and is followed by a brief focus upon some economics issues – namely, self-interest, bonuses and mathematical economics. We then introduce certain issues relating to Schumpeter's creative destruction and its relevance in the financial crisis. Our chapter is completed with an overview of the insights of the economist Hyman Minsky and the Austrian School on finance through the business cycle.

◼ Culture and conformity

In her excellent book on the financial crisis, Gillian Tett[2] reports that the Royal Bank of Scotland was an aggressive investor in CDOs. She tells us that Ron den Braber, a statistician working on CDOs at the bank, expressed doubts about the bank's models in terms of their underpinning exposure to super-senior debt. Tett quotes Mr den Braber as recalling, 'I started saying things gently. In banks you don't use the word "error", but what I was trying to say was important. The problem is that in banks you have this kind of mentality, this group think, and people just keep going with what they know, and they don't want to listen to bad news'. Shortly afterwards he was asked to leave the bank. The same fate befell Peter Moores, the head of group regulatory risk at HBOS, who expressed risk concerns emanating from the exposure of the firm to the UK housing market.

Even when things do go wrong, how many boards of directors at banks and at other businesses underestimate their losses and their needs for further funds? Galbraith[3] reminds us that 'the euphoric episode is protected and sustained by the will of those who are involved, in order to justify the circumstances that are making them rich. And it is equally protected by the will to ignore, exorcise, or condemn those who express doubts.'

Most interesting in the observation of Ron den Braber is the comment on group think. This quality may be valuable in terms of creating a common culture. But all too often the selection of the top management team based on the one-of-us school of thought can engender a conformity which is conducive to a situation in which no-one challenges the prescribed wisdom. Indeed, many corporations encourage this lookalike style in their recruitment and promotion. In describing the innovation that turned out to be the credit default swap, Tett introduces her readers, on the very first page of the very first chapter, to a meeting of several dozen young bankers from J. P. Morgan offices in New York, London and Tokyo. The gathering at the Boca Raton hotel on Florida's Gold Coast was a brainstorming affair where 'one step of the breakthrough occurred' that gave birth to the CDS phenomenon. Tett adds that some of the rookie bankers 'have only the haziest, alcohol-fuddled memories of that weekend'. It was, of course, also a bonding session – sowing seeds of behaviour, conformity and co-operation. Friendship among men is often based on shared activities, instead of emotional sharing which is how women's friendships are often characterised. The top man, the most powerful in the group, is reinforced as the alpha male and this was how it seemed at J. P. Morgan's Boca Raton brainstorming session.

Whilst conformity, shared backgrounds, common ways of thinking and an absence of challenge may be considered desirable in business, it may be dangerous. At RBS and HBOS, risk officers raised doubts about their banks' potential stability only to be asked to leave their employment. Although fiction, one can understand the hustler behaviour portrayed in such films as *Wall Street*, *Boiler Room* or *Glengarry Glen Ross* where illegality, conformity and greed converge. Of course, fiction often imitates fact. It is a small step to imagine the attractions of the challenge of a banking career with potential big bonuses, working with MBA and university colleagues, and many will happily conform to achieve this well-paid goal. The ease with which subjects fall into the conformity trap has been demonstrated by the experiments of Solomon Asch[4], the obedience to authority figures experiments of Stanley Milgram[5] and the Stanford prison experiments of Haney, Banks and Zimbardo[6]. Although all of these pieces of work have been criticised, their implications about the darker side of human nature are evident. At their ultimate extreme, they are the stuff of Hitler's Nazi Germany mentality.

In a fascinating study of the culture of investment banks, Karen Ho[7], a social anthropologist, attempted to observe and draw conclusions from an examination of Wall Street practices and attitudes. In doing so, she draws on the ideas of Pierre Bourdieu[8] who developed the concept of the habitus, the notion that a group develops a system of dispositions, a way of being that produces practices and constructs of its social world. In a review of Karen Ho's book, Gillian Tett[9] describes the concept of habitus as a way by which a society develops a cognitive map to order its world: it is based on actual experience but participants are only dimly aware of it because they are not necessarily regularly asking themselves questions relating to their actions and beliefs. In her study, Ho describes it as looking at how investment bankers have developed the investment banking ethos as a set of experiences that frame them and empower them to make deals affecting corporate America. She attempts to show how the backgrounds and thought processes of investment bankers converge with workplace status and job experiences to shape an understanding of Wall Street working styles, analysis and client recommendations. She observes that 'recruited from elite universities and represented as the smartest, investment bankers enter into a Wall Street workplace of rampant insecurity, intense hard work, and exorbitant pay for performance compensation.' She goes on to say that 'Wall Street work environments ... are notorious for downsizing privileged investment bankers, even during bull markets, multiple times a year ... And yet – Wall Street investment bankers understand the necessity of constantly performing in notoriously insecure work environments not as a liability but as a challenge. Bankers, recruited as they are only from the Ivy League and a few comparable schools like MIT and Stanford, are trained to view themselves as the best and brightest, for whom intense deal-making ... becomes a sign of their smartness and superiority as well as a way to cope with an anxious environment. Empowered by cultural capital, extensive elite networks, and an organisational structure of exorbitant compensation ... investment bankers often successfully weather and negotiate (and create) crises until the next resurgence.'

Ho's ethnography of Wall Street involves her in blending into the background, listening in a non-judgemental way and drawing conclusions. Inevitably it is not possible for the social anthropologist to arrive at a purely objective view of the world. Nonetheless there are interesting accounts of the implicit caste system at investment banks where the front office elite dominates the middle and back offices, descriptions of how university and business school networks evolve, and tales of bankers becoming dazzled by their own self-importance and deluded by their own rhetoric.

Karen Ho concludes her study by observing that 'it is the very privileged subjectivities of investment bankers – their elite biographies, experiences, and hierarchical representation – that empower and legitimate their authority over inefficient corporate America. When enmeshed within the organisational culture of Wall Street, particular dispositions are constructed and investment bankers are motivated to engage in intense deal-making and market responsiveness as signs of their superiority. These ... depend on continual global boasting, marketing, and leveraging in order to grow and become dominant. Wall Street-led financial booms are made possible by the very financial ideologies and transactions which eventually implode under the accumulated weight of broken promises, failed shareholder value, and the mining of capital without replenishing it.' And her very last paragraph states that 'it has become painstakingly clear that the practices of US investment banks have global ripple effects, and ... produced a highly unequal, new world order. It remains to be seen whether or not the global financial crises of 2008 are seismic enough to radically change the power relations on Wall Street and beyond.'

Obviously elements of subjectivity have to pervade such an analysis. However, one cannot dismiss such an interesting and insightful study even though one may not be convinced by all of Ho's observations and conclusions.

The culture of Wall Street through time is presented in Steve Fraser's[10] *Wall Street: A Cultural History*. And the culture of the investment bank trading desks in the 'me, me, me' age and the incentives of big bonuses is more than brilliantly described by such authors as Lewis[11], Partnoy[12], Anderson[13], Ishikawa[14], Preston[15] and Augar[16]. The culture is perceived as one of turning a quick buck with little or no regard for the other party to the deal. It is one of doing the deal in line with bank tactics discussed at the beginning of each day and it is one of not asking questions as to the rationale for the deal from a client standpoint or, even, whether it makes sense for the bank itself. The dealers are just conforming to the bank's explicit tactics at that point with their eyes and emotions almost exclusively on the profitability of their own dealing book at the time and what it means for their own bonus. The Alex strip in the *Daily Telegraph* is both funny and instructive on the issue of investment banker attitudes.

Lehrer[17] reports that recent research on how the brain deals with financial market movements indicates a neural (that is, to do with the nervous system) signal that seems to be associated with investment decisions. This flows from dopamine-rich areas of the brain which are concerned with learning and dealing with what-if scenarios. Take, for example, this situation. A dealer has decided to wager 10 per cent of their total portfolio in the market. As the dealer sees the market rising dramatically, learning signals start to appear. The dealer enjoys their profits but the dopamine-laden brain cells focus upon the profits missed. Why didn't they do a bigger deal? This is experienced as a feeling of regret. It seems that, as a result, dealers adapt their investment tactics to the ebb and flow – to the trend or current – of the market. With booming markets, players increase their investments. Failing to invest creates more regret. These signals are the main cause of financial bubbles. When the market keeps leaping up, investors keep leaping into the market with bigger and bigger investments. In the boom they stop thinking about the possible losses. Ultimately, of course, the bubble bursts. At this point, the brain becomes aware that some very expensive prediction errors have been made. The investor dumps assets that are declining in value. And as other investors do the same, financial panic is upon us. We refer our readers to Press Cuttings 11.1 and 11.2.

| Press cutting 11.1 | *Financial Times*, 25 November 2009   **FT** |

Alpha males must trade on more than machismo

John Coates

Male traders, like animals in the wild, take more risk when their testosterone levels rise. Research by myself and my colleagues found that moderately elevated levels of this hormone increased the profits of high-frequency traders – although at higher levels it can cause overconfidence and risky behaviour, morphing traders into Masters of the Universe.

What we could not say, however, was whether testosterone was having its beneficial effects by increasing the trader's skill or merely by increasing his appetite for risk.

In a study published on Wednesday in PLoS ONE we found that testosterone had little to do with trading skill. Traders with higher testosterone did indeed do better at this type of trading, because they took more risk. But there was no link between the hormone and their trading skills, as measured by the Sharpe ratio (of which more later). Testosterone alone was not enough.

Showing this requires an understanding of how to judge whether a trader's profits are due to skill or luck – a vital question for banks and hedge funds when allocating capital and paying bonuses.

Trading managers commonly equate skill with a trader's profit and loss

→

(P&L). This measure is simple, but also misleading and dangerous. Knowing that a trader made $100m says nothing about the skill involved unless we know how much risk they took. What if that trader could just as easily have lost $500m?

A better way of sorting the skilful from the brave is to look at the Sharpe ratio, a measure of the steadiness of returns calculated as the P&L divided by the variability of P&L. The higher the variability (or risk), the lower the Sharpe. A trader making $100m but whose P&L regularly swings back and forth by $500m will have a low Sharpe ratio, around 0.20. A trader making $100m but whose P&L varies less, swinging by $100m, will have a higher ratio, around 1.0.

I and my colleague Lionel Page looked at the Sharpe ratios of a group of male high-frequency traders between 2005 and 2007. The experienced traders among them achieved an average Sharpe of 1.02, significantly higher than their benchmark index, Germany's Dax, which averaged 0.53. Furthermore, these traders continued to make money in 2008, a year when many banks and hedge funds gave back five years of returns.

We thought testosterone levels might predict the traders' Sharpe ratios. But they did not. Testosterone levels predicted the amount of risk taken, but not skill.

How were these traders harnessing a high-testosterone/high-risk style of trading into high Sharpe ratios? We found that a trader's Sharpe ratios increased markedly with the number of years they had traded, with first years having a Sharpe around zero, second years matching the Dax, and the most experienced, those in their 12th year, achieving a ratio close to 2.00. Were the traders getting better or were employers culling low Sharpe traders? We found traders increased their Sharpe ratios significantly during the two years of the study – indicating they were learning to make more money per unit of risk.

Learning was encouraged by the compensation scheme at the trading company where they worked. Banks, with their yearly bonuses, may attract traders with an appetite for risk rather than prudence; but the traders in our study received only profit sharing, so if they lose money for the firm they lose it for themselves. These traders have, therefore, a strong incentive to damp the swings in their earnings.

As an aside, learning, like outperformance, is incompatible with the efficient markets hypothesis, according to which the markets follow a random walk and you can no more learn to trade them than you can improve at flipping coins. Our data therefore suggest the markets are not in fact random.

More usefully, the data also suggest that banks could use an improving Sharpe ratio over time as a measure that indicates a trader has developed a skill worth paying for. A high tolerance for risk – predicted by pre-natal testosterone exposure – is needed, but, like height or speed in sports, may count for little without proper training and management. In trading as in sports, biology needs the guiding hand of experience and the right incentives.

Press cutting 11.2   *Financial Times*, 26 November 2009   **FT**

Beneath all the toxic acronyms lies a basic cultural issue

Donald MacKenzie

Of all the 'toxic assets' at the heart of the credit crisis, one kind proved most toxic of all: collateralised debt obligations made up of asset-backed securities (or ABS CDOs to those in the know).

They are like a kind of Russian doll. A CDO, or collateralised debt obligation, is an instrument that involves packaging a pool of assets and selling tranches of securities based on the cash flow from the pool. In an ABS CDO, each of those underlying assets is itself a tranche of an asset-backed security, which is already a packaged instrument, most commonly based on a large pool of mortgages. By 2005, ABS CDOs had become the main source of demand for the riskier tranches of mortgage-backed securities, and the International Monetary Fund calculates that by October 2008 losses on these Russian-doll instruments totalled $290bn, the largest single category of the losses that triggered the global banking crisis.

Why were ABS CDOs so toxic? For the past 10 years, I have interviewed many market participants for my research on the sociology of financial markets. One thing that is striking is that different groups of participants understand financial instruments in very different ways and each with their own 'evaluation cultures', their own distinctive ways of making sense of and valuing financial instruments.

ABS CDOs fell into the gap between two evaluation cultures. ABS specialists and CDO specialists each have rich and sophisticated ways of understanding financial instruments, but those ways were, and are, different, in spite of the fact that ABS and CDOs are instruments with very similar structures.

A gap between evaluation cultures such as this is enticing, because money – arbitrage profits – can be made there. Often, this involves the modern equivalent of the age-old practice of buying something cheaply in one culture and selling it expensively in another. What was being arbitraged by ABS CDOs was an unintentional side-effect of the way ABS CDOs were evaluated, especially by the rating agencies, using the techniques of the CDO culture. These were honed originally for the analysis of a different kind of CDO, in which the underlying assets were loans made to corporations or bonds issued by them.

The models the agencies employed made it possible to create an ABS CDO that was mostly triple A rated out of tranches of mortgage-backed securities with only low investment-grade (triple B or triple B minus) ratings. This arbitrage was not magic or alchemy, but the effect of the assumption of only modest levels of correlation – somewhat higher than those assumed for corporate loans or bonds, but still not very high – between different mortgage-backed securities. Everyone understood that default on any particular triple B or triple B minus tranche was perfectly conceivable, but ABS CDOs could withstand limited numbers of these defaults. Crucially, the models implied that large scale defaults were unlikely, so permitting triple A ratings. It's rather like how it is perfectly possible for one coin to turn up tails, but very unlikely for 20 independently tossed coins all to do so.

→

In retrospect, the chain of disaster is clear: ABS CDOs helped permit mortgage-backed securities to become riskier, and those securities in turn facilitated ever riskier mortgage lending. But it was not seen clearly at the time because ABS CDOs fell into the gap between cultures. ABS specialists, for example, were certainly worried by the deteriorating quality of US mortgage lending and of the resultant ABS, but paid little attention to the potentially precarious situation of ABS CDOs. Those whose job it was to construct the latter had to turn a blind eye. As one of my interviewees put it, 'So, you know, you talk to people [CDO arrangers], and they're complaining about the quality [of ABS] . . . But they've got a mandate to do the CDO, they've got to get it done. They've got to buy something because they want their fees.'

CDO specialists did not spot the growing danger for different reasons. Some looked down on ABS specialists as mathematically unsophisticated. The understanding that ABS specialists had of the institutional realities of US mortgage lending was not sufficiently valued. In the months before the crisis, CDO specialists also had their anxieties, but these focused on innovative new products, not the hugely larger volumes of ABS CDOs, which were a 'very boring part of the market', as another interviewee said. The gaps between evaluation cultures are dangerous as well as enticing. To understand them, we need the techniques of the sociologist or anthropologist, not just the economist. We need to talk to people, to grasp how they think and calculate, to try to get 'inside their heads', to find out how their evaluation cultures differ.

By doing so, we'll also discover things that are not said, tacit assumptions that are made, people who are not spoken to, and the perilous gaps that in consequence open up.

■ Self-interest

We can trace ideas of self-interest as a driver of economic systems back to the classic writings of Adam Smith[18]. To quote the great economist, Smith observes that 'man has almost constant occasion for the help of his brethren, and it is in vain for him to expect it from their benevolence alone . . . It is not from the benevolence of the butcher, the brewer, or the baker that we expect our dinner, but from their regard to their own interest. We address ourselves not to their humanity, but to their self-love, and never talk to them of our own necessities, but of their advantages.' Thus economic man looks after his own interests. If he has something to offer, he seeks to exchange it for something in another man's possession, usually money – which enables him, in turn, to exchange it to better his condition. 'The quantity of every commodity brought to market naturally suits itself to the effectual demand.' Supply adjusts to meet demand. In pursuing their business interests, the entrepreneur is governed by the principle of self-interest.

Certainly, Smith did not regard this as the best of all possible worlds. His sympathy for the working class is very clear when he observes that 'rent and profit eat up wages and the two superior orders of people oppress the interior one'. And he was far from satisfied with the distribution of wealth and income. He was suspicious of manufacturers who had 'generally an interest to deceive and even to oppress the public, and who accordingly have, upon many occasions, both deceived and oppressed it.' And his doubts about the means by which businesspeople pursue their self-interest is brilliantly observed in the oft-quoted words 'people of the same trade seldom meet together even for merriment and diversion, but the conversation ends in a conspiracy against the public, or in some contrivance to raise prices ... But though the law cannot hinder people of the same trade from sometimes assembling together, it ought to do nothing to facilitate such assemblies, much less to render them necessary.'

When Smith's *magnum opus* appeared in 1776, the Industrial Revolution had only just begun. James Watt had patented a steam engine seven years earlier. Samuel Crompton's spinning mule was devised in 1779 and Edmund Cartwright's power loom was almost a decade in the future. It was the year of America's Declaration of Independence and final victory at Yorktown in 1781 was five years off. It was more than a decade before the French Revolution. It was more than four decades before *Frankenstein* was published. The world has changed greatly since Smith first began to lecture at Glasgow University in 1751. Some of his teachings have certainly ceased to hold good – hardly surprising. Perhaps more surprising is how many still make wonderful sense over two-and-a-half centuries on. And some were prophetic in terms of the evolution of economic thought. For example, Smith is suspicious of his own theory of the pursuit of self-interest and profit in the context of the joint stock enterprise rather than with respect to the small individual business. Referring to joint stock companies, Adam Smith observes that 'the directors of such companies being the managers rather of other people's money than of their own, it cannot well be expected that they should watch over it with the same anxious vigilance with which the partners in a private copartnery frequently watch over their own. Like the stewards of a rich man, they are apt to consider attention to small matters as not for their master's honour, and very easily give themselves a dispensation from having it. Negligence and profusion, therefore, must always prevail, more or less, in the management of the affairs of such a company.' Was Smith foreseeing theories related to the divorce of ownership and control?

Work in this area was pioneered and articulated by Berle and Means[19] and published in 1932 (updated in 1967). In accordance with Smith's self-interest idea, Berle and Means observe that 'whereas the organization of feudal economic life rested upon an elaborate system of binding customs, the organization under the system of private enterprise has rested upon the self interest of the property owner ... Such self-interest has long been regarded as the best guarantee of economic efficiency. It has been assumed that, if the individual is protected in the right both to use his own property as he sees fit and to receive the full fruits of its use, his desire for personal gain, for profits, can be relied upon as an effective incentive to his efficient use of any industrial property he may possess.'

However, in the modern corporation listed on the stock exchange, ownership (by shareholders) and control (by directors and executives) have been separated. In this circumstance, Berle and Means suggest that the typical shareholder is uninterested in the daily affairs of the company. Thus, those individuals that are directly interested in the daily affairs of the company, that is, the management and the directors, have the oppor-tunity to manage corporate resources to their own advantage without full and effective involvement and scrutiny. It means that 'the property owner who invests in a modern corporation surrenders his wealth to those in control of the corporation in which he may become merely ... a recipient of the wages of capital ... [The shareholders] have surrendered the right that the corporation should be operated in their sole interest.' Berle and Means conclude that owners will not be most beneficially rewarded by such a structure.

At the heart of the issue of the divorce of ownership and control is the key question raised by Berle and Means, namely, 'Have we justification for the assumption that those in control of a modern corporation will also choose to operate it in the interests of the owners?' The answer to this question will depend on the degree to which the self-interest of those in control runs parallel to the interest of ownership ... If we are to assume that the desire for personal profit is the prime force motivating control, we must conclude that the interests of control are different from and often radically opposed to those of ownership; that the owners most emphatically will not be served by a profit-seeking controlling group.' To a large extent, their words are prophetic of the massive directors' emoluments and so-called share incentive schemes that have become too typical of corporations in this era of ownership and control divorce.

Berle and Means insights are also prophetic and again applicable years beyond their original writing. Consider their conclusion that 'the economic power in the hands of the few persons who control a giant corporation is a tremendous force which can harm or benefit a multitude of individuals, affect whole districts, shift the currents of trade, bring ruin to one community and prosperity to another. The organizations which they control have passed far beyond the realm of private enterprise.' Surely relevant to the noughties financial crash.

The theme of the divorce of ownership and control and its consequences is one aspect of agency conflict referring to the fact that managers act as agents for absentee owners. The implications of agency conflict in financial economics were presented by Jensen and Meckling[20] in 1976. Their main postulate of agency conflict concerned relations between shareholders and bondholders. Potential conflict between these two classes of investors arises because managers may make decisions on dividends, financing, and investment that transfer wealth from bondholders to stockholders. Such decisions may clearly create gains for stockholders and losses for bondholders. For example, a corporate decision to borrow billions of euros to pay shareholders a big one-off dividend could result in such shareholders being better off at the expense of bondholders. There have been cases like this which have resulted in equity value soaring. The bond price drop would reflect the combination of a greater risk of default (the firms total interest and principal payments would rise substantially) and a smaller payoff to bondholders if default were to occur (fewer assets remaining to satisfy total bondholder claims).

Another aspect of the agency problem is the fact that one party to a contract often knows something relevant to the transaction of which the other party is unaware. Such information asymmetries are widely encountered in business. For example, they occur in relationships between the shareholders and the managers of a firm, between the issuer and the purchaser of a security, between the insurer and the insured, and between a lender and a borrower. To counter the problem of information asymmetry, various mechanisms and institutions have evolved. These include the use of bankers to certify the quality of the securities they issue, the use of rating agencies, utmost good faith insurance contracts aimed to ensure that all parties declare everything relevant to their agreement. One key aspect of these solutions is the reputation of the parties concerned. This may be destroyed in the event that the so-called reputable party were to use inside information to exploit the ignorant party. Clearly, the financial crisis revealed a number of problems of this sort – not least, as we have seen, in respect of rating agencies.

The economic idea of self-interest and its application in the modern corporation has led to the emergence of share incentive schemes for executives and also to bonuses for performance. Intuitively, this seems a sensible idea. The firm performs better so the executive gains and the shareholder gains. The bonus system would seem to be advantageous to shareholder and to executive alike – that is, to principal and to agent. This is often referred to as goal congruence. We now examine this, in the context of Wall Street and City of London incentive structures.

■ Bonuses

Consider the following deal for a bank. The bank has a 60 per cent chance of making GBP50 million profit and a 40 per cent chance of losing GBP50 million on a deal. Logically the deal structure implies a net expected profit GBP10 million derived from [60 per cent of GBP50 million] – [40 per cent of GBP50 million] = GBP10 million and, according to the expected payoff, the bank concerned should proceed with the deal.

Consider a further deal. It is based upon one cited in Cassidy[21]. This deal has the prospect of a 98 per cent chance of a profit of GBP150 million and a 2 per cent chance of ending up with a GBP20 billion loss. In this case, the bank's expected payoff is in negative territory to the extent of over GBP150 million, given by [0.98 × GBP150 million] – [0.02 × GBP20 billion] = minus GBP253 million. The bank should surely reject the deal. But if we assume, at the same time, that the key executive making the decision has a remuneration package worth GBP500,000 per annum plus 5 per cent of deal profits, what now? If the executive proceeds with the deal, there is a 98 per cent chance it will pay off and they will earn their basic salary of GBP500,000 per year plus a GBP7,500,000 bonus, that is GBP8 million. If the deal fails, the bank will write off GBP20 billion, but the executive will still earn GBP500,000. With this kind of remuneration structure and with the criterion of pure self-interest executives will logically become big risk-takers in the bank's name.

Clearly it is self-interest that is driving this decision which is hardly an optimal one for the bank and its shareholders. Rather than attributing this to a failure of economics, the bank's control systems and risk management procedures stand accused. But it has to be a really big risk management officer to stand up and make the point as we have just done. Imagine doing so with the Lehman Brothers' CEO, Dick Fuld, at the other side of the desk. Furthermore, with debt to equity ratios anything like those at Lehmans (25 to 1), Merrill Lynch (21 to 1) or Bear Stearns (28 to 1) the incentives to take on bigger and riskier deals, of the kind exemplified above, are even further magnified.

Bonus carrots like the one exemplified give executives colossal temptations to take on excessive risk and, even, to bet the bank. Many bonus schemes and stock option schemes too give key executives an asymmetric and leveraged bet on the value of the firm's assets. Should the bank's investments pay off, such key executives pocket fortunes. If the business suffers a mammoth loss, the equity shareholders may be wiped out and the debt holders and other creditors experience significant losses. But if systemic risk is on the horizon, the financial institution may be rescued at taxpayers' expense. In the approach of Akerlof and Romer[22], this would amount to a form of looting in which 'bankruptcy for profit will occur if poor accounting, lax regulation, or low penalties for abuse give owners an incentive to pay themselves more than their firms are worth and then default on their debt obligations'. Perverse incentive structures like the ones set out above are common on Wall Street and in the City of London. Salary and bonus packages out of all proportion to the basic requirements of the job and its performance abound. Again, to quote Akerlof and Romer, 'bankruptcy for profit can easily become a more attractive strategy ... than maximising true economic values. If so, the normal economics of maximising economic value is replaced by the topsy-turvy economics of maximising current extractable value.' And current extractable value is all about bank bonus packages. This plea that there needs to be limitations on bonuses is not written out of envy but out of a desire to ensure that current extractable value (the bonus) does not create further situations that could put the whole financial system in jeopardy again.

In a scathing critique of non-executive directors who fail to curb this kind of situation, not just for banks but for listed companies in general, Galbraith[23] refers to the 'board of directors selected by management; fully subordinate to management but heard as the voice of the shareholders'. He goes on to say that 'they are reliably acquiescent. Given a fee and some food, the directors are routinely informed by management on what has been decided or is already known. Approval is assumed, including for management compensation – compensation set by management for itself. This, not surprisingly, can be munificent.' Galbraith goes on to observe that 'to affirm this fiction, stockholders are invited each year to the annual meeting, which, indeed, resembles a religious rite. There is ceremonial expression and, with rare exceptions, no negative response. Infidels who urge action are set aside; the management position is routinely approved.' Galbraith concludes this section with the précis of his view: 'no one should be in doubt: Shareholders – owners – and their alleged directors in any sizeable enterprise are fully subordinate to the management. Though the impression of owner authority is offered, it does not, in fact, exist. An accepted fraud.' Galbraith's vitriolic prose may overstate his case but his point is certainly worthy of consideration and discussion. It reminds us of a joke which goes as follows: what's the difference between a non-executive director and a supermarket trolley? And the answer is – the supermarket trolley has a mind of its own. We have observed earlier that a new breed of questioning, non-acquiescent non-executive is required – especially in banks.

Galbraith certainly affirms the Berle and Means contention. Corporate power has passed, in the modern corporation, to its management at the expense of its owners. Galbraith continues as follows: '... the belief that ownership has a final authority persisted, as it still does. At the annual meeting shareholders are provided with information on performance, earnings, managerial intention and other matters, including many that are already known. The resemblance is to a Covenanted Baptist Church service. Management authority remains unimpaired, including the setting of its own compensation in cash or stock options. In recent times, executive compensation so approved has run into millions of dollars annually in an environment in which there is no adverse view of making money. Here, to repeat, the basic fact of the twenty-first century – a corporate system based on the unrestrained power of self-enrichment ... Corporate power lies with management – a bureaucracy in control of its task and its compensation. Rewards that can verge on larceny.' Again, if we set aside the venom of Galbraith's prose, the issue raised is a topic justifying serious attention. And it is reinforced by Press Cutting 11.3.

Press cutting 11.3	*Financial Times*, 31 July 2009 **FT**

Loss-making banks award bonuses

Greg Farrell in New York

Citigroup and Merrill Lynch, which together lost $55bn in 2008, paid bonuses of $1m (€700,000, £600,000) or more each to 1,400 employees, according to a New York state report yesterday on banks propped up with taxpayer funds.

The study, compiled by Andrew Cuomo, New York attorney-general, showed that JPMorgan Chase and Goldman Sachs, which both finished in the black last year, paid the most million-dollar bonuses – 1,626 and 953, respectively.

But the totals at a profitable bank such as Goldman were nearly matched by two of the year's biggest losers on Wall Street. Citi, which suffered a $27.7bn loss, paid million-dollar bonuses to 738 employees. Merrill, which lost $27.6bn, paid 696 bonuses of $1m or more. 'There is no clear rhyme or reason to the way banks compensate and reward their employees,' Mr Cuomo said. 'Compensation for bank employees has become unmoored from the banks' financial performance.'

Republican Edolphus Towns, head of the House of Representatives committee on government oversight and reform, pledged to hold hearings in September on the matter, suggesting the controversy over banker bonuses was likely to continue later this year.

Earlier, Mr Cuomo had detailed the number of million-dollar bonus payments made at Merrill in the last days of 2008, before it was acquired by Bank of America. In his new report, sent to Mr Towns' committee, Mr Cuomo detailed the number and size of bonuses at eight other banks that received billions from the federal Troubled Asset Relief Programme (Tarp) fund last October.

JP Morgan which earned $5.6bn in 2008, set aside $8.7bn for bonuses. The report shows JP Morgan paid out bonuses in excess of $3m to more than 200 employees The bank received $25bn in Tarp funds last year, and paid the money back last month.

At Goldman, the bonus pool last year was $4.8bn, more than twice the $2.3bn it earned for the year. Goldman paid $3m or more to 212 employees. It paid back $10bn in Tarp funds last month. Citigroup set aside $5.3bn for its bonus pool, and paid bonuses of $3m or more to 124 employees. Like Bank of America, Citigroup received $45bn in Tarp funds in 2008 and has converted some of that funding into common equity.

→

BofA paid bonuses of $3m to 28 employees and million-dollar bonuses to 172. The bank reported a profit of $4bn in 2008 and set aside $3.3bn for bonuses.	Morgan Stanley earned $1.7bn last year and set aside $4.5bn for bonuses. It received $10bn in Tarp funds last year, and paid back the money in June.

Even the institutional shareholders, represented by fund managers, are a large enough body to challenge executive excess, but are they likely to rock the boat? Motivated by their own self-interest, they are not greatly inclined to attack the issue of excessive remuneration because their own remuneration is benchmarked on that of the very directors of the companies in which their institutions hold shares. Add into the equation similar collegiate backgrounds and interests and their complacency is understandable. Whether it should be is another matter entirely.

■ Mathematical economics

Advances in mathematical economics took place in the decades following World War II. Paul Samuelson's[24] book *Foundations of Economic Analysis* was greatly influential. As Cassidy puts it, 'the thrust of Samuelson's book was that economic decision-makers could be treated as rational automatons who attempt to maximise mathematical functions. (In the case of firms, it is profit function; in the case of consumers, it is a happiness, or utility function).' Samuelson's approach made a big impact on the young Robert Lucas who later became a Chicago professor and was a Nobel prize winner for economics. Lucas is quoted[25] as saying, of Samuelson's textbook: 'Like so many others in my cohort, I internalised its view that if I couldn't formulate a problem in economic theory mathematically, I didn't know what I was doing. I came to the position that mathematical analysis is not one of many ways of doing economic theory: it is the only way. Economic theory is mathematical analysis. Everything else is just pictures and talk.'

Lucas took the efficient market hypothesis and extended its approach to the overall economy. The basic idea was that rational economic decision makers are well aware of how the economy works. Decision makers are aware of macroeconomic linkages, for example between wages, unemployment, inflation and interest rates. All have the same mathematical models of the economy in their minds and they use these to form expectations of wages, prices and so on. This is essentially the rational expectations hypothesis, pioneered by fellow-economist, John Muth[26]. Using rational expectations ideas, Lucas developed mathematical descriptions of how workers, firms and governments behave. This would never be 100 per cent correct but would be a useful economic model with explanatory power. So, for example, if the expectation is of an expansion in money supply or a cut in interest rates, workers and businesses would be able to predict the results and their responses would exactly offset the policy change. Using this line of reasoning, the government may be argued to be powerless, or a source of trouble. Its policies would make little difference to the economy – unless they were unpredicted, in which case they would destabilise the economy. The corollary that government attempts to manage the economy were unnecessary and could be counterproductive, followed.

In such an efficient markets/rational expectations mathematical model of the world, stock market bubbles, illiquidity in markets and banks being frightened of lending are not part of the underlying assumptions. Why not? Because prices in stock markets, money markets and so on would adjust to reach a level which would precisely compensate for perceived risk. No more bubbles. No more credit crunches. The market clearing price ensures that. And it was this assumption that kept on cropping up in mathematical models of the economy. It led to swathes of economic model-building based upon nice straight line relationships. William Buiter[27] puts it brilliantly when he suggests that, referring to economic models, 'it would soon become clear that any potentially policy-relevant model would be highly non-linear, and that the interaction of these non-linearities and uncertainty makes for deep conceptual and technical problems. Macroeconomists are brave, but not that brave. So they took these non-linear stochastic dynamic equilibrium models into the basement and beat them with a rubber hose until they behaved. This was achieved by completely stripping the model of its non-linearities and by achieving the transubstantiation of complex convolutions of random variables and non-linear mappings into well-behaved additive stochastic disturbances.' As Buiter summarises, it 'linearise and trivialise'.

Taking this point and referring back to Figure 7.2 concerning the risk/return trade-off, we would in reality expect this to be non-linear. In the earlier chapter we were simplifying. The shape of the trade-off would be more like that specified by the continuous line in Figure 11.1. In this figure, the dotted line represents the linear relationship. If valuation of assets, for example equities, is based upon investors discounting future cash flows at a discount rate based on perceived risk, it is arguable that the discount rate used would be the rate based on the linear trade-off in the exhibit whereas the more logical rate would be the curved solid line. This reasoning can be used to help explain bubbles and their bursting since, given some shock to the system, investors move their risk perception from a linear one to the non-linear trade-off.

Add into the equation the fact that, immediately following the shock, investors lower estimates of future cash flow and we have a triple-whammy to valuation – higher discounting for risk (even the linear bit may move upwards), reignited awareness of the non-linear aspect and lower future outturns. Hardly surprising that bubbles burst so precipitously – having advanced relatively slowly.

The thrust of the argument is simple. It is that unjustified emphasis on the linear has been a feature of recent research in macroeconomics and in financial economics. Far more interesting would be the pursuit of the non-linear, what is going on when shocks to the system create these difficult-to-model movements. All too often researchers nowadays seem to treat them with little attention, regarding them as aberrant outliers. Incidentally, we would not in any way criticise the achievements of the pioneering mathematical economist, Robert Lucas. The argument is that many of his followers have linearised and trivialised.

■ Creative destruction

We now turn briefly to the economic concept developed by Joseph Schumpeter because we hypothesise that it played a bigger part than is realised in the financial crisis. Schumpeter was

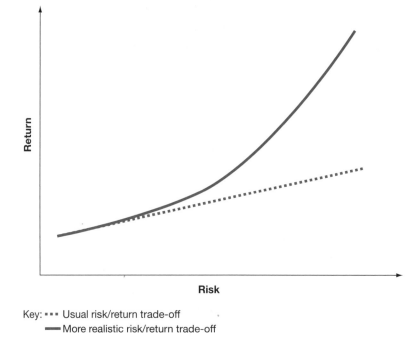

Key: ▪▪▪ Usual risk/return trade-off
    ━ More realistic risk/return trade-off

Figure 11.1 The realistic risk/return trade-off

born in what is now the Czech Republic in 1883 and he died in 1950. As a child he moved to Vienna, Austria, when his mother remarried and his aristocratic stepfather was influential in his entry to élite colleges, where he stood out as an excellent student. This led to academic life where he became professor of economics and government at various universities and after World War I, he became Austrian Minister of Finance and subsequently a bank president. The bank's failure in 1924 forced Schumpeter back to academia. In the 1930s he moved to America to escape Nazism and he spent the rest of his career as a professor at Harvard University.

According to Schumpeter's creative destruction, business failures can ultimately serve to create stronger economies and a wealthier society by weeding out inefficient and uncompetitive businesses to make way for new, innovative business. His idea that recession, or an economic downturn, in which unemployment rises as firms face receding profits, might, somewhat counter-intuitively, be positive for an economy in the long run. As Schumpeter[28] claimed, 'the process of industrial mutation ... incessantly revolutionises the economic structure from within, incessantly destroying the old one, incessantly creating a new one.'

Although not proven, or even investigated at the time of writing, we seriously wonder whether some bailout funds were directed at firms which were due to receive their creative destruction death knell. For example, was it possible that the rescue of General Motors and Ford was sparked because of a massive wall of credit default swaps on the two US automobile companies? If this were the case and if they were to default on their obligations, the knock-on effect might well have been further bank failures. And the banks which would have failed would have been those that were offering credit default swap insurance. Furthermore, as the motor companies' balance sheets eroded, the increasing cost of such swaps would have had negative consequences for them in terms of their abilities to raise new borrowings. Such knock-on impacts would have the effect of pushing them nearer bankruptcy.

This kind of hypothesis has an impact in creative destruction. Do government bailouts like those received by General Motors and Chrysler have an adverse long-run effect on economic efficiency because they keep ailing businesses alive too long? But the bailouts were, perhaps, engineered to avoid bank failures. And these potential failures flowed from excess risk-taking via credit default instruments. Is this a potent argument in favour of requiring that an insurable interest must be present in all such instruments? If this were enacted as a requirement, it would reduce the possibility that banks take on too much risk via the CDS. It may reduce the potential for bankers' profits from betting that a company may fail and thereby (because the credit default swap price would not be there) increase the likelihood that a weakish company would be able to raise needed finance to pull it through a short-term problem. It may, also, because it should mean less likelihood of a government bailout, give a superior chance of the process of creative destruction driving the economy forward in the longer run.

■ The insights of Hyman Minsky

The Crash of 2007 reignited an interest in the ideas of Hyman Minsky, a prominent member of the post-Keynesian school of economics. Most economists are of the view that economic crises are the outcome of various external shocks. Minsky differed. To him, even in the absence of shocks, the capitalist economy has an inbuilt tendency to move to instability, leading to economic crisis.

Hyman Minsky was born in 1919 and died in 1996. He was an American economist whose research attempted to provide an understanding and explanation of the characteristics of financial crises. Minsky believed that risk attitudes changed gradually during the cycle. Early in the business cycle, when expansion has barely begun, people tend to hedge their bets. Debt use would be conservative and cash margins of safety relatively high. As expansion kicks in, people become more speculative and debt usage grows. For these first two stages of the financial cycle, Minsky coins the terms hedge finance and speculative finance, respectively.

As expansion becomes a boom, however, with higher asset prices providing ever greater confidence to borrow more, so we enter Minsky's final stage of Ponzi finance. The end of the boom usually precedes recession and, with it, a return to hedge finance. Minsky's three stages of capitalist finance may be summarised as below:

1. **Hedge finance:**
    - early cycle, with clear memories of recession still there;
    - conservative estimates of cash inflows when making financing decisions – business plans provide more than enough cash generation to pay off cash commitments;
    - cash in hand is held to cover possible setbacks;

- debt tends to be conservative and at long-term fixed interest rates;

- cash is held to pay off interest and principal;

- margin of safety is high.

2. **Speculative finance:**

- mid-cycle, after several years of growth;

- estimates of cash inflows are more aggressive – debt levels rise – expected cash inflows provide just enough cover to make interest payments on debts with principal rolled over;

- cash in hand shrinks;

- debt becomes shorter term and therefore needs regular refinancing – borrowers become exposed to short-term changes in lender's willingness to extend loans;

- margin of safety becomes lower.

3. **Ponzi finance:**

- late cycle – very distant memories of recession;

- estimates of cash generation not expected to cover cash commitments;

- cash for emergencies depends on more borrowing;

- debt is short term and rolled over;

- widespread borrowing against asset collateral;

- strongly rising asset prices needed to underpin debt payments;

- margin of safety is low.

Is this familiar? Does it sound like the expansion that ended in 2007?

The financial structure of a capitalist economy becomes, according to Minsky, more fragile during the period of prosperity. The longer the prosperity, the more fragile the economy. Minsky's line of argument, through hedge finance and ultimately to Ponzi finance and back, is the core of his Financial Instability Hypothesis[29] (FIH).

Minsky essentially proposed theories linking financial market fragility, the normal cycle of the economy and speculative investment bubbles. He proposed that, in periods of growth, as corporate cash flows rise beyond what is needed to pay off debt, the roots of a speculative explosion or bubble are laid. Soon after, debts exceed what borrowers can pay off from incoming revenues and this precipitates a financial crisis as assets are realised to meet debt service. Asset prices would clearly decline. Immediately following the burst of the bubble, banks and other lenders tighten credit availability, even to companies that can afford to service loans. Then the economy contracts.

Minsky argued that economic swings, booms and busts are inevitable in a free market economy, unless governments intervene to control them via central bank action, regulation and other means. He strongly opposed the financial deregulation witnessed since the 1980s. Application of Minsky's Financial Instability Hypothesis, as it is called, to the crisis of 2007–8 is not difficult. Even though this scenario reasonably describes the recent Crash, it does not provide an entirely empirically tested explanation using previous phenomena.

Minsky's opponents claim that his hypothesis places the blame for instability on the capitalist system without deductive logical explanations. The presence of the central bank can provide the foundation for financial stability by dampening booms – but may also be responsible for instability by failing to do so. We continue to hope that, with competent regulation, crises can be avoided. Perfect stability can never be achieved. But utter instability should be avoidable. The well-timed touch on the tiller is an absolute necessity. This view is directly opposed to Minsky's. His basic assumption was that capitalism is unstable. It is claimed that his framework describes but it fails to explain. Let this not be misinterpreted. We have great respect for the insights of Hyman Minsky. Indeed we incorporate them into our final chapter focusing upon lessons from the 2007/9 financial crash Minsky's contributions to our insights of finance are well summarised in Barbera[30].

■ The Austrian School of Economics

At this point we feel it is important to remind readers of the boom/bust interpretations of the Austrian School of Economics. To them central banking is the ultimate cause of the boom/bust economic cycle resulting from the central banks failure to set interest rates appropriately. According to the Austrian school, low interest rates stimulate borrowing. The associated expansion of credit causes an expansion in the supply of money and moves towards boom conditions during which artificially higher stimulated borrowing seeks out less good investment opportunities. The boom creates the means for widespread malinvestment. Resources are misallocated to areas that would fail to attract investment under normal money supply stability. The correction (the recession or bust) follows when credit creation is curtailed. The money supply contracts sharply as markets are cleared and resources are reallocated back to efficient uses. The key players in developing the Austrian business cycle were von Mises and Hayek.

Both Minsky and the Austrian School have something in common. They point the finger at banks for the boom and bust in the economy. However, whilst Minsky targets commercial banks (his merchants of debt), the Austrian School saddles central banks with the guilt for maintaining interest rates at unrealistic levels.

■ An eclectic view

We believe that there is room for a mixed view. To this end we would hypothesise that there are areas in which Minsky's stages in finance might be augmented. We set out our syncretic approach which draws from Minsky and the Austrian School plus observations (which, we admit, need to be verified empirically) from the recent financial crisis and earlier episodes. We use Minksky's three stages but we have redesignated them as Recovery finance (rather than Hedge finance), Normal finance (rather than Speculative finance) and Boom finance (rather than Ponzi finance). We do this because we perceive Minsky's terms as carrying unnecessarily emotive or pejorative implications which have led to his theory being less accepted than It deserves to be. So, we believe that the features specified above relating to Minsky's categorisation should be complemented by the following:

- **Recovery finance**
  - bank loan criteria and control systems tighten;
  - leverage of financial institutions and non-financial firms moves to more conservative levels through rights issues and/or budget tightening;
  - regulation of financial institutions tightens as memories of recession are still easily recalled;
  - interest rates are relatively low to hasten recovery;
  - firms are choosy about investment decisions;
  - resource allocation is generally good;
  - mortgage funds fairly tight.
- **Normal finance**
  - bank lending criteria and control systems still satisfactory but loosening up as competition hots up;
  - leverage of financial institutions and non-financial firms moves upwards but still not unsatisfactory in general;
  - regulation becomes more relaxed;
  - interest rates still reasonable but should be edging up from previous part of the cycle;
  - firm's investment decisions becoming less satisfactory;
  - resource allocation still satisfactory;
  - mortgage monies reasonably available for medium to good borrowers.
- **Boom finance**
  - bank lending criteria and control systems become lax as competition becomes fierce;
  - leverage of financial institutions and non-financial firms becomes high and in many cases far too high;
  - regulation becomes lax as governments and politicians rush to curry popularity – lobbying becomes easy;
  - interest rates become too low given the level of economic activity;
  - resource misallocation as too many investments made in low-quality projects oiled by interest rates that are too low and appraisal standards become lax;
  - mortgage monies widely and cheaply available to low-quality borrowers;
  - financial innovation, usually a variant on an old debt theme, makes for heightened risk;
  - banking institutions take on too much debt fuelling potential problems.

■ Final words on self-interest

In a devastating critique of the culture which encouraged the pursuit of self-interest with the carrot of significant incentives, Dowd and Hutchinson[31] paint a picture of a process which raises questions about the banks' business practices that prevailed prior to the financial crisis. They tell us that 'problems were especially apparent in the subprime mortgage market, where a blatantly undesirable outcome arose from a process in which participants' activities at each stage were economically rational:

■ Low-income consumers took on mortgages they had no prospect of affording because they believed from the experience of others that house prices would rise sufficiently to bail them out. In any case, being often near bankruptcy the potential profit from successful speculation often appeared to them greater than the potential loss from default.

■ The encyclopaedia salesmen and used car dealers who functioned as mortgage brokers sold subprime mortgages because they got a generous commission for selling them (better than for the technologically obsolescent encyclopaedias or even used cars) and were not responsible for the credit risk.

■ Investment banks packaged the subprime mortgages into multiple-tranche mortgage-backed securities because they received fat fees for doing so and, again, had no responsibility for the credit risk.

■ Rating agencies gave the upper tranches of mortgage debt favourable ratings because they made a great deal of money from providing ratings for asset-backed securities, needed to keep in the favour of the investment banks who bought them this attractive business and had mathematical models (either their own or the investment banks') "proving" that the default rates of the securitised mortgages would be low.

■ Investment bank and rating agency mathematicians produced models "proving" that default rates would be low, ignoring the real-world correlations between defaults on low quality consumer debt, because they had succumbed to the group-think affecting everyone else – and because they were well paid and the alternative was to return to a miserable low-paid existence in academia.

■ Finally, the investors bought asset-backed securities because they could achieve a higher return on them in the short term than their borrowing costs, and could tell their funding sources (in the case of hedge funds) or bosses (in the case of foreign banks) that they were taking very little risk because of the securities' high rating.

Each step of the process was rational (albeit operating on imperfect information), yet because incentives were hopelessly misaligned, the final result was an irrational, twisted market in which loans that would not be repaid were securitised and sold to investors seeking an above-market return at below-market risk, a combination that in the long run cannot exist.'

There are clearly big lessons here for avoidance of the next financial crisis.

Chapter 12

Bank failures in the USA

■ Introduction

There have been too many failures of US financial institutions to present a chapter of case studies on all the stories for all of the failures. Inevitably we have had to choose those that seem most interesting. This, inevitably, means that coverage has to include – Bear Stearns, Lehman Brothers, AIG and Fannie Mae and Freddie Mac.

With this brief background, the case studies in this chapter follow. To some extent they speak for themselves. For tutorial or seminar discussion, it would be possible to use these as they are or to supplement them with further material. So, without more ado the cases that comprise this section are:

> Case 12.1 – Bear Stearns
> Case 12.2 – Lehman Brothers
> Case 12.3 – American International Group (AIG)
> Case 12.4 – Fannie Mae and Freddie Mac

These American failures mainly involved excessive indulgence in credit default swaps, CDOs and MBSs – a surfeit of securitisation.

Insights on some of the cases in this chapter and on the financial crisis are provided in Milne[1]. And Andrew Ross Sorkin[2] recreates the story of the US bailouts and the air of panic and fear pervading September 2008 as if it were a thriller. For a close-up of the difficult task of taking the necessary action to relieve the crisis, see *On the Brink* by Henry Paulson[3].

Case 12.1 Bear Stearns

■ Introduction

Bear Stearns, headquartered in New York City, was a global investment bank and securities brokerage and trading house until its collapse and sale to J. P. Morgan Chase in 2008. Its key business areas, based on net revenues were capital markets – equities, fixed income, investment banking – accounting for just short of 80 per cent, wealth management giving rise to 10 per cent, and global clearing services bringing in approximately 12 per cent.

Bear Stearns was one of the pioneers of securitisation and trading of asset-backed securities. In 2006 and 2007, the bank increased its exposure to mortgage-backed assets, in particular subprime mortgages. In March of 2008, the Federal Reserve Bank of New York provided an emergency loan in an attempt to avert collapse. Bear Stearns could not be saved and was sold to J. P. Morgan Chase for ten dollars per share. This contrasted with a 52-week high of USD133.20 per share – but that was before its collapse in profit and asset values were revealed. However the exit price was better than the original offer from J. P. Morgan Chase of two dollars per share.

The failure of Bear Stearns was the first act in the tale of the meltdown of the investment bank industry which climaxed in September 2008 and led to the subsequent global financial crisis. At the beginning of 2010, J. P. Morgan Chase discontinued the Bear Stearns name. It was the end of a history that dated back to 1923.

In 1923, Joseph Bear, Robert Stearns and Harold Mayer started the firm Bear Stearns as an equity trading house. The firm prospered and survived the Wall Street Crash of 1929 without laying off any employees. In 1933 the firm started a corporate bond business under Cy Lewis, who later became the firm's leader. In 1955 Bear Stearns opened its first international office in Amsterdam. By 1985, when Bear Stearns became a publicly traded company, it was a fully-fledged investment bank with headquarters in Manhattan at 383 Madison Avenue.

■ Recent history

Bear Stearns was the smallest of the five main US investment banks, employing over 15,000 people. It was well known for its aggressive style. Unlike commercial banks, investment banks do not have depositors' funds to use. For many years Bear Stearns, like their main rivals in their segment of the banking business, largely financed their highly leveraged operations by means of short-term borrowing – either in unsecured commercial paper or in the overnight repo market, most recently secured by mortgage-related assets (for definitions see Glossary). If the market value of these assets fell, lenders would require more collateral. Each of the US investment banks was potentially vulnerable to a short-term funding crisis. This means that maintaining their reputation and the confidence of lenders was extremely important. Up to 2007, Bear Stearns seems to have managed to achieve this with post-tax profits coming in at USD1.4 billion in 2004, USD1.5 billion in 2005 and as much as USD2.1 billion in 2006.

In June 2007, two highly-leveraged hedge funds run by Bear Stearns Asset Management were having trouble meeting margin calls for increased collateral. These two funds were the High Grade Structured Credit Strategies Fund and the Enhanced Leverage Fund. They had largely invested in CDOs and their liquidity was falling fast. On 22 June, 2007, Bear Stearns pledged a collateralised loan of up to USD3.2 billion to bail out the High Grade Structured Credit Fund, while negotiating with other banks to loan money against collateral to the Enhanced Leverage Fund. The Bear Stearns CEO was hesitant about this bailout and was very worried about the damage to the company's reputation. At the same time, Merrill Lynch, with USD850 million worth of similar collateral, was only able to auction USD100 million of it. There was cause for concern. Would Bear Stearns have to liquidate more of its CDOs? Would a mark-down of similar assets in other portfolios follow? Would CDO contagion run through already bombed out markets? Would these markets seize up completely? As a result, the two funds had to suspend subscriptions and redemptions.

On 17 July 2007, Bear Stearns disclosed that the two funds had lost virtually all of their value driven by a decline in the CDO market. Although Bear Stearns itself was not legally liable, it had provided assets to bail out the two funds. Bear Sterns fired the manager of the funds, Ralph Cioffi. He protested there had been no default on the funds' underlying investments. However, where confidence is crucial, securities need not actually default to lose value and their market price had bombed. On 1 August 2007, the Co-President of Bear Stearns, Warren Spector, who had ultimate responsibility for the hedge funds, was also fired.

At about this time, the Securities and Exchange Committee announced an inquiry into Bear Stearns. The firm had USD525 billion in assets but only USD12 billion in equity, a leverage ratio of 44 times. These problems affected the firm's share price. It had stood at USD143 on 2 July 2007, but was down to USD106 by 3 August 2007 when Standard and Poor's announced it was changing its outlook on Bear Stearns from stable to negative. In early December the shares were still trading at over USD100.

In June 2008, Ralph Cioffi and his colleague, Matthew Tannin, were arrested on criminal charges including securities fraud. The core of the case was the extent to which fund managers could legitimately put a positive spin on bad news. In November 2009, a jury found Cioffi and Tannin not guilty on all charges. Their acquittal was a serious setback for the US prosecuting authorities.

■ Into the abyss

On 8 January 2008, Bear Stearns declared a loss of USD857 million, the first quarterly loss in its 85-year history. Standard and Poor's promptly downgraded the firm's credit rating from AA to A. By now the shares were down to USD76 per share. The 73-year-old Jimmy Cayne, who personally owned just under five per cent of the firm (now worth nearly USD500 million), resigned as CEO after 14 years, though he remained as non-executive chairman of the board. Alan Schwartz became the new CEO.

On 14 February 2008, UBS, the largest Swiss bank, reported a fourth quarter loss of USD11.3 billion after writing off USD13.7 billion on US mortgages. UBS had lost USD2 billion on Alt-A mortgages on which it had a further USD26.6 billion of exposure. By writing down the value of its Alt-A mortgages, UBS set an example which other banks followed in valuing downwards similar mortgages on their own books. Since these were used as collateral for short-term borrowings, if their value was reduced, lenders were likely to make margin calls for cash or ask for more collateral. Bear Stearns, whose equity was then quoted at USD93 per share, held USD6 billion of such loans. Lehman Brothers held USD15 billion.

On 29 February 2008, a small hedge fund called Peloton Partners went bust. It had received the award of hedge fund of the year in 2007. As a result, there was a huge sell-off of high-quality securities at low prices. Mark-to-market accounting rules, at that time, forced companies to recognise unrealised book losses even on assets which they intended to hold to maturity and to use the latest market prices to do so, even in highly distressed markets. So, like others in the same boat, Bear Stearns would have to recognise large unrealised losses in its first quarter results, due on 20 March 2008.

On 5 March 2008, the Carlyle Capital Group, a USD22 billion hedge fund, was having trouble meeting margin calls in Amsterdam. The hedge fund was controlled by, and 15 per cent owned by, the Carlyle Group, a large private equity firm. The margin calls arose from the hedge fund's large holdings in residential mortgage-backed securities that were becoming increasingly hard to value. What hard to value generally means is that there is no market at all in the security. By 7 March 2008, trading in the hedge fund's shares was suspended and by 16 March 2008, it had been forced into compulsory liquidation. These things can happen very quickly.

On Friday 7 March 2008 the Federal Reserve Bank, the US central bank, announced that, 'to address heightened liquidity pressures' it would inject up to USD200 billion into the banking system by offering one month loans of cash at low interest rates and allowing banks to pledge CDOs, CDSs and MBSs as collateral.

On Monday 10 March 2008, the Office of the Comptroller of the Currency called banks it supervised, asking about their exposure to Bear Stearns. This was a big blow to confidence. Moody's downgraded various mortgage bonds underwritten by Bear Stearns and Bear's shares fell by 11 per cent to USD62.30. The cost of credit insurance on Bear Stearns debt rose to 7 per cent per annum. Not a good sign.

On Tuesday 11 March 2008, the Federal Reserve agreed to make USD200 billion in government securities available as from 27 March to securities firms for a period of 28 days. Until now this facility had only been on an overnight basis. This was in addition to the measures of the previous Friday. In effect, the Fed was offering temporarily to swap risky toxic assets for safe Treasury securities. The Fed had not done anything like this since the Great Depression. The news unnerved the markets, the general feeling being that the Fed must be very worried about Bear Stearns.

Thursday 13 March 2008, was a very difficult day. In the morning Alan Schwartz, Bear's CEO, talked to Tim Geithner, the President of the Federal Reserve Bank of New York, about finding a potential buyer for the firm. All through the day trading partners withdrew funds, with a devastating effect on liquidity. By the end of the afternoon, Bear Stearns had run out of cash. On Thursday night and into early Friday morning there were discussions between Ben Bernanke, the Chairman of the Federal Reserve, Tim Geithner, President of the Federal Reserve Bank of New York, Hank Paulson, Secretary of the Treasury and Christopher Cox, CEO of the SEC. They were worried that since Bear Stearns was counterparty to trillions of dollars of swaps, if the firm declared bankruptcy it could trigger serious instability in global financial markets. To avoid the potential panic and probable meltdown, they eventually announced a deal whereby the Fed (aided by the government) would supply

USD30 billion to J. P. Morgan Chase to help finance Bear Stearns for an initial period of up to 28 days. Being an investment bank, Bear Stearns did not have access to the Federal Reserve's lender of last resort facilities. At the time, it was hoped that this might give it a much-needed breathing space. But it was not to be.

When the US markets opened on Friday 14 March 2008, at first the Bear Sterns share price rose by about 10 per cent to USD64. But this soon changed, and by 10.30 am the price had more than halved to only USD30. Bear Stearns announced it would bring forward the report of its first quarter results to Monday 17 March 2008. But to no avail. Credit rating agencies reduced their view on Bear Stearns. Standard and Poor's downgraded by three levels, to BBB. By the end of the day, funds had drained away and it was clear the firm could not survive the weekend.

■ J. P. Morgan to the rescue

Indeed, over the weekend there were intensive talks. The outcome was an offer from J. P. Morgan Chase to buy Bear Stearns for USD2 per share, a huge reduction from Friday's closing price. The New York Federal Reserve Bank was to provide USD30 billion of funding. On the Sunday afternoon, the Fed also announced that, starting the next day, it would be opening the discount window to securities firms directly by which they would provide funds against security – and the quality of security need not be AAA. But this was too late to save Bear Stearns.

J. P. Morgan Chase agreed to indemnify each current and former director and officer of Bear Stearns from liability for anything arising prior to the completion of the merger. This was important to the managers. The top management of Bear Stearns had to consider their 14,000 employees and their USD70 billion of loan creditors as well as their shareholders. The board agreed to the USD2 a share offer, but the deal was also subject to shareholder approval. With plenty of overlap between the two firms, many of Bear Stearns' employees could expect to lose their jobs over the course of the next few months.

The loan creditors would be protected if J. P. Morgan were to take over Bear Stearns and guarantee their debt. If Bear Stearns opted for bankruptcy they would lose heavily as the assets, when liquidated, would not realise anything like their face value.

From the shareholders' point of view, voting against the takeover might give them a chance of a higher price. But that would be what the press called a 'nuclear card', since bankruptcy could topple the whole financial system. This nuclear card put the shareholders in a stronger bargaining position than had been apparent over the weekend.

On the Monday morning, 17 March 2008, the bondholders in Bear Stearns were buying Bear Sterns shares in order to become shareholders themselves and to try to ensure a positive vote on the takeover. Any agreed price, even as low as USD2 per share, would suit them fine. J. P. Morgan Chase too was buying Bear Stearns shares, since it turned out that their guarantee, as worded, left them dangerously exposed to a continuing liability even if the deal did not go through. Bear Stearns' shares traded at USD3.50 on the Monday morning and closed the day of 17 March 2008 at USD4.81 per share – even though the official J. P. Morgan Chase offer was only USD2.00 per share. On the Tuesday morning the shares traded as high as USD8, and closed on Thursday 20 March at just under USD6. The following day – Good Friday – was a bank holiday.

The final offer, agreed over the Easter holiday weekend (21 to 24 March 2008), was USD10 per share. J. P. Morgan Chase, which had originally offered USD290 million for the equity ended up paying USD1.45 billion. Bear Sterns was one of the early failures in the financial crisis and things were going to get worse. For a very good overview of the failure of Bear Stearns, see William D. Cohan's book, *House of Cards*[4].

Case 12.2   Lehman Brothers

■ Introduction

Lehman Brothers was a global investment bank which declared bankruptcy in 2008. The firm's worldwide headquarters were in New York with regional bases in London, Tokyo and offices located throughout the world.

In 1844, the 23-year-old Henry Lehman, the son of a Jewish cattle merchant, emigrated from Germany to the USA. He settled in Montgomery, Alabama, and he opened a dry-goods store. In 1847, with the arrival of his brother Emanuel Lehman, the firm adopted the name H. Lehman and Bro. And with the subsequent arrival of their youngest brother, Mayer Lehman, in 1850, the firm adopted the name Lehman Brothers.

In the decade following, cotton was a growing and important crop in the USA. The Lehman brothers were enterprising. They began to accept raw cotton from customers as payment for goods. And this led to a second business trading in cotton. Within a few years this part of the business became the most significant part of Lehman Brothers.

In 1858, the firm moved to Manhattan in New York City. Lehman Brothers helped found the New York Cotton Exchange, became a member of the Coffee Exchange and, in 1887, became a member of the New York Stock Exchange. Among the companies Lehman brought to the stockmarket in the early 20th century were Sears Roebuck, F. W. Woolworth and Studebaker.

Traditionally a family firm, Philip Lehman, its head in 1924 opened it up to non-family as top managers. On the retirement of Philip Lehman in 1925, Bobbie Lehman led the firm through the 1920s and it weathered the Great Depression of the thirties. The firm focused on start-up capital and helped finance the new film industry and the growing oil industry. In the 1950s, Lehman underwrote the stock exchange offering of Digital Equipment Corporation, the leading player in the minicomputer market throughout the 1960s and 1970s. Bobbie Lehman died in 1969 and left the firm with no clear succession plans.

In 1977 the firm merged with Kuhn Loeb to form the fourth largest investment bank in the USA. In 1984 it was taken over by Shearson/American Express which, four years later, purchased E. F. Hutton. Shearson Lehman Hutton made leveraged finance and venture capital a strong part of its portfolio.

In 1994 the management of American Express, its holding company, decided to divest itself of Lehman Brothers Kuhn Loeb which was floated on the stock exchange as Lehman Brothers Holdings Inc., with Richard (Dick) Fuld as CEO.

Beginning with USD2 billion in assets under management, the firm made various acquisitions and grew organically. Prior to its bankruptcy, the firm was reported to have had in excess of USD275 billion in assets under management. Altogether, since going public in 1994, the firm had increased net revenues over 603 per cent from USD2.73 billion to USD19.2 billion and it had increased employee headcount by 236 per cent from 8,500 to 28,600. Reported profit after tax from 2003 through 2007 totalled USD16 billion, growing from USD1.7 billion in 2003 to USD4.2 billion in 2007. At the operating income level, reported profit grew from USD2.5 billion in 2003 and reached USD6.0 billion in 2007.

■ Bankruptcy

Lehman Brothers filed for bankruptcy protection on 15 September, 2008. This is the largest bankruptcy in US history, with Lehman holding over USD600 billion in assets. So how did it come about?

Like many of its rival investment banks, Lehmans had borrowed vast amounts to fund its investing in the years leading to 2008. A big portion of this was in property and housing-related assets. It was vulnerable to even a small downturn in the market. Lehman had leverage. And it had leverage in spades. Its ratio of assets to shareholders' equity had increased from 24 to 1 in 2003 reaching 31 to 1 by 2007. High leverage generates tremendous profits growth during the boom, but it creates tremendous problems when profits head south. Lehman's leverage meant that a mere 3.23 per cent decline in the value of its assets would wipe out entirely the value of shareholders' equity.

It is worth remembering that investment banks were not subject to the same prudential regulation as commercial banks. And it is also worth recalling that, like most investment banks it depended upon constantly renewing very short-term borrowings.

In fact, in August 2007, Lehman closed its subprime lender, BNC Mortgage, eliminating 1,200 jobs in 23 locations and taking a USD25 million after-tax charge and a USD27 million reduction in goodwill in so doing. This was, of course, a response to the weakening property market. But there was worse to come. Lehman was holding toxic assets galore. It had begun with subprime mortgage loans and it had escalated into collateralised debt obligations and credit default swaps. It had far too much subprime and other lower-rated mortgage tranches. Huge losses were accruing in lower-rated mortgage-backed securities throughout 2008. In its second quarter of 2008, Lehman reported losses of USD2.8 billion as it sold off USD6 billion of toxic assets. In the first half of 2008, Lehman's share price lost 73 per cent of its value as the housing market continued to worsen. In August 2008, Lehman indicated its intention to lay off 6 per cent of its workforce, 1,500 people.

Throughout 2008, Dick Fuld complained about short selling of his firm's shares. In particular, David Einhorn, founder of the hedge fund Greenlight Capital, had publicly criticised Lehman's accounting, while aggressively short selling its stock.

Lehman shares shot up later in the month. On 22 August 2008 they closed up 5 per cent and recorded a 16 per cent jump due to reports that the state-controlled Korea Development Bank was considering buying the firm. Gains were rapidly eroded on news that Korea Development Bank was having difficulties meeting its regulators requests and attracting partners for the deal. On 9 September 2008 it was reported that the Korean bank had put talks on hold. Lehman shares ended the day down 45 per cent to USD7.79 per share. US share indices were down around 3½ per cent on the day.

Next day, Wednesday 10 September 2008, Lehman announced a loss of USD3.9 billion for the third quarter and its intent to sell off an interest in its investment management business and a plan to float on the stockmarket USD30 billion of real estate assets. Of course, there were big doubts about property valuations at the time and the plan seemed less than credible to most investors. There was also a dividend cut from 68 cents per share to 5 cents per share to save USD450 million. Shareholders smelt a rat. Lehman's shares dropped 7 per cent on the day.

On Thursday 11 September 2008, it was obvious that the radical plan to save the bank was unlikely to work. The share price fell a further 40 per cent, to close at USD4.21 per share. On Friday, the share price closed down again, at USD3.65 per share. This was 2 per cent of their one-time peak of USD180 per share.

On Friday 12 September 2008, the US government tried to organise a private sector rescue of Lehman. But the government itself would not provide the financial support to maintain the firm as a going concern. Bank of America reckoned it would need USD65 billion of government support to enable it to acquire Lehman. If government support were not forthcoming, it appeared that Bank of America would pursue the acquisition of Merrill Lynch, the financial position of which also seemed precarious. The deal was to be via a USD50 billion share swap valuing Merrill Lynch at USD29 per share, much higher than its closing price of USD17 per share.

Barclays, the UK bank, was also in talks with Lehman Brothers. But it was unwilling to go ahead without some government support. Moreover, its British regulator, the FSA, refused to waive the requirement to get takeover approval from its shareholders, which would take time. Barclays was keen to acquire some of Lehman's US interests in investment banking, fixed income, equity and trading, research and certain support functions – but not the investment management arm or the real estate holdings.

On the weekend beginning 13 September 2008, Tim Geithner, then president of the Federal Reserve Bank of New York, called a meeting on the future of Lehman. This included possible liquidation of its assets. Lehman indicated that it had been in talks with both Bank of America and Barclays for its possible sale. It appears that Barclays interest stalled when it was vetoed by the Bank of England and the Financial Services Authority. But it revived after the weekend.

On Monday 15 September 2008, Lehman filed for bankruptcy, which the Court approved on Friday of the same week. With assets of USD639 billion, it was the largest bankruptcy in US history. The firm had about 24,000 employees (5,000 in the UK). It transpired that Lehman had about 3,000 legal entities globally – more than 100 in Luxembourg alone. The firm was reckoned to have 1.2 million derivatives contracts with a face value of USD6 trillion. Many of Lehman's counterparties were outside the USA.

On television screens all round the world, Monday 15 September 2008 brought pictures of Lehman employees leaving the office at 745 Seventh Avenue with boxes of personal possessions. Images continued being broadcast throughout the day and again on Tuesday. Lehman shares fell by over 90 per cent on 15 September 2008 and the Dow Jones index fell by 5 per cent.

On Tuesday 16 September 2008, Barclays announced that it would acquire a stripped clean portion of Lehman for USD1.75 billion which included the North American assets that they wanted plus the office building. Nomura acquired the European, Asia and Middle-East businesses of Lehman's. On September 17 2008, the New York Stock Exchange delisted Lehman Brothers. Alarm over counterparty risk on Lehman's 1.2 million derivative contracts turned to panic. Markets were guessing which banks would be likely to be hurt – and, maybe, wiped out – by counterparty failure. Panic and fear combined to paralyse money markets. Bank A did not wish to lend to bank B because of the fear that bank B would be likely to fail as a result of its exposure to Lehman Brothers. This became a feature of markets in the latter half of September 2008.

Lehman's collapse was the event that signalled a very serious crisis. Indeed it triggered a global panic. The opaqueness of mortgage-backed securities and credit default swaps made it impossible for banks to tell how much other banks had invested in toxic loans or what their losses might be. Hedge funds in New York and London found their assets frozen. Around the globe banks were not prepared to lend to other banks. The inter-bank lending market almost completely dried up and there was a huge contraction in credit. This was the credit crunch. Stock markets went into meltdown, wiping USD600 billion off equity values.

After the event, the question arose, was it a mistake for the US government to let Lehman go bust? US government agencies professed to be conscious of the danger of systemic breakdown, but almost certainly misjudged its gravity. Tim Geithner, President of the Federal Reserve Bank of New York, was reputed to have said that central banks do liquidity, they don't do insolvency.

There are major lessons to be learned from the Lehman story. First of all, Lehman was running massive risk to achieve its returns. At the point of its failure, the firm had a balance sheet with USD613 billion in debts and USD639 billion in assets. Of these assets, property accounted for USD43 billion – maybe more. The point that we have made earlier about leverage is reinforced.

Repo 105

It appears, however, that Lehman's had been using an accounting device in its published figures to reduce its reported level of leverage. This was revealed in the 2,200 page report of Anton Valukas, appointed by a US court to examine Lehman's failure. Mr Valukas' report begins on a high point – Lehman's biggest profit in its 158-year history, its 2007 reported annual profit after tax of USD4 billion. At the centre of the accounting ruse was Repo 105. This was used from 2001 onwards according to the Valukas report and, as the lengthy document reveals, it started as 'a lazy way of managing the balance sheet' but it became crucial as the bank tried to survive the financial crisis. At the end of each quarter, Lehman sold some of its loans and investments temporarily to other financial institutions for cash using a short-term repurchase agreement – or repo – and then bought them back a few days later.

Normally the assets would still be included on the bank's balance sheet but, because they were valued at 105 per cent or more of the cash received, the transactions counted as a sale under accounting rules and Lehman was able to report a less risky balance sheet with lower leverage.

The bank stuck roughly to a limit of USD25 billion using Repo 105 until early 2007. But the investment bank increased its use in the first and second quarters of 2008 when Lehman was hiding USD50 billion of assets from investors, the government, rating agencies and regulators. Lehman was reporting its reduced leverage as it told shareholders of its massive USD2.8 billion second-quarter loss without revealing that it had bought the assets back once its books were signed off. Lehman also used a similar device – called Repo 108 – which works exactly like the 105 device but involved a different percentage on the deal.

Essentially the accounting trick involves reducing balance sheet liabilities (debt) and, at the same time, reducing balance sheet assets. The effect of this is that if debt and assets are reduced, the net effect is to lower the level of leverage and make the financial position of the firm look less risky.

The auditors, Ernst and Young, knew about Repo 105 and were aware that the bank was using the accounting trick. The Ernst and Young partner responsible for the Lehman audit told Mr Valukas his firm did not 'approve' Repo 105 but 'became comfortable with the policy for purposes of auditing financial statements'.

Mr Valukas concluded that there was a potential case against Ernst and Young for malpractice for alleged 'failure to question and challenge improper disclosures' by Lehman. It seems that about USD50 billion of assets were hidden from investors at the last use of the device.

The Valukas investigation also seemed to indicate that there might be grounds for claims against Dick Fuld, the bank's chief executive, and three of Lehman's former finance directors for allowing the filing of financial statements that omitted or misrepresented the Repo 105 activities and for failing to tell the bank's directors about the gimmick. The report said that Mr Fuld was told in June 2008 by Bart McDale, Lehman's chief operating officer, that the bank relied too heavily on Repo 105. However, it does seem that Repo 105 was a legitimate accounting tool. The argument that the device was in accordance with accounting rules and that the auditors recognised the presentation as being acceptable would lead to the possible conclusion that Lehman's directors were not at fault. Press Cuttings 12.1 and 12.2 relate to Repo 105.

Press cutting 12.1   *Financial Tiimes*, 12 March 2010   **FT**

Valukas report finds few heroes

Justin Baer and Henny Sender in New York

Anton Valukas's 2,200-page report to the bankruptcy court on Lehman Brothers will not be the first account of the legendary securities firm's demise to captivate Wall Street.

For the many Lehman creditors with millions of dollars in claims at stake, his may be the only one that counts.

The examiner earlier this year submitted his report to the court, where it remained sealed until many of the key players agreed to release their rights to keep aspects of the document confidential.

In Mr Valukas's grim synopsis of Lehman's final days, there are few heroes and numerous alleged culprits.

'There are many reasons Lehman failed, and the responsibility is shared,' Mr Valukas wrote in his report, which was made public by the court on Thursday. 'Lehman was more the consequence than the cause of a deteriorating economic climate.'

Mr Valukas took aim at many of Lehman's leaders, including Dick Fuld, the firm's long-time chief executive, and former finance chiefs Chris O'Meara, Erin Callan and Ian Lowitt, and alleged he found colorable claims, or instances where there is enough credible evidence to support a claim, against each of the executives.

In his report, Mr Valukas claimed that Lehman's financial plight 'was exacerbated by Lehman executives, whose conduct ranged from serious but non-culpable errors of business judgment to actionable balance sheet manipulation; by the investment bank business model, which rewarded excessive risk taking and leverage; and by government agencies, who by their own admission might better have anticipated or mitigated the outcome.'

By the time Lehman imploded, $25bn in capital was supporting $700bn of assets and liabilities, a leverage ratio that was regarded as extremely high. In an effort to maintain favourable ratings from the rating agencies, Lehman engaged in what was referred to internally as Repo 105, a sort of window dressing which involved getting $50bn of assets off the firm's balance sheet at the end of both the 2008 first- and second-quarter balance sheets. The examiner quotes a Lehman executive saying, 'there was no substance to the transactions'.

The examiner alleged: 'Lehman did not disclose, however, that it had been using an accounting device (known within Lehman as "Repo 105") to manage its balance sheet – by temporarily removing approximately $50bn of assets from the balance sheet at the end of the first and second quarters of 2008.'

The examiner also alleged that a 'limited amount of assets' were 'improperly transferred' to Barclays, the UK bank that acquired Lehman's US brokerage business following the collapse.

Barclays declined to comment.

In a statement, Mr Fuld's attorney, Patricia Hynes, of Allen & Overy, said:

'The examiner believes the Lehman estate has a colorable claim against Dick Fuld because Lehman did not provide enhanced disclosures about certain financing arrangements called Repo 105 transactions.

'Mr Fuld did not know what those transactions were – he didn't structure or negotiate them, nor was he aware of their accounting treatment. Furthermore, the evidence available to the Examiner shows that the Repo 105 transactions were done in accordance with an internal accounting policy, supported by legal opinions and approved by Ernst & Young, Lehman's independent outside auditor. At no time did Lehman's senior financial officers, legal counsel or Ernst & Young raise any concerns about the use of Repo 105 with Mr Fuld who throughout his career faithfully and diligently worked in the interests of Lehman and its stakeholders.'

'In the three months during which he held the job, Mr Lowitt worked diligently and faithfully to discharge all of his duties as Lehman's CFO,' according to a statement from Mr Lowitt's lawyer. 'Any suggestion that Mr Lowitt breached his fiduciary duties is baseless.'

Mr O'Meara could not be reached for comment. A lawyer representing Ms Callan declined to comment.

In addition, the examiner's report reiterates allegations that shortly after Lehman raised $6bn in a public offer in early June, Hank Paulson, then Treasury secretary, warned Mr Fuld that if Lehman reported further losses in the third quarter, without having a buyer or a definitive survival plan in place, Lehman's existence would be in jeopardy.

Press cutting 12.2   *Financial Times*, 16 March 2010   **FT**

Global harmony a distant prospect despite Lehman outrage

Gillian Tett

Anton Valukas's 2,200 page report on the demise of Lehman Brothers has provoked outrage among many investors and politicians.

Among some senior American and European bankers, however, the main reaction has been a wince – or a groan.

For while the revelations about Lehman's use of accounting and regulatory tricks might startle many non-bankers, one dirty secret that hangs over the industry is that the type of cross-border games at Lehman were simply an (arguably) extreme version of what has occurred at many other companies.

And the dirtier secret still – and one that should cause some politicians to hang their heads – is that these games are unlikely to disappear.

For the conditions which gave rise to the type of cross-border arbitrage that Lehman exploited – namely a fragmented global regulatory and accounting regime – do not seem to be on their way out. On the contrary, on current trends this fragmentation may soon increase. And that not only defies common sense, but flies in the face of one of the most basic lessons of the Lehman report.

One of the juiciest details in the report by Mr Valukas, the court-appointed

→

examiner, is the description of how Lehman used a device dubbed 'Repo 105', a type of repo transaction which allowed the bank to reduce apparent leverage.

This was apparently deemed legal by the UK offices of Linklaters, and was thus widely used by Lehman, even though some lawyers question its validity under US law.

What drove Repo 105, in other words, was a form of 'forum shopping'. And on the face of it, this situation suggests that there is now an urgent need for global financial leaders to close this type of loophole, by introducing more harmony between accounting rules and banking laws in Europe and the US (or, at the very least, between London and New York).

A year ago, most financial bureaucrats appeared determined to do just that. Most notably, during early 2009 a plethora of committees linked to the Basel group – the global body that unites supervisors and central bankers – were working hard to produce unified banking reforms supposed to prevent the use of tricks such as Repo 105.

Back then, efforts were also underway in the accounting industry to introduce more transatlantic harmony, between the US system (which revolves around generally accepted accounting principles) and that used in Europe (centred on International Financial Reporting Standards).

But in recent months, this drive by western bureaucrats to introduce more global harmony in the financial system has been repeatedly undercut by national politics – with the result that fragmentation, not harmonisation, is becoming the new order of the day.

In the US, for example, the chief accounting body has unilaterally changed the way that American banks account for toxic assets – setting those banks at odds with Europe, yet again. Meanwhile, in the banking world, national politicians have unveiled unilateral measures which have also undermined the Basel initiatives. Just look, for example, at the proposals by Paul Volcker, an adviser to the Obama administration, on proprietary trading, which – yet again – also seem likely to put the US on a different track to Europe.

Now, it is possible that this unilateralism will turn out to be short-lived, and that common sense will eventually triumph; it is also likely that, in the short term, many bankers will be circumspect about exploiting all the existing cross-border loopholes (or those which may soon be created as a result of this unilateralism).

But don't bet on that restraint lasting for ever; once the current hullabaloo dies down, it is a fair bet that profit-hungry or desperate financiers will start sniffing around again for new areas of regulatory arbitrage.

So, if politicians want to fix the fundamental problems revealed by the Lehman report, it will not be enough to bash the bankers, brainwash them or lock them up; nor will it be enough to simply give the regulators sharper teeth. What is really needed, above all else, is a new drive for harmonisation. Whether that happens, however, is still anyone's guess.

■ Property

It is also interesting to note that Lehman Brothers was committing big amounts in loans and equity in property companies. For example, Lehman invested USD2 billion in deals with Sun Cal, a Southern California developer which was responsible for the McAllister Ranch, a 6,000 home, multimillion dollar recreational community that now stands fenced off and unfinished – at the time of writing, a ghost estate. The remarkable thing about this kind of investment was that Lehman was already so deeply exposed to real estate via its subprime mortgage securities and investments plus its credit default swap positions based on pyramids of real property that one would have expected that someone in the bank would have been calling for a halt to further property exposure. 'High risk, high return' is an adage often heard. It should be remembered that it has an obverse. 'High risk, high chance of wipeout.'

■ The CEO

But it might have been difficult to say that to Lehman's CEO, Dick Fuld. New York born and bred, he had graduated from the University of Colorado and earned his MBA at NYU Stern School of Business. Joining Lehman aged 25, he was CEO on its stockmarket reappearance in 1994. Fuld was then aged 46. Since we have never met Dick Fuld we draw on a pen picture by Larry McDonald[5] who worked at Lehman Brothers. 'Quite simply, people were afraid of him ... And this was a fear based upon reputation, because through the years Fuld had fired many, many people, for a thousand different reasons ... There were secondhand accounts of his rages and threats. It was like hearing the life story of some caged lion ... Fuld lived in an enormous Greenwich mansion, over 9,000 square feet, valued at USD10 million. He had four other homes, including a mansion on Jupiter Island, one of Florida's garrisons of the big muckety-mucks in Hobe Sound, thirty miles north of Palm Beach. Dick picked it up five years previously for USD13.75 million ... He also owned a vast USD21 million Park Avenue apartment with three wood-burning fireplaces, and a spectacular ski chalet near Sun Valley, Idaho. His art collection was valued at USD200 million, including a collection of postwar and contemporary drawings worth tens of millions, one of them by Jackson Pollock.' He was well paid too. Lehman's accounts record USD34 million in 2007 and USD40.5 million in 2006 – almost USD500 million in total from 1993 to 2007. Yes, it might have been difficult to suggest to Mr Fuld that Lehman Brothers was pursuing too risky a strategy.

To round off this piece on Lehman Brothers, may we quote from a *Washington Post* article by Allan Sloan and Roddy Boyd[6]. They observe that 'it's tempting to blame Fuld for everything that's gone wrong at Lehman. After all, the man took credit for the firm's successes (while throwing the occasional victim under the bus when there were problems), and got a corporate rock star compensation package. By Fortune's math, Fuld had realised almost a half-billion dollars in cash – USD489.7 million, to be precise – by cashing in stock options and restricted stock that he was granted. (That's a pre-tax number.) He's also knocked down wads of regular old money.' Dick Fuld's management style was aggressive but we think that the first item in parentheses in the above quote is a metaphor. Sloan and Boyd go on to say that 'a significant part of Lehman's problem doesn't stem from Fuld's management – it's because the firm suffered collateral damage from Washington's decision a decade ago to repeal the Glass-Steagall Act, adopted during the Great Depression to separate investment banking from commercial banking.' We think that this is irony. What do you think?

Press cutting 12.3   *Financial Times*, 22 December 2008   FT

Overpaid CEO award

Take your pick. The crop of entries for the inaugural Lex Overpaid CEO of the year award was richer than any could have dared imagine. The term 'rewards for failure' scarcely did justice to a broken model of executive compensation that brought the global financial system to within an ace of collapse. From Europe, Sir Fred Goodwin, ousted as chief executive of Royal Bank of Scotland in October, was a popular choice among readers, after taking home a total of £8.2m in 2007 and 2006. Ditto the bosses of the Icelandic banks: they managed to sink not just their own companies, but an entire country.

But their packages look positively stingy when compared to the payouts offered to the disgraced titans of the US financial sector. Daniel Mudd, who pocketed $23m for his last two years' service at Fannie Mae, and Dick Syron, paid $33m by Freddie Mac over the same period, were both stand-out candidates. They were the two men who arguably did most to stoke the housing bubble that pushed the world's largest economy into recession. Both men made enough to set up their descendants for generations. Then they threw the government-sponsored enterprises into the arms of the taxpayer.

In the end, though, there could only be one winner: Dick Fuld. The Lehman Brothers boss made many tens of millions of dollars in the years preceding the bank's collapse in September, an event that triggered an earthquake in global markets. His stubborn refusal to sell the bank when he had the chance was the single worst trade of the year. Picking up $34m in 2007 and $40.5m in 2006, (nodded through by Sir Christopher Gent, a member of the board's four-person compensation committee), he set a high standard for the 2009 award. All suggestions for shortlistable candidates for next year should be e-mailed to lex@ft.com or posted online at www.ft.com/overpaidceos.

Case 12.3 American International Group (AIG)

■ Introduction

AIG is the largest US writer of commercial and industrial insurance. Its history dates from 1919. Cornelius Vander Starr established his insurance business in Shanghai, China. The firm thrived until AIG was forced to leave China in 1949 as Mao Zedong's Communist People's Liberation Army advanced to Shanghai. Starr moved the AIG headquarters to New York. The company expanded into Europe, Asia, Latin America and the Middle East.

In 1962, Starr ceded management of AIG's US holdings to Maurice Greenberg (known as Hank) who moved AIG's focus from personal insurance to higher margin corporate business. Greenberg also moved to selling insurance via independent brokers rather than agents, thereby eliminating retainers. This emphasis positively impacted the income statement and Starr named Greenberg his successor in 1968 and AIG went public in 1969.

In 2005, AIG was the subject of a series of fraud investigations conducted by the Securities and Exchange Commission, the US Justice Department, and New York State Attorney. Greenberg was ousted midst this accounting scandal. The action led to a USD1.6 billion fine for AIG and criminal charges for some executives. Greenberg's successor as CEO was Martin J. Sullivan. And, during the financial crisis of June 2008, after disclosing losses and in the wake of a dramatically falling stock price, Sullivan resigned and was replaced by Robert B. Willumstad, Chairman of AIG from 2006. In his turn, Willumstad was forced out by the US government and was replaced by Edward M. Libby on 17 September 2008. At its peak, AIG had around USD1,000 billion of assets: it made profits of USD14 billion and employed over 100,000 people in 130 countries.

AIG's business of insurance is a fairly straightforward one. It competes in almost every class of insurance. Remarkably, because AIG executives saw the real estate downturn on the horizon, it withdrew from the business of offering insurance on bonds with a subprime exposure. This occurred in 2005. But its massive exposure to the 2007/8 crisis was not generated by its core operations. It was its Financial Products (FP) division which was responsible for AIG's fall from grace culminating in its bailout and resultant 79.9 per cent equity ownership by the US government. Because of this, we focus substantially on FP in the remainder of this section.

■ AIG Financial Products Corporation

FP was created in 1987, when a derivates expert, Howard Sosin, quit the investment bank Drexel Burnham Lambert three years in advance of its junk bond operation folding and filing for bankruptcy in 1990. Sosin sought a strong financial player with a high credit rating. He found Greenberg and AIG amenable to his ideas and took his team of 13 Drexel employees, including the 32-year-old Joseph Cassano, to the insurance giant. Dramatically, Cassano earned the sobriquet 'one of the ten most wanted culprits of the 2008 financial collapse' from a CNN journalist. What did Cassano do to earn such an epithet?

FP was essentially a hedge fund with many of its trades remunerated, as is the hedge fund practice, with a 38 per cent of profit bonus pool and with AIG getting the rest. The FP group argued that, with AIG's AAA credit rating, its cost of capital was lower than many competitors enabling it to take more risk. Moreover, AIG was an insurance company and was not subject to the same capital reserve ratio requirements as banks. That meant that AIG would need virtually no additional capital requirement when it insured super-senior debt, the very top tranche of debt – see Figure 5.1. Neither was FP likely to face tough questions from its regulators. In fact, it was regulated by the Office for Thrift Supervision (OFS). And OFS executives had limited training, exposure and expertise at the field of cutting-edge of derivative products.

To Greenberg, the triple AAA rating was sacrosanct. He realised that a hedge fund within AIG could endanger it if things went wrong. Greenberg formed a shadow group to study Sosin's financial deals so that they could readily be reverse engineered should problems ensue. This precipitated numerous disagreements and wrangling. Sosin viewed the tight control on FP as unjustified. Things came to a head in 1994 with Sosin's resignation and he took many other FP founders with him when he left. After his exit, Cassano became chief operating officer of FP and the division decamped to London where regulation was even less onerous.

Cassano was not the detailed quant finance man that was Sosin's specialism. Less innovative, less cutting-edge than Sosin, Cassano was a networker and an organiser. He became deeply interested in rival J. P. Morgan's new credit derivative product called the broad index secured trust offering (presumably to get the acronym Bistro). With banks taking hits to the income statement from bad debts in the 1997 Asian financial crisis, J. P. Morgan was looking for a way to reduce exposure to bad loans – as was Cassano's FP group.

The FP team concluded that J. P. Morgan's Bistro was, essentially, what we think of now as a credit default swap. They were right: that's what it was. Cassano liked the product. The FP group took the view that the chance of a tide of defaults occurring simultaneously was remote – except with another Great Depression. Therefore, the FP group concluded, holders of credit default swaps could anticipate millions of dollars a year of inflows – rather like insurance premiums – for relatively low risk. Cassano, who had become CEO of FP in 2001, took AIG into writing credit default swaps. In fact, J. P. Morgan offered FP its total super-senior risk book either via a form of purchase of securities or via signing credit derivative contracts. Cassano agreed. One wonders whether J. P. Morgan executives felt somewhat uneasy about their super-senior exposure. We have no answer to that question. Commenting on the event, Tett[7] describes this as a watershed event. She goes on to describe and simplify the deal thus: 'AIG would earn a relatively paltry fee for providing this service, of just 0.02 cents on the dollar each year. But, that said, if 0.02 cents are multiplied a few billion times, it adds up to an appreciable income stream, particularly if almost no reserves are required to cover the risk. Once again, the magic of derivatives had produced a "win-win" solution. Only many years later did it become clear that Cassano's trade set AIG on the path to near-ruin.' To move on the risk of the Bistro deal, the FP team sold on its super-senior risk to other insurance companies, banks and reinsurance companies.

Lobbying of the regulators by J. P. Morgan made these Bistro-style credit default swap instruments even more interesting. They convinced regulators that AAA credit default swaps (rated as such by a 'nationally recognised credit-rating agency') entailed less risk and therefore required fewer reserves to be held by banks to meet the exposure. The argument was bought by the Office of the Comptroller of the Currency (OCC) and the Federal Reserve Bank. The practical effect of this relaxation was that whilst banks had typically been forced to hold USD800 million reserves for every USD10 billion corporate loans on their books, that sum would now fall to USD160 million for AAA-rated credit default swaps. Tett[8] reports that 'some bankers started to joke that "Bistro" really stood for BIS Total Rip Off', referring to the Bank for International Settlements (BIS), which had overseen the Basel Accord.' The CDS business at AIG thrived – at least for a time. AIG's FP was the biggest player in credit default swaps and, of course, the traders bonuses were astronomical.

Like most CDS and CDO players, AIG was no exception in terms of failing to set aside an adequate fund of capital against potential losses. And, like many other CDS and CDO players, FP executives at AIG believed that their strategy was invulnerable – a win, win, win situation. Compared to its investment bank rivals in the CDS and CDO market, AIG was different. AIG was not an investment bank and not financing itself from short-term money markets. Indeed, AIG had relatively little debt and around USD40 billion in cash in hand. It seemed too big to fail. AIG was also different from its rivals in that it specialised in insuring super-senior debt, the very top tranche of debt.

By mid-2007 AIG was holding around USD560 billion of super-senior risk. This was a colossal figure and little known outside the firm. Tett[9] reports that when some of the J. P. Morgan Bistro team 'saw it they assumed it was a typo. "It's got to be fifty-six billion, hasn't it?" one asked'.

In the autumn of 2007, many banks' auditors were forcing them to write down their holdings of super-senior risk. At first, AIG refused to follow suit. But in February 2008, AIG was forced by its auditors to admit to a 'material weakness' in its accounts. AIG was then facing claims galore and it announced write-downs of super-senior assets of USD43 billion. Needless to say, Joseph Cassano departed the company.

Confidence in the CDS and CDO markets was deteriorating – and fast. The credit ratings agencies were downgrading billions and billions of dollars' worth of CDOs including those with AAA ratings – including, therefore, super-senior debt. In 2007 one its biggest counterparties, Goldman Sachs, demanded that AIG put up billions of dollars in collateral as required in the wording of its swaps contracts. AIG disclosed this dispute in November 2007.

The position progressively worsened through 2008. Practice in the swaps business enables highly-rated firms to enter into swaps without depositing collateral with their trading counterparties. (This is different to the reserves required under the Basel rules.) If the credit rating becomes significantly impaired or if large losses accrue to one of the swap counterparties then that firm is required, under the swap small print, to post collateral to make good the accrued losses. So, when (as described above) CDS and CDO ratings were downgraded and AIG's own credit rating became imperiled, the company was required to post additional collateral with trading counterparties. Despite unsuccessful attempts to raise funds, the liquidity crisis was clear.

AIG's problem was worsened because so many institutions were linked together through CDS deals. Lehman Brothers had more than USD700 billion worth of swaps, many backed by AIG. When mortgage-backed securities started to default, AIG had to make good on billions of dollars of credit default swaps. It became apparent that it could not cover its losses.

■ The end is nigh

As noted above, AIG's widespread underwriting of the CDS and CDO markets made it a backstop in the business. Banks and hedge funds were playing both sides of the CDS and CDO businesses. They were buying and trading them and making profits and losses in so doing. AIG was providing the initiating swaps and holding on to them. Had it been allowed to default, the many parties who had bought CDS contracts from AIG would have suffered vast losses in the value of the contracts they had purchased, causing them, in turn, to default. AIG was essentially, via the CDS market, underwriting so-called triple A debt. In traditional insurance, if one car driver crashes, it is not a harbinger of other drivers doing the same – there is no correlation. But with bond underwriting, with one default it may cause such a large loss for the underwriters that other bonds underwritten by them become riskier and are downgraded. In short, one of the problems with the CDS market is that it can readily precipitate a chain reaction of defaults.

If AIG were allowed to collapse it would have resulted in a domino effect in the banking, the insurance and reinsurance markets globally. It would have meant that great swathes of business that has to be insured, from aircraft and ships to lorries and cars, would have been immobilised. The argument that AIG was too big to fail was easily reached.

The US Federal Reserve Bank announced the creation of a secured credit facility of up to USD85 billion to prevent the company's collapse thus enabling AIG to meet its obligations to swap trading partners. The credit facility was secured on the stock of AIG-owned subsidiaries, and gave the Fed warrants for a 79.9 per cent equity stake in AIG and the right to demand suspension of dividends. The AIG board accepted the terms of the Fed's rescue package. This was the second largest government bailout of a company in US history, behind the bailout of Fannie Mae and Freddie Mac a week earlier.

AIG's share price had fallen by 95 per cent to just USD1.25 on 16 September 2008, from a 52-week peak of USD70.13. The company had reported losses of over USD13 billion for the first six months of the year. AIG confessed that its Financial Products division had entered into credit default swaps to insure USD441 billion worth of securities that had originally been rated AAA; USD57.8 billion of this represented structured debt securities backed by subprime loans. You now know why Cassano was called one of the ten most wanted culprits of the financial collapse. One wonders whether members of the board of directors of AIG were fully (or even partially) aware what was going on at FP. That would be an interesting story.

Another interesting little story by Iain Dey[10] appeared in the *Sunday Times* which suggested that 'conspiracy theorists have claimed that the business was only saved because its collapse could have tipped Goldman Sachs, the giant investment bank, towards the brink of financial disaster. About USD12.8 billion of the AIG rescue package was needed to meet contractual obligations to Goldman'. And Goldman wanted its pound of flesh.

From September to November 2008, AIG's credit default swap spreads were rising implying an increased risk of its failure. Since then, AIG has borrowed more to keep itself afloat and it has sold off various assets. At the time of writing, its CDS spreads have stabilised. It is estimated that the US government's total exposure to AIG hit USD152 billion but has since fallen, at the time of writing, to nearer USD120 billion and, of course, it remains 79.9 per cent government owned.

CASE 12.4 Fannie Mae and Freddie Mac

■ Introduction

The Federal National Mortgage Association (FNMA), commonly known as Fannie Mae, was established in 1938 as a mechanism to facilitate liquidity in the US mortgage market and provide greater access to low-income families in the ongoing grip of depression. It was part of Franklin D. Roosevelt's New Deal. In 1968, the government converted Fannie Mae into a private shareholder-owned corporation in order to remove its finances from the balance sheet of the federal budget.

The corporation's purpose is to purchase and securitise mortgages in order to ensure that funds are consistently available to the institutions that lend money to home buyers. Prior to 1968, Fannie Mae was the guarantor of government-issued mortgages but, following its privatisation, that responsibility passed to the newly-created Government National Mortgage Association, also known as Ginnie Mae for short. As a result, Fannie Mae ceased to be the guarantor of government-issued mortgages. In 1970, the US government created the Federal Home Loan Mortgage Corporation (FHLMC), known as Freddie Mac, to compete with Fannie Mae and facilitate a more robust and efficient secondary mortgage market. Since the creation of these government-sponsored enterprises (GSEs), there has been debate about their role in the mortgage market, their relationship with government, and whether or not they are necessary. This debate resurfaced during the collapse of the US housing market and subprime mortgage crisis of 2007. Despite this, Fannie Mae, Ginnie Mae and Freddie Mac have played a significant role in increasing home ownership rates in the US to among the highest in the world. All three became stock market quoted firms.

The role of the aforementioned GSEs is to buy mortgages in the secondary market, pool them, and sell them as mortgage-backed securities to investors on the open market. This secondary mortgage market tends to increase the supply of money available for mortgage lending and increase the money available for new home purchases.

Fannie Mae and Freddie Mac's primary method of making money is by charging a guarantee fee on loans that it has purchased and securitised into mortgage-backed security bonds. Investors, or purchasers of Fannie and Freddie MBS, are willing to let Fannie Mae and Freddie Mac charge a fee for assuming the credit risk – that is, Freddie Mac's guarantee that the principal and interest on the underlying loan will be paid back regardless of whether the borrower actually repays.

Fannie and Freddie may also securitise mortgages from their own loan portfolios and sell the resultant mortgage-backed security to investors in the secondary mortgage market, again with a guarantee that the stated principal and interest payments will be passed through to the investor on time. By purchasing the mortgages, Fannie Mae and Freddie Mac provide banks and other financial institutions with fresh money to make new loans, giving the US housing and credit markets ongoing liquidity. For Fannie and Freddie to provide their guarantee to mortgage-backed securities that they issue, they set guidelines for the loans that they will accept for purchase, called conforming loans – see Chapter 5. Mortgages that do not meet these guidelines are called non-conforming. The secondary market for non-conforming loans was traditionally in larger mortgages (termed jumbo) than the maximum mortgage that Fannie Mae and Freddie Mac would purchase. In 2008, the decision was made to allow eligible MBS to include up to 10 per cent jumbo mortgages.

■ Mortgage securitisation

In fact, the process of mortgage securitisation began with Ginnie Mae. In 1970, it issued an innovative bond known as a residential mortgage-backed security (RMBS). Put simply, a bond is a piece of paper (or, as it is sometimes called, a note) that promises its holder or bearer (originally the lender) a series of interest payments over a specified period plus full repayment of principal at an agreed date. It can be argued that any entity that generates a fairly predictable set of cash flows could issue a bond. Prior to 1970, the main issuers were governments and companies. Ginnie Mae's innovation was to take a number of mortgages, pool the monthly payments generated, and use the cash flow to back the bond. Assuming that most home-owners keep up their monthly payments, it would not matter too much if a few defaulted. There should still be enough money coming in to pay bondholders the interest due to them. Note that individual home loans underpinning these mortgage bonds were government-guaranteed. So the credit risk attached to them is greatly reduced. They received high credit ratings, and they paid an interest rate slightly above that for Treasury bonds. These mortgage bonds proved popular with institutional investors, such as pension funds. Given the success of Ginnie Mae's innovation, Fannie Mae and Freddie Mac followed suit and the mortgage bond market expanded rapidly. With the principle of securitisation established, Wall Street firms sought other cash flows that could be packaged into saleable bonds. In 1977, Salomon Brothers and Bank of America managed the first securitisation of home loans that were not government-guaranteed. And new securitised products followed.

In 1983, Freddie Mac issued the first collateralised mortgage obligation (CMO). This was a bond mutual fund in which the cash flows from a pool of mortgages and mortgage-backed securities were split into a number of different layers, or tranches. Purchasers of senior tranches obtained first claim on the underlying cash flows. Buyers of the mezzanine tranches were next in line. Holders of the junior tranches were entitled to what was left. In 1985, Sperry Lease Finance Corporation issued the first asset-backed security (ABS) when it issued bonds backed by the cash flows from a pool of computer equipment leases. Nowadays, the process has been carried much further. Sports businesses, such as soccer and baseball clubs, have issued bonds backed by the cash flows arising from future season ticket sales.

The evolution of a secondary market in mortgages and other types of credits led banks to sell on many of the loans they held on their books – from private equity loans to credit card debt. The originate-to-hold model of banking was being replaced by the originate-to-distribute model. But it was the GSEs that had let the genie out of the bottle.

■ Political pressure

Unfortunately, Fannie and Freddie's business model came under political pressure. Fannie and Freddie were underwriting over one half of all US mortgages. In 1999, the Clinton administration set itself the task of expanding mortgage loans to low- and moderate-income borrowers. This was to be achieved by increasing the ratios of lender portfolios in distressed inner city areas designated in the Community Reinvestment Act of 1977 – see Chapter 5. Lobbyists and politicians pressed Fannie and Freddie to ease credit requirements for mortgages and to make loans to subprime borrowers at interest rates which would be higher than for conventional loans. It seemed that some shareholders were also in favour of this because it seemed to increase potential profit streams. Of course, it might also increase bad debts.

The argument was that Fannie and Freddie's underwriting standards for conforming mortgages would provide safe and stable cash flows which should enable them to lend to buyers who did not have prime credit. Fannie and Freddie succumbed somewhat but argued that their underwriting standards for prime loans would have to be brought to the subprime market. But political pressure continued, using the drip by drip mode of influence.

In 1999, Steven A. Holmes in the *New York Times* reported that with the move by Fannie Mae towards the subprime market, it was taking on significantly more risk, which might not pose any difficulties during flush economic times. But the government-subsidised corporation might run into trouble in an economic downturn, prompting a government rescue similar to that of the savings and loan industry in the 1980s. Alex Berenson of the *New York Times* reported in 2003 that Fannie Mae's risk was becoming much larger than commonly believed.

In 2002, President George W. Bush signed the Single-Family Affordable Housing Tax Credit Act, dubbed 'Renewing the Dream'. The programme would give around USD2.4 billion in tax credits over the next five years to investors and builders to develop affordable single-family housing in distressed areas. All of this was stoking up trouble for Fannie and Freddie.

In September 2003, the Bush Administration recommended what it called the most significant regulatory overhaul in the housing finance industry since the savings and loan crisis. Under its plan, a new agency would be created within the Treasury Department to assume supervision of Fannie and Freddie. The new agency would have the authority to set capital reserve requirements for the companies and to determine whether they were adequately managing the risks of their portfolios.

On 16 December 2003, President George W. Bush signed the American Dream Downpayment Act, a new programme that provided grants to help home buyers with downpayment and closing costs. The Act would release funds for the programme for fiscal years 2004–2007. President Bush also tripled the funding for organisations that help families help themselves to become home-owners in their communities. This substantially increased the financial commitment made by the government-sponsored enterprises involved in the secondary mortgage market toward the minority market. Billions of dollars were heading from government towards the subprime market.

And so it went on. The US government, through its tentacles of agencies, was selling the idea of the key step in the American Dream being home-ownership. The American public was lapping it up through the well-oiled wheels of the subprime mortgage market and now there were exhortations from Bush politicians to Fannie and Freddie to come and join the party.

■ The financial crisis

Then in 2007, the subprime mortgage crisis began. An increasing number of borrowers, often with poor credit scores, were unable to pay their mortgages – particularly those with adjustable rate mortgages (ARM). This caused a very significant increase in home foreclosures. House prices declined as increasing foreclosures added weight to the already increasing inventory of homes for sale. This led to a return to superior mortgage appraisal criteria. Stricter lending standards made it increasingly difficult for borrowers to get mortgages. The depreciation in home prices led to growing losses for Fannie and Freddie which, between them, were guaranteeing over 50 per cent of US mortgages. In July 2008, the US government tried to ease market fears stressing that 'Fannie Mae and Freddie Mac play a central role in the US housing finance system', This was what America already knew. And they also knew that there was a colossal housing bubble bursting. US stockholders were selling Fannie and Freddie shares. The US Treasury Department and the Federal Reserve took steps to bolster confidence in the corporations, granting both access to Federal Reserve low-interest loans and removing various prohibitions on them.

Fannie and Freddie received no direct government funding or backing. Their securities carried no government guarantee of being repaid. This was explicitly stated in the law authorising GSEs. On 11 July 2008, the *New York Times* reported that government officials were considering a plan for the US government to take over Fannie Mae and Freddie Mac should their financial situations worsen due to the US housing crisis. These officials also stated that the government had considered a guarantee for the USD5 trillion debt owned or guaranteed by Fannie and Freddie. Despite these efforts, by August 2008, shares of both Fannie and Freddie had tumbled more than 90 per cent from their one-year-prior levels.

With this background, the major question for Fannie and Freddie was whether they were too big to be allowed to fail. The answer came shortly afterwards with the government takeover (called conservatorship) of the two GSEs. The federal takeover of Fannie Mae and Freddie Mac involved the placing into conservatorship of the two government-sponsored enterprises by the US Treasury in September 2008. The government was providing a backstop for Fannie and Freddie. It was one of the many amazing crashes and bailouts occurring in that month.

On 7 September 2008 the director of the Federal Housing Finance Agency (FHFA), James B. Lockhart III, announced his decision to place the two GSEs into conservatorship run by the FHFA. At the same time, United States Treasury Secretary Henry Paulson stated that placing the two GSEs into conservatorship was a decision he fully supported. He added that 'I attribute the need for today's action primarily to the inherent conflict and flawed model embedded in the GSE structure, and to the ongoing housing correction.'

The combined Fannie and Freddie losses of USD14.9 billion and market concerns about their ability to raise capital and debt threatened to disrupt the US housing financial market. The Treasury committed to invest as much as USD200 billion in preferred stock and extend credit through 2009 to keep the GSEs solvent and operating. The two GSEs had outstanding more than USD5 trillion in mortgage backed securities (MBSs) and debt – not all subprime, of course.

The agreement that the Treasury made with both GSEs specifies that in exchange for future support and capital investments of up to USD100 billion in each GSE, at the inception of the conservatorship, each GSE shall issue to the Treasury USD1 billion of senior preferred stock, with a 10 per cent coupon, without cost to the Treasury. Also, each GSE contracted to issue common stock warrants representing an ownership stake of 79.9 per cent at an exercise price of one-thousandth of a US cent (USD0.00001) per share, and with a warrant of 20 years.

The conservatorship action and commitment by the US government to underwrite the two GSEs with up to USD200 billion in additional capital turned out to be the first big event in a tumultuous month among US-based investment banking, financial institutions and federal regulatory bodies. By 15 September 2008, the 158-year-old Lehman Brothers holding company filed for bankruptcy with intent to liquidate its assets, leaving its financially sound subsidiaries operational and outside of the bankruptcy filing. The 94-year-old Merrill Lynch accepted a purchase offer by Bank of America for approximately USD50 billion, a big drop from the year-earlier market valuation of about USD100 billion. And a credit rating downgrade of the insurer American International Group (AIG) led to a 16 September 2008 rescue agreement with the Federal Reserve Bank for a USD85 billion secured loan facility, in exchange for warrants for 79.9 per cent of its equity. September 2008 was a dark month in US financial history.

Chapter 13

Bank failures in the UK

■ Introduction

Just as the USA had its fair share of bank failures, so did Britain. The UK chapter contains only three case studies versus four in respect of the USA and their downfall seems to have been driven by different factors. The first case study, Northern Rock, a mortgage bank, was playing a dangerous game – but not in CDS, CDO and alphabet soup markets. However, they were selling on mortgages for repackaging and when this market stalled, they felt the adverse consequences. There were, though, other issues afoot for the Rock. The two other banks are interesting. HBOS decided to play the alphabet soup game, with dire consequences, to say nothing of grandiose lending with diminishing credit controls. And RBS, also a player in the alphabet soup of CDSs, CDOs and so on, sought to undertake one of the worst acquisitions known to man or beast at the same time as the financial crisis was unfolding. In all instances their hubris was overtaken by their nemesis. In other words, pride comes before a fall. But, in each case, the basic issues related and discussed on introductory courses on banking and on project appraisal were ignored. Incompetence of the highest order? What do you think? The case studies that follow in this chapter are:

Case 13.1 Northern Rock
Case 13.2 HBOS
Case 13.3 Royal Bank of Scotland (RBS)

CASE 13.1 Northern Rock

■ Introduction

Northern Rock is a mortgage bank which can trace its origins back to the 1860s when it operated as a building society. Conceived with the intention of taking customers deposits and lending them to borrowers for the purposes of purchasing their home, Northern Rock was focused very much upon the north east of England. The building society's source of finance was entirely customers' deposits until the deregulation of the financial sector in the 1980s. Its ownership then was with the depositors themselves – a typical building society, also called mutual society. In 1997, Northern Rock was transformed into a public company with the flotation of its shares on the London stock market. All qualifying depositors with Northern Rock received a windfall of 500 shares, worth GBP2,250 at the issue price of GBP4.50 per share and, at the same time, new shares were sold to the public. The demutualisation proved popular and was three times oversubscribed.

The mortgage bank did not provide the full range of services of a typical UK bank, like Lloyds, but specialised in residential mortgages, commercial mortgages, buy-to-let and unsecured personal loans and, on the liabilities side, taking savings accounts deposits and, after deregulation, borrowing in capital markets.

Under its new chief executive Adam Applegarth, appointed in 2001, Northern Rock became a growth story. Within three years of its demutualisation, it was one of Britain's top 100 companies and a constituent of the FTSE-100 share index. Applegarth, at 38, was the second youngest CEO of a FTSE-100 company. And the Rock's strategy aimed for more growth. To meet this objective, it needed to offer house buyers a better mortgage deal than competitors and it needed to be able to finance its growing ambitions.

■ Risky business model

Traditionally, building societies worked to a rule of thumb of advancing loans of two-and-a-half times a borrower's income and up to 75 per cent of the value of the property mortgaged. But by the year 2000, mortgage banks had, in the light of fairly solid house price rises, eased their rule of thumb nearer to advancing three times the borrower's income and 90 to 95 per cent of the value of the property mortgaged. Northern Rock pursued its growth objective by offering an even higher package, with its mortgage brand called 'Together'. This was a 125 per cent deal based on 95 per cent of the property value plus a 30 per cent top-up unsecured loan and loan up to six times income. In a world of increasing house prices, as was then the case, borrowers were making mental notes of when their property would rise by 25 per cent and then they would be in positive territory. 'Together' was marketed with passion with salespersons highly incentivised.

The other side of the equation concerned Northern Rock's ability to provide money to lend. Its conservative competitor, Lloyds TSB, raised 25 per cent of mortgage banking money from the wholesale money markets (generally meaning the London inter-bank market on three months terms with an interest rate based upon three month LIBOR – London inter bank offer rate) and 75 per cent from deposits by mortgage bank depositors. This was far too conservative for the Rock. Applegarth's financing was to aim for 75 per cent of its lending funds from wholesale markets and 25 per cent from deposits. Effectively, the 75 per cent was achieved by raising 50 per cent from securitisation and tapping the three money wholesale money markets (at three month LIBOR) for the remaining 25 per cent. The securitisation process involved bundling mortgages together and selling them on to, for example Lehman Brothers, for a commission. Of course, as we saw in Chapter 6, the investment bank would then create collateralised debt obligations from these mortgages plus other debt and sell it on (remember, at a AAA rating too).

Securitisation is invisible to borrowers. The terms and conditions of the mortgage remain the same and borrowers continue to deal with the same mortgage bank that granted the loan. Securitisation helped Northern Rock expand its lending book. Every so often, the

Rock would sell on its mortgages by securitisation and this would release further funds to be on-lent. To bridge the gap between securitisations, it would borrow money short term from other banks in the wholesale money markets. The strategy worked – at least for a time. The Rock's share price soared. Its market share of mortgage lending doubled in three years.

In 2000, the Rock recorded pre-tax profit of GBP250 million. By 2005, the figure had risen to GBP494 million. In the first half of 2007, it held 20 per cent of the UK mortgage market and the largest share of new mortgages. As profits rose to GBP587 million, the share price powered ahead to GBP12.60 per share, valuing the Rock at over GBP6 billion. In addition to growth, Adam Applegarth kept a tight control on costs and, on the basis of costs to revenue, the Rock was top of the league. As a keen sportsman, this was just what Applegarth liked.

But warning signals were to be raised. In March 2007, HSBC reported one portfolio of purchased subprime mortgages as showing much higher delinquency than had been priced into the previous valuation of the products. In April 2007, the second largest subprime lender in the USA, New Century Financial, had declared bankruptcy. In June 2007, Bear Stearns failed to support one of its hedge funds. In July 2007, the carry trade (borrowing in currencies where interest is low and depositing money in currrencies where interest is high) experienced a six standard deviation move. With this background, questions began to be asked about the Rock's business model. Could the growth rate be sustained? If subprime mortgages start to look dodgy and other packages look as weak as HSBC revealed in March 2007, what would this do to the securitisation of mortgages, which provided 50 per cent of the Rock's finance? If house prices stop rising – and maybe move into reverse – the Together brand could become a millstone for the Rock since it was offering a 125 per cent loan to value figure.

And there was an interest rate problem too. The Rock was mismatching maturity, lending long-term and borrowing substantially short-term. It was also mismatching its lending and borrowing rates. Its mortgage loans were linked to the Bank of England base rate, but its borrowings from the money markets were linked to LIBOR. The cost of the latter was going up faster than the base rate. Figure 13.1 summarises the problem. This adverse gap between base rate and LIBOR led the Rock to issue a profits warning on 27 June 2007.

■ Crunch time

As August 2007 began, Northern Rock appeared to the outside world to be functioning normally. However, a bombshell fell. On 9 August 2007, the inter-bank lending market ceased functioning. Banks stopped lending to one another. This had been triggered by the announcement from BNP Paribas, the large French bank, that it was suspending three of its asset-backed security funds, explaining that it could no longer value them accurately due to problems in the US subprime mortgage market. Furthermore, the credit default swap market was caught in a tsunami as valuations were adversely affected by suspicions of widespread potential failures and this had led to a complete standstill in the market. The ramifications of the market seizure were severe. Banks were ceasing lending to each

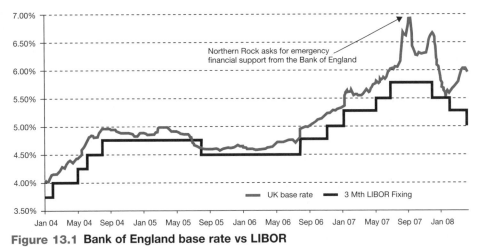

Figure 13.1 Bank of England base rate vs LIBOR

Source: J. C. Rathbone Associates Limited (www.jcra.co.uk)

other, suspicious of how much toxic debt (CDOs and CDS) other banks were holding. The implications were far-reaching for Northern Rock. The problems clearly derived from the Rock's business model based on borrowing from short-term wholesale money markets and its loan securitisation policy. Its funding model required mortgages to be securitised, and the next securitisation was scheduled for September 2007. Would it be able to do the securitisation and what might happen if it couldn't?

On the following day, Friday 10 August 2007, the Financial Services Authority (FSA) contacted financial businesses that it reckoned could be at risk from the freezing of the money markets. Northern Rock was one of those companies contacted. The Rock replied the next working day, 13 August, confirming potential difficulties. The FSA and Northern Rock were then in ongoing discussion. The next day, Tuesday 14 August, discussions expanded to embrace the tripartite authorities, the Treasury, the Bank of England and the FSA with the Governor of the Bank of England alerted.

On 15 August 2007, newspaper articles appeared asking searching questions of Northern Rock. The big issue was just how much trouble was Northern Rock in? The Rock's share price had fallen 12 per cent after the profits warning in June and a further 13 per cent since then indicated that the answer was 'a lot'. Northern Rock was being hammered by the liquidity crisis in the wholesale credit markets, where the bulk of its funds for mortgage lending was raised. These markets were virtually shut and, without this source of funds, the Rock did not have a business. Lack of liquidity was a problem for the mortgage market, but Northern Rock's business model left it more exposed than others. It could still raise wholesale funds at LIBOR but, at that moment, doing so was uneconomical. LIBOR had jumped to 6.37 per cent. In other words, after costs, Northern Rock would have to lend at about 6.75 per cent to make the smallest of profits. Rivals could undercut it. Northern Rock had little control of its destiny.

On Wednesday 15 August, more detailed discussions ensued, with the Chancellor of the Exchequer being informed. Come Thursday 16 August, the Northern Rock Chairman, Matt Ridley, was discussing the possibility of a support operation with the Governor of the Bank of England. It was agreed that Northern Rock was sailing into extremely stormy weather and its options were limited.

During this period, three courses of action were identified, namely:

■ Northern Rock resolves its own liquidity problems via its business model and its own actions in short-term wholesale money markets and by securitising its debt.

■ Northern Rock obtains a takeover bid from a major bank

■ Northern Rock receives a support facility from the central bank guaranteed by the government.

The first solution was pursued until 10 September 2007. But it achieved zero success. The search for a bid from a major bank was on. Then there was Bank of England liquidity support. This way forward was also considered until 10 September 2007. Two institutions expressed some interest, but one quickly withdrew. The other, Lloyds TSB, showed continued interest. It is not clear as to the depth and commitment of discussions but certainly any takeover would have been conditional on a Bank of England backstop loan facility reported to be in the order of GBP30 billion for a two-year period at market rates. This proposition was not acceptable to the Bank of England Governor, it not being the function of a central bank to aid the takeover of one bank by another via loans or guarantees – and certainly not for GBP30 billion. On Monday 10 September, Northern Rock and the tripartite authorities agreed that only one option remained – a support facility from the Bank of England. Plans were that an announcement would be made the following week.

■ Britain's first bank run since 1866

However, things were not this smooth. On Thursday 13 September 2007, BBC Business Editor, Robert Peston, released the news ahead of schedule. Northern Rock was to be bailed out. Such news caused a host of Rock investors to go to their local branch and withdraw their savings. Friday 14 September was metaphorically tempestuous. Queues were forming outside every branch of Northern Rock across Britain. And they got longer by the minute. Frightened investors wanted to withdraw their savings. Of course, the Bank of England had already announced that it was supporting the Rock. Far from being reassured, investors wanted the simple solution. 'Give me the money.' Television pictures of scared savers queuing to get their investments out encouraged others to do the same. In one day GBP1 billion was withdrawn. Shortly afterwards, on 17 September, the panic ceased when the British Chancellor of the Exchequer guaranteed the bank's deposits. But Britain had experienced its first bank run since Overend Gurney in 1866. Clearly, that's another story. It is briefly told in Kindleberger[1] and in Ferguson[2]

Earlier that week, on Wednesday 12 September 2007, Northern Rock formally asked the Bank of England, as lender of last resort in the UK, for a liquidity support facility due to problems in raising funds in the money market to replace maturing borrowings. Northern Rock borrowed GBP3 billion from the Bank of England in the first few days.

On Monday 17 September, worried savers continued to flock to some Northern Rock bank branches to withdraw their savings. It was reported that an estimated GBP2 billion had been withdrawn since the bank applied to the Bank of England for emergency funds. By early afternoon in London, Northern Rock's shares, which had lost 32 per cent on the previous Friday, fell a further 40 per cent from 438 pence to 263 pence. Later that day, Alistair Darling, the Chancellor of the Exchequer, announced that the British Government and the Bank of England would guarantee all deposits held at Northern Rock. Its shares promptly rose by 16 per cent after this was announced.

In November 2007, there were numerous exits from the Board of Directors of the Rock. Chief Executive, Adam Applegarth, remained in a caretaker role until December 2007. Despite having received conditional takeover bids from various parties, Northern Rock announced that all had been materially below the previous trading value and estimated present value and none got a green light to proceed. In December 2007, the Government prepared emergency legislation to nationalise the Bank, in the event that the takeover bids fail. On 12 January 2008, the Treasury recruited Ron Sandler, the former Lloyd's of London chief executive, to lead Northern Rock, in the event of its formal nationalisation.

On 6 February 2008, the Office for National Statistics announced that it was treating Northern Rock as a public corporation (like the BBC), causing the loans (some GBP25 billion) and guarantees (around GBP30 billion) extended by the Bank of England and the value of the company's mortgage book (GBP55 billion), totalling GBP110 billion, to be added to the National Debt, reflecting the fact that the Rock was effectively nationalised.

On 17 February 2008, Alistair Darling, the Chancellor of the Exchequer, announced that Northern Rock was actually to be nationalised. The government became the sole shareholder through UK Financial Investments Limited, and the Bank became managed at arm's length on a commercial basis with an independent board under Ron Sandler.

Prior to the markets opening on 18 February 2008, trading in Northern Rock's ordinary and preference shares on the London Stock Exchange was suspended with compensation (if any) to be arbitrated upon. On 22 February 2008, Northern Rock was formally nationalised. On 31 March 2008, the bank released its annual report for 2007. It showed a loss of GBP167 million.

In October 2009, the European Commission agreed the corporate plan to aim to restructure the bank with the intention of eventually selling it on.

■ Why did things go so wrong?

A number of issues underpinned the Rock's failure. First, its business strategy was based upon lending long term with funding from short-term borrowings. On top of this, its originate to distribute mode of operation meant that it would be a holder of subprime mortgages until securitisation took place and this meant that the Rock would be vulnerable whilst waiting to distribute. What if liquidity dries up and its potential purchaser of mortgages does not want to buy them?

When money markets froze, the Rock suffered a double whammy on each of the above fronts. It is worth mentioning that there had been harbingers of this possibility since early 2007 when problems with an HSBC portfolio of subprime mortgages and BNP had indicated difficulties.

Furthermore, the Together mortgage, with its 125 per cent loan to value would inevitably create problems when house prices started to fall. Because of its popularity, when the crisis arose it left the Rock with a handful of second-rate assets awaiting securitisation in a market that no longer wanted to play. Also, because of its competitive generosity, the Together model became the mortgage of choice for the weakest subprime borrowers.

Add to this the dash for growth strategy and, like any business pitching for high growth, it can become vulnerable and found itself unable to finance expansion when money became tight. For a non-financial business, the problem arises because demands for capital to finance growth exceed internally generated sources – profits. Hence the need to arrange outside funding. In the Rock's financial business, assets were being securitised. With securitisation markets showing signs of indigestion, this was making life impossible. And when that happened, the Rock's business model imploded.

Should the regulatory authorities – The Treasury, the FSA and the Bank of England – have stepped in to slow the Rock down? Well, the FSA acknowledged that there were failings in its regulation of Northern Rock in the months immediately preceding the September 2007 run. In its review of the Rock's crisis, the House of Commons Treasury Committee made a number of observations about these failings. For example:

- There were warning signals about the risks associated with Northern Rock's business model, both from its rapid growth and from its share price drops from February 2007 onwards. The FSA exercised 'regulatory engagement' with the Rock but, between them, they failed to tackle the fundamental weakness in its funding strategy and risk management.

- The FSA failed to supervise the Rock properly and its procedures were inadequate to supervise a bank where its business had grown so rapidly and was so clearly underresourced.

- The FSA was unhappy with the stress-tests conducted on Northern Rock but it failed to communicate the strength of these concerns to the Northern Rock board.

- The FSA should have been more concerned that the Rock chairman and its chief executive did not possess any relevant financial qualifications.

- It concluded that the current regulatory regime for liquidity of UK banks is flawed and requires urgent review.

The Rock's business strategy needed an early warning system of when the housing market was likely to move into reverse. It needed financial controls – which seemed to be lacking, as revealed in Press Cutting 13.1. It needed a risk management system which the chief executive trusted, believed in and acted upon. This seems to have been utterly absent at the Rock. The point is that the riskier the business model, the greater the need for a trusted, listened to and acted upon, risk management early warning system. And it needs the chief executive's ear and confidence. As is so often the case, top management hubris is a forerunner of nemesis in the form of the corporate grim reaper.

Brian Walters[3] tells the story in much more detail and with the advantage of a view from the inside track since he once worked for Northern Rock.

Press cutting 13.1 *Financial Times*, 14 April 2010 **FT**

Northern Rock lacked proper financial controls

Brooke Masters and Sharlene Goff

During the boom years, critics of fast-growing mortgage lender Northern Rock often wondered how it could lend so aggressively while maintaining impressively low rates of bad loans.

Now a Financial Services Authority case against two of the failed lender's senior executives demonstrates that some of those criticisms were on the mark.

In January 2007, Northern Rock left nearly 2,000 troubled mortgages out of its statistics by reclassifying them into a category that was not publicly reported, the FSA said. Had those mortgages been included, the bank's arrears rate would have risen from 0.42 per cent to 0.68 per cent in January 2007. The misreporting had still not been corrected six months later, the FSA said.

While the misleading statistics did not cause the September 2007 run that led eventually to Northern Rock's takeover by the government, the cases against David Baker, former deputy chief executive, and Richard Barclay, former credit director, depict an institution without proper controls and under tremendous pressure to maintain its public image and the flow of funding.

At the peak of the housing bubble in late 2006 – just months before Northern Rock's fall from grace – the bank was the fifth-largest UK mortgage lender, the FSA said.

It offered credit-hungry borrowers high multiples of their income and large loan-to-value ratios. Its 'Together' portfolio – which accounted for about a quarter of lending – offered loans worth up to almost six times salary and up to 125 per cent of the property's value.

The rapid expansion meant the bank had not been able to build up a sizeable deposit base and was heavily reliant on the wholesale money markets for funding. Prior to its collapse, about 70 per cent of Northern Rock's mortgage lending was based on wholesale funding, with some 20 per cent secured on a short time horizon of about three or six months.

That meant that when the wholesale markets seized up in late 2007, Northern Rock was unable to renegotiate its maturing debt and the bank's liquidity dried up almost overnight. While the disappearance of funding afflicted the whole banking industry, Northern Rock fell first and hardest.

The bank's reliance on the money markets may also have been an incentive for its efforts to keep its financial position as clean as possible, and its arrears record as low. The bank routinely boasted that its arrears rate was half the Council of Mortgage Lenders average.

'The price of funding would have been influenced by the quality of its loan book and a key determinant of that was its arrears record,' said Ray Boulger, at John Charcol, the mortgage broker.

According to the FSA, some of the arrears reporting problems started

→

in 2005, when staff in the bank's debt management unit felt 'pressure … to achieve arrears targets.' They created a new category for troubled loans where a possession order had been obtained but not enforced, the FSA final notice said.

Those 'pending possession' loans were omitted from public disclosure and their numbers grew substantially in 2006. But Mr Barclay did not alert senior management until early 2007.

The FSA said Mr Barclay also failed to investigate the widespread use of a discretionary 'capitalisation' process to rehabilitate under-performing loans and keep them out of the arrears statistics.

That involved restructuring the loans so that any missed payments and fines were added to the amount owed. The loans would then be counted as normally performing debts. Ordinarily, such a restructuring would only take place once regular payments had restarted, but in some cases loans were being capitalised even if the ordinary requirements had not been met.

The FSA said there were 6,870 capitalisations each month, many of them contrary to the bank's secured lending policies. Mr Barclay's lawyer declined to comment.

Mr Baker's spokesman said that he was unaware of the capitalisation issues and that he only learnt of the pending possessions problem in late December 2006. He then decided to give the debt unit six months to fix the issue rather than tell Adam Applegarth, chief executive, and the board. He then gave the incorrect figures to investors and analysts on a January 2007 company webcast.

'I now recognise that this decision, taken to resolve and not hide, the reporting error, did not make these loans immediately transparent. I made an error of judgment and I regret it,' Mr Baker said in a statement.

Northern Rock, now government owned, said in a statement that 'The company has fully co-operated with the FSA throughout its investigation and … will not be subject to any sanction … The company's leadership team and risk control environment have now been significantly strengthened.'

The FSA said it was unable to quantify the impact of the arrears under-reporting on investors. The case has no direct effect on legal efforts by Northern Rock shareholders to force the government to pay them compensation for the 2008 takeover.

But Roger Lawson, a board member of the Northern Rock shareholders action group, said accurate arrears data 'might have made a difference' to investors who bought Northern Rock shares shortly before its collapse

'We thought the business was a very sound business and we had read they had a better default rate than similar institutions. It was just one factor, but it might have made a difference'.

Case 13.2 HBOS

■ Introduction

HBOS plc is a banking and insurance company in the UK. It is now a wholly-owned subsidiary of the Lloyds Banking Group (LBG), having been taken over in January 2009 as part of the financial crisis rescue. At the time of writing LBG is 57 per cent owned by the UK government. It is the holding company of Bank of Scotland plc, and owner of the Halifax mortgage brand, HBOS Australia, and HBOS Insurance & Investment Group.

HBOS was formed in 2001 by the merger of Halifax plc and the Bank of Scotland. The merger made HBOS a fifth force in British banking as it created a group of comparable size to the established big four UK retail banks – HSBC, Lloyds, RBS and Barclays. It also became the UK's largest mortgage lender, a position that Halifax had held for some time.

Indeed, Halifax was the UK's largest pure building society when it merged earlier with the Leeds Permanent Building Society in 1995 and listed on the stock market in 1997. With the Bank of Scotland merger in 2001, property lending remained a very significant business for the enlarged bank. James Crosby, an actuary who had been a fund manager and founding director of a leading wealth management company, joined Halifax and became chief executive of HBOS in 1999.

In that year, Halifax recruited Andy Hornby, previously retail managing director at Asda, the supermarket company. He was to head the Halifax mortgage business, a position he held in the new group after the merger. He was elevated to HBOS chief operating officer in 2005 and again, in 2006, to chief executive when James Crosby left the group. Crosby was knighted for his contribution to financial services. Between 2001 and 2005, he had presided over a doubling of HBOS reported profit. On leaving he said, 'Now I know what I know, I wish I'd been bolder.'[4] As subsequent events would show, he had probably been more than bold enough.

■ A changed business model

HBOS, at its peak, was earning profit before tax of GBP5.7 billion, it had an equity capitalisation of over GBP35 billion, it had ten million customers, a UK current account market share of 13 per cent, 74,000 staff, 1,200 branches and retail deposits (June 2008) of GBP258 billion, 15 per cent of the UK's total customer savings. On the other side of the equation, consumer lending moved ahead more aggressively than savings. Thanks to a focus on buy-to-let and self-certified loans in which employment and income checks are waived, HBOS mortgage market share reached 20 per cent. HBOS had forsaken the matched loan and deposit business model. Its retail and corporate deposits now covered about half the liabilities on its group balance sheet, the rest coming from wholesale markets and securitisation. This was managed by the HBOS treasury department, a group of debt, derivatives and currency traders who, amongst other things, packaged and repackaged mortgages, bought and sold credit default swaps and collateralised debt obligations as well as being responsible for HBOS funding and liquidity. One of its key responsibilities was to deal with the HBOS funding gap – the difference between internally generated funds and cash required. By September 2008 this was as much as GBP200 billion and the annual refinancing requirement was GBP20 billion.

At the end of 1998, the top eight UK banks held more in deposits than they lent out to borrowers. At the end of 2007, loans exceeded deposits by over GBP500 billion – a clear transformation in the business model. The causes of this derived from relaxed banking regulations and the growth of securitisation. The effects were to make UK banks, like US investment banks, highly leveraged and dependent upon the money markets to bridge their funding gap.

UK banks were copying the techniques of US investment banks. This involved packaging their own mortgage loans and other loans to corporations in different industries (although including property companies which featured very highly in their portfolios) plus their own private equity lending into CDOs and selling them to investors through SIVs and other conduits – as described in Chapter 5. And, like US banks, they were diluting the previously highly-developed rigour of credit analysis routines and loan screening. The argument advanced for dumping a set of loan appraisal routines developed over decades of banking was that if the loan were to be repackaged into a CDO and sold on to someone else, and one can still get a triple A rating for it, why bother with time-consuming credit analysis of the loan? Why set high standards of credit analysis – or do it at all – if the lending is sold on to third parties? The argument was all too frequently bought by bankers – ultimately with all too negative consequences for banks. In the business of banking there is a technical term for loans which are in arrears and likely to go bad – it is delinquent loans. We believe that downgrading credit analysis was tantamount to delinquent banking. We referred briefly to this in Chapter 7.

At the same time, UK banks claimed that they were increasing profits and reducing funding costs by selling and buying in the American mortgage-backed securities market. Using a mixture of their own and borrowed capital, they invested in American mortgage-backed securities, holding some on their books and repackaging others into CDOs, placing them in SIVs and selling them on to outside investors. They contended that they were cutting their funding costs by borrowing capital at one price and lending it on to house buyers and others at a higher rate. But as they were buying US mortgage-backed securities, they were taking on an exposure to the US housing market. Hardly surprising, they were getting a higher return on their investment because they were taking on more risk.

From 2001 to 2006 it worked well for the UK banks but it was risky – highly so. If, for any reason, there were problems with payments to the SIV or if liquidity in the money markets dried up, underwriting agreements required banks to stand behind the SIVs. These conditions occurred in 2007/8. The US real estate market retreated and the asset-backed commercial paper market on which the banks depended to fund their SIVs dried up.

■ Days of reckoning

The first warning of the problem in the US property market came in February 2007, with a trading statement from HSBC disclosing substantial subprime related credit losses. HSBC had a large consumer credit business in the USA and the market took this announcement in its stride.

In August 2007, HBOS decided to absorb Grampian, its off-balance sheet funding vehicle. Grampian had assets of USD37 billion including a significant amount of US mortgage-backed securities, but when the commercial paper market exhibited difficulties, HBOS decided that it was more cost effective to fund Grampain itself. Investors were surprised. They knew very little about Grampian. Under accounting rules, HBOS did not have to disclose it in its annual report. The bank described the matter as a business decision of 'no material adverse impact'.

Financial markets were more alarmed in February 2008 when, in reporting profits for 2007, HBOS wrote down the value of mortgage-backed securities by GBP726 million and in April set aside a further GBP2.8 billion. It revealed that at the end of March 2008 it held mortgage-backed securities worth GBP20.7 billion, of which half related to US mortgages.

The Northern Rock affair, HSBC's problem and the HBOS case alerted investors to UK banks' exposures to the potential problems of securitisation, short-term funding and CDS and CDO markets. During the first half of 2008, falling house prices and weakness in CDS, CDO and MBS markets led to fears that write-downs would leave the banks without enough capital to meet the levels required by banking regulators. In March 2008, UK banks share prices came under pressure, with HBOS and mortgage lenders Alliance and Leicester and Bradford & Bingley particularly badly hit. In April there were rumours of rights issues and profit warnings from the UK banks.

In the second half of 2008 the HBOS funding requirement was causing big problems. Banking rules required that the value of a bank's capital to be at least 4 per cent of the value of the risks on its book – the Tier 1 capital ratio. Market conditions were difficult. The Grampian story, the write-downs, a rights issue – in July 2008 of 1.5 billion shares at 275p each to raise GBP4.1 billion, problems in the global property and credit markets and expectations of more write-downs to come put HBOS on the market's sell list. Counterparties became reluctant to deal with the bank. There were bear raids on HBOS shares during September 2008 in which hedge funds were suspected of targeted selling. After the collapse of Lehman, the price of HBOS credit default swaps soared, implying probable failure. The share price sank from 283 pence on Friday 12 September to 88 pence three trading days later. Its price had been 450 pence six months earlier.

■ The takeover and the bailout

Come September 2008, HBOS was not a viable independent entity. The UK government concluded that a bank of its size and importance could not be allowed to fail. With governments guaranteeing bank deposits in some countries, for example, Ireland, with banks being nationalised elsewhere, for example Iceland, with US banks failing (Lehmans) and institutions being bailed out (AIG), it was hardly surprising that the UK government concluded that HBOS would have to be nationalised. Or taken over. The preferred takeover partner was Lloyds TSB, a well-run retail banking and insurance group with financial strength and a low-risk business model. Under its past leadership of Sir Brian Pitman and from 2003 Eric Daniels, a former Citigroup banker, Lloyds TSB had concentrated on its core businesses and, unlike its UK counterparts, avoided building an investment bank or allowing its treasury to engage in high-risk practices. In June 2008 Lloyds TSB was able to report no direct exposure to US subprime asset-backed securities, limited indirect exposure through asset-backed CDOs and a modest exposure to SIVs and asset-backed commercial paper. Its funding gap was estimated at GBP67 billion, one third the level of HBOS, and its annual refinancing needs were in the region of GBP10 billion.

HBOS and Lloyds TSB were rumoured to have had discussions for several years about a merger but had always concluded that a combined UK market share of 28 per cent in mortgages, 35 per cent in current accounts and 22 per cent in savings would raise competition concerns.

The situation of HBOS was now so dire that after the intervention of the UK Prime Minister and the Chancellor of the Exchequer, and with the sanction of the FSA, the government agreed to waive competition concerns. On 27 September 2008, the companies said that there would be an all-share takeover by Lloyds TSB on terms that were later revised after a further fall in the HBOS share price. HBOS chairman Lord Stevenson and chief executive Andy Hornby were to leave after the merger was completed.

On 13 October 2008, the UK government announced that because of the unprecedented banking crisis, the Treasury would infuse GBP37 billion as new capital in a bailout of Royal Bank of Scotland, Lloyds TSB and HBOS to prevent a financial sector collapse. But this sum was dwarfed by semi-permanent guarantees (which banks would have to pay an annual premium for) totalling GBP400 billion to insure against losses on banks' already-made loans and holdings of toxic assets. An open offer and placing of shares (essentially to the UK government but existing equity shareholders could participate – but the issue price was above market price, so that was unlikely) was arranged. This took the total government ownership in Lloyds Banking Group equity, after the merger, to 40 per cent plus a substantial holding of preference shares carrying a 12 per cent per annum interest rate as part of the government guarantee scheme. Under a similar guarantee scheme, RBS equity became 60 per cent government-owned.

Later still, as market conditions eased and it looked less likely that the financial world was going to implode completely, Lloyds TSB managers concluded that it would make sense for it to quit the government's guarantee scheme and preference shareholdings which were attracting a hefty cost. Following a further rights issue, this was achieved and the government equity shareholding advanced to 57 per cent.

■ Risk management

In the five years between 2002 and 2007, the HBOS asset base almost doubled from GBP355 billion to GBP666 billion, with much of the growth funded from the wholesale market. This growth and its mode of financing increased the HBOS risk profile. This was revealed by Paul Moore, who had been head of regulatory risk at HBOS from 2002 to 2004. In an interview in October 2008 on the BBC's *Money Programme*, Mr Moore said the speed of growth reflected a new premier sales and marketing culture. 'I think it was a major change – to change a bank from a fuddy-duddy, musty old place to a shopping centre, to a supermarket-type culture,' he said. 'The retail bank was going at breakneck speed and an internal risk and compliance function feels like a man in a rowing boat trying to slow down an oil tanker.' He further revealed that he thought a concern of everyone was whether the business was under control.

Later still, in February 2009, Paul Moore continued his revelations to a House of Commons Treasury Select Committee. He said: 'Anyone whose eyes were not blinded by money, power, pride, who really looked carefully knew there was something wrong ... [and it]

could only ultimately lead to disaster.' He continued 'Whatever the very specific, final and direct causes of the financial crisis, I strongly believe the real underlying cause of all the problems was simply this – a total failure of all key aspects of governance.' And he did not stop there: 'This crisis was caused not because many bright people did not see it coming but because there has been a completely inadequate separation and balance of powers between the executive and all those accounting for their actions and reining them in, i.e. internal control functions such as finance, risk, compliance and internal audit, non-executive chairmen and directors, external auditors, the FSA, shareholders and politicians.' In his written evidence Mr Moore said: 'At the beginning of 2004, the regulatory risk profile of HBOS was higher than it had ever been; and higher than the board's appetite for risk should have been.' Mr Moore added that he was determined that the board should understand the risks and present a plan to reduce them. In his evidence he wrote: 'I was obliged to raise the numerous issues of actual or potential breach of FSA regulations and had to challenge unacceptable practices... [it] was bound to upset some people.' Eventually Mr Moore presented his report to the HBOS Audit Committee. It appears that Mr Moore was shortly afterward relieved of his job.

The FSA issued a statement to the effect that 'the allegations of Mr Moore were taken seriously and were properly and professionally investigated.' Reference to Chapter 7 will show that the problems inherent in practical risk management in banks are indeed complicated.

■ What went wrong?

HBOS financed its aggressive growth mainly from short-term wholesale markets. It ignored warnings from its group risk manager. The bank invested heavily in CDSs and CDOs, with a large exposure to US mortgages. Its losses in late 2007 and early 2008 put its capital adequacy ratios at risk. In July 2008, a GBP4 billion rights issue was a huge flop, with shareholders subscribing for only 8.3 per cent. When markets panicked after Lehman Brothers went bust in mid-September 2008, HBOS came under tremendous pressure. Bear raids forced the price of the equity shares lower.

The government decided that either another bank should take HBOS over or else it should be nationalised. The preferred acquirer was Lloyds TSB, and as an incentive the government offered to waive competition rules. Later, the European Commission decided that this hasty act had been *ultra vires* and required phased disposals by Lloyds. A secret GBP25 billion government loan to HBOS at this time was only revealed a year later.

The government put in GBP4 billion as 12 per cent preference capital. A condition was that the new Lloyds Banking Group could not pay any ordinary dividends until it had fully repaid the preference shares. Both HBOS and Lloyds share prices at once fell sharply. To improve capital ratios, the government also invested GBP13 billion of ordinary capital. Lloyds took a punt on HBOS and seems to have lost out heavily. Under government pressure, a bank well known for being cautious and boring ended up acquiring the most risky of all UK banks – except possibly RBS.

Case 13.3 **Royal Bank of Scotland (RBS)**

■ Introduction

The Royal Bank of Scotland was founded in 1727 by a Royal Charter of King George I. Unlike English commercial banks, RBS has been granted the right to issue banknotes in Scotland – and in Northern Ireland through its Ulster Bank subsidiary, which dates back even further than RBS – to 1650.

Following its disastrous passage through the 2007/8 crisis, it is now 84 per cent held by HM Treasury although voting rights are at 75 per cent in order to retain its stock exchange listing.

At its peak, RBS was the fifth largest bank in the world by market capitalisation and was ranked by Forbes as the tenth largest company in the world in 2000. Prior to its fall from grace, it operated a variety of banking brands offering personal and business banking, private banking, insurance and corporate finance in Europe, North America and Asia. In the UK and in Ireland, its main subsidiary companies were The Royal Bank of Scotland, National Westminster Bank, Ulster Bank, Drummonds and Coutts & Co. In the United States, it owned Citizens Financial Group and from 2004 to 2009, it was the second largest shareholder in the Bank of China, itself the world's fifth largest bank by market capitalisation in February 2008. It also owns various strongly-branded insurance companies.

■ The NatWest takeover

During the late 1990s there was a wave of consolidation in the financial services sector. In 1999, the Bank of Scotland launched a takeover bid for English rival, National Westminster Bank (NatWest). The Bank of Scotland planned to fund the deal by selling off various NatWest subsidiary companies, including Ulster Bank and Coutts. The Royal Bank tabled a counter-offer, setting off a hostile takeover battle. A key difference between the competing offers was that the Royal Bank's plan was to retain all NatWest subsidiaries. Although NatWest was significantly larger than either Scottish bank, it had a recent history of poor financial performance. In February 2000, RBS finally won the takeover battle and moved up the UK bank league table to number two behind HSBC. Rationalisation and elimination of duplication meant the loss of 18,000 jobs in the UK alone.

■ Investment banking

Until its acquisition of NatWest, RBS had kept well away from investment banking, although it offered a well-respected business in corporate lending, interest-rate trading and foreign exchange dealing. When RBS acquired NatWest it inherited Greenwich Capital, an underwriter and dealer in US Treasury bonds, mortgages and other asset-backed securities. Greenwich was about to be sold as part of NatWest's plan to return cash to shareholders. RBS cancelled the sale and began its plan to build a Global Banking and Markets division (GBM). 'The strategy for GBM ... was to start in the UK and cement our position in the UK capital markets, in sterling bonds ... then go into Europe ... and build our position in loans and bonds in Europe. Then to start in America, again to build our position in loans and bonds and finally Asia.'[5]

The strategy of GBM was to use the RBS position as a large commercial lender to sell other services to clients and to broaden its international reach. They targeted the UK, then built up operations in France and Germany lending to private equity groups and in the process becoming the biggest player in European leveraged finance. In the US, Greenwich gave RBS the opportunity to move into such sectors as trading US Treasury bonds, asset-backed securities, investment-grade corporate bonds and mortgage-backed securities. RBS was also expanding globally in leveraged finance. The bank was, in fact, building a significant exposure to the activities that were at the heart of the global banking maelstrom of 2007/8. And it was to pay a heavy price for this commitment.

Under the leadership of Johnny Cameron, who had joined RBS from investment bank Dresdner Kleinwort Benson in 1998, the GBM division showed an average growth rate in profits of 17 per cent per annum in the six years to 2006. In March 2007, when GBM profits accounted for 40 per cent of RBS group profit, Cameron boasted: 'That is a huge number. It is bigger than Coca-Cola's profits! Compared to other banks it is, for example, twice the size of BarCap – we make more or less twice as much money as BarCap with just over half as many people.'[6] At this time, GBM was the second largest issuer of subprime mortgages in the world – equipped with SIVs and all the other incendiary trappings of a future débâcle.

The financial crisis of 2007/8 was to undermine, with staggering losses, RBS efforts in the investment banking domain. And it was to do it at the very moment that its ill-timed takeover of ABN Amro was to create nothing but problems for the Scottish bank. Like many of its banking peers, RBS was also pushing its leverage (its liabilities to equity) to the hilt and this magnified its losses and, hence, its problems.

■ The ABN Amro acquisition

Having eliminated 18,000 jobs at NatWest, RBS chief executive officer, Sir Fred Goodwin needed another project to get his teeth into. So successful was his axe-wielding at NatWest that he had earned the sobriquet 'Fred the Shred'. Perhaps he expected to rationalise operations at ABN Amro, the largest Dutch bank, just as well. Like NatWest's history before the acquisition of RBS, ABN Amro's recent financial performance was becalmed. RBS again hit the takeover trail. In a bitterly fought battle, which raged from April to October 2007, with Barclays as its rival suitor, the RBS consortium, which included Belgian bank Fortis and the Spanish group Banco Santander, the consortium emerged as Pyrrhic victors. Further details of the acquisition appear in the Fortis case study under the subheading 'The ABN Amro takeover'. Rather than repeat ourselves, readers are referred to that section. There were no commentators who thought that the ABN Amro was a snip at the GBP49 billion paid for it. And there were some who reckoned it was one the worst takeovers of all time.

Before RBS had secured the ABN Amro deal, the Dutch bank had sold on to Bank of America the asset which RBS most prized – its Chicago-based La Salle banking unit. This left the Edinburgh-based RBS with only an underperforming London-based investment banking franchise and some small Asian businesses. Even worse, once the financial crisis started to bite in the summer of 2007, it became apparent that ABN Amro would not deliver expected earnings. But RBS went ahead with the takeover without trying to amend its terms.

By the time the deal was completed, many banks' shares were trading at around book value. This made the initial price paid by RBS – at three times book value – look even more of a folly. RBS began to struggle under the acquisition's costs and with the toxic assets it acquired with ABN Amro. Why the RBS-led consortium did not drop this bid when ABN Amro sold off its US-based La Salle subsidiary is a mystery. One can surmise that the takeover chase was so thrilling and so intense that the dopamine-driven executives at RBS *et al.* were spurred by the pursuit of their quarry and rationality was forgotten. It would not have been the first time that this kind of thing has happened in takeover situations. Furthermore, the acquisition resulted in writedowns of goodwill of around GBP20 billion for RBS. This would adversely affect shareholders' funds on the RBS group balance sheet and also key financial ratios which are of prime importance to banks. This should certainly have been apparent to RBS executives before the time of the takeover. The RBS-ABN Amro deal is also unusual in that it led to the fall of not just one buyer but two: the Belgian-Dutch bank Fortis was nationalised by the Dutch government to avert a liquidity crisis. Press Cutting 13.2 contains an interesting angle on the RBS-ABN Amro deal and on other issues too.

Press cutting 13.2　　　　　*Financial Times*, 26 August 2009　**FT**

Banks brought down by a new Peter Principle

John Kay

Forty years ago, Dr Lawrence Peter enunciated what he immodestly called the Peter Principle. Individuals would find their level of incompetence. If you were good at doing a job, you would be promoted until you were appointed to a job you weren't good at.

The recent failures of financial institutions suggests an organisational analogue. Financial institutions diversify into their level of incompetence. They extend their scope into activities they understand less until they are tripped up by one they cannot do. It was almost refreshing when the Chelsea Building Society announced large losses because it had been a victim of mortgage fraud. The bank's problems related to its core business. Most financial institutions that have come close to failure have done so as a result of losses in essentially peripheral activities.

The principle of diversification into incompetence applies from the largest financial institution to the smallest. AIG was America's leading insurance company. The company did not just undertake credit insurance, but was the largest trader in the credit default swap market. That is how its financial products group, employing 120 people in London, brought about the collapse of a business that employed 120,000.

The very name of the Dunfermline Building Society evokes prudence, its base the home town of that canniest of Scotsmen, Andrew Carnegie. For more than a century, the society collected savings to lend to careful homebuyers. What were they thinking of when they decided that 2007 was the perfect moment for aggressive development of their commercial lending portfolio?

Hypo Real Estate was Germany's largest property lender: it is hard to think of a duller but more profitable dominant position. So the bank bought a business that specialised in raising funds on wholesale money markets to lend to public authorities. No doubt its advisers offered an explanation of how you can make lots of money doing that. But whatever the explanation was, it was wrong, and led to Europe's most costly bank bail-out.

The boredom factor is important. Much of traditional banking is quite boring. The desire to find new challenges is an admirable human trait. It is, however, very expensive for shareholders to allow their chief executives to indulge it.

Public sector bodies are usually constrained in their activities, so deregulation is often a trigger for expensive experimentation. In Britain, many of the efficiency gains from privatisation were squandered in diversification: I watched senior managers spending 80 per cent of their time on activities that generated 1 per cent of turnover and minus 10 per cent of profit. But it is more fun to go on jollies to Buenos Aires than to fix leaking pipes.

To win an auction when you don't know what you are bidding for is often to lose. This winner's curse is often behind bad acquisitions because the successful purchaser is the bidder most willing to pay too much. Hence the contest between Royal Bank of Scotland and Barclays as to which bank would court bankruptcy by buying ABN Amro. Ignorance of products may also be a problem. When you are the newcomer and know little, the business that gravitates to you will be the business no one else wants.

But the driving factor is hubris. Jim Collins's well-timed study of *How the Mighty Fall* applies to every business I have mentioned. The financial services industry is particularly vulnerable to hubris because sections of it are not very competitive, and randomness plays a large role in the outcome of speculative transactions. It is therefore particularly easy for those who work in financial institutions to make the mistake of believing that their success is the result of exceptional skill rather than good fortune. What more natural to believe than that extraordinary talent will find pots of gold under other rainbows? Until vanity is vanquished, I anticipate that diversification to the level of incompetence will continue to be a powerful element in business behaviour.

■ 2008 financial crisis

As if the ABN Amro disaster were not enough, market rumours of disastrous losses at GMB on writing of credit default swaps, its holdings of collateralised debt obligations and other toxic assets led to credit default swaps on RBS itself rising in value – thus implying increasing default probabilities. In April 2008, RBS announced a rights issue aimed to raise GBP12 billion in new capital to offset value losses of GBP5.9 billion on toxic asset holdings and to shore up its reserves following write-downs pursuant to the purchase of ABN Amro. This was, at the time, the largest rights issue in British corporate history. The bank also announced that it would consider divesting some of its subsidiaries to raise further funds, notably its insurance business. But it was not enough to plug the gap in the RBS balance sheet.

In October 2008, following a further failed rights issue, underwritten by the UK government, it was announced that the government would take its stake in RBS to 58 per cent. The aim was to increase Tier 1 capital. The issue to existing shareholders, having failed to secure more than minimal take-up, the government found itself owning almost 60 per cent of the bank's equity share capital.

The UK Treasury would pump in GBP37 billion of new capital to RBS, HBOS and Lloyds TSB to avert a banking collapse. The government stressed, however, that it was not standard public ownership and that the banks would return to private investors at the right time. At RBS, this infusion of funds and the giving of a guarantee on specified losses from toxic assets was paid for in equity shares in RBS and in preference shares with a 12 per cent coupon rate in the banking group. The guarantee was part of the Government Asset Protection Scheme, rather like the USA's Troubled Asset Relief Program.

Following these clear failures, Sir Fred Goodwin offered his resignation which was accepted, and chairman Sir Tom McKillop indicated he would stand down in March 2009. Goodwin was replaced by Stephen Hester, previously chief executive of British Land. He took over at RBS in November 2008.

Following negotiations between RBS and the UK government, it was announced, on 19 January 2009, that its holding of preference shares in RBS that it had acquired in October 2008 would be converted into ordinary shares. This would remove the 12 per cent coupon payment (GBP600 million per annum) on the shares but would increase the government's equity stake. On the same day, RBS released a trading statement in which it expected full-year trading losses (before write-downs) to be between GBP7 and 8 billion. The group also announced write-downs on goodwill mainly related to the takeover of ABN Amro of around GBP20 billion. The combined total of GBP28 billion represented the biggest ever annual loss in UK corporate history. The RBS share price fell over 66 per cent in one day to 10.9 pence per share, from a year high of 354p per share, itself a drop of 97 per cent. At the time of writing (June 2010), the RBS share has ascended from its nadir and traded in a 52 week range from 28 pence per share to 59 pence per share.

■ What went wrong?

Philip Augar[7] summarised the RBS débâcle thus. 'It was a sorry end to a fast ride. Under Goodwin's leadership RBS had conducted an aggressive acquisition strategy, including the hostile takeover of NatWest in 1999 and participation in the consortium break-up of ABN Amro in 2007. This was achieved on the back of thin capital ratios and a leveraged balance sheet. The strategy had worked well in benign markets but the sea change in 2007 exposed the risks that had been run in the markets division and the high-rolling nature of an acquisition-led strategy. ABN Amro was the deal that broke the camel's back. RBS paid a top-of-the-market price for a second-grade investment bank'... 'The timing of the deal could not have been worse, coinciding with failing markets, mortgage-related write-downs and difficult funding conditions.'

New chief executive Stephen Hester, a well-regarded banker, admitted that RBS had overextended itself. Hester planned to review the bank from back to basics principles and to rationalise it to a more focused, less capital-intensive and less risky core, involving significant job losses in investment banking.

Chapter 14

Bank failures in Europe

■ Introduction

In this chapter, two of the case studies focus upon individual banks and two look at the problems affecting two countries. The bank cases involve Fortis, mainly a Benelux business, and UBS, an international bank centred in Switzerland. Fortis was a member of the consortium of bidders for ABN Amro which comprises a major part of Case Study 13.3 at the end of the previous chapter. The UBS case focuses upon one of the major players in the alphabet soup game. The two other cases in Chapter 14 look at banks in individual countries. The first focuses upon Icelandic banks where unprofessional banking standards and crony lending coupled with currency problems created massive problems. As in the last chapter, had the bankers had the least inkling of basic economics and credit analysis and had they applied this to their businesses, their banks would have survived unscathed. The final case, on Irish banks is fascinating. The economy of Ireland was in the midst of a property boom to end all property booms and banking standards in some of its institutions seemed abysmal. Add crony lending and substandard regulation and the mix is a lethal one. In order, the cases are:

    Case 14.1 Fortis
    Case 14.2 UBS
    Case 14.3 Icelandic banks
    Case 14.4 Irish banks

Case 14.1 Fortis

■ Introduction

Fortis is a banking, insurance, and investment management business with the Benelux countries as its home base. Fortis banking operations included retail, commercial and merchant banking. Its insurance products included life, health and property and it was listed on stock exchanges in Amsterdam, Brussels and Luxembourg.

Fortis came into being in 1990, as the result of a merger of AMEV, a Dutch insurer and VSB, a Dutch banking group plus, later that same year, AG, a Belgian insurer. Fortis acquired the Dutch investment bank, Mees Pierson, in 1996 from ABN Amro. It made various other acquisitions including Générale de Banque in 1999, and expanded into Poland, Turkey, Asia and Africa. As of 2006, its profits were EUR4.56 billion and its market value was over EUR45 billion.

On 8 October 2007 a consortium of three banks, Royal Bank of Scotland Group, Fortis and Banco Santander (headquartered in Spain) announced that it had been successful in its acquisition of ABN Amro, the Dutch bank. A hostile fight for the bank had raged from April to October with Barclays as the consortium's contender. Details on the takeover appear below.

■ The ABN Amro takeover

ABN Amro executives had been seriously contemplating the bank's position since 2005. ABN Amro was still falling well short of its target of having a return on equity that would put it among the top five of its peer group. This target had been set by CEO Rijkman Groenink on his appointment in 2000. From 2000 until 2005, the ABN Amro stock price stagnated and, although profits improved marginally, they fell short of aspirations.

The 2006 financial results did not improve matters. Operating expenses increased at a greater rate than operating revenue. Non-performing loans increased year on year by 192 per cent. Net profits were up, but only thanks to profits on assets sold off.

There had been calls from active investors (the hedge fund, TCI, in particular) over the prior couple of years, for ABN Amro to break up, or merge, or to put itself up for sale. On 21 February 2007 TCI had asked the chairman of the Supervisory Board to investigate a merger, acquisition or breakup of ABN Amro. TCI observed that the current stock price did not reflect the true value of the underlying assets. TCI requested that the chairman put the proposition on the agenda of the annual shareholders' meeting of April 2007. Matters moved ahead quickly and, on 20 March 2007 the British bank Barclays and ABN Amro both confirmed they were in exclusive talks about a merger. On 28 March 2007 ABN Amro published the agenda for the shareholders' meeting. It included the items requested by TCI, with the recommendation not to follow up the request for a breakup of the company.

On 18 April 2007 the British bank, Royal Bank of Scotland (RBS) contacted ABN Amro proposing a deal in which a consortium of banks, including RBS, Belgium's Fortis and Spain's Banco Santander would jointly bid for ABN Amro and thereafter take geographical parts of the company between them. According to the proposal, RBS would take ABN Amro's Chicago operations, La Salle, and the wholesale operations; while Banco Santander would take the Brazilian operations and Fortis, the operations in the Netherlands.

On 23 April 2007 ABN Amro and Barclays announced further detail of the proposed acquisition of ABN Amro by Barclays. The deal was valued at EUR67 billion. Part of the proposal was the sale of La Salle to Bank of America for EUR21 billion. On 25 April 2007 the RBS-led consortium brought out their own offer, worth EUR72 billion, if ABN Amro would abandon its sale plans of La Salle to Bank of America. During the shareholders' meeting the next day, a majority of about 68 per cent of the shareholders voted in favour of the proposals requested by TCI.

The La Salle proposition was clearly an obstructive tactic. It was a way of blocking the RBS bid, which turned around further access to the US markets – the group's existing US brands included Citizens Bank and Charter One. On 3 May 2007 the Dutch Investors' Association, with the support of shareholders representing 20 per cent of ABN Amro shares, took its case to the Dutch commercial court in Amsterdam, asking for an injunction against the La Salle sale. The court ruled that the sale of La Salle was effectively part of the current merger talks between Barclays and ABN Amro, and that the ABN Amro shareholders should be able to approve other possibilities in a general meeting of shareholders. And, in July 2007, the Dutch Supreme Court eliminated any uncertainty about the situation when it ruled that Bank of America's acquisition of La Salle Bank could proceed. Bank of America absorbed La Salle with effect from 1 October 2007.

On 23 July Barclays raised its offer for ABN Amro to EUR67.5 billion (that is EUR67.5 billion for ABN Amro minus La Salle but plus cash from the sale thereof). But this was still short of the RBS consortium's offer. The new Barclay's offer was worth EUR35.73 per share and included 37 per cent cash, but was below the EUR38.40 per share offer made, a week earlier by the RBS consortium. These offers did not include the La Salle business since ABN Amro could now proceed with the sale of La Salle to Bank of America. The RBS consortium would have to settle for ABN Amro's investment banking division and its Asian network – but not La Salle. On 30 July 2007, ABN Amro withdrew its support for Barclay's offer which was lower than the offer from the RBS consortium. The ABN Amro board stated that the Barclay's offer matched ABN Amro's strategic vision, but the board could not recommend it from a financial point of view. The bid from RBS, Fortis and Banco Santander was 9.8 per cent higher than Barclay's offer. On 5 October 2007 Barclays withdrew its bid, clearing the way for the RBS-led consortium bid to go through, along with its planned break-up of ABN Amro. Fortis would have ABN Amro's Dutch and Belgian operations, Banco Santander would have Banco Real in Brazil and Banca Antonveneta in Italy, and RBS would have ABN Amro's wholesale division and other operations, including the Asian business.

On 8 October 2007 the RBS consortium declared victory in the bid after the shareholders representing 86 per cent of ABN Amro shares accepted their offer. The successful offer was paid for by over 93 per cent cash. Rijkman Froenink, chairman of the Management Board of ABN Amro, who had heavily backed the Barclay's offer, decided to step down.

To fund the takeover bid, Fortis arranged a EUR13 billion rights issue in October 2007. In April 2008, RBS announced the largest rights issue in British corporate history, which aimed to raise GBP12 billion to offset a write-down of GBP5.9 billion resulting from bad investments and to shore up its reserves following the purchase of ABN Amro.

In October 2008, British Prime Minister, Gordon Brown announced a UK government bailout of the British financial system. The UK Treasury would put in GBP37 billion of new capital into RBS, Lloyds TSB and HBOS to avert a financial collapse. This resulted in government ownership in RBS of 58 per cent. Sir Fred Goodwin, RBS chief executive officer, resigned.

In January 2009, RBS announced a loss of GBP28 billion of which GBP20 billion was due to ABN Amro asset write-downs versus the acquisition price. At this time the UK government took its ownership in RBS to 70 per cent.

The question remains. RBS, the prime mover in the takeover bid could have withdrawn their bid on the news of the La Salle sale to Bank of America. After all, they claimed that this was what they wanted. That they failed to do so may justifiably be viewed as a clear indication that it was seeking takeover victory at all costs. Never mind the RBS shareholders. It happens all too often. A clear maximum price needs to be specified. A clear statement of what is required from the deal needs to be specified. Failure to adhere to these goals is the root cause of so many acquisition disasters. Hubris, evidenced by the takeover victory, quickly led to corporate nemesis. The RBS board, especially its apex, must surely wonder whether things could have got any worse.

■ Fortis problems in the wake of ABN Amro takeover

The price paid for ABN Amro totalled EUR70 billion, an amount widely reckoned to be on the high side. After the deal, it was agreed that Fortis would get the retail and business activities in the Benelux countries and the international investment company. Integration of the retail activities into Fortis Bank would be subject to permission of De Nederlandsche Bank (DNB), the Dutch central bank, and some business activities would have to be sold on because of EU competition regulations on market share. Fortis would then use the ABN Amro brand name for its retail operations in the Netherlands. To finance its share of the purchase price, Fortis issued new shares via a rights issue (therefore available to existing Fortis shareholders) at EUR15 per share to raise EUR13 billion.

Like RBS, Fortis was expecting big write-offs relating to the ABN Amro acquisition. The price paid included a huge amount for intangibles that could not, under accounting rules prevailing, be put on the Fortis group balance sheet. After the write-downs, Fortis would be in danger of failing to meet the standards for capital required by banks. Also, the sale of the business activities as requested by EU regulations would create a EUR300 million loss.

Additionally, by June 2008, with the financial crisis on the immediate horizon, Fortis needed to raise further equity to the extent of an additional EUR8.3 billion. A further rights issue at EUR10 per share was called for. The raising of the additional EUR8.3 billion was partly achieved by eliminating the year's dividend, saving EUR1.5 billion. Previously, Fortis CEO Jean Votron had stated and repeated that the dividend would be untouched. For years, the reliability of the Fortis dividend had been one of the strong points for its share price. It was widely reckoned to be as safe as houses (sic). Eliminating it rocked shareholder confidence and the share value dropped from over EUR12 to just over EUR10 on 26 June (reducing the value of the company by over EUR4 billion, with more declines to come later).

Many commentators reckoned that in drawing up the ABN Amro takeover, Fortis and RBS management had disregarded the effects on shareholders' funds (the total of shares issued plus undistributed profits and reserves less losses). Investors were amazed that Fortis needed more money so soon after the earlier share issue and they were loathe to put up more cash, feeling that Fortis had proved unreliable. Many shareholders had raised loans to pay for the earlier share issue and were counting on the dividend. To say that they were furious is an understatement.

On 11 July 2008 the Fortis CEO, Jean Votron, stepped down. The value of Fortis, as reflected in the share price, was, at that time, one third of what it had been before the ABN Amro acquisition, and reflected a value just below what Fortis had paid for ABN Amro's Benelux activities alone. The share price continued to waiver below EUR10 per share. Votron was succeeded as CEO by Herman Verwilst, who reassured shareholders that Fortis was solid and to be relied upon. Maurice Lippens, chairman of the Supervisory Board, had personally bought a large amount of shares at just below EUR9 per share. But, as the markets in general declined, so did the Fortis share price. On Thursday 25 September 2008 Fortis shares plunged to EUR5.5. This was attributed to a rumour that Dutch bank Rabobank had been asked to help out with Fortis's difficulties. The rumour was denied by both Fortis and Rabobank. CEO Verwilst held a press conference to reassure analysts and stockholders. He did not produce actual figures but reaffirmed that Fortis was solid and that there was no reason at all to believe a bankruptcy was at hand. Nonetheless, the shares plunged again, closing around EUR5. The new CEO stepped down that same evening and Filip Dierckx was named as the incoming CEO. Again, in one week Fortis shares dropped 35 per cent. A joke circulated in Belgium to the effect that one should wait indoors near the telephone because the next call could be for you to become the new Fortis CEO.

Fortis issued a shareholder circular on 20 November in which it stated that, on Friday 26 September 2008 liquidity problems became evidenced by large withdrawals on the part of business customers, due to the Fortis bankruptcy rumours. On Friday September 26, EUR20 billion was withdrawn, with an additional withdrawal of EUR30 billion expected for the following Monday. The firm declared that there were no solvency problems, only liquidity problems.

The Belgian government was now pleading that Fortis should band up with a stronger partner. Easier said than done. In preliminary discussions, ING offered EUR1.50 per share and BNP Paribas EUR2 per share for Fortis. These talks were curtailed as governments themselves intervened. Fortis was nationalised on 28 September 2008 with the three Benelux countries investing a total of EUR11.2 billion into the bank. Press releases reported that Belgium, Netherlands and Luxembourg governments would invest respectively EUR4.7 billion, EUR4 billion and EUR2.5 billion in the Belgian, Dutch and Luxembourg parts of Fortis. At the same time, it was announced that plans to integrate the retail activities of ABN Amro into Fortis had been stopped and that these activities would be sold. A sale at less than EUR12 billion would have adverse consequences for the Tier 1 ratio of Fortis.

In the week of 20 November 2008 large withdrawals by business customers continued, causing further liquidity problems. Emergency credit of EUR66 billion was provided to save the day.

Government wrangling was a feature of the Fortis bailout and the ongoing legal cases will keep the courts in business for a few years to come. Having said that, asset sales have continued. In fact, the Dutch government sold the Fortis insurance division for EUR350 million in June 2009.

In an extremely complicated deal in October 2008, the French bank, BNP Paribas, took a majority stake in the Fortis Belgian and Luxembourg banking ends of its activities. The Belgian and Luxembourg governments were reduced to minority shareholders with blocking power in exchange for shares in BNP Paribas. Effectively, the governments sold a 75 per cent stake to BNP Paribas, at a valuation of EUR11 billion for the total company, to be paid in BNP Paribas shares, making the Belgian government the largest shareholder in BNP Paribas at 12 per cent.

Negotiations with BNP Paribas were not easy, the French being adamant that they wanted only the banking parts and no part of the toxic assets held by the bank. Finally, the government shareholders agreed to let the remaining Fortis Group retained deal with these toxic assets – Fortis had caused the problem so Fortis could clear it up – and sold on only the bank, shorn of the toxic assets, to BNP Paribas.

Case 14.2 UBS

■ Introduction

Headquartered in Zurich and Basel in Switzerland, UBS is a diversified international bank and financial services provider. It is the world's number two manager of private wealth assets and is the second-largest bank in Europe. UBS has retail offices throughout the USA and in over 50 other countries. The acronym UBS is an abbreviation, which originated from its predecessor firm, Union Bank of Switzerland, which merged with Swiss Bank Corporation (SBC) in 1998. Some 38 per cent of its employees work in the Americas, 34 per cent in Switzerland, 15 per cent in the rest of Europe and 13 per cent in Asia Pacific. Its operational segments embrace wealth management, investment banking, asset management, retail banking and commercial banking. At the middle of 2007, its equity market capitalisation was CHF151 billion.

Prior to that year UBS, along with many other investment banks like RBS, had piled into CDOs, where it incurred vast losses. UBS turned to the government of Singapore for fresh funding amounting to USD11 billion, and in November 2008, following further large losses, UBS accepted financial aid from the Swiss government.

As mentioned above, UBS was the result of the merger of the Union Bank of Switzerland and the Swiss Bank Corporation in June 1998. Prior to the merger, SBC had built a global investment banking business through its purchases of Dillion Read in New York and S. G. Warburg in London. In 2000, UBS acquired Paine Webber Group to become one of the world's largest private client wealth management businesses. In June 2003, all UBS business groups rebranded under the UBS name. UBS Paine Webber, UBS Warburg, UBS Asset Management and others became UBS.

■ Dubious practices

A number of pieces of financial history, extracted from archive material, depict UBS as having a somewhat chequered past. Listed below are some of these instances. For example, in January 1997, Christoph Meili, a security officer at the Union Bank of Switzerland found employees shredding archives of a subsidiary that had previously had extensive dealings with Nazi Germany. This was in violation of a Swiss law, adopted in December 1996, protecting such material. Union Bank of Switzerland acknowledged that it had 'made a deplorable mistake', but stated that the destroyed archives were not related to the Holocaust. Criminal proceedings began against archive personnel and against Meili for possible violation of bank secrecy, which is a criminal offence in Switzerland. Both of these proceedings were discontinued in September 1997.

In 1997, a lawsuit by the World Jewish Congress against Swiss banks was launched to retrieve deposits made by victims of Nazi persecution prior to and during World War II. Negotiations involving Union Bank of Switzerland and competitor, Credit Suisse, resulted in a settlement of USD1.25 billion in 1998.

In April 2005, UBS lost a discrimination lawsuit. The plaintiff Laura Zubulake, a former institutional equities saleswoman in the USA, alleged that her manager had undermined and removed her from professional responsibilities and treated her differently from men in the same job. An important point in the case was that UBS had not preserved relevant e-mails. The federal judge was unimpressed by this and, in October 2005, the parties agreed to settle the case privately out of court.

In a *Business Week* article published on 26 February 2007, there was a story that UBS was under investigation following discovery that traders working for two or more unidentified hedge funds were paying a UBS employee for information on impending ratings changes on stocks. In March 2007, an executive director in the firm's equity research department was charged, along with 13 other individuals from various firms, with insider-trading fraud of more than USD15 million.

In an article published by Reuters on 23 February 2008, the Brazilian public prosecutor announced that several employees of UBS as well others from a Credit Suisse company and AIG were under investigation by federal authorities. Earlier in 2007, police had arrested 20 people, including bankers at UBS, Credit Suisse and AIG Private Bank after the discovery of illegal activities including money laundering, tax evasion, fraudulent banking and operating without a banking licence.

In June 2008, the US Federal Bureau of Investigation made a formal request to travel to Switzerland to probe a multi-million dollar tax evasion case involving UBS. The *New York Times* reported that the case involved around 20,000 citizens in the USA. This investigation flowed from information revealed in 2006 by a UBS client under investigation for US tax evasion. Contiguous to this, in February 2009, the US government filed a suit against UBS to reveal the names of 52,000 American customers, alleging that the bank and these customers conspired to defraud the Internal Revenue Services and federal government of legitimately-owed US taxes. In August 2009, UBS announced a settlement deal that concluded its litigation with the IRS. This involved the revealing of many of the names of the offending US citizens and payment of fines and restitution of USD780 million.

Embarrassed by the above and seeking change, UBS issued, in January 2010, a new code of conduct and business ethics which all employees must sign. The code addresses financial crime, competition, confidentiality, human rights and environmental issues. The code lays out sanctions against employees who violate it, embracing warnings, demotions or dismissal. According to the UBS chairman of the board and group CEO, the code is an 'integral part of changing the way UBS conducts business'.

■ The financial crisis hits UBS

Along with Citigroup, RBS and Merrill Lynch, UBS was one of the most aggressive players in the CDO market. And not just in CDOs. Entering the financial crisis, the ratio of assets to equity at UBS was 46.9 times – the median ratio for US banks was 35 times. Also symptomatic of UBS aggressiveness was its formation in 2005 of a hedge fund, Dillon Real Capital Management, and expansion by UBS, again in 2005, into the securitisation business. Their growth was rapid indeed.

With the rise of the super-senior debt difficulties, UBS initially decided to sell the risk on in the market place but later this was reversed and UBS became a net holder of CDO risk. In line with the Basel Accord, UBS took a relaxed view in respect of assets with high credit ratings, like super-senior risk. Basel allowed banks to use their own models to work out the risk and estimate how much capital they needed to hold as protection. The UBS risk group used VaR and Gaussian analysis to model risk. This was the case for many other banks too. Its models indicated that super-senior assets would not lose more than 2 per cent of value, even in a worst-case scenario. So, the bank decided it needed to maintain only a small amount of capital to back the risk. UBS was even more aggressive. UBS executives were aware that if they bought insurance from monoline insurers against that 2 per cent risk, the super-senior effectively became risk-free. That would remove the need to hold any capital at all to back the risk. The bank proceeded to put oceans of super-senior on its books. No problem. Well, so they thought.

The UBS team went further on the CDO front. UBS internal rules required mark-to-market valuation of its trading assets – that is the value of assets held on the trading book had to be revalued at current market prices. But it was often difficult to get market prices for senior CDO notes as they rarely traded. What the UBS trading team decided to do was to make estimates of what a CDO ought to be worth using its own internal models. Such prices would be adjusted over time. With a rising market, this resulted in their reporting profits in this area. Such profits were small in percentage terms but with USD50 billion of super-senior assets on its book, most on the CDO trading desk, overall profits were large.

As Gillian Tett[1] observes, 'now and then, risk managers expressed surprise as the mountain grew. Their concerns were dismissed. The conservative and bureaucratic UBS managers put great stock in the fact that the super-senior notes carried a triple-A tag. The result was that vast quantities of risk completely disappeared from the bank's internal risk reports.' Tett goes on to report that one member of the UBS board said, 'We were just told by our risk people that these instruments are triple A, like Treasury bonds. People did not ask too many questions.'

With all of this CDO risk on their books as an asset, the problem ballooned when markets stalled and values fell. In April 2008, UBS announced that it was writing down USD19 billion on its CDOs and investments related to American subprime and other mortgages. As a result, its credit rating was cut. The bank also said it would call on its shareholders for CHF15 billion in additional funds to shore up its Tier 1 capital ratio. In May 2008, UBS announced plans to cut 5,500 jobs by the middle of 2009 as a result of the economic crisis.

In October 2008, UBS announced that it had arranged CHF6 billion of further new capital through mandatory convertible notes placed with the Swiss Confederation. The Swiss National Bank and UBS made an agreement to transfer USD60 billion of illiquid securities and various assets from UBS to a separate fund entity.

In November 2008, UBS announced that from 2009 no more than one-third of any cash bonus would be paid out in the year it is earned with the rest held in reserve. Share incentives would vest after three years and top executives would have to hold on to 75 per cent of any such vested shares. Share bonuses would also be subject to malus charges – the opposite of bonus and that means deductions for subsequent losses.

In February 2009, UBS announced that it lost nearly CHF20 billion in 2008, the biggest annual loss in corporate history in Switzerland. The loss was later revised to CHF21 billion. Due to the global financial crisis, UBS has had to take USD50 billion in write-downs and has cut 11,000 jobs since 2007.

During 2009, UBS further strengthened its capital base by placing 293 million shares with a number of large institutional investors. In August 2009, the Swiss government announced that it was selling its CHF6 billion stake in UBS, making a significant profit.

In passing, it is worth noting that the problems of UBS during the financial crisis and retold in this section are very similar in terms of exposés and the subsequent débâcle to those encountered at US banks, Citigroup and Merrill Lynch and at UK banks HBOS and RBS, although the latter British bank saddled itself with the dire consequences of a takeover too far – namely its purchase of ABN Amro.

Case 14.3 Icelandic banks

■ Introduction

Iceland is a small country. Its population is a mere 300,000. Just before the crash it was experiencing mid-teens inflation and this was not a new experience. Iceland has few proven natural resources apart from fish and hot water, and its economy is one-third the size of Luxembourg's. But in the run-up to the credit crunch, Iceland experienced a massive bubble. There was a brief period when the country's economic output per person was higher than that of the US. At the same time its currency, the krona, was overvalued according to numerous purchasing power parity (PPP) criteria. PPP suggests an inverse relationship between inflation and currency strength. Empirically, it seems to hold long-term but there are substantial short-term deviations – meaning short-term overvaluation or undervaluation.

In early 2007, the krona was rated as one of the most overvalued currencies in the world. According to the Big Mac Index, as late as July 2008, a burger cost the equivalent of USD6 in Iceland versus USD3.57 in the US. This excess currency strength derived substantially from the carry trade, essentially hot money speculation looking for high interest rates. But this is a risky strategy. The carry trade involves borrowing in currencies where the interest rate is low and depositing money in currencies where the interest rate is high. However, basic economics suggests a relationship between the quoted interest rate in a particular currency, the real international interest rate and local inflation. For developed economies with no exchange controls to prevent money from moving from one currency to another, the following equation would apply:

$$\text{Quoted interest rate in} = \text{International real interest} + \text{Inflation in the}$$
$$\text{currency X} \qquad \text{rate (with no inflation} \qquad \text{country of}$$
$$\text{built in)} \qquad \text{currency X}$$

To be more precise, the right-hand side of the equation should have a further term equal to (the international real interest rate) multiplied by (inflation in the country of currency X) added to it. But, since the international real interest rate is small, the above multiplication is usually very small.

So, according to the above formula, the interest rate in krona was high because of Iceland's high inflation rate. Borrowing in Japanese yen may have a low interest rate attached because yen inflation is low. Borrowing at 2 per cent per annum in yen and transferring the money to krona at 16 per cent per annum may appear attractive at first sight – you gain 14 per cent per annum. But you only gain 14 per cent if exchange rates remain constant, enabling you to ship back krona deposited into yen borrowed at the same rate as shipped from yen to krona at the outset. Admittedly, if the krona gains against the yen, you will make more than 14 per cent per annum. But what if the krona falls in value against the yen? Well, if the krona falls by around 14 per cent against the yen, you may come out even. But remember that the krona was vastly overvalued at the time of our story. According to PPP (using the Big Mac Index) the krona could easily fall by 40 per cent against the dollar. And maybe by a similar amount against the yen – but that depends on dollar/yen PPP standings. Anyway, the risk should be clear. Carry trade players – and there were a lot of them – in banks and hedge funds were placing monies borrowed from low interest rate currencies into krona and hoping for no fall in the krona. Clearly carry trade speculators run big risks. And, carry traders need to monitor their investments carefully against possible FX losses. And they have to be prepared to move fast if the market looks like going against them. This is hot money trading. And hot money can vanish rapidly. The carry traders will have to unload their krona positions before a fall in the krona happens. Understanding this background is essential to a full comprehension of the Iceland position because speculators suddenly reversed their views on the krona as 2008 progressed.

Iceland had attracted vast amounts of carry trade money deposited in local currency and, on the strength of this success, Icelandic banks were flush with cash. The Iceland banks also marketed deposit accounts with attractive rates in euros, sterling and so on. They were offering higher deposit rates than competing international banks in euros, sterling and so on.

Three hundred thousand British depositors put money into online sterling bank accounts (for example, Icesave, sponsored by the Icelandic bank, Landsbanki) attracted by high interest rates, forgetting that high interest rates, and high risk go together. Meanwhile, many ordinary Icelanders, with salaries in krona, took out 100 per cent mortgages in dollars, euros and yen, unaware perhaps that PPP was likely to reassert itself in the future. Repayment of the mortgage would then cost more in terms of krona. Did they realise the nature of the currency mismatch? Salaries in krona versus mortgage payments in dollars, euros or yen. Accidents waiting to happen abounded in Iceland in 2008.

■ The root of the problem

In 1998 and 1999 Iceland's state-owned banks were privatised and Landsbanki, Glitnir and Kaupthing joined the local stock market. In 2001, Icelandic banks were deregulated. The banks promptly increased debt as foreign businesses were acquired.

The Iceland bank crisis was precipitated in 2008 when banks became unable to refinance their debts. The three major banks held foreign debt in excess of EUR50 billion – that is, EUR160,000 for every Iceland resident. It compares with Iceland's gross domestic product of EUR8.5 billion. Even in March 2008, the cost of deposit insurance for monies in Landsbanki and Kaupthing was running at between 6 and 8.5 per cent of the sum deposited above the rate for other European banks.

Iceland's banks were financing their expansion with loans on the interbank lending market and, more recently, from deposits from outside of Iceland – as described earlier. Households had taken on a large amount of debt, equivalent to 213 per cent of disposable income and this drove inflation. This was further exacerbated by the practice of the Central Bank of Iceland issuing liquidity loans to banks on the basis of newly-issued unsecured bonds. In other words, the Central Bank was printing money on demand.

Consumer prices were rising at 14 per cent per annum at September 2008, compared with a government target of 2.5 per cent and the Central Bank of Iceland interest rate was 15.5 per cent for krona. Icelandic money supply (M3) grew at 56.5 per cent in the 12 months to September 2008, compared with 5.0 per cent per annum real GDP growth. Iceland was in a bubble and Iceland was in trouble. Its krona was vastly overvalued. Its population was on a debt-driven spending spree and the carry trade was moving in reverse in 2008. In fact, the Icelandic krona had declined by more than 35 per cent against the euro from January to September 2008.

The three Icelandic banks were funding themselves from their Central Bank, from deposits in euros, sterling and US dollars and so on and from the interbank wholesale market, again in euros, sterling and US dollars. If the Icelandic banks had lent the same amounts as they had borrowed in the same currencies for the same maturities, then incoming cash flows would have been equal to cash flows out at the same times and in the same currencies. But the banks were nowhere near this sophisticated. They exhibited mismatches in currency terms, in maturities and in amounts. With net asset positions in krona, the risk was self-evident. An overvalued currency implies a drop in that currency sometime in the future. The problems for Icelandic banks became a triple whammy – more assets held in a potentially depreciating currency and more liabilities in foreign currencies plus the need to roll over debt in the interbank market plus pervasive maturity mismatches. Another accident waiting to happen. As the financial community became increasingly aware of the potential problems, so the accident became more certain.

■ Accident

Icelandic banks appear not to have been holders of either subprime debt or toxic instruments. But they did experience credit default swaps – not as holders but as the subject of the CDS. As Thorvaldsson[2], a former CEO of the UK end of Kaupthing, comments: '… when the first CDS was written on Kaupthing, the price of this insurance was 20 basis points or 0.20 per cent. If you held a million dollar bond, issued by Kaupthing, on which you wanted to insure yourself against a possible default, you needed to pay an annual fee of 0.20 per cent of one million, or USD2000. The pricing of a CDS was highly correlated to the prices of the bonds you were issuing, of course. If the Kaupthing CDS was trading at 0.20 per cent, you would expect the bank to sell its bonds at 0.20 per cent margin over LIBOR rates … By paying a small amount of money in our example USD2000, a hedge fund could potentially make one million dollars on the downfall of Kaupthing.' He continues: '… the CDS spreads also became an indicator of a bank's riskiness on the basis of the spreads. In theory that sounds right; in practice there were so many factors influencing the spreads, including manipulation, that it was far from reliable. But it was a great quantifiable measure for the newspapers when they wanted to make the point about how risky the market perceived the Icelandic banks to be.' And, of course, the perception of riskiness rose and the CDS spreads widened. Even in 2006, well before the crash, Iceland experienced a mini-crisis with widespread drops in confidence in the currency and the banks – justifiably so it later transpired. Headlines such as 'Iceland melting' abounded in market reports. Others offered the opinion that 'Kaupthing Bank with a balance sheet 2.5 times Iceland's GDP is too large to be rescued by the sovereign.' Amidst all of this, Kaupthing's CDS spread widened to 1 per cent and above. Hedge fund gurus were negative on the country and the krona. Hugh Hendry was reported in a *Times* (of London) interview in 2006 that he wanted to become known as 'the man who bankrupted Iceland'.

If Icelandic financial institutions survived 2006 and 2007, they failed to do so in 2008. As with many banks around the world, the Icelandic banks found it impossible to roll over their loans in the interbank market, their creditors insisting on repayment while no other banks were willing to make new loans. In such a situation, a bank would normally have to ask for a loan from the central bank as the lender of last resort. But in Iceland the banks were, in 2008, so much larger than the national economy that the Central Bank of Iceland and the Iceland government could not guarantee repayment of the banks' debts, making the collapse of the banks inevitable.

In late September 2008, it was announced that the Glitnir bank would be nationalised. The following week, control of Landsbanki and Glitnir was given to receivers appointed by the Financial Supervisory Authority (FME). Soon after that, the same organisation placed Iceland's largest bank, Kaupthing, into receivership too. Commenting on the need for emergency measures, Prime Minister Geir Haarde said on 6 October 2008 that the Icelandic economy, in the worst case, could be sucked with the banks into the whirlpool and the result could have been national bankruptcy, he further affirmed that the actions taken by the government had ensured that the Icelandic state would not go bankrupt. In the middle of 2008, Iceland's external debt was 9.553 trillion Icelandic krona (EUR50 billion), more than 80 per cent of which was in the banking sector. This compares with Iceland's 2007 gross domestic product of 1.293 trillion krona (EUR8.5 billion).

Immediately following, the krona fell sharply in value and foreign currency transactions were suspended for weeks on end. The market capitalisation of the Icelandic stock exchange dropped by more than 90 per cent. As one would expect, the four rating agencies that monitor Iceland were responding negatively and lowered the country's standing as shown in Table 14.1.

On Wednesday night, 8 October 2008, the Central Bank of Iceland abandoned its attempt to peg the krona at 131 krona to the euro. By 9 October, the Icelandic krona was trading at 340 to the euro, although by 28 November it had perked up a little to a rate of 280 krona to the euro. But the Central Bank of Iceland would only give you 182.5 krona to the euro. The reason for this difference in quotation was all down to new exchange control rules instituted by the Central Bank.

The new foreign exchange rules obliged Icelandic residents to deposit foreign currency they received with an Icelandic bank on a krona account. But there is evidence that some Icelandic exporters had been operating an informal offshore foreign exchange market, trading pounds and euros for krona outside of Icelandic FX controls or keeping money in sterling and euro accounts. On 28 November 2008 the Central Bank of Iceland imposed a new set of currency regulations, banning movements of capital to and from Iceland without a licence from the Central Bank.

The FME acted to ring-fence the Icelandic operations of Landsbanki and Glitnir. NBI (originally known as Nýi Landsbanki – New Landsbanki) was set up on 9 October 2008 with 200 billion krona in equity and 2,300 billion krona of assets. Nýi Glitnir was set up on 15 October with 110 billion krona in equity and 1,200 billion of assets. Discussions with Icelandic pension funds to sell Kaupthing as a going concern broke down on 17 October

Table 14.1 Icelandic sovereign debt rating

	29 Sept 2008	10 Oct 2008
Fitch	A+	BBB−
Moody's	Aa1	A1
R&I	AA	BBB−
S&P	A−	BBB

2008 and Nýja Kaupping was set up on 22 October 2008 with 75 billion krona in equity and 700 billion krona of assets. The equity in all three new banks came from the Icelandic government. The new banks, following nationalisation, will also have to reimburse their predecessors for the net value of the transferred assets.

IMF loans have been necessary to prop up the ailing economic condition of Iceland. It has been said that Iceland's banks, its fishing industry and its agriculture, to say nothing of most companies, were insolvent in 2009. And the plight of the average Icelander in 2009/10 was something that would not have been imaginable two years earlier. With over 25 per cent of mortgages in default and the government depending upon foreign emergency loans, there is little light at the end of the tunnel.

Of course, IMF support is usual in these situations. Also, international help has been forthcoming, with Russia strategically interested. With the Arctic ice-cap melting faster than anticipated, there is an expectation that ice-locked sea-lanes may be clear by 2015 and some studies indicate that the whole summer ice-cap could disappear by 2040. Furthermore, 25 per cent of the world's undiscovered oil and gas is reckoned to lie beneath the Arctic Ocean. And, minerals and diamonds lie under the ice. The USA, Canada, Russia, Norway and other northern countries (including Iceland) can lay claim to substantial potential resources. So, longer term, Iceland may be a winner. But, in the short term, its dependence upon international funding has, to a large extent, mortgaged its future. Its ability to weather the storm will be sorely tested.

Before departing Iceland, there are other lessons to be learned from its financial débâcle which reveals an amazing degree of amateurism (even by the standards encountered elsewhere). We briefly describe these below.

■ Cronyism

Summarising the extreme cronyism of the Icelandic business system, Boyes[3] estimates that the financial elite of the country consisted of a mere 30 people. And he describes the following scenario relating to an Icelandic bank takeover.

1. Icelandic bank with dubious credentials bids for established foreign bank using borrowed money;
2. Targeted bank eagerly takes the offered cash, claiming to be acting in the interest of shareholders, [then] registers doubts with FSA or other regulatory body;
3. FSA contacts Icelandic regulator, who offers reassurance;
4. Icelandic regulator attends school reunion with Icelandic banker.'

And this pattern of cronyism seems to have pervaded the banking practices of Kaupthing as revealed by its loan book. The *Daily Telegraph*[4] of 4 August 2009 revealed leaked internal documents that showed that Kaupthing had lent billions of euros to companies linked to a key director and top shareholders.

■ Kaupthing leaked documents

The papers cast light on Kaupthing's highly unusual lending practices. They revealed that its largest loans, totalling more than EUR6.4 billion (GBP5.45 billion), were given to companies connected to just six clients, four of whom were major shareholders in the company. Kaupthing made some of these loans with partial or no collateral, the largest of which was given to Exista, its own biggest shareholder with a stake of over 20 per cent.

The bank was also lending millions of pounds to individuals and holding companies so that they could buy shares in Kaupthing itself – effectively propping up its own share price. The 205-page leaked document, which appeared on the internet, was allegedly presented at an internal meeting at Kaupthing on 25 September 2008. It details the loans to companies and high-profile individuals such as Kevin Stanford, Robert Tchenguiz, the Candy brothers and Simon Halabi.

Among some of the bank's biggest borrowers were companies connected to:

■ Lydur Gudmundsson, who founded the Bakkavor food empire that employs 20,000, mainly in the UK. Mr Gudmundsson sat on the boards of Kaupthing and of Exista and was granted loans worth EUR1.86 billion for companies linked to him and his brother, Agust.

■ A note relating to a EUR791.2 million loan to Exista itself indicates that the 'bulk of the loans are unsecured and with no covenants'.

■ Robert Tchenguiz, the bank's biggest client, was a London-based entrepreneur with property interests and was also a board member of Exista. Kaupthing lent EUR1.74 billion to finance private investments.

■ Kevin Stanford, the retail entrepreneur and director of House of Fraser, was Kaupthing's fourth largest shareholder. He was lent EUR519 million to buy shares, substantially in Kaupthing itself, using those same shares as collateral.

Also, companies belonging to the bank's second biggest shareholder, Olafur Olafsson, were lent EUR636 million, but one of the assets pledged as security appears to be a 9.71 per cent share in Kaupthing itself. Another sizeable shareholder was Skuli Thorvaldsson, who borrowed EUR790 million to buy 22 million shares in the bank and 94 million shares in Exista.

There is no suggestion that any of the above shareholders acted illegally. But questions must stand about the financial correctness and business sense of the bank's practices. Clearly, credit analysis and bank control systems must have been almost non-existent.

Kaupthing's widespread practice of lending large sums for customers to buy shares in the bank itself, using those same shares as collateral, would push up the share price and mean that many of the bank's top shareholders did not fully own their stakes. In addition, there appeared to be a haphazard approach to risk whereby little or no collateral was offered for substantial loans. In a section of the leaked document relating to credit ratings, many loans to key borrowers were marked 'exception list' or 'margin N/A'. A note detailing one loan to Exista admits that the 'bulk of the loans are unsecured and with no covenants.'

Furthermore, many loans were so-called bullet loans, where borrowers did not have to pay any interest until the end of the loans' maturity – and this was often rolled-over. This seems like a new meaning to the term bullet loan. It normally refers to loans where the principal is repaid in one shot at the end of the loan, but interest is paid year by year.

In accordance with the *Daily Telegraph*'s revelations[5] in its 11 August edition, Table 14.2 shows the breakdown of loan facilities given by Kaupthing versus shareholdings in the bank. A salutary indication of banking practices gone mad.

■ The unravelling

So, what created the bursting of Iceland's bubble? Indeed, why do bubbles burst anyway? We cannot do better than quote, once again, Kindleberger[6] summarising Hyman Minsky[7]. The former is much more readable than the latter although the latter's insights are deep indeed. 'According to Minsky, events leading up to a crisis start with a "displacement", some exogenous, outside shock to the macroeconomic system. The nature of this displacement varies from one speculative boom to another. It may be the outbreak or end of a war, a bumper harvest or crop failure, the widespread adoption of an invention with pervasive effects – canals, railroads, the automobile – some political event or surprising financial success' – or failure. For example, the unravelling of the carry trade. For example, banking incompetence worthy of the exploits of Laurel and Hardy, or Frank Spencer, or Mr Bean. Or would that comparison flatter Icelandic bankers?

Table 14.2 Loan facilities and shareholdings in Kaupthing

Loans to companies connected to or merely to:	Loan facility EUR million	Percentage shareholding in Kaupthing
Exista and Robert Tchenguiz (London-based entrepreneur and property developer)	3200	23.0
Skulli Thorvaldsson (Icelandic investor)	790	2.96
Olafur Olafsson (Icelandic transport investor)	636	9.88
Kevin Stanford (British retail entrepreneur)	519	4.3
Jon Helgi Gudmundsson (Icelandic retailer)	255	3.7
Mohammed Binhalifa Al-thani (Sheikh of Qatar)	194	5.01
		49

Case 14.4 Irish banks

■ Introduction

The Republic of Ireland is a small country with a population of around 4 million, most of whom (98 per cent or so) are Catholics. A member country of the European Union, it was one of the original members of the eurozone with its previous currency, the punt, being replaced by the euro on 1 January 1999. The GDP of the country grew by an estimated 6 per cent per annum for each of the years 2005 to 2007.

Ireland, like many other European countries, experienced a property boom which built up from the mid-1990s and continued until 2006. However, in the period from 1980 to 1990 house prices in the Irish Republic had fallen in real terms.

The property lift-off began in 1994. Three main factors drove the price explosion. The first was demographic. Ireland had a baby boom during the late 1960s and in the 1970s. The impact on total population was cooled in the late 1980s as economic stagnation caused outward migration. But, as the economy took off from 1994 onwards, the baby boom generation was reaching maturity and this was coupled with Irish emigrants returning to their homeland. This led to a rapid increase in the young-adult population and gave a strong push to housing demand. The second factor was rapidly rising real disposable incomes. This was a consequence of rising real wages, a rapid increase in the numbers at work and large reductions in income taxes. Indeed, the numbers in work increased by half between 1994 and 2001. Much of this was due to the entry of married women into employment. At an after-tax level, the real terms increase in spending power between 1987 and 2000 was over 50 per cent. The third driving force to the rise in house prices was a fall in mortgage rates and the increasing availability of 100 per cent loan to value mortgages. Following Ireland's entry into the European Monetary Union and then into the eurozone, its real interest rates (that is, net of inflation) were frequently at net negative levels.

To put some flesh on the skeleton, the average home price increased by 2.3 times in real terms between 1994 and 2002 – or three times with general inflation included. In each of the years 2003 and 2004, the rise was 13 per cent. Between 2000 and 2006, prices tripled, although 2007 recorded a setback. The Celtic Tiger was riding a property boom.

Average prices in the capital, Dublin, moved from EUR80,000 in 1994 to EUR300,000 in 2002 and to EUR420,000 in 2005. Dublin prices are reckoned to be some 35 per cent higher than in the rest of Ireland.

■ Banking background

Ireland has a history of a cosy relationship between bankers, regulators and politicians – cronies playing golf together, partying together, horse riding together and drinking and gossiping together. Ross[8] begins his excellent overview of the local financial crisis with a portrait of the banking elite and so-called regulators which ends with a telling phrase

– 'here was the Irish aristocracy in action, wining and dining their regulators in undisturbed luxury just as a local volcano was erupting before their eyes.' Of course, the local volcano was the bubbling financial crisis.

Lest one thinks that such friendliness between regulators and regulated was novel, Ross goes on to say that 'rogue bankers were not sudden arrivals to the Ireland of 2008. Regulators being fêted by bankers was nothing new. There had been bailouts before, and small cliques had frequently seized control of banks – all to the detriment of taxpayers. Nor were today's bankers the first buccaneers to create a culture of the cavalier pursuit of quick riches. They were the inheritors of that culture. Ireland has a shameful banking history … For over thirty years Ireland has been cursed by banking scandals … banking skulduggery is endemic.' Two such examples related to the Deposit Interest Retention Tax (DIRT) and the Cayman Islands back to back loan.

The rules of DIRT, introduced in Ireland in 1986, required banks to withhold tax at source on interest paid to borrowers and pass it to the tax authorities. Non-residents were allowed to sign a form stating that they did not ordinarily live in Ireland and escape the tax. It seems that filling in the forms became a national hobby and, by the mid-nineties, 17 per cent of bank deposits were held by non-residents. According to O'Toole[9], the official files of the Department of Finance contained references stating that 'half the non-resident accounts are thought to be bogus'. The same Department's estimates of the amounts held in non-resident accounts amounted to 2 billion Irish punts (about GBP1.8 billion) in 1993. It is easy to imagine that this wealth was, in fact, held by high net worth Irishmen and women and that the tax authorities did not really wish to probe the Irish élite too closely.

This last sentiment is also applicable to the Cayman trick. It was used to hide income and assets from the Irish tax authorities and, at the same time, to provide interest payments which were deductible in calculating Irish tax payable. It involved the merchant bank Guinness Mahon's Cayman Trust and the Irish branch of Ansbacher, also a merchant. Using the intermediary Dublin end of Guinness and Mahon, money would be placed with them for onward relay to the Cayman Islands where it would be deposited. In return, Ansbacher would lend the same sum, in Ireland, to the original depositor. This is known as a back to back loan. Interest on this latter borrowing would be tax deductible in the Republic of Ireland. At the same time the income from the deposit in the Caymans would be hidden from the Irish tax authorities. The deposits in the Cayman Islands are reported by O'Toole to have included monies placed by the three-times Taoiseach of the Republic of Ireland, Charles Haughey. Hardly surprising that the Irish élite was using this back to back loan way of evading tax or that the Irish tax authorities were less than wholehearted in tracking depositors in the Caymans. Other examples of O'Toole's skulduggery point are available in his text.

Ireland's two major banks are Bank of Ireland Group (BOI) and Allied Irish Banks (AIB). The latter should not be confused with a more recent arrival on the scene – namely Anglo Irish Bank. The two largest banks faced minor competition from foreign banks but the truth is that these new entrants only achieved niche status.

Prior to the 2007/8 financial crisis, many smaller Irish banks failed and one of the above major players, Allied Irish Banks, was rescued by the government in 1985. By Irish standards, it was reckoned to be too big to fail. Ross provides interesting coverage on a number of rather dubious minor banking groups.

Before moving on to an overview of the financial crisis in Ireland it should be clear that the housing boom led to a growing mortgage business, however the massive property-related lending was not just related to owner-occupiers or buy-to-let landlords but also to property developers and building materials companies. Having said this, tax and EU subsidies had also encouraged a significant number of multinational businesses to locate some of their operations in the Republic of Ireland. It would be wrong to think of Ireland as being entirely a property play – far from it.

■ Anglo Irish Bank

This section could be subtitled as the rise and fall of Sean FitzPatrick who is now a well-known character in the Irish Republic. According to Ross, 'he was a little man with a little bank that became a rather big bank.' Having come from humble beginnings, studied commerce at University College Dublin (UCD) and later qualified as a chartered accountant, he is often called South Dublin's answer to North Dublin's Charlie Haughey because both followed similar university and professional backgrounds although their paths diverged thereafter, Haughey becoming Taoiseach of Ireland three times. The term Taoiseach means Ireland's first minister, equivalent to Britain's Prime Minister or the title President elsewhere. Haughey's life spanned 1926 to 2006.

Sean FitzPatrick was born in 1948 and, like many small men, was said to display Adlerian characteristics with an over-compensation directed towards power and status. After a brief post-qualification spell with a firm of practising accountants, Seanie (as he became known) joined Irish Bank of Commerce, a very small outfit but with a stock exchange listing. He was the bank's accountant and the job grew as the Irish Bank of Commerce expanded as a result of various acquisitions. His career path developed as he became financial controller and, in 1980, chief executive of the bank. In 1986, following a merger with another bank trading as Anglo Irish, the newly created Anglo Irish Bank emerged with Sean FitzPatrick as chief executive. Followed by further acquisitions and frenzied growth in lending, substantially to the property industry, particularly to property developers, Anglo Irish Bank looked like a supreme success story with 2007 profits of EUR998 million. FitzPatrick had built the business from meagre profit levels and was now chairman with stock in the firm, a salary of EUR539,000 and a reputation in the local media where he was being fêted as businessman of the year and given similar accolades. Ross portrays the years of growth with great insight and skill and is well worth reading.

But Anglo Irish Bank was making property loans which were secured on other properties being developed. Its loan book was unbalanced, with vast amounts outstanding to a few favoured clients. According to Ross, it was described by one London investment firm as a property junkie – a building society on crack.

The year 2007 was the beginning of the great reckoning for Ireland's housing market. Prices were 7.3 per cent down. But dividends for Ireland's top banks continued their upward trajectory. Then 2008 brought bank failures in the US and the UK. Bear Stearns collapsed in March 2008. Shortly afterwards things were looking distinctly dodgy in Ireland.

Enter a new character. He is Sean Quinn, who was Ireland's richest man having made billions from nothing at all. In 1973 he had started to extract gravel from below his family farm. Gravel is, of course, an input in numerous building materials. This was a good business to be in, given the takeoff of property in Ireland. Quinn expanded and diversified his business interests. His conglomerate ranged over cement, property, glass, plastics, hotels, stockbroking, financial services, insurance and, of course, gravel. Quinn's business vehicle was, remarkably, not a company listed on a stock exchange but a privately held group. In early 2007, Quinn was a big investor in Anglo Irish Bank shares – but not through the usual route of holding stock in his own, or a nominee, name on Anglo's share register. Quinn held his investment via contracts for difference (CFDs) which, basically, pay out if the shares rise in a specified period or requires the investor to pay up if the shares fall.

As 2007 progressed and 2008 arrived, the Anglo Irish Bank share price was dropping fast, driven by the weakening housing market. Through the CFDs, Quinn had a position on 25 per cent of Anglo Irish shares – a quarter of the company. Quinn converted 60 per cent of his CFD position into ordinary shares in Anglo Irish and at the same time took a loss of a billion euros in so doing. The Anglo Irish top team got news of this. What would Quinn do next? If he sold out of the remaining CFDs (representing 10 per cent of Anglo Irish shares), what effect would this have on Anglo's share price?

Somehow, Anglo managed to put together ten rich backers. The plan was that they would take up Quinn's shares at a cost of around EUR451 million. Where would the money come from? Anglo Irish would lend them the EUR451 million. Three-quarters of this was to be secured on the Anglo shares to be purchased and the other quarter was to be secured against the individuals' personal assets. The ten Anglo backers were christened the Golden Circle. Of course, the whole thing was illegal. Anglo Irish was lending money to buy shares in itself in a share support operation. Unbelievably, Anglo Irish's August 2008 interim statement was bullish in the extreme forecasting increasing earnings per share for the year and claiming no exposure to subprime lending or off-balance sheet vehicles.

As more and more adverse news emerged about the global banking crisis, shares in banks – good and bad – toppled. The *Financial Times* Lex column was scathing of Anglo Irish and its exposure to the property market. Come September 2008 and the failure of Lehman Brothers, the world was gripped by expectations of another Great Depression. It is nigh on impossible to describe how people felt. But from Wall Street to main street, from the City of London to the man on the Clapham omnibus, from Reykjavik to Milan, there was a feeling that we were facing the abyss. Financial Armageddon. Economic Meltdown. Bankruptcies and Unemployment.

Sean FitzPatrick was praying for a financial saviour. He aired the idea of a merger with the ailing Irish Nationwide Bank which had a loan book amounting to 15 per cent of Anglo's.

Seanie arranged a meeting with Ireland's Minister for Finance, Brian Lenihan. FitzPatrick's idea was a merger to save the beleaguered smaller bank – plus an injection of capital from the government to help save Irish Nationwide. Good try but not good enough, was the reply. And anyway, mergers were hardly the top priority for the Irish Minister for Finance.

On 29 September 2008, Anglo Irish lost 46 per cent of its value in the stock market. Government ministers foresaw a doomsday scenario. In it Anglo Irish Bank would tumble, bringing down Bank of Ireland and AIB through interbank loans. Bank of Ireland had a loan book of about EUR135 billion, AIB had a loan book of EUR130 billion, Anglo had EUR72 billion or so, EBS Building Society EUR17 billion and Irish Nationwide EUR10 billion or so. Ministers, perhaps reminded of the Northern Rock situation in Britain, foresaw queues outside Ireland's banks with customers wanting their money back as soon as possible. To avert the cataclysm, the government decided to guarantee all liabilities – that is, to customers, inter-bank exposures and bond indebtedness – of the six big Irish banks. The stock market effect was understandable. Anglo Irish rose 60 per cent next day (from EUR2.30 to EUR3.84 per share) and Bank of Ireland and AIB rose 21 per cent and 18 per cent respectively.

An austerity budget and a recapitalisation of Ireland's banks by the state followed. The cavalry had arrived. But not before the Irish stock market had lost 66 per cent of its value in 2008, property had fallen by 9 per cent and banking stock had been trashed in the year. Bank of Ireland went from EUR10.19 to 83 cents per share in 2008. AIB dropped from EUR15.67 per share to EUR1.73. Anglo Irish went from EUR10.94 per share to 17 cents. But what of our anti-hero?

The story gets worse. It was later revealed that Sean FitzPatrick had borrowed EUR122 million of unreported loans from Anglo Irish Bank over the past eight years. These borrowings did not appear in Anglo's annual report. They should have shown up under directors' loans. But each year, as 30 September (Anglo Irish's year end) approached, FitzPatrick moved the loan from Anglo Irish to the Irish Nationwide. He would leave the loan there for a short time then return it to Anglo Irish. Could the auditors have found this?

At Anglo Irish's 2008 year end, it was thought that there had been a run on its deposits. Although denied, rumours of big withdrawals continued. They were justified. Anglo Irish had covered up the run. Anglo Irish arranged a deposit of EUR7.5 billion from Irish Life and Permanent (ILP). The trick was that ILP would make a customer deposit with Anglo Irish and Anglo would make an investment deposit with ILP. This would inflate Anglo Irish's customer deposit base at the year end and – maybe – disguise the depletion therein.

Days after the government guarantee, Sean FitzPatrick told Irish radio that 'it would be very easy for me to say sorry. But the cause of our problem was global so I couldn't say sorry with any degree of sincerity and decency but I do say thank you (to the Irish taxpayer).' In March 2010, FitzPatrick was arrested and questioned over allegations of financial impropriety.

Unsurprisingly, FitzPatrick's resignation from Anglo Irish Bank was received on 18 December 2008. O'Toole[10] is scathing of the whole affair. He estimates that 'at least two generations of Irish people would be made to pay for the blind folly and greed of a closed élite.' He goes on to say that 'the decision to guarantee all of Anglo's obligations was particularly breathtaking. Banks like BOI and AIB were clearly a crucial part of the real Irish economy. Anglo was a bubble bank, a chimerical creation of years of swagger and self-delusion.' O'Toole offers the opinion that 'the Financial Regulator certainly had a good idea of what was going on ... (from) daily liquidity reports provided to his office.'

Anglo Irish bank was nationalised 100 per cent in January 2009. It announced a loss of EUR12.7 billion for the 15 months to 31 December 2009 – the largest in Irish corporate history.

■ Irish Nationwide

The story of Ireland's banking and property boom and bust is peopled by an interesting range of characters whose stories are revealed in histories of the Celtic Tiger by Ross, O'Toole, Cooper, Murphy and Devlin and McDonald and Sheridan. We include here a cameo of Michael Fingleton of Irish Nationwide. This was the firm used by Sean FitzPatrick to remove his loan from the books of Anglo Irish Bank at Anglo's year end.

Michael Fingleton, known as Fingers, had graduated from University College Dublin with a commerce degree. He was recruited by and became general manager of the small Irish Industrial Building Society. In 1975 he qualified as a barrister. In the early seventies, Irish Industrial Building Society, renamed Irish Nationwide in 1975, had a staff of five and assets equivalent to EUR2 million. In 2004, it had assets of EUR8.5 billion and reported profits of EUR135 million rising to EUR391 million in 2007.

Fingers cultivated the image of a personality banker, never missing an opportunity to hobnob with politicians and seeking media photo calls. He saw politicians as a way of getting things done and he saw the media as a way of publicising himself and the Irish Nationwide. The building society became a provider of mortgages to politicians, journalists and celebrities. Fingers usually arranged speedy loans for those with good connections. He gained access to the corridors of power and to the media world. Fingleton and the Nationwide became household names. And he had ready access to politicians.

After two rival building societies had embarked on public flotations (in 1994 and 1998), their members received windfall gains. Investors, trying to identify the next in line to do so, homed in on Irish Nationwide. Deposits poured in. Hopes were of EUR15,000 for each qualifying member on flotation. The rumour was that this had attracted 125,000 savers, increasing the capital base. To ward off too many carpetbaggers, a minimum deposit of EUR20,000 over two years was introduced.

A change in the law was needed for Irish Nationwide to take its preferred route of selling out to a bank. As the law stood, no sale could take place until five years after the society gave up its mutual status. Michael Fingleton was delighted in 2006 when Ireland passed the Building Societies Bill which would enable the Irish Nationwide to be sold. But things were getting rocky. In 2007, much of the unravelling was happening. Amongst potential bidders were Icelandic banks and their interest expired rapidly as they needed government rescues.

Fingleton had two pressing problems. Investors with Irish Nationwide were becoming more agitated about when they were going to get their windfall. And the strategy of an unbalanced portfolio of lending to property developers was looking disastrous. In the past, these same developers had been the source of growing profit. Now they were transformed into a reservoir of bad debt.

Fingleton, previously lionised in the Irish media, was now being vilified. Questions were being asked. How was a building society – a mutual where investors' deposits fund loans to buy houses – allowed to become a property developers' bank? How and why was Fingleton himself being paid millions of euros and Irish Nationwide facing wipeout? There were many ex-tigers who were now being characterised in the Irish press as scurrying mice (that's the polite version of what was said).

As can be seen in Table 14.3, Irish Nationwide's loan book of over EUR10 billion was reckoned to have over EUR8 billion of bad or doubtful debts and was to be rescued 100 per cent by the Irish government in 2010.

■ The bailout

As the Celtic Tiger lost its roar, the Irish government was confronted with the problem of a swathe of bad property loans on the books of its leading banks. The banks were falling short of capital ratio requirements amidst destruction of stock market values. The banks needed recapitalisation. The bailout occurred in two chunks, with a short-term recapitalisation which put monies into AIB and Bank of Ireland, both of which had lent substantial sums to failed property developers and, at the same time, there was the nationalisation of Anglo Irish. The second phase of the bailout, announced on 30 March 2010, would involve banks transferring some EUR77.1 billion of their loan books to Ireland's state-owned bad bank (National Asset Management Agency – NAMA) plus EUR8.5 billion to be transferred immediately – this latter sum reflecting some 1,200 loans with a nominal value of EUR16 billion. The larger amount (EUR77.1 billion of loans) was expected to be transferred to NAMA by February 2011 in exchange for the equivalent of around EUR43 billion of government-backed loans. The effect, in terms of estimated short-term control of major Irish banks, is shown in Table 14.3.

At the time of announcement of the bailout, the Irish Finance minister, Brian Lenihan, told parliament that banks had 'made appalling lending decisions' during the boom years. He did, however, single out BOI as a ray of hope with 'a strong future'. He also said that the financial regulator had 'failed abysmally'. To maintain required banking ratios, further capital raising of, possibly, EUR7.4 billion at AIB and EUR2.7 billion at BOI is likely to be required from shareholders.

Before we leave Ireland's banks, it is worth mentioning that the country suffered a drop in GDP in 2009 of around 7.1 per cent and that with a ratio of budget deficit to GDP for 2009/10 estimated at 11.8 per cent, an austerity plan was implemented. Remember

Table 14.3 Republic of Ireland's 2010 bank bailout

Bank	Total loan book (EUR billion)	Transferred to NAMA – book value (EUR billion)	Transferred at discount of (%)	Government stake before 2010 bailout	Government stake after 2010 bailout
Bank of Ireland	135.5	15.5	35	15%	40%*
Allied Irish Bank	129.0	24.1	43	25%	70%*
Anglo Irish Bank	72.3	28.4	50	100%	100%
Irish Nationwide	10.5	8.3	58	0%	100%†
EBS Building Society	17.0	0.8	37	0%	100%†
Other banks	?	about 4.0	?		

Banks sell EUR81 billion (book value) of loans to NAMA.

In return NAMA pays banks a discounted price of up to EUR51.3 billion in government loans.

* brokers estimates as reported by *Financial Times*, 31 March 2010
† control via special shares

that, given its membership of the eurozone, unilateral devaluation is not possible, without quitting the currency zone. The austerity plan involved a combination of pay cuts, tax rises and curtailed public spending worth, in total, around 6 per cent of GDP. It is an ambitious plan. But given the openness of Ireland's economy it could work – but don't hold your breath. And let us hope that banking shenanigans are a thing of Ireland's past. And let us hope that the Chinese proverb is kept in mind – 'he who rides the tiger can never dismount'.

On the topic of Irish banks, there are other books which are worth reading – for example, *Banksters* by Murphy and Devlin[11], *The Builders* by McDonald and Sheridan[12] and also *Who Runs Ireland?* by Cooper[13]. Readers are also referred to Press Cutting 14.1.

Press cutting 14.1　　　　　　　　*Financial Times*, 14 June 2010　**FT**

Ireland's financial lessons

A profligate government in thrall to out-of-control property developers lavishes incentives on the construction industry to keep tax revenues flowing. Clueless banks raid wholesale markets for funds, and drop lending standards as the cash is pushed towards those favoured developers. Deferential regulators merely look on. That, in a nutshell, is how the seeds of Ireland's financial crisis – the most severe of any country outside Iceland – were sown between 2003 and 2008.

Now two reports into the fiasco flesh out the narrative. Their joint and separate conclusions are that this vicious circle meant the crisis was almost entirely home-made. Much of the Irish banking sector – and especially the two chief victims of the crisis, Anglo Irish Bank and building society Irish Nationwide – was heading straight towards insolvency even before the collapse of Lehman Brothers.

The reports – by Patrick Honohan, governor of the Irish central bank, and by banking experts Klaus Regling and Max Watson – make uncomfortable reading for everyone involved. Unvarnished accounts of such crises usually do. They may not necessarily tell us anything we don't know already about how the Celtic Tiger came to collapse so destructively and spectacularly, but they offer sober analysis and help to prepare the ground for a full and honest reckoning.

As with the nation's reluctant but comprehensive embrace of austerity measures to right its economy, there are also important global lessons from these accounts. One is that countries experience financial crises in different ways, requiring tailored solutions to the problems. Another is the calamity of regulatory deference. Ireland's regulator had no more than two staff involved in prudential supervision of each large credit institution it supervised, and, perhaps as a result, emphasised process over outcomes. A third is the need for a full accounting of the financial crisis. Perhaps Ireland's example will prompt other countries to offer an equally robust account of their own banking failures. It is the least taxpayers deserve.

Chapter **15**

The Great Depression

■ Introduction

In this chapter, we attempt to summarise some of the key aspects of the Great Depression. At the end of the chapter we draw conclusions based on similarities and differences between the Great Depression and the financial crisis beginning in 2007/8.

Milton and Rose Friedman[1] start their analysis of the Great Depression with the following introduction: 'The depression that started in mid-1929 was a catastrophe of unprecedented dimensions for the United States. The dollar income of the nation was cut in half before the economy hit bottom in 1933. Total output fell by a third, and unemployment reached the unprecedented level of 25 per cent of the work force. The depression was no less a catastrophe for the rest of the world. As it spread to other countries, it brought lower output, higher unemployment, hunger, and misery everywhere. In Germany the depression helped Adolf Hitler rise to power, paving the way for World War II. In Japan it strengthened the military clique that was dedicated to creating a Greater East Asia coprosperity sphere. In China it led to monetary changes that accelerated the final hyperinflation that sealed the doom of the Chiang Kai-shek regime and brought the communists to power.' Liaquat Ahamed[2] says that 'no other period of peace-time economic turmoil since has even come close to approaching the depth and breadth of that cataclysm.'

An interpretation often aired is that the depression began on Black Thursday, 24 October 1929, when the New York stock market fell 9 per cent. It was followed by Black Monday, 28 October when the market fell by a further 13 per cent only to be succeeded by Black Tuesday, the following day, when the market managed to lose another 12 per cent. After a few more downs and ups, the market ended in 1933 at about one-sixth of its 1929 level. The market crash was significant but was it the beginning of the depression? Of course, one answer is to say that it depends what you mean by the beginning. As Friedman and Friedman[3] point out, 'business activity reached its peak in August 1929, two months before the stock market crashed, and had already fallen appreciably by then.' Industrial production was falling months before the Wall Street Crash. The market's dramatic decline deflated an unsustainable speculative bubble. The immediate aftermath of the crash put Keynes' animal spirits[4] on hold. It created uncertainty in the minds of investors, businessmen and consumers. And their risk-averse stance was to draw in their horns. It clobbered their willingness to invest and to spend. It courted the desire to conserve cash resources for unexpected emergencies.

Figure 15.1, based upon the work of Friedman and Schwartz[5], shows a number of interesting data. Immediately following World War I, the US experienced recession

conditions. These persisted until 1921. Real incomes, money supply and industrial production were in decline. But as the twenties got up and running, things
changed. Up until 1929 real incomes rose steadily as did money supply and industrial
production. This was the Roaring Twenties really roaring. Of course, as can be seen,
the picture deteriorates as we move into the thirties. But that part of the story is still
to come. First of all, we look at the Roaring Twenties, the years preceding the Great
Depression.

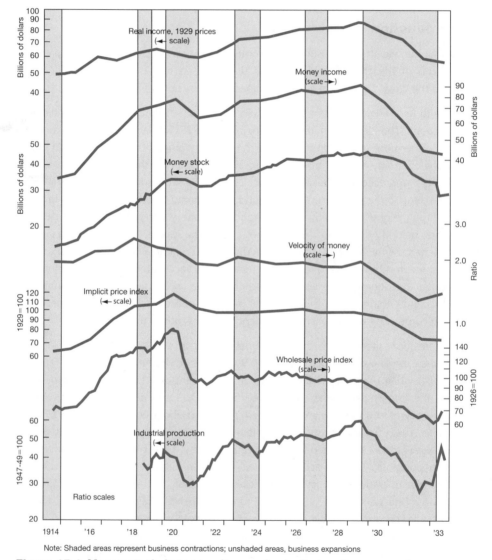

Note: Shaded areas represent business contractions; unshaded areas, business expansions

**Figure 15.1 Money stock, income prices and velocity in reference cycle
expansions and contractions 1914–33**

Source: Milton Friedman and Anna Jacobson Schwartz, 'The Great Contraction 1929–33', Princeton University
Press, 1963.

■ The Roaring Twenties

The Roaring Twenties was particularly manifest in North America, Britain, France and Germany. The term conjures up the decade's social, artistic and cultural change. Words spring to mind as one mentions the twenties. The Jazz Age, the flapper, prohibition and speakeasies, Art Deco and, finally, the Wall Street Crash. The era was also distinguished by inventions in consumer products, strong industrial growth, accelerating consumer demand, aspirations and lifestyle changes.

At the end of World War I, soldiers returned to their own countries with wartime wages and many new products on which to spend it. At first, following wartime levels of production, there was a brief but deep reverse in output levels, known as the Post-World War I recession. Quickly, however, North American economies rebounded as returning soldiers re-entered the labour force and factories were retooled to produce consumer goods. The Democratic presidency of Woodrow Wilson saw the USA through World War I and it continued until 1921. His tenure was followed by three consecutive Republican administrations. All three courted a close relationship between government and business. In 1921, when President Warren Harding took office, the economy was in recession, with an unemployment rate of 20 per cent and high inflation. Harding proposed a reduction in national debt, reduced taxes, protection of farming interests and a cut back on immigration. Harding did not live long enough to see the full impact of these changes, dying in office in 1923. His adminis-tration's policy changes laid the foundations of the twenties boom.

Before World War I, the top marginal tax rate was 7 per cent. It was increased to 77 per cent in 1916 to finance the War effort. This was reversed in 1925 when the top rate was reduced to 25 per cent. One of the main initiatives of both the Harding and Coolidge administrations was the rolling back of income taxes on the wealthy. The big tax cut was achieved under President Coolidge's administration. Harding and Coolidge both aimed their economic policy at sustained growth through most of the decade.

The economic policies of these two administrations pulled the USA from acute recession to sustained recovery. The Federal Reserve expanded credit by setting relatively low interest rates and low reserve asset requirements. The money supply actually increased by about 60 per cent during the period from 1923 to 1929. This was a period of great economic prosperity.

Via mass production, technology made new products affordable to the middle class. Sales of motor cars, radios, movies and output from the chemical industries soared during the 1920s. Of major importance was the automobile industry. Before World War I, cars were a luxury. In the twenties, mass-produced vehicles became common throughout North America. By 1927, Ford ended production of the Model T after selling 15 million. The automobile's effects were widespread, contributing to growth of such industries as highway building, motels, service stations, used car dealerships and new housing which extended towns and cities to new boundaries.

The growth of radio was comparable and radio advertising became a source of mass marketing. Its influence affected the growth of mass culture. Although cinema appeared in 1895 it was during the twenties that Hollywood boomed, developing a new form of entertainment that overwhelmed the old vaudeville. Going to the movies was cheap and accessible. There were queues around cinemas and the wonder of talking pictures arrived in 1927.

New technologies led to expanded new infrastructures. Road construction was crucial to the motor vehicle industry. Dusty roads were upgraded to highways. Expressways were constructed. Americans emerged with surplus money and a desire to spend it. As can be seen from Figure 15.1, real incomes rose by around 55 per cent from 1921 to 1929. All of this spurred the marketing of consumer goods. Electrification slowed down during the war but was now expanded in America and Europe. Many industries switched from coal power to electricity. New power plants were constructed. And electricity production took off. Telephone lines criss-crossed America and inside plumbing and modern sewerage were installed in many regions for the first time. These infrastructure programmes were mostly funded by central and local government. And all of this hastened urbanisation. At the same time the United States paid down war debts and reduced taxation.

From 1925, there was another manifestation of growing affluence. This was the Florida land boom. Galbraith[6] tells us that 'there, in the mid-twenties, Miami, Miami Beach, Coral Gables, the East Coast as far north as Palm Beach, and other cities over on the Gulf had been struck by the great Florida real estate boom. The Florida boom contained all of the elements of the classic speculative bubble ... Florida had a better winter climate than New York, Chicago, or Minneapolis. Higher incomes and better transportation were making it increasingly accessible ... Through 1925 the pursuit of effortless riches brought people to Florida in satisfactorily increasing numbers. More land was subdivided each week. What was loosely called sea-shore became five, ten, or fifteen miles from the nearest brine. Suburbs became an astonishing distance from town ... However, in the spring of 1926, the supply of new buyers, so essential to the reality of increasing prices, began to fail.' Were buyers becoming aware that a few miles from the coast wasn't exactly sea-front? Galbraith goes on to tell us that 'farmers who had sold their land at a handsome price and had condemned themselves as it later sold for double, treble, quadruple the original price, now on occasion got it back through a whole chain of subsequent defaults ... The Florida boom was the first indication of the mood of the twenties and the conviction that God intended the American middle class to be rich. But that this mood survived the Florida collapse is still more remarkable.' As Galbraith reminds us, Florida land was dealt on the basis of the purchaser putting only 10 per cent of the value on the table. Galbraith goes on to say that 'the trading was in "binders". Not the land itself but the right to buy the land at a stated price was traded. This right to buy – which was obtained by a down payment of ten per cent of the purchase price – could be sold. It then conferred on the speculators the full benefit of the increases in values. After the value of the lot had risen he could resell the binder for what he had paid plus the full amount of the increase in price.' But if the value of the land falls merely by 10 per cent, the purchaser loses all that he put up. The Florida land rush ended in 1926 – a deflated bubble.

There was a feature of twenties USA that was truly strange. It was amazing that a country orientated towards freedom denied the manufacture, sale, import and export of alcohol.

It was prohibited by the Eighteenth Amendment to the United States Constitution and it came into force in 1920 in an attempt to alleviate various social problems. This was termed Prohibition. Its introduction was supported by churches and temperance leagues. The continued desire for alcohol during Prohibition proved to be a fertile source of profit for organised crime. The names of gangsters such as Al Capone and Lucky Luciano spring to mind. Many famous families in the USA owed their wealth to illegal speakeasies in the prohibition years. These were basically bars, which were illegal, and were commonly operated with connections to organised crime and alcohol smuggling. While US agents raided such establishments and arrested many ordinary citizens and smugglers, they rarely managed to trap the big bosses. The business of running speakeasies was lucrative and such establishments flourished throughout the USA. Speakeasies differentiated their marketing by offering food, live bands and floor shows. Police were frequently bribed by speakeasy operators to leave them alone or to give them advance warning of raids. Prohibition continued until 1933. It was another manifestation that made the Roaring Twenties so exciting.

Maybe the narrow-mindedness of Prohibition led to the temporary self-exile of many great writers, especially those who enjoyed their booze. Ernest Hemingway and Scott Fitzgerald both decamped for long periods to Europe. Sad to relate, F. Scott Fitzgerald died at the age of 44 but, at his best, as in *The Great Gatsby*[7] and *Tender is the Night*[8], was one of America's greatest novelists. If you haven't read these two great books, try them. As you admire the structure of these novels and Fitzgerald's style, drink up the flavour of the . Roaring Twenties.

Before we leave this roaring decade, it is imperative to discuss trading on margin. We came across it in relation to the Florida land bubble. During the boom years, the stock market had become an increasing preoccupation of a fair number of Americans. Buying on margin was a technique introduced by stockbrokers to enable clients to put down only 10 per cent of the amount of a stock market purchase. This was attractive to Joe Public who responded by playing the market. Possibly 15 per cent of US citizens were stockholders. And from 1926 to 1929 the stock market raced upwards by nearly 400 per cent. Obviously the relaxed credit terms fuelled this take-off. Also popular among investors were investment trusts, companies which invested in stock market quoted firms. The investment trusts had discovered gearing and were using it. If investors have a margin of 10 per cent and if, for example, the investment trust has assets financed by 70 per cent borrowings from a bank and 30 per cent raised from shareholders you can see a potential problem when markets go into reverse, as they did in 1929. If the investment trust's portfolio of 1000 falls by 30 per cent it would have to sell everything to repay the remaining 700 to repay the bank. The investment trust's equity of 300 has been wiped out. If the actual investor in the trust bought stock at 100 on the basis of 10 down and 90 later (that is, 10 per cent margin) – oh dear. The investor now has worthless shares but still owes 90 (he only put down 10 per cent margin). You might say that's not such a problem if the investor bought the shares two years ago at, say, 25 rather than 100. In this case the investor owns worthless stock and still owes 22.5. So it is still a problem. And the fact was that most investors had bought in more recently. Incidentally, if you think that the investment trust's portfolio was unlikely to fall by 33 per cent quickly, think again. On the first page of this chapter we related that the stockmarket fell, on individual days of the Wall Street Crash, by 9 per cent, 13 per cent and 12 per cent. And that was in less than a week in October 1929.

To make matters worse, frequently the investment trusts invested in the equity of other investment trusts. With so much trading on margin, this was creating an upside down pyramid of debt. Push it and it will crash. The wonders of debt had been discovered by the man on the subway. He knew how debt and gearing worked now and he wasn't enjoying the lesson. The Roaring Twenties were going out with a bang. Or was it a Crash?

■ The Wall Street Crash

Before we get into the Wall Street Crash itself, we preface our discussion with a brief reference to US presidents during the twenties. The Crash occurred shortly after Calvin Coolidge's presidency – in fact, during Herbert Hoover's tenure. Coolidge, a Republican, was inaugurated as president after the death of fellow Republican president, Warren Harding. He was easily elected when he ran on a basis of order and prosperity. The first presidential inauguration broadcast on radio was Coolidge's on 12 February 1924. As can be seen from Figure 15.1, Coolidge was in office through a period of great prosperity in the USA. Some would say his administration was a period of economic and social success – some would say excess. He was president from 1923 (although he was inaugurated in 1924) to 4 March 1929. Coolidge presided over the chunk of the 1920s that was viewed by many Americans as the best time of their lives. Soon after he was elected, he gained a reputation as a small-government conservative. As one of Coolidge's biographers, Claude Fuess[9], put it, 'he embodied the spirit and hopes of the middle class, could interpret their longings and express their opinions. That he did represent the genius of the average is the most convincing proof of his strength.' Many, such as Ferrell[10], Greenberg[11] and McCoy[12], have criticised Coolidge for his laissez-faire style. His reputation was reassessed during the Reagan administration – see Sobel[13] and Greenberg[14] – but evaluation of his presidency is still divided between those who approve of his government programmes and those who believe his government failed to regulate and control the economy – again see Greenberg[15].

Coolidge was followed in the White House by Herbert Hoover. In the presidential election of 1928, he easily won the Republican nomination. The nation was prosperous at the time and he achieved a landslide victory.

When the Wall Street Crash of 1929 struck, less than six months after he took office, Hoover expected to combat the situation with a programme of farm subsidies and public works. Indeed, more public works were started in his four years as president than in the previous 30 years. Increasing taxes sharply to meet the demands of the budget did not endear him to the electorate. Neither did it solve the economic problem. Anyway, we have moved ahead too quickly. We return to the Wall Street Crash of 1929.

The stock market had experienced massive gains from 1926 to 1928. Market indices moved up nearly 400 per cent. As we have mentioned, relaxed credit terms from banks and brokers fuelled the buying frenzy – as it had driven the Florida land boom. But in October 1929, the market returned to sanity.

On 24 October 1929, often called Black Thursday, the market began its wipeout. In truth the market crashed over a period of five days. The first sign of trouble occurred on Black Thursday. At the time, the stock exchange typically traded around 4 million shares each trading day. On Black Thursday, a record 12.9 million shares changed hands. The systems for tracking the market prices could not keep up with the trading volume and this may have contributed to panic selling. At one point, ticker-tapes were running nearly 90 minutes behind the market. By the end of the day, the market was down 33 points or around 9 per cent.

The next big market correction occurred on 28 October 1929, also known as Black Monday. Following Black Thursday, the market perked up a bit on Friday. This led to a sense of security over the weekend as investors felt the market might rebound. However, conditions quickly deteriorated again on Black Monday and high volumes of trading again put pressure on the flow of information. On Black Monday, trading volume was near 9.25 million shares. Market confidence was evaporating – and fast. By the end of the day, the market was down another 13 per cent.

Black Tuesday, 29 October 1929, is the day that many suggest dealt a final blow to the Roaring Twenties and was the beginning of the Great Depression. On Black Tuesday, a record 16.4 million shares changed hands. The ticker tape machines fell behind by nearly three hours. With hopes of a market recovery gone, panic selling continued and the market fell another 12 per cent.

Over the next month, the market continued its decline. The market would not bottom out until July 1932, when the Dow hit 41 from a high of 381 in 1929 – a decline of nearly 90 per cent. It would take another 22 years before the Dow would climb above the levels seen in 1929.

Why do values fall so rapidly after a bubble bursts? Generally there is a steady rise in prices as the bubble forms. But when it deflates, the fall begins in a symmetrical way to the build up. However the downswing gains intensity and falls become asymmetrical. This occurs where there are substantial borrowings used to underpin buying in the upswing. As prices drop there are either margin calls or the value of collateral becomes insufficient to cover bank loans. Either way, borrowers become forced sellers. Pepper and Oliver[16] sum up the position when they refer to stages in the process which they list in order of intensity as:

- Borrowers become forced sellers of assets
- People start to go bankrupt
- Others retrench as they observe the pain of bankruptcy
- Banks suffer from bad debts
- Bankers become cautious about making new loans. They have more than enough trouble with bad debts on existing loans. The last thing they want is a bad debt on a new loan. Loan officers become afraid of jeopardising their careers if they are not very cautious about new loans
- Both the demand for and the supply of new loans subside

- As bad debts multiply, banks may lack capital to make new loans
- As bad debts multiply further, banks have to call in existing loans because they have insufficient capital to support their current business
- Banks fail because the level of bad debts has wiped out their capital
- Depositors lose money as banks fail.

This process both explains the intensity of market declines and it also goes some way to explain how declines in economic activity can easily follow the deflation of bubbles.

■ The Great Depression unfolds

The Great Depression was a severe worldwide economic depression spanning the decade from 1929 to World War II. In truth, its timing varied across nations. In most countries it started around 1929 and lasted until the late 1930s or even the early 1940s. It was by far the longest, deepest and most global depression of the 20th century.

The Great Depression had devastating effects in every country, rich and poor. Income tax revenues, profits and prices dropped. International trade plunged by around 60 per cent. Unemployment in the USA rose to 25 per cent. In some countries it rose to 33 per cent. Cities around the world were hit hard, especially those dependent upon heavy industry. Construction was halted in many countries. Farming suffered as crop prices fell by around 60 per cent with plummeting demand and in agricultural areas there were few alternative sources of jobs. Areas dependent on primary sector industries, such as farming, mining and logging, were devastated. For many countries, the adverse effects of the Great Depression lasted until the start of World War II.

Although some date the start of the Great Depression to the sudden collapse of the US stock market prices on Black Thursday, 24 October 1929, through to Black Tuesday, there are others who see its genesis in the preceding excesses of the Roaring Twenties. We would put ourselves in this latter category.

The economy was suffering. By May 1930, car sales had declined to below their levels in 1928. As can be seen in Figure 15.1, the thirties were bringing bad news for the US economy. Money terms incomes were falling. Real terms incomes were falling. Industrial production was heading south. The velocity of circulation of money was falling. Prices were falling.

If you owe 100 and there's inflation, the real terms value of your debt falls. If you owe 100 and there's deflation – negative inflation – then the real value of your debt increases. Householders with debt will certainly lose their confidence – their animal spirits. With consumers less confident and with industrial production falling significantly – look at Figure 15.1 – what do you suppose this was doing to the animal spirits of the entrepreneur? They headed south too. Unfortunately this also seems to have been the case for the Hoover administration. So, we had a deflationary spiral, falling commodity and farming prices, and unemployment which hit almost 25 per cent in the USA (in 1932).

The decline in the US economy was a key factor that pulled down other countries' economies. Attempts to shore up the economies of individual nations through protectionist policies and retaliatory tariffs exacerbated the collapse in global trade. A steady decline set in which reached bottom by March 1933. But how do we get cause and effect running from the Wall Street Crash?

In the wake of the Wall Street Crash, there were bank failures. Also, remember that investors were buying shares on the basis of 10 today and 90 later. With the fall in stock prices, the banks and brokers made their 90 per cent margin calls. To meet them investors had to sell shares and this further depressed markets. Banks were writing off bad debts. Banks were stopping lending. Cash was drying up. Wages were not getting paid and people were being laid off. If the money supply had been increased by the central bank, some of these worst effects may have been alleviated. But this did not happen. In fact, in the 1930s, Figure 15.1 shows us that the US money stock was actually in retreat. And this is one of the oft-quoted reasons for the Great Depression. But there are others. So, let's examine them in turn. Broadly there are two main reasons advanced.

First, there are demand-driven theories associated with Keynesian economics, but there are also those who point to the breakdown of international trade and under-consumption and previous over-investment, causing the earlier bubble. There was now a large-scale loss of confidence that led to a reduction in consumption and investment spending. Aggregate demand fell and with monetary policy and fiscal policy not helping, demand remained at low levels for long periods. Add to this panic and deflation and we have a picture of an economy badly battered and heading downhill with no help from the government.

Second, there are the monetarists, who believe that the Great Depression started as an ordinary recession, but policy mistakes by monetary authorities, especially the US central bank, caused a shrinking of the money supply which exacerbated the economic situation, making a recession a colossal depression. Add to this the fact that debt deflation was causing those who borrowed to owe ever more in real terms and the problem is severe.

To look at things further, John Maynard Keynes[17] argued in *The General Theory of Employment, Interest and Money* that lower aggregate expenditures in the economy contributed to a massive decline in income and to employment. In such a situation, the economy reached equilibrium at low levels of economic activity and high unemployment. Keynes' solution was simple. Keep people fully employed with governments running deficits when the economy is slowing to make up for the private sector not doing enough to keep production at normal levels. Keynes called for governments to pick up the slack by increasing government spending and/or cutting taxes.

As the Great Depression wore on, Franklin D. Roosevelt, Democratic president from 1932 through to 1945, tried public works, farm subsidies and other devices to restart the economy, but never completely gave up trying to balance the budget. This may have improved the economy, but Roosevelt did not spend enough to bring the economy out of recession until the start of World War II.

Many have argued that the sharp decline in international trade after 1930 helped to worsen the Great Depression, especially for countries significantly dependent on foreign trade. Most economists partly blame the American Smoot-Hawley Tariff Act, a US act of 1930 establishing a protectionism tariff regime. Retaliatory measures by other countries, such as Germany and Britain, lowered international trade and this had the effect of exporting the US depression around the world. While foreign trade was a small part of overall economic activity in the USA and was concentrated in a few areas like farming, it was a much larger factor for many other countries. The average US tariff on dutiable imports for 1921–1925 was 26 per cent. Under Smoot-Hawley, it jumped to 50 per cent in 1931–1935. US exports declined from over USD5 billion in 1929 to USD1.7 billion in 1933. Prices also fell. In fact, the physical volume of exports fell by half. Hardest hit were farm commodities – wheat, cotton, tobacco and lumber. The collapse of farm exports led to many American farmers defaulting on their loans, leading to bank runs for small rural banks. This was a feature of the early years of the Great Depression. John Steinbeck's book *The Grapes of Wrath*[18] conveys the plight of Great Depression farmers. And it's a terrific novel.

Debt deflation was another big adverse factor of the Great Depression. Irving Fisher argued that one of the main characteristics of the Great Depression was over-indebtedness and deflation. For Fisher[19], loose credit and over-indebtedness were features of asset bubbles and speculative times. He outlined nine factors interacting with one another under conditions of debt and deflation to create the mechanics of a move from boom to bust. The events proceeded as follows:

1. Debt liquidation and distressed selling.
2. Contraction of the money supply as bank loans are paid off.
3. A fall in the level of asset prices.
4. A still greater fall in the net worth of business, precipitating bankruptcies.
5. A fall in profits.
6. A reduction in output, in trade and in employment.
7. Pessimism and loss of confidence.
8. Hoarding of money.
9. A fall in nominal interest rates and a rise, during deflation, in real interest rates.

Recalling the margin requirements for stock purchases preceding the Great Depression, margin requirements were only 10 per cent; brokerage firms would lend USD9 for every USD1 an investor had deposited. When the market fell, brokers called in these loans, which often could not be paid back. Banks began to fail as borrowers defaulted on debt and depositors attempted to withdraw their deposits. This triggered multiple bank runs. Government guarantees and Federal Reserve banking regulations to prevent such panics were not used or were ineffective. After the Wall Street Crash and during the first ten months of 1930, 744 US banks failed. A total of 9,000 banks failed during the 1930s. In the face of bad loans and worsening future prospects, the surviving banks became even more conservative in their lending. Banks built up their reserves and made fewer loans, which intensified deflationary pressures. A vicious cycle developed and the downward spiral accelerated.

Strangely, the liquidation of debt could not keep up with the fall of prices which it caused. The overall effect of the stampede to liquidate lowered prices. The effort of individuals to lessen their burden of debt effectively increased it for others. This process actually made the depression worse. The debt deflation aspect of the Great Depression was significant indeed.

Monetarists argue that the Great Depression was mainly caused by monetary contraction caused by poor policy-making at the US Federal Reserve and the continuing crisis in the banking system. In this view, the Federal Reserve allowed the money supply to shrink by one-third from 1929 to 1933, thereby transforming a normal recession into the Great Depression. Friedman and Schwartz[20] argued that the downward turn in the economy, just before the Wall Street Crash, would have been just another recession had the Fed followed a reasonably logical stance. The Federal Reserve did not act sufficiently at that time because the amount of credit it could issue was limited by laws which required partial gold backing of that credit. This takes us conveniently on to the gold standard. It is useful to explain this from basics since nowadays it is not widely taught.

■ The gold standard

The international monetary system that operated immediately prior to World War I was termed the gold standard. Then, countries accepted two major assets – gold and sterling – in settlement of international debt. So the term gold/sterling standard might be more appropriate.

Most major countries operated the gold standard system. A unit of a country's currency was defined as a certain weight – a part of an ounce – of gold. It also provided that gold could be obtained from the treasuries of these countries in exchange for money and coin of the country concerned.

The pound sterling could be converted into 113.0015 grains of fine gold, and the US dollar into 23.22 grains. The pound was effectively defined as 113.0015/23.22 times as much gold as the dollar – or 4.8665 times as much gold. Through gold equivalents, the pound was worth USD4.8665. This amount of dollars was termed the 'par value' of the pound.

A country is said to be on the gold standard when its central bank is obliged to give gold in exchange for its currency when presented to it. When the UK was on the gold standard before 1914, anyone could go to the Bank of England and demand gold in exchange for bank notes. The UK came off the gold standard in 1914, but in 1925 it returned to a modified version termed the 'gold bullion standard'. Individual bank notes were no longer convertible into gold, but gold bars of 400 ounces were sold and bought by the Bank of England. Other countries adopted either this system or the gold exchange standard, under which their central banks would exchange home currency for the currency of some other country on the gold standard rather than for gold itself. The UK abandoned the gold standard in 1931.

The gold standard was a keystone in the classical economic theory of equilibrium in international trade. The currency of countries on the gold standard was freely convertible into gold at a fixed exchange rate and enabled all international debt settlement to be in gold. A balance of payments surplus caused an inflow of gold into the central bank. This enabled it to expand its domestic money supply without fear of having insufficient gold to meet its liabilities. The increase in the quantity of money tended to raise prices, making exports less competitive and resulting in a fall in the demand for exports and therefore a reduction in the balance of payments surplus. In the event of a deficit in the balance of payments, the reverse was expected to happen. The outflow of gold would be accompanied by a relative money supply contraction, resulting in exports becoming more competitive and the deficit automatically becoming corrected.

World War I had a serious effect on the international monetary system. The UK was forced to abandon the gold standard because of the wartime deficit on its balance of payments, and its reluctance at that time to provide gold to settle international differences. This was, perhaps, the beginning of a reduction in confidence in sterling as an international reserve asset.

Many other countries abandoned the gold standard temporarily, but none had the same significance as the action of the UK because sterling had financed 90 per cent of international trade payments. The UK government, recognising the importance of sterling and of UK institutions in international finance, wished to return to the gold standard as soon as possible. Delay occurred because of the recession in the US in 1920 and 1921, coupled with the post-war inflation, which reversed itself as rapidly as it had occurred. Recovery came in the US, and a degree of recovery also occurred in Britain. After its disastrous hyperinflation, taking the value of its currency from 60 marks to the dollar in May 1921 to 4.2 trillion to the dollar at the end of 1923, Germany also experienced stabilisation and returned to the gold standard in 1924. Interesting to note, as of October 1923, Germany's hyperinflation was running at a monthly rate of 29,500 per cent – that is, 20.9 per cent per day. And, with compound interest, that means that prices double in 3.7 days. An overview of Germany's hyperinflation during the Weimar Republic period is provided by Adam Fergusson[21].

The gold standard to which major countries returned in the mid-1920s was different from that which had existed before World War I. The major difference was that instead of two international reserve assets – gold and sterling – there were several. Both the US and France had become much more important in international finance, and dollar and franc deposits were used for much international financing.

Another important difference was that flexibility in costs and prices no longer existed as it had before World War I. This was especially important in the UK which had returned to the gold standard based on pre-war par values. The British pound was internationally overvalued. But only with a decline in relative costs and prices could the former par value of the pound have been maintained in the long run. Given that this flexibility in costs and prices was lacking, confidence in sterling deteriorated, culminating in the UK abandoning the gold standard in 1931. Most other countries followed the UK example in quitting the gold standard.

The US had imposed import restrictions in 1922 and again in 1930. Countries heavily dependent upon exports found their incomes falling sharply, their unemployment levels rising and their consumption falling. They could finance their essential imports neither from their exports nor from their reserves.

Add to a world economic system under strain the precariousness of an international monetary system, balanced like an inverse pyramid upon a relatively small base of gold holdings, and our structure is weak indeed. Strains on those countries without substantial gold holdings could cause difficulties for the gold exchange standard countries. Moreover, strains on a gold standard country resulting in a flow of gold reserves to another country could easily precipitate a financial crisis. Many economists are convinced that the supply of gold at that time was inadequate to support the international financial structure of the day.

Exchange rates were out of line with cost structures in different countries. The UK's return to the old par value for sterling was undoubtedly an error. France's devaluation of the franc in the 1920s was too great. Fundamental disequilibria existed. And the system was inadequate to cope with them. Faced with an overvalued currency in deep depression, one of the UK's responses was to abandon the gold standard and allow its currency to float against other currencies.

■ Franklin D. Roosevelt

We gave brief pictures of presidencies in the twenties earlier in this chapter. Following Hoover's presidency and with the US economy in the jaws of the Great Depression, the Republican occupation of the White House moved to the Democrats.

Roosevelt won his first of four presidential elections in 1932. He saw the USA through much of World War II, and died in office of a cerebral haemorrhage shortly before the war ended.

In his first term (1933–1936), Roosevelt launched the New Deal. This was a series of economic programmes. They were responses to the Great Depression and focused upon the 3Rs: relief, recovery and reform. This meant relief for the unemployed and poor, recovery for the economy to normal levels, and reform of the financial system to prevent a repeat of the Depression.

Following election, one of the things Roosevelt did was devalue the dollar against gold, raising the price of gold from USD20.67 per ounce to USD35 per ounce, where it stayed for 35 years. The Emergency Banking Act gave him the power to control foreign exchange transactions; he required all American citizens to surrender all gold and gold certificates, other than rare coins.

After 1933 there was some recovery, but it was slow; and there was another recession in 1937/8. Real GDP did not regain its pre-Depression level until 1937, and did not catch up with its pre-Depression trend until 1942. At the worst point of previous recessions, the unemployed had rarely reached 10 per cent of the workforce. During the Great Depression, having reached more than 25 per cent by 1933, unemployment stayed above 15 per cent for six more years, until 1939. It was only after the US entry into World War II in December 1941 that unemployment levels started to plummet.

■ Summing up

One of the most interesting things to emerge from our précis on the Great Depression is how remarkably strongly it resembles, at least in the run-up to October 1929, the recent financial crisis. The things that followed each crash were different. We attempt to show this similarity in Table 15.1 and we contrast it with Figure 1.1.

What we see in the run-up to both is an amazing similarity in certain key economic aspects. For example, in both cases, there was an expansion of credit, buoyant growth, rises in real incomes and a boom – in the Great Depression in stocks and in the recent financial crisis in housing prices. In each case there was a shock to the system – in 1929 industrial production moved into reverse and this led to an exit from the stock market and in 2007 the reversal in housing led to a frantic unwinding of credit default swap positions. In both cases, before the Crash there was a takeoff in dangerous debt products – in 1929 geared investment trusts and trading on very generous margin terms, in 2007 the toxic debt written by so many banking institutions plus the proliferation of personal debt.

After the crashes, things were somewhat different. In the earlier affair, there were widespread bank failures, tight money supply, deflation, protectionism and widespread unemployment. In the aftermath of the 2007/8 crisis, governments seemed to have learned lessons from the thirties. Banks have been propped up, money has been put into the system to overcome the credit crunch and every effort has been made to avoid deflation, protectionism and excessive unemployment.

Table 15.1 Key features of the Roaring Twenties and then the Great Depression

Up to October 1929

- Expansion of credit availability
- Emergence of dangerous debt products – the investment trust and trading on margin
- Rise in real incomes
- Rise in money stock
- Rise in industrial production
- Stock market boom reaching bubble proportions
- Shock to the system – industrial production goes into reverse

From October 1929

- Crash
- Bank failures
- Money supply tight, then tighter still from 1930 to 1933
- Deflation
- Protectionism
- Widespread unemployment

It is interesting to note that, in writing about the panic of 1907, Bruner and Carr[22] observed a number of features about that crash which were common to the two later crashes, namely:

- complex interconnections making it difficult to see what was going on. The linkages also enable contagion to flow from one market to another;
- buoyant growth preceding the crash;
- excessive debt in the financial system;
- prominent people failing to do the necessary things to put the system right and, in fact, by their unwitting actions making things worse. We suspect that this was true for 1907 and for 1929 but not for 2007/8 – unless inflation takes off in the wake of governments pumping in money and failing to mop it up quickly enough;
- the unexpected economic shock causing a sudden reversal of the outlook of individuals;
- the shift from optimism to pessimism and the attendant loss of confidence generating a downward spiral. Again, for the most recent setback, the fairly prompt actions of governments have prevented this being as bad as it might have been;
- failure of collective action meaning that policies have been inadequate to meet the economic challenge. Again, it is possible that, in the most recent crisis, the worst has been averted by timely government actions.

Before leaving the Great Depression, it is worth recalling the observation of Friedman and Friedman[23] who observed that 'instead of actively expanding the money supply by more than the usual amount to offset the contraction, the [Federal Reserve] System allowed the quantity of money to decline slowly throughout 1930. Compared to the decline of roughly one-third in the quantity of money from late 1930 to early 1933, the decline in the quantity of money up to October 1930 seems mild – a mere 2.6 per cent ... it was a larger decline than had occurred during or preceding all but a few of the earlier recessions. The combined effect of the aftermath of the stock market crash and the slow decline in the quantity of money during 1930 was a rather severe recession. Even if the recession had come to an end in late 1930 or early 1931, as it might well have done if a monetary collapse had not occurred, it would have ranked as one of the most severe recessions on record.'

Let us hope that the work of Friedman and Schwartz[24] (upon which the above is based) has taught us a lesson that we should remember. We do not cut money supply in a recession. It can turn a recession into a depression. As a reminder, a recession is often defined as two successive quarters with negative growth (a drop in real GDP) and a depression is defined loosely as a prolonged period of abnormally low economic activity and abnormally high unemployment.

And just in case the reader wonders what qualifies as a great depression, we think that it signifies many years of depression. If there's a definition in the economic texts, we couldn't find it. It is interesting to note that there have been worse times than the thirties. Press Cutting 15.1 reminds us of this.

Press cutting 15.1   *Financial Times*, 23 December 2009   **FT**

Call this a recession? At least it isn't the Dark Ages

Bryan Ward-Perkins

As we face an uncertain and worrying New Year, we can at least console ourselves with the fact that we are not living 1,600 years ago, and about to begin the year 410. In this year Rome was sacked, and the empire gave up trying to defend Britain. While this marks the glorious beginnings of 'English history', as Anglo-Saxon barbarians began their inexorable conquest of lowland Britain, it was also the start of a recession that puts all recent crises in the shade.

The economic indicators for fifth-century Britain are scanty, and derive exclusively from archaeology, but they are consistent and extremely bleak. Under the Roman empire, the province had benefited from the use of a sophisticated coinage in three metals – gold, silver and copper – lubricating the economy with a guaranteed and abundant medium of exchange. In the first decade of the fifth century new coins ceased to reach Britain from the imperial mints on the continent, and while some attempts were made to produce local substitutes, these efforts were soon abandoned. For about 300 years, from around AD 420, Britain's economy functioned without coin.

Core manufacturing declined in a similar way. There was some continuity of production of the high-class metalwork needed by a warrior aristocracy to mark its wealth and status; but at the level of purely functional products there was startling change, all of it for the worse. Roman Britain had enjoyed an abundance of simple iron goods, documented by the many hob-nail boots and coffin-nails found in Roman cemeteries. These, like the coinage, disappeared early in the fifth century, as too did the industries that had produced abundant attractive and functional wheel-turned pottery. From the early fifth century, and for about 250 years, the potter's wheel – that most basic tool, which enables thin-walled and smoothly finished vessels to be made in bulk – disappeared altogether from Britain. The only pots remaining were shaped by hand, and fired, not in kilns as in Roman times, but in open 'clamps' (a smart word for a pile of pots in a bonfire).

We do not know for certain what all this meant for population numbers in the countryside, because from the fifth to the eighth century people had so few goods that they are remarkably difficult to find in the archaeological record; but we do know its effect on urban populations. Roman Britain had a dense network of towns, ranging from larger settlements, like London and Cirencester, which also served an administrative function, to small commercial centres that had grown up along the roads and waterways. By 450 all of these had disappeared, or were well on the way to extinction. Canterbury, the only town in Britain that has established a good claim to continuous settlement from Roman times to the present, impresses us much more for the ephemeral nature of its fifth to seventh-century huts than for their truly urban character. Again it was only in the eighth century, with the (re)emergence of trading towns such as London and Saxon Southampton, that urban life returned to Britain.

For two or three hundred years, beginning at the start of the fifth century, the economy of Britain reverted to levels not experienced since well before the Roman invasion of AD 43. The most startling features of the fifth-century crash are its suddenness and its scale. We might not be surprised if, on leaving the empire, Britain had reverted to an economy similar to that which it had enjoyed in the immediately pre-Roman Iron Age. But southern Britain just before the Roman invasion was a considerably more sophisticated place economically than Britain in the fifth and sixth centuries: it had a native silver coinage; pottery industries that produced wheel-turned vessels and sold them widely; and even the beginnings of settlements recognisable as towns. Nothing of the kind existed in the fifth and sixth centuries; and it was only really in the eighth century that the British economy crawled back to the levels it had already reached before Emperor Claudius's invasion. It is impossible to say with any confidence when Britain finally returned to levels of economic complexity comparable to those of the highest point of Roman times, but it might be as late as around the year 1000 or 1100. If so, the post-Roman recession lasted for 600–700 years.

We can take some cheer from this sad story – so far our own problems pale into insignificance. But *Schadenfreude* is never a very satisfying emotion, and in this case it would be decidedly misplaced. The reason the Romano-British economy collapsed so dramatically should give us pause for thought. Almost certainly the suddenness and the catastrophic scale of the crash were caused by the levels of sophistication and specialisation reached by the economy in Roman times. The Romano-British population had grown used to buying their pottery, nails, and other basic goods from specialist producers, based often many miles away, and these producers in their turn relied on widespread markets to sustain their specialised production. When insecurity came in the fifth century, this impressive house of cards collapsed, leaving a population without the goods they wanted and without the skills and infrastructure needed to produce them locally. It took centuries to reconstruct networks of specialisation and exchange comparable to those of the Roman period.

The more complex an economy is, the more fragile it is, and the more cataclysmic its disintegration can be. Our economy is, of course, in a different league of complexity to that of Roman Britain. Our pottery and metal goods are likely to have been made, not many miles away, but on the other side of the globe, while our main medium of exchange is electronic, and sometimes based on smoke and mirrors. If our economy ever truly collapses, the consequences will make fifth-century Britain seem like a picnic.

Chapter 16

Government responses to the crisis

■ Introduction

In this chapter we attempt to set out government responses to the problems that confronted them in the wake of the financial crisis. The credit crunch, essentially a freeze in interbank lending immediately following the Lehman Brothers failure, brought the global financial system to the brink of collapse. Responses by the Federal Reserve System, the Bank of England and the European Central Bank were speedy and dramatic. The practical issues involved in the rescue aimed to achieve the following:

- to end the panic;
- to free up interbank lending in order to restore normal financial flows;
- to prevent economic activity from collapsing;
- to ensure that banks had adequate capital;
- to lay the foundation for a sustained recovery;
- to inject a monetary stimulus to provide sufficient liquidity and prevent deflation;
- to provide a fiscal stimulus to maintain demand and prevent or mitigate the effects of a recession.

All of the above required large-scale government intervention. In a nutshell, it would involve throwing money at the problem and mopping it up afterwards. At the time of writing (June 2010) the first part of this has been done – the second part is to come. We look at the intervention in the USA, Britain and the eurozone in turn. But it is our intention not to duplicate the specific coverage of individual bank bailouts that we have already covered in Chapters 12, 13 and 14.

■ US responses

In the US, there were a number of schemes devised to shore-up the banking system. The first to be put into practice was TARP (the Troubled Asset Relief Program). TARP was designed to allow the US Treasury to purchase or insure up to USD700 billion of troubled assets, defined as toxic assets including credit default swaps, residential and commercial mortgages and any securities, obligations, or other financial instruments that the Federal Reserve System deems as necessary to promote financial market stability. It was a requirement that such TARP assets had to be issued on or before 14 March 2008. This meant that the US Treasury could purchase illiquid, difficult-to-value assets from banks and other financial institutions.

TARP did not allow banks to recover losses already incurred on troubled assets. US government officials expected that once trading of these assets resumed, their prices would stabilise and ultimately increase. The idea of future gains from troubled assets was based upon the assumption that these assets were oversold rather than being subject to potential widespread default. TARP was planned to operate as a revolving purchase facility. The Treasury would have a set spending limit, USD250 billion at the start of the programme with provisions for this to be expanded if required subject to Presidential and Congressional assent. The scheme required financial institutions selling assets to the US Treasury to issue equity warrants or senior debt securities to the Treasury. An important goal of TARP was to encourage banks to resume lending again at levels before the crisis, both to each other and to businesses and to consumers.

In the original plan presented by Treasury Secretary Henry Paulson, the government would buy troubled assets held by banks and subsequently sell them to private investors or companies as markets revived. This plan was shelved when Paulson met with UK Prime Minister Gordon Brown who, in attempting to extricate Britain from the credit crunch had pursued a different strategy. Britain had put capital into banks via equity and preferred stock in order to clean up their balance sheets. This plan seemed more attractive than TARP because if the US Treasury offered to pay the current market price for these assets, the banks may refuse to sell, since it would lock in their losses. The point here was that, even under mark-to-market accounting, some commercial banks held some assets on their balance sheets at book values even though they could not sell them at those prices. Selling assets would force banks to recognise the losses in their financial accounts.

The US government chose to recapitalise banks by offering cash in exchange for preferred shares with further guarantee packages to Citigroup and Bank of America and to other commercial banks as time went on. For their part, many US financial institutions arranged rights issues by which existing shareholders injected more funds into stricken banks.

The government bailout of AIG, and Fannie Mae and Freddie Mac have been detailed in Chapter 12, as have the failures of Bear Stearns and Lehman Brothers.

After some relaxation of mark-to-market accounting rules, banks continued to hold their toxic assets. Matters improved for the banks following stress tests of US commercial banks in the spring of 2009 with results released in May 2009. The purpose of what was officially termed the Supervisory Capital Assessment Program and applied to 19 leading banks was to test whether the banks could withstand a severe economic downturn, quantify the amount of capital they would need in a worst-case scenario, and force them to raise that capital. But the most important outcome was that it restored some confidence in the financial system. Perhaps there was a hidden agenda here. Since the government had certified the banks' financial positions and since the banks would have to raise capital as the programme demanded, the government could expect no further bailout being necessary.

With many banks having exited the scene – Lehman Brothers, Bear Stearns, Merrill Lynch, Washington Mutual and Wachovia, plus a host of non-bank mortgage lenders – competition was reduced. The survivors could gain a larger market share and earn higher fees and margins. Furthermore, the Fed was pumping cheap money into the economy. All of this meant higher revenues and lower costs – to say nothing of continuing bonuses.

With low interest rates, banks could obtain depositors funds at very low cost. They could borrow cheaply from each other. They could borrow cheaply via the Federal Reserve discount window. They were enabled to sell bonds at low interest rates. They could swap asset-backed securities for cash from the Fed. They could sell their mortgages to Fannie and Freddie, which could then sell debt to the Fed.

So much cash was readily available to the banks, they could not run out of money. Since short-term interest rates fell below long-term interest rates, the essential rule of banking, borrowing short and lending long, was now a formula for pretty certain success. Banks were able to recapitalise themselves from current operations and repay government emergency financing.

The stress test results and the emergency bailouts made it clear that government would not let a major bank fail and that the government would bail out banks with their ongoing management and structures. They could go back to business as usual. Washington was there as a backstop if things got tough. The panic that had begun with Lehman's failure ended with utter conviction that the government would not let other major banks fail. This increased moral hazard. As the economy began to bottom out it became easier for banks to make money again. The US government had not only thrown money at the problem but, some would argue, had given Wall Street a blank cheque and had demanded very little in return. The same people were in the banks. The bonuses were still there. The Wall Street-Washington revolving door was still there. Most of the banks had received a 'get out of jail free' card.

The total cost to the US government of saving the banking system has variously been estimated at between USD1.5 and USD2 trillion. Which is much below earlier estimates – presumably falling as markets have improved. Despite the tremendous cost of bailing out the US financial system, the cost of letting it collapse would surely have been even higher.

■ British responses

As we have seen, the actions of the British government in recapitalising its banks rather than buying toxic assets from troubled financial institutions influenced the US government in replacing TARP with a similar programme. But, like its neighbour on the other side of the Atlantic, Britain was also mindful of the bullet points set out on the first page of this chapter. Given panic financial conditions and a credit crunch in which interbank lending was stalled there was a clear need to restore confidence.

The collapse of Lehman Brothers in September 2008 had paralysed banks and markets. Bankers had no idea to what extent other banks, to whom they might lend, were exposed to losses on holdings of toxic assets and derivatives related to them. The frozen markets were not just a question of liquidity. Confidence was blown away. Nobody knew which banks – even large ones – might turn out to be insolvent, with unrealised and, as yet, unacknowledged losses exceeding their equity capital.

In the autumn of 2008, banks worldwide were facing a double problem in meeting the Basel II required Tier 1 capital ratio requirements. The market value of bank shares was plummeting, while the perceived extent of their risks was rising sharply. They needed either to take risks off their books, or raise more equity capital – or both. By Friday 10 October 2008, the Dow Jones Index had lost 22 per cent of its value in a single week. This scale of decline was reminiscent of the Wall Street Crash of October 1929.

Some regulators required their banks to increase their equity capital. In other cases the banks themselves made rights issues requesting their shareholders to boost their equity capital. In the UK this was true of all four of the largest banks – Barclays, HSBC, Lloyds and RBS.

In some cases the government itself invested money in buying equity shares having under-written potentially failing rights offerings. The British government ended up owning 43 per cent of the equity in Lloyds, after its rescue takeover of HBOS, and 84 per cent in RBS. The stated intention was that such holdings would be sold to the public in due course. Taxpayers might eventually have to bear any losses if the ultimate sales proceeds from the government's equity shareholdings failed to exceed what the government had invested – although the prospects did seem reasonable for a profitable outturn because the govern-ment's purchases were at low levels. Even when the government put in a large amount of new capital, there was, for many months, doubt as to whether it would be enough. This was partly because of continuing uncertainty about the ultimate extent of losses on toxic assets, and partly because regulators were under pressure to increase further the capital ratios required of banks.

A further important problem was that banks themselves were keen to de-leverage their highly-geared balance sheets. They wanted to use any new equity capital, whether from existing shareholders or from governments, to reduce their liabilities, not to enable them to increase their assets by lending more to retail and wholesale customers. Potential borrowers' financial positions often now seemed much riskier than had been the case only a few months earlier, hence less creditworthy. Now, the UK government was asking commercial banks to lend. But customer requests frequently seemed unsound in the new austerity climate.

In the crisis, governments tried to provide a big monetary stimulus, in addition to some fiscal stimulus, both by slashing interest rates and by open market operations. The official name given to the latter was quantitative easing though the media preferred to call it simply printing money.

In the UK, the Bank of England cut interest rates from 5 per cent to ½ per cent between October 2008 and March 2009 – a reduction of 4½ per cent in just six months. In the US, the Federal Reserve (starting earlier) cut interest rates by 5 per cent over a longer time-frame – between late summer of 2007 and the end of 2008. This solution was not directly open to the 16 individual countries in the eurozone. But the ECB in Frankfurt, moving rather more cautiously, reduced interest rates by 3 per cent. Earlier that year, the ECB had actually increased interest rates in July 2008, by ¼ per cent to 4¼ per cent. See Figure 16.1.

Like several other government measures, interest rates take time to work through the economy – probably between 12 and 18 months. And if there were to be deflation – which was a matter of widespread concern – real interest rates could still be high even if the nominal rates were ½ per cent or even zero. One obvious problem is that once nominal interest rates reach zero the authorities cannot use further reductions to steer the economy. Having said this, historically, negative interest rates have been known in some countries.

Quantitative easing involved the central bank in offering cash to buy government debt and other debt held by banks and financial institutions. This aimed to increase the banks' capacity to lend – though their willingness to do so still remained uncertain. In the US, the amount involved in this kind of stimulus amounted to USD800 billion (more than 5 per cent of GDP. In the UK, it was GBP200 billion (about 13 per cent of GDP). At the time US annual GDP was about USD14 trillion. The GDP of the UK was about GBP1.5 trillion.

The intent was also that quantitative easing would offset the threat of deflation, which, as well as increasing the real burden of debt (and, of wages paid by businesses) might cause people to delay spending in the expectation of continuing falling prices. Again, quantitative easing would take some time to work through the economy. Even more than a year after the programme had started, it was hard to detect much effect on consumer spending – though it was certainly buoying up asset prices and stock markets. Of course,

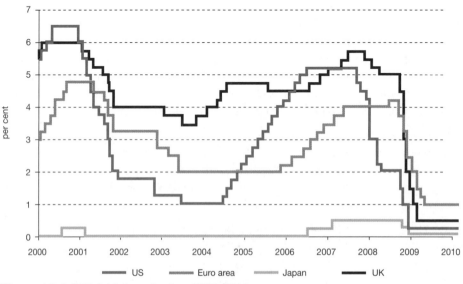

Figure 16.1 Official interest rates 2000–2010

one problem in assessing the impact of government actions is telling what would have happened without them.

A potential worry was whether the authorities would be willing and able to reverse the process at the right time when the velocity of circulation of money picked up. This had dropped in the wake of the financial crisis. Without care on this front, quantitative easing could push up inflation – and maybe, quite considerably. Throughout history inflation has been a tempting way for governments to seek popularity be easing the burden of too much debt. Some cynics, or realists perhaps, have reminded us that besides achieving prosperity there are popular, and often used, routes to escape government debt – namely inflation and consequent devaluation (which works in those cases where the debt is in the currency of the borrower) and/or default.

Would it be unduly cynical to think that political leaders would deliberately set out to create inflation? Might there be a temptation to delay unwinding quantitative easing? Since very few people in office have had practical experience of the problem it would be quite an achievement were they to get it exactly right.

In the UK, the government implemented a cut in Value Added Tax from 17 per cent to 15 per cent for 13 months from December 2008 until the end of 2009. It was widely viewed as a waste of the GBP12 billion (less than 1 per cent of GDP) it would cost. Even if retailers passed on the cut, such a small reduction in retail prices was likely to be swamped by the huge discounts retailers were offering – faced, as they were, with seasonally high stocks which they were having trouble selling to risk-averse, confidence-deprived customers. Moreover, the requirement to change hundreds of prices almost overnight at the height of the Christmas season (and then to reverse them at the height of the New Year Sales a year later) was an unwelcome distraction for retailers. On the other hand, this marginal help to the cash flow of retail customers would at least continue all through 2009. It was a gesture.

■ Eurozone responses

First of all a little bit of background. On 1 January 1999, a single European currency, the euro, was introduced in 11 EU countries, with further entrants joining later. The original members of the eurozone were Austria, Belgium, Finland, France, Germany, Ireland, Italy, Luxembourg, Netherlands, Portugal and Spain. Joining the single currency area two years later was Greece and more recently new members have been Slovenia, Cyprus, Malta and Slovakia, taking membership to 16 as of June 2010.

All of the original countries in the eurozone progressively phased out their old currencies and they were replaced on 1 January 2002 by the euro. On this date, euro banknotes and coins were introduced and old national banknotes and coins were withdrawn from circulation. Eurozone members share a single interest rate, set by the European Central Bank (ECB), and, of course, a single foreign exchange rate. The ECB is responsible for the monetary policy of the eurozone countries – but not fiscal policies.

We now need to introduce a bit of economics here. It's on the topic of purchasing power parity and it's straightforward. At its simplest, this theory suggests that exchange rates move to make good changes in inflation rates. Take an example in which there are no costs of transporting goods. If the US dollar/sterling exchange rate is USD1.70 equals GBP1 and British widgets sell at GBP10 each, the US-produced widget should be marketed at USD17 to be in line on price. If this were initially the case, and inflation in Britain and the US amounted to 8 per cent and 4 per cent per annum, respectively, the widget prices (assuming they were to move in line with inflation) would be GBP10.80 and USD17.68, respectively. However, an exchange rate movement which took account of these relative inflations would ensure continuing competitiveness; such a rate would have to be USD1.6370 = GBP1.

There are a number of reservations about purchasing power parity. First, the prices of individual goods and services rarely move exactly in line with general inflation, whether it be measured by retail prices, wholesale prices or whatever. Furthermore, the index that would be most relevant would be one based upon export prices.

To reiterate, purchasing power parity suggests that the exchange rate changes to compensate for differences in inflation between two countries. Thus, if country A has a higher inflation rate than its trading partners, the exchange rate of the former should weaken to compensate for this relativity. If country A's exchange rate falls, and if that fall is an exact compensation for inflation differentials, its real effective exchange rate is said to remain constant. Purchasing power parity suggests that real effective exchange rates might remain constant through time.

But, as is often the case in economics, we have a problem. When tested against evidence from economic statistics, purchasing power parity is found to hold up moderately well in the long term. But in the short term there are substantial deviations; so much so that using purchasing power parity as a short-term predictor of exchange rates is utterly unjustified. Having said this, its use as a long-term forecasting device seems better merited by the evidence. As mentioned above, purchasing power parity suggests that exchange rates change to compensate for differences in inflation between two countries.

The message for the eurozone is simple. Since eurozone members have a common currency, the countries using the euro should have common inflation rates. And if their inflation rates are different, it is likely to be the case that the eurozone member with the low inflation rate will have lower costs and probably export more than its eurozone partners with high inflation rates. Maybe this problem will not be so great if inflation rate differences are relatively minor – but if they escalate into big differences, so does the economic problem.

When the common currency was instigated, the conversion rates for the old national currency into the euro was set at such a level as to ensure competitiveness between themselves. In the jargon, this rate was an equilibrium rate. And, although there are minor differences between economists' views, an equilibrium exchange rate is normally taken as one which would create a current account balance of payments result of zero (techni-cally, this may not be precisely so but it isn't far out). And this would mean that exports and imports of goods and services would be equal. (Again, near enough so.) Incidentally, there are other problems with the theory and the position of some countries. For example,

Norway has adequate exports of oil and gas that are so big as to defy the implication of purchasing power parity. There are quite a few countries like this.

Anyway, to maintain equilibrium, in the eurozone, different countries should exhibit similar inflation rates – or more or less so. Inevitably, in reality, different inflation rates exist within a country. Inflation in the South East of England may be different from that in the North East. Inflation in New York may differ from that in the Mid West. The actual cost of living and pay rates may be very different. But we would expect that the actual inflation rate differences would not be excessive.

Returning to the actual picture of inflation in the eurozone, the scale of the problem becomes clear. Labour costs in Germany rose 7 per cent between 2000 and 2008 versus 34 per cent in Ireland, 30 per cent in Spain, Portugal and Italy, 28 per cent in Greece and the Netherlands and 20 per cent in France. Over this period, Germany recorded an accumulated figure of exports minus imports of EUR1261 billion while Spain saw a deficit of EUR598 billion and Greece also achieved a minus figure amounting to EUR273 billion.

This picture is brought into relief if one tracks the real effective exchange of certain eurozone members from the beginning of the euro project up to the end of 2009. Remember, the real effective exchange rate is arrived at by looking at the actual exchange rate versus an index of foreign prices versus home prices. Also remember that if purchasing power parity is holding, the real effective exchange rate remains constant. Figure 16.2 shows the real effective exchange rate for certain countries in the eurozone. The conclusion that can be drawn from the figure is that Spain, Ireland, Portugal and Greece have all become relatively weak competitively at the euro exchange rate given their excessive inflation versus Germany, which has controlled inflation and is competitively strong versus its eurozone partners.

The impact of these relative competitive positions for eurozone countries can be seen in Figure 16.3 which shows exports as a percentage of GDP from 1999 to 2009. Clearly Germany has been a winner and Greece, in particular, has been a loser.

A further tabulation shows the effect of all of this upon the balance of payments current account as a percentage of GDP and various countries' budget deficits (government inflows versus outflows) as a percentage of GDP. This appears in Table 16.1 which also shows consumer price increases for the last available year, unemployment rates and interest rates. The table shows data for the USA and the UK as well as some eurozone countries. What is clear from the table is the massive impact of inflation relativities within the eurozone. Of the countries in Table 16.1, the plight of Greece and Spain stand out with high negatives showing up on budget deficit data. The same is true for Britain and the USA. What is also apparent are Germany and the Netherlands' current account positivity on balance of payments. And, also, on the interest rates front some big differences in eurozone ten-year interest rates. This is interesting. Since eurozone countries all have the same currency and all have interest rates set by the ECB, why should longer-term interest rates diverge so much? After all, short-term rates are exactly the same. Shouldn't German long-term rates be the same as Greek long-term interest rates? The answer is yes … but, what if something odd happened. Like Greece quitting the eurozone. If this were to happen and Greece went back to its old national currency – the drachma – there would

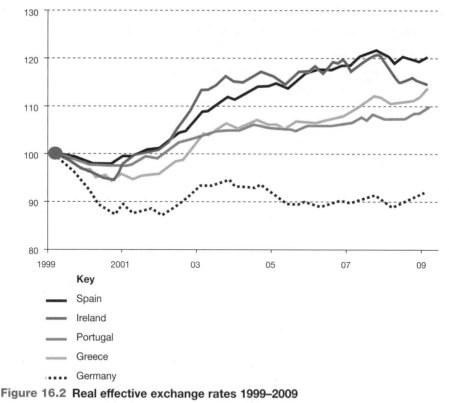

Key

— Spain

— Ireland

— Portugal

— Greece

...... Germany

Figure 16.2 Real effective exchange rates 1999–2009

Source: European Central Bank

be every chance that the drachma would fall in value against the euro to make Greek exports competitive again. Is the interest rate market charging Greece a higher rate than other eurozone members because it expects that to happen? Is the premium the market charges Greece something to do with political risk? Maybe a bit of each – probably more to do with Greece exiting the eurozone. Incidentally, note that European countries outside the eurozone do have the luxury of currency depreciation – Britain, for example – as a way of helping them move towards the solution of their economic problems.

Our table (Table 16.1) was compiled just after the eurozone put together a rescue package for Greece, which was experiencing a borrowing crisis of the highest order. A couple of weeks before the date of the table, Greece was paying 14 per cent for ten-year borrowing. Afterwards, its rate had fallen to 7.7 per cent.

Turning to the Greek rescue package mentioned in the previous paragraph, there was speculation and gambling via credit default swaps that Greece might default on its debt or leave the eurozone. This sovereign crisis also threatened to spread to Portugal, Spain, Ireland and maybe elsewhere.

By 7 May 2010, as yields on weak eurozone countries' government bonds rose sharply, there was a real threat that foreign financing for these countries would stop. This raised fears about the exposures of banks to these eurozone countries – the PIGS, Portugal, Italy,

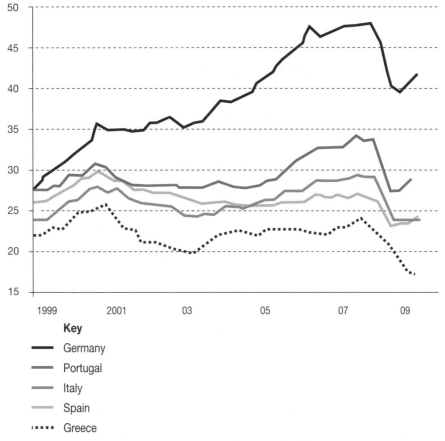

Figure 16.3 Export of goods and services (as % of GDP)
Source: Thomson Reuters Datastream

Greece and Spain, also known as Club Med. If the acronym were written PIIGS, it would justifiably include Ireland.

Not being a country per se, the eurozone did not have an economic framework designed to cope with this kind of problem. But EU finance ministers acted quickly to contain the crisis – for now anyway. They agreed to create a stabilisation fund, worth up to EUR500 billion. This included EUR60 billion to be financed by EU bonds that could be raised fairly quickly – this amount being as much as could be sold over three years without breaching the EU's budget ceiling. This element had to be approved by EU members, such as Britain, which does not use the euro, because their taxpayers would be on the hook were the money not repaid in full. The stabilisation fund would be supplemented by up to EUR250 billion more from the IMF.

In addition, the ECB said it would purchase government bonds to restore calm to markets. The ECB also reopened credit lines that had been put in place in the autumn of 2008 with the Federal Reserve, the Bank of England, the Bank of Canada and the Swiss National Bank.

Financial markets responded positively. Germany's stock market closed more than 5 per cent higher on 10 May 2010. France's stock market index rose by almost 10 per cent;

Table 16.1 Economic data for various countries (table prepared end May 2010)

	Consumer price increases %	Unemploy-ment rate %	Interest rates		Balance of payment current account versus GDP %	Budget deficit versus GDP %
			3 month rate %	10 year rate %		
Austria	+1.9	4.9	0.70	2.99	+1.6	−5.0
Belgium	+1.8	11.6	0.70	3.16	−0.1	−6.0
France	+1.7	10.1	0.70	2.91	−2.1	−8.4
Germany	+1.0	7.8	0.70	2.64	+5.3	−5.6
Greece	+4.8	12.1	0.70	7.70	−7.0	−10.2
Italy	+1.5	8.3	0.70	4.01	−2.6	−5.3
Netherlands	+1.1	5.6	0.70	2.88	+5.5	−6.2
Spain	+1.5	19.1	0.70	4.20	−3.9	−11.5
Euro area	+1.5	10.0	0.70	2.59		−7.1
USA	+2.2	9.9	0.29	3.23	−3.3	−11.0
Britain	+3.7	8.0	0.72	3.54	−1.0	−12.8

big French banks were heavily exposed to Greece and would stand to benefit significantly from rescue guarantee. The yield on ten-year Greek government bonds plunged from more than 12 per cent to less than 8 per cent. Yields on comparable Irish, Italian, Portuguese and Spanish bonds also fell sharply.

However, the rescue plan had question marks associated with it. Much of the finer detail was missing. And the package only buys time for troubled governments to cut their budget deficits and put in place structural reforms needed to improve their lost export competitiveness. If they fail, there could be more trouble ahead. We do not think that we have heard the last of this problem yet. Further eurozone bank bailout funds are likely to be required. And whether all of the existing members of the euro will still be euro members in ten years' time is a moot point.

Possible routes out of the problem might include:

■ austerity programmes to continue in the high inflation countries. At best the risk is social tension. At worse, the risk is political upheaval and possible overthrow of existing regimes – in other words, revolution;

■ the high inflation countries could quit the euro and return to their old national currencies. There would be short-term turmoil in the capital markets but this would settle down;

■ there might be a halfway house which would be politically acceptable whereby weaker eurozone countries would adopt a new 'soft euro' which would involve a depreciation against the existing euro – the 'hard euro'. We suspect that this would lead eventually to a return to national currencies for weaker eurozone members;

■ new accessions to the euro to be put on hold – maybe permanently.

We rule out the other possibility, which would be for Germany, in particular, to run high inflation for a few years to catch up to that already experienced in the PIIGS. In theory it could work, but in practice it's highly unlikely. It's thinking the unthinkable.

Is it also unthinkable that these strains could create pressure to curtail the whole European Union project? Note that we used the word curtail – not abandon. There are iconoclasts who have long expressed doubt about the expansion of the project. Their voices will be heard louder now. And if the project is curtailed, would it be such a bad thing?

■ The extent of total bailouts

The total amounts invested by governments in rescue packages for banks have been huge. Including capital injections, asset purchases and guarantees on debt (which are likely only to be partially required) but excluding deposit guarantees which will probably not be called upon in any case, Table 16.2 (prepared in January 2010) attempts to put numbers on the problem. Because of the inclusion of guarantees of debt, the figures shown in the table are higher than government bailout estimates elsewhere in this book. It should be borne in mind that the statistics set out therein are a moving feast. New things are happening continually but, having said that, some of the data – especially in terms of percentages of GDP – are truly staggering. On this criterion, Ireland's position at the top of the league would not be surprising to those who have read the case study in Chapter 14. Britain's position as second in the table is not so surprising when it is remembered that financial services had taken over as the largest sector in the UK economy and two of its leading banks were colossal players in a market that they did not understand and in which they failed to control the extent of their exposure. The UK's problem is mitigated because much of its debt is much longer term than other countries' debt. This buys it time to solve the problem and it means that lenders are not likely to be knocking on the door imminently. Incidentally, we would point out that our table does not contain figures for all countries. We are sure that if we had the data for Iceland, Britain would drop one place in the league table. Maybe Ireland would too.

Clearly, what began as a financial crisis, affecting banks, became an economic crisis, causing recession worldwide. It developed into a political crisis with sovereign states at risk of default. Will governments mop up the money in a timely manner? Will governments create inflation by failing to do this? And thereby make it easier to repay debt. We are rather worried. So are Roubini and Das – see Press Cutting 16.1. So is Martin Wolf – see Press Cutting 16.2.

Table 16.2 Government rescue packages for some countries (including guarantees on debt but excluding deposit guarantees)

Country	% of GDP	USD billions
Ireland	244	648
United Kingdom	69	1,476
Sweden	49	196
Netherlands	43	339
Slovenia	39	18
Austria	37	139
Finland	30	75
Spain	26	374
Canada	22	361
Germany	20	669
Norway	20	71
United States	18	2,684
South Korea	16	160
Portugal	15	34
Greece	12	39
Luxembourg	8	4
France	7	183
Belgium	6	27
Denmark	6	19
Japan	4	225
Italy	3	73

Table shows figures at January 2010.

Press cutting 16.1   *Financial Times*, 1 June 2010   FT

Solutions for a crisis in its sovereign stage

Nouriel Roubini and Arnab Das

The largest financial crisis in history is spreading from private to sovereign entities. At best, Europe's recovery will suffer and the collapsing euro will subtract from growth in its key trading partners. At worst, a disintegration of the single currency or a wave of disorderly defaults could unhinge the financial system and precipitate a double-dip recession.

How did it come to this? Starting in the 1970s, financial liberalisation and innovation eased credit constraints on the public and private sectors. Households in advanced economies – where real income growth was anaemic – could use debt to spend beyond their means. The process was fed by ever laxer regulation, increasingly frequent and expensive government and International Monetary Fund bail-outs in response to increasingly frequent and expensive crises, and easy monetary policy from the 1990s. Political support for this democratisation of credit and home-ownership compounded the trend after 2000.

Paradigm shifts were invoked to justify debt-fuelled global growth: the transition from cold war to Washington Consensus; the re-integration of emerging markets into the global economy; the 'Goldilocks' combination of high growth and low inflation; a much-ballyhooed convergence ahead of monetary union across Europe; and rapid financial innovation.

The result was a consumption binge in deficit countries and an export surge in surplus countries, with vendor financing courtesy of the latter. Global output and growth, corporate profits, household income and wealth, and public revenue and spending temporarily shot well above equilibrium. Wishful thinking allowed asset prices to reach absurd heights and pushed risk premiums to incredible lows. When the asset and credit bubbles burst, it became clear that the world faced a lower speed limit on growth than we had banked on.

Now, governments everywhere are releveraging to socialise private losses and jump-start private demand. But public debt is ultimately a private burden: governments subsist by taxing private income and wealth, or through the ultimate capital levy of inflation or outright default. Eventually governments must deleverage too, or else public debt will explode, precipitating further, deeper public and private-sector crises.

This is already happening in the frontline of the crisis, eurozone sovereign debt. Greece is first over the edge; Ireland, Portugal and Spain trail close behind. Italy, while not yet illiquid, faces solvency risks. Even France and Germany have rising deficits. UK budget cuts are starting. Eventually Japan and the US will have to cut too.

In the early part of the crisis, governments acted in unison to restore confidence and economic activity. The Group of 20 coalesced after the crash of 2008–09; we all were in the same boat together, sinking fast.

But in 2010, national imperatives reasserted themselves. Co-ordination is now lacking: Germany is banning naked short selling unilaterally and the US is pursuing its own financial sector reform. Surplus countries are unwilling to stimulate consumption, while deficit countries are building unsustainable public debt.

The eurozone offers an object lesson in how not to respond to a systemic crisis. Member states started going it alone when they carved up pan-European banks along national lines in 2008. After much dithering and denial over Greece, leaders orchestrated an overwhelming show of force; a €750bn bail-out bolstered confidence for one day. But the rules went out of the window. Sovereign rescues are legitimised by an escape clause from the 'no bail-out' rule intended for acts of God, not man-made debt. The European Central Bank began buying government bonds days after insisting it would not. Tensions in the Franco-German axis are palpable.

Instead of Balkanised local responses, we need a comprehensive solution to this global problem.

First, the eurozone must get its act together. It must deregulate, liberalise, reform the south and stoke demand in the north to restore dynamism and growth; ease monetary policy to prevent deflation and boost competitiveness; implement sovereign debt restructuring mechanisms to limit moral hazard from bail-outs; and put expansion of the eurozone on ice.

Second, creditors need to take a hit, and debtors adjust. This is a solvency problem, demanding a grand work-out. Greece is the tip of the iceberg; banks in Spain and elsewhere in Europe stand knee-deep in bad debt, while problems persist in US residential and global commercial property.

Third, fiscal sustainability must be restored, with a focus on timetables and scenarios for revenues and spending, ageing-related costs and contingencies

→

for future shocks, rather than on fiscal rules.

Fourth, it is time for radical reform of finance. The majority of proposals on the table are inadequate or irrelevant. Large financial institutions must be unbundled; they are too big, interconnected and complex to manage. Investors and customers can find all the traditional banking, investment banking, hedge fund, mutual fund and insurance services they need in specialised firms. We need to go back to Glass-Steagal on steroids.

Last, the global economy must be rebalanced. Deficit countries need to boost savings and investment; surplus countries to stimulate consumption. The quid pro quo for fiscal and financial reform in deficit countries must be deregulation of product, service and labour markets to boost incomes in surplus countries.

Press cutting 16.2

Financial Times, 29 May 2010   **FT**

An ABC of financial shocks and fiscal aftershocks

Martin Wolf

'Is the crisis over, Daddy?'

'Not really, Bobby. Just look at the news of market turmoil.'

'Why isn't it over, Daddy?'

'The crisis began in August 2007 and reached its worst in autumn of 2008. By historical standards, that is not so long for such a big crisis.'

'Not so long, Daddy? Did you not say that the guarantees and capital injections, the money-printing by central banks – "unconventional policy", you called it – and the borrowing by governments had fixed the crisis?'

'Bobby, you don't pay enough attention,' replied his father, a bit impatiently. 'What I said is that these actions would stop the crisis from becoming a depression. I was right, as usual.'

Bobby smiled, affectionately.

'Stop smirking,' said his father. 'Take the rich western countries: their output shrank by 3.3 per cent last year – the worst performance since the Second World War. You do know about the war, don't you?'

'Oh yes. We have studied it at least three times at school.'

'Well, the Organisation for Economic Co-operation and Development – I know, that's a mouthful – said this week that the output of the rich countries might grow by 2.7 per cent this year. The world economy is forecast to grow 4.6 per cent after a 0.9 per cent decline in 2009. This is better than almost anybody expected even half a year ago.'

'If that's true,' replied the boy, 'why do all these people talk about "instability"? What's that about?'

'You know about aftershocks following earthquakes. Well, fiscal crises can be the aftershocks of financial crises. And then they can cause financial aftershocks, in their turn.'

Bobby was beginning to find this lecture interesting, to his surprise. 'So how does that work, Daddy?'

'Well, think about what happened before the financial earthquake of 2007–09: there were huge rises in property prices and booms in construction; there was an explosion of private debt; and there was a big increase in financial complexity. So, when property prices fell, we had the big panic. But two other things happened:

governments received more revenue than they had expected, most of which they spent; and they borrowed easily, too.

'In the new eurozone, all governments found they could borrow as if they were Germany's. Households and businesses could also borrow on German terms. So they bought and built. In the good times, wages also soared.'

Bobby yawned. His father drove on.

'So what happened after the crisis? Fiscal deficits exploded to levels never before seen in peacetime, particularly in countries affected by the bubbles – the US, UK, Ireland and Spain. So the threat of a fiscal crisis emerged.

'What triggered this aftershock was the revelation that Greece had lied about its fiscal position, followed by the inability of the eurozone to respond: Germans were outraged at the idea that they should rescue irresponsible profligates; others thought the Germans inflexible bullies. So the Europeans made the same mistake as the Americans had made when responding to financial worries: they let the crisis get ahead of them.'

'But they bailed out Greece,' said the boy. 'So why all the turbulence?'

'The big point is that investors are not altogether stupid: they know these are temporary patches; they know Greek indebtedness is going to worsen; they know that other countries in peripheral Europe will find it hard to grow out of their plight; they know that solidarity among eurozone member countries is fraying; they know Germans are very angry; and they know that inadequately capitalised banks are vulnerable to sovereign risks. All this makes the euro seem a worse bet. So it has fallen in value.'

'I understand that,' replied Bobby. 'But won't that help the eurozone?'

'Yes,' agreed his father. 'But it will worsen prospects elsewhere – in the UK and US, for example. And then there's the worry that these countries have huge fiscal difficulties, too. The markets don't

seem to mind now. But they might change their view. Worse, they don't know what to fear: will it end up in deflation, default, inflation, financial shocks, or all of these? Markets are unpredictable, like children.'

Bobby decided not to respond to this teasing. 'So,' he asked thoughtfully, 'what's going to happen next?'

'If I knew that, I wouldn't be a mere economic journalist,' his father said.

Bobby smiled: a familiar remark.

His father did not notice. 'Maybe, the momentum gained by the US and the big emerging markets, especially China, will let the world ride through the shocks. The OECD calls the outlook "moderately encouraging".'

'Alternatively, you could argue that the massive fiscal deficits are unsustainable and that attempts to rein them in, in the eurozone and UK, are going to cause renewed recession and political strife. We have also barely begun reducing private debts, which will take years. The banks are far too big and have too many doubtful assets on their books. Meanwhile, emerging countries are too small and weak to be locomotives for the world. Some people worry that China is overheating or suffering from huge asset price bubbles, too, though I disagree. And then there is geopolitical uncertainty over North Korea and Iran. In short, markets are volatile because of all the uncertainty out there.'

Bobby was beginning to find this familiar: his father tended to see the gloomy side. But he could be wrong, as his mother enjoyed pointing out.

'Anyway,' concluded his father, 'these aftershocks are likely to go on for years, with fiscal worries undermining confidence in the financial sector and back again. It will affect you, too: western governments are going to be short of money for decades. It's going to be miserable. But you can learn Chinese and go east.'

Bobby groaned. It sounded like hard work. But he went off quietly to bed. What nightmares disturbed him?

Chapter 17

Lessons and major issues

■ Introduction

In this chapter we start by bringing together some of the key general lessons from our analysis. This is followed by warnings for various players in the financial crisis. We offer counsel relevant to governments, bankers, regulators, household borrowers and academics. Finally, we end the chapter with an overview of major issues that are worthy of detailed discussion and possible action.

■ Financial crises

Charles Kindleberger[1] begins his scholarly study of manias and crashes with a chapter headed 'Financial crisis: a hardy perennial'. He is clear that financial crises are a regular feature of the economic world. The regularity of boom and bust is documented by Reinhart and Rogoff[2]. Their analysis is of a system that fails frequently. As we have pointed out in Chapters 9 and 11, there are widely-accepted patterns to the build-up to financial crises. Given this background, failure would seem to emanate from a collective memory lapse. Or, maybe, participants get carried away on a wave of euphoria that no-one wants to end – perhaps, propelled forward by greed and turning a deaf ear to doubters.

Kindleberger[3] observes that 'financial crises are associated with the peaks of business cycles'. We see no reason to disagree. Kindleberger goes on to say that 'markets generally work, but occasionally they break down. When they do, they require government intervention to provide the public good of stability.' And at the end of his text, Kindleberger tells us that 'economists think they know how to handle financial crises: throw money at them, and after the crisis is over, mop the money up ... Central banks can create money, and when the lender of last resort is a central bank, the problem is usually a technical, rather than a political one.' We would concur with Kindleberger's advice. On the issue of whether it is a technical or political problem it does seem that in the USA it has taken on the nature of a party political issue with Republicans and Democrats divided over the preferred course of action.

On the question of bubbles in the economy, Galbraith[4] observes that 'boom and bust were said to be predictable manifestations of the business cycle'. True, but if predictable means putting an approximate date on the timing of transformation from boom to bust, this is surely difficult indeed. Bubbles follow fairly well-trodden routes and these have been summarised in Chapter 9. It does no harm to recall the statement by Keynes[5] that 'speculators may do no harm as bubbles on a steady stream of enterprise. But the position is serious when enterprise becomes the bubble on a whirlpool of speculation.' From our case studies of bank collapses, this seems to have occurred, in one way or another, in all of our examples. The quotation is a lesson in itself for governments, bankers, regulators and businesspeople. It needs to be borne in mind. But that fact is that they all wish to sustain the euphoric phase that is making them rich and powerful and they all wish to condemn or marginalise the doubters.

In our experience, when you hear the repeated mantra 'this time is different' or 'the new paradigm' or 'the new economy' or 'we have defeated boom and bust', or some new variant on this cant, you know that the good times being experienced are unsustainable and the bursting of the bubble is not far away. In bubble times the assumption is that because money is the measure of capitalist achievement, this leads to the corollary that money is associated with superior intelligence. On this point Galbraith[6] is worth quoting. 'We compulsively associate unusual intelligence with the leadership of great financial institutions ... The larger the capital assets and income flows controlled, the deeper the presumed financial, economic and social perception.' He goes on to say that 'only after the spectacular collapse does the truth emerge ... financial genius is before the fall.'

From bust to boom and back again, governments, commercial and investment banks, central banks and regulators make repeated mistakes in terms of their approaches to the economy, lending, controls, susceptibility to lobbying, and falling in love with debt and financial innovation. One of the key lessons for all of the above parties and for the economics and academic professions is the importance of Hyman Minsky's model[7] of finance through the cycle. This appears in our Chapter 11 as do some augmentations to his model on our part. During the boom period, bank competition overheats, resulting all too easily in an environment of lax regulation, in moves to negative real interest rates, indiscipline in bank lending involving relaxed credit analysis and overexposure to individual industrial sectors. Crony lending becomes a feature of banking in less sophisticated markets. Even in advanced markets, debt reaches unacceptable levels in banking as well as some non-financial businesses. At the peak of the cycle the whole picture is one of awful lending and awful internal control by banks. And this is not just the case for retail and wholesale banking. The mortgage business reaches binge proportions as lenders lower their standards, in particular in respect of subprime mortgagees. Galbraith[8] observed that 'the world of finance hails the invention of the wheel over and over again, often in a slightly more unstable version. All financial innovation involves, in one form or another, the creation of debt secured in greater or lesser adequacy by real assets.'

In writing this book, your author became more aware of the way in which bankers had manipulated their shareholders to enable them (the bank executives) to receive rewards out of all proportion to their input, based upon dubious short-term profits which were unrealised and may not actually accrue. The prevalence of perverse bonus structures was surprising. These were conducive to taking on excess risk which might be good for bank bonuses but could result in liquidation for the bank and wipeout for shareholders. Stiglitz[9] puts it succinctly when he says that 'bank officers' incentives were not consistent with the objectives of other shareholders and society more generally.' We outlined examples of the problem in Chapter 11.

The crisis in the financial system was not helped by naive accounting rules which allowed cavalier off-balance sheet treatments of structured investment vehicles and similar leveraged funds which enabled banks to present a picture of lower leverage than was truly the case. Add to this the inflated values of assets permitted in bank published accounts – see Chapter 8 – and up-front recognition of profits on longer-term deals in internal management accounts which are used to compute bonuses – again, see Chapter 8 – and it is clear that accounting has a lot to answer for. The outlawing of material amounts of window dressing is another serious lesson for accounting rule-makers.

A major lesson for regulators, failure on which was clearly evident in the recent crash, concerns risk monitoring. We agree with Pozen's advice[10] that financial risk monitoring should concentrate on four key factors 'inflated prices of real estate, institutions with very high leverage, asset-liability mismatches and fast-growing products or institutions'. All of these lessons so far are consistent with Ritholz's ingredients[11] for financial catastrophe, which include:

- massive use of leverage;
- excessive risk-taking;
- abuse of lax regulation;
- off-balance-sheet accounting;
- inept risk management;
- shortsighted (and greedy) incentives;
- interconnectedness and complexity that screams 'systemic risk' to any policy-maker within earshot.

The concurrent presence of these factors inevitably implies that the system is waiting for a shock of some sort to create an implosion of significant magnitude.

After the crash comes a phase in which the banking élite attempts to pass the blame for the incident on to other agencies or forces outside of banking markets – such as subprime lenders and borrowers. Sooner, rather than later, the truth emerges and the dubious and risky strategies of the banks become apparent – see Chapter 11. After this phase comes reform and regulation with two schools of thought confronting each other – Wall Street pitching for self-regulation or light regulation and the government interested in serious regulation and its pound of flesh.

There are other lessons which have emanated from other authors' analyses. For example, Bruner and Carr[12] explore key drivers of the crash of 1909 and draw parallels with the recent implosion. Their seven drivers are all apparent in respect of the financial crisis of 2007/8 although their last element, the failure of collective action, seems not to have been so obvious this time round, especially if, by this term, one means a failure of action by governments after the event. Indeed, this time round, governments acted fairly quickly and decisively in their rescue programmes and they seem to have learned much from the

Great Depression. Bruner and Carr's key elements were listed in more detail in Chapter 16. They include:

- complexity, making the nature of events opaque;
- buoyant growth;
- excessive debt;
- adverse leadership;
- the unexpected economic shock;
- the shift from optimism to pessimism;
- failure of collective action.

Stiglitz[13] proposes seven principles, gleaned from the most recent crisis, for an effective stimulus plan to drive the economy out of difficulties. The reader will recall that Kindleberger expressed the opinion that the way to handle the crisis was to throw money at it and, when the crisis is over, to mop it up. How the injection of cash is done is the thesis of Stiglitz's recommendations. They include the following:

- It should be fast. It is imperative to get money into the economy quickly.
- It should be effective. This means a big bang for the buck. Every dollar spent should give rise to a large increase in employment and output. Stiglitz reminds us that 'the amount by which national income increases for every dollar spent is called the multiplier: in standard Keynesian analysis, a dollar of government spending gives rise to more than a dollar's increase in national output.' But the multiplier effect may be short term or it may be deferred. Stiglitz explains. 'On average, the short-run multiplier for the US economy is around 1.5. If the government spends a billion dollars now GDP this year will go up by $1.5 billion. Long-run multipliers are larger. Not all spending has the same multiplier: spending on foreign contractors … has a low multiplier, because much of their consumption takes place outside the United States; so do tax cuts for the rich – who save much of what they receive. Increased unemployment benefits have a high multiplier, because those who find themselves suddenly short of income are going to spend almost every dollar they receive … spending money to bail out the banks without getting something in return gives money to the richest Americans and has almost no multiplier … '
- It should address the country's long-term problems.
- It should focus on investment. A stimulus package will increase a country's deficit, but the country will be in a better shape in the long run as a result of the stimulus and, in the short run, output and employment are increased.
- It should be fair. Stiglitz points out that middle-class Americans have fared far worse in recent years compared to those at the top. In his opinion, the stimulus should target less well-off groups. Of course, what is fair is subjective.
- It should deal with the short-term exigencies created by the crisis. Stiglitz words are telling here. 'In a downturn, states often run out of money and have to start cutting jobs. The jobless are left without health care insurance. People struggling to make

mortgage payments could go under if they lose their job or someone in their family gets sick. A well-designed stimulus should deal with as many of these issues as possible.'

■ The stimulus plan should be targeted at areas of potential job loss.

We would endorse these principles and recommendations.

Finally, in this section, we must reiterate as one of the great lessons on the recent financial crisis all of the warnings that we made in Chapters 10 and 11 about the use of Gaussian models in fat tail financial markets, the efficient market hypothesis and rational economic man. We have been deluding ourselves for far too long on these issues. We would also be deluding ourselves if we thought that there would not be another financial crisis in the future. Memories of markets are short.

At the risk of reiterating the lessons of the crisis, we now direct them, in summary form, under the headings of the various parties to whom they should be most pertinent.

■ Lessons for governments

Undoubtedly governments made massive mistakes in the run-up to the financial crisis. We have articulated these in earlier chapters. We see it appropriate now to summarise, in bullet point form, major lessons for governments. They are as follows:

■ Financial crises are not a new phenomenon. Repeatedly governments have taken their collective eyes off the ball and failed to see them coming. They occur at the peak of business cycles. This is the time for maximum attention and action if crisis is to be thwarted.

■ Markets usually work well but, occasionally, they break down and when they do, government intervention is necessary if stability is to be restored.

■ The route to the restoration of stability is achieved by throwing money at the crisis but – just as important – mopping it up effectively afterwards to avoid the corollary of excessive inflation. Having said this, often in the past, the injection of money into the system has led to increased government debt problems. Although in many cases this has been followed by timely repayment, it has often been corrected by inflation reducing the real value of the debt. And default has also frequently occurred. We would hardly counsel governments to pursue this latter course.

■ Governments love to be loved. Their desire for popularity should not stop them from realising that they have to take away the punch bowl before the party gets into full swing.

■ Watch out for times when enterprise becomes the bubble on a whirlpool of speculation. Marginal businesses occur all over the place. Resource allocation is poor. The government needs to curb such situations. And when such situations are apparent, it is a good indicator that we are in the late stage of a bubble. A shock will soon defuse it.

■ Beware the four words 'this time is different' and other platitudes that we mentioned earlier in this chapter. When heard, it's for sure that the punch bowl should be taken away – and quick.

■ When the banks and the business world are piling high debt on their balance sheets, when average debt to equity ratios are well beyond norms and financial innovation is all the rage, this is surely indicative of a boom out of control. Action is necessary. But politicians often find it difficult to choose the necessary corrective route because of the insistence of friendly lobbyists bearing gifts, because of the congratulatory cant of sycophants and flatterers and the belief in their own rhetoric and their role in creating a successful economy. This is a time to beware.

■ Governments should never forget Hyman Minsky's model of finance and should be guided by it.

■ The list of suggestions from Joseph Stiglitz, recounted in this chapter, are wise counsel for the saving of the endangered ship.

■ We would also suggest that conservative economic policy throughout the cycle is to be recommended, including prudent national finances with something in reserve for when things turn down. In terms of inflation measures, attention to all definitions of inflation, including ones with housing costs built in as well as more usual measures, are recommended to give a more complete picture of the economy.

■ Interest rates set at too low a level, a good source of popularity, is likely to create runaway prices for housing and stock markets. This is a sure way to hasten economic problems. And what do we mean by interest rates being too low? We reckon a good indicator of a correct interest rate is given by:

Inflation + between 1 and 2 per cent

■ This gives a reasonable guide for fair value risk-free rates. For corporate and individual borrowers, add in a further factor for risk – reflecting a borrower's status and likelihood of repaying. Of course, there will be times when the above guidelines would be disregarded. For example, when recession or depression are envisaged, the premium might be cut dramatically.

■ There is a need for clear regulation of banks and financial institutions. Responsibility for insuring that systemic failure is avoided and the economy remains on a steady course is not enhanced by having numerous regulatory agencies. Effective control can easily slip through the gaps between different agencies and we end up with them all blaming each other. Does it sound familiar? It happened in the 2007/8 crisis.

■ Confidence in the financial system is a must. Governments must pursue this on all possible occasions.

■ Governments have to avoid encouraging mortgage lending to poor credit risks. It creates indiscipline at the lender's level and at the borrower level too. It is an accident waiting to happen.

■ Overlooking the unintended consequences of government actions is a danger. Moral hazard is a case in point. Banks may have to be bailed out but because they know this they may take on risks that are too high. Encouraging lending to borrowers with low FICO scores is another danger. Taking on too much risk by weak borrowers is likely to create excessive problems for them when minor setbacks occur. The list goes on. And everything on it will be things that make the government popular but are likely to stoke up future financial problems.

■ Lessons for banks

■ Maintaining discipline in lending hardly needs to be mentioned. But the profusion of crony loans, especially in less sophisticated markets, brought some banks into bailout territory.

■ Credit analysis is too important to be shortcut and overexposure to individual customers and to industry classification are too important not to be monitored with constant zeal.

■ Bank debt must never be allowed to reach the levels that perpetuated pre-crisis. Debt to equity ratios must be kept under control. Anything else will hasten a repeat of the financial crisis.

■ Patterns of awful bank lending and awful control must be guarded against. Weak internal lending standards and controls at the peak of cycles have been manifest again and again whether in respect of corporate lending or mortgage lending.

■ Rewards out of all proportion to inputs in terms of banker bonuses based on dubious short-term profits should be eradicated. This needs to be done by the banks themselves. Failure to do so will likely hasten government regulation. If this occurs, bankers have no one but themselves to blame.

■ Financial innovation based on some variant of high debt secured on weak assets is a feature of boom finance. With banks selling toxic assets to each other, they can pass the parcel on to a greater fool until the music stops. This is a high-risk strategy (probably driven by exorbitant dealer bonuses and exuberance at doing the deal) and likely to end in tears. Perverse bonus structures are probably the driver of such practices. Bankers cannot go on hoping that governments will bail them out for ever. They may be reluctant to do so next time round.

■ Lessons for regulators

■ Cavalier off-balance sheet treatments and structured investment vehicles need to be controlled and regulators need to patrol these with utmost vigilance.

■ Debt to equity ratios for shadow banking institutions need to be regulated just as if they were banks. If it looks like a bank, regulate it like a bank.

■ Consider rules that prevent investment banks proprietary trading for their own account rather than for their clients.

■ Misuse of mark-to-market accounting has to be policed with concern.

■ Material amounts of window dressing in corporate and bank financial statements must be outlawed.

■ Regulators have to be on their guard in respect of inflated real estate values, high financial leverage, asset liability mismatches and fast-growing financial products and institutions. Regulators failed on these scores last time around. Their practices must be improved if next time is not to be a bigger meltdown.

- Ritzholz's seven elements of potential financial blow-up must be borne in mind by all regulators at all times. These have already been quoted in this chapter.

- Rating agencies must never again be allowed to behave in such an uneducated and unprofessional manner as in the run-up to the financial crisis. Rating agencies activities should be audited (maybe 1 in 5 ratings or so) by a regulator paid for by central government out of a levy on the agencies.

- Calls for light regulation, self-regulation and further deregulation must be disregarded.

■ Lessons for household borrowers

- Household borrowers who have defaulted on their obligations have been treated extremely lightly in many countries. They should beware because governments and lenders cannot, and in our opinion should not, be picking up the bills for borrowings that householders took on but could not afford. They won't do it next time round.

- Liar loans were a feature of the run up to the 2007/8 financial crisis. This is a crime and also extremely stupid – especially if governments do not bail out the liars next time around.

- Household borrowers should not assume that things are unlikely to go wrong. It is well to keep something in reserve for the rainy day. House prices do move into reverse. They are certainly not a one-way bet. It is as well for borrowers to be vigilant here and not to take on large commitments based on house prices continuing to escalate year in year out. And it is as well to remember that the year in which house prices do go into reverse will likely be the year that the economy hits trouble and this could put one's employment at risk. Beware the double whammy.

■ Lessons for academics

- Lecturers in economics and in finance have been teaching their students with models based upon the normal distributions for a long time. Whilst the models may work on most occasions, it fails miserably when crises occur. This caveat has to be writ large so that all students understand the frailties of the models. We cannot immutably depend upon Gaussian outturns in financial markets. Remember – fat tails.

- Economists and finance lecturers have been discussing the efficient market hypothesis and rational expectations with their students for years. The reverence that the model has attained in some of our leading business schools and universities and with many eminent professors is hardly justified by its track record in the real world of financial markets.

- Rational economic man is another exaggerated claim in our studies of how decisions are made. Work in the area of behavioural finance has already shown that the cold logic of choosing a maximising course of action with a focus on future outturns and with a disregard of past costs (sunk costs) may be how the world should work. But it is categorically not the way it works in reality.

- The building of economic models with a focus upon the linear, an expulsion of the non-linear and outliers has pushed too much research towards the trivial. Willem

Buiter[14] coined the phrase 'linearise and trivialise'. Couple this with the willing acceptance of research based upon short-term data (as was the case with respect to credit default swaps) and it is possible that business schools and university research resources are being misused in pursuit of trivial and unrealistic propositions. In business schools, research is ultimately concerned with the way the real world works, rather than pursuing beautiful, simplifying descriptions which seem to be deductively enticing but fail when tested with empirical data. Buiter's warning on linearise and trivialise models and ours on the exclusion of outliers are worth remembering. A rigorous pursuit of the whys and wherefores of the non-linear and the nature of outlier data is time well spent.

■ Major issues

In Table 17.1, we present some major issues which need to be resolved in terms of taking action to limit future financial crises. As can be seen from the table we have listed 20 such problem areas. In the table, we have three action columns, one based on the risky extreme (the right-hand column which is, under virtually all of our headings, how things were at the time of the crisis) which contrasts with a risk-averse posture (the left-hand column which is, generally, more defensive than is absolutely necessary) and a middle column which displays a more likely course.

We are not suggesting for one moment that all of the issues that we have raised should be implemented according to our middle way criterion. What we are saying is that there are big issues that need to be considered. It's worth remembering that a 'do nothing' route is always feasible and defensible. We would also suggest that good regulation should be set in the context of cost-benefit analysis criteria. Using a steamroller to crack a nut is not a recommended option.

In particular, the issue that we would suggest is of prime importance is the CDS market. Credit default swaps can be used to enable speculative firms to mount a bear raid on a debt instrument which could threaten the very existence of the firm (or country) liable under the debt. Just before writing this chapter, raids on Greek credit default swaps pushed the cost of Greece's borrowing in the bond markets from some 5 per cent to 16 per cent over a seven-day period. The reason is that there is an arbitrage linkage between credit default swap prices and actual bond borrowing rates. Arbitrage should, and does, drive them together. Imagine a similar situation for company X which is experiencing hard times but has every opportunity of survival. Needing new borrowings, company X plans a debt issue. However, an investment bank hears rumours to this effect and draws the conclusion that its survival is very much in danger. The investment bank undertakes a bear raid in the CDS market on company X bonds. The effect of this is that other players in the market perceive this as an implication that company X is nearer default than was previously thought. The cost of CDS insurance rises and, through an arbitrage mechanism, so does the cost of debt finance to company X. It is possible that at 5 per cent, the debt issue originally planned looked feasible in terms of company X's survival plans. But if CDS speculation were to push the debt cost to company X up to, say 12 per cent, the very survival of company X may be threatened. Some may perceive this as being just another

Table 17.1 Major issues

Issue	Risk-averse extreme	Middle way	Risky extreme
(1) Credit default swaps	Require an insurable interest. Effectively this would reduce the CDS market to an insurance only market and available for hedging only – not speculation.	All CDS contracts to be dealt via a clearing house as is the case with financial futures. That means continuous marking to market and margin requirements as for financial futures. Require banks to hold 100 per cent tier 1 capital backing for CDS positions, thereby limiting risk.	Leave as is.
(2) Glass-Steagall type acts	Bring them back as a part-solution to the too-big-to-fail problem. Investment banks to have no lender of last resort protection. Investment banks to be regulated with tighter controls because they are more likely to fail.	Banks to choose status on split. Only commercial banks to have lender of last resort aid. Higher ratio requirements for investment banks.	Leave as is.
(3) Break up banks	Do it. Linked to (2) above, based upon size criteria for all banks, whether commercial banks or investment banks	This is the too-big-to-fail argument. Break up on higher size criterion than that in risk-averse extreme column	Leave as is.
(4) Shadow banking system	If it looks like a bank, regulate it just like a bank	As per left-hand column	Leave as is.
(5) Bonuses	Cap or curb. Absolute maximum. For lower outturns base it relative to profit outturn of the group – not the division. Could amalgamate with middle way criterion. Bonus pot to be based on audited income statement prepared on the realisation and conservatism principles.	Cap as in left-hand column. Or impose very high marginal tax rates over, say, USD1 million and then rising to up to 80 per cent for very high payouts.	Leave as is.

(6) Backdated bonus tax	Based on bonuses already paid in the three years prior to 2007. Payable on bonuses in excess of USD1 million per year. Internationally co-ordinated.	Do nothing	Leave as is.
(7) Rating agencies	To avoid all conflicts of interest, nationalise them.	Regular random audit of individual ratings. Audit could be as high as 1 in 5 at outset.	Leave as is.
(8) Levy or lender of last resort tax	Levy based on risk levels undertaken by banks. Also levy to pay for crisis of 2007/8. Internationally co-ordinated.	As per left-hand column.	Leave system as is – that is, without levy.
(9) Subprime mortgage lending	Use FICO criteria to define subprime. Set maximum lending levels of 75 per cent for loan to value and three times multiple of income. Ban teaser loans. Ban self-certification. Require independent audit of loan making. Ban loan intermediaries.	Rather like the risk-averse extreme but with slightly more liberal criteria. Teaser loans not allowed. Self-certification not allowed. There is a need for governments to stop trying to be popular by pushing low grade minority group lending. This was a big driver of the last crisis and lessons need to be learned.	Leave as is.
(10) Securitisation including CDOs and CLOs	Ban.	Could ban securitisation of subprime mortgages and other subprime loans, but prefer to require originating banks of all securitised loans to keep some skin in the game, say 10 to 15 per cent of a CDO. This would mean that only 85 per cent to 90 per cent would be available for securitisation.	Leave as is.

(11) Accounting	Ban all window dressing (including Repo 105 and similar devices) of a material size, say 1 per cent of profit or 3 per cent of turnover, whichever is lower. Ban off-balance sheet accounting. Bring all kinds of SIV onto the accounts. More careful consideration of mark-to-market rules. Special aspect of interim audits to ensure compliance.	As per left-hand column.	Leave as is.
(12) Bank debt to equity ratios	Tighten up and set higher standards. Special regular audits.	Tighter controls for investment banks especially.	Leave as is.
(13) Derivatives	Require all derivatives, except foreign exchange forwards and some simple swaps, to have same trading structure as financial futures with similar margin rules. This includes CDSs, CDOs, CLOs etc.	Require broad regulation of derivatives markets, with one or two exceptions, applying to private markets as well as those traded on public exchanges. Broadly similar to risk-averse extreme.	Leave as is.
(14) Risk monitoring	Designate an agency to focus upon key predictors of systemic failure, for example high leverage, inflated real property and equity prices, asset liability mismatches and fast-growing products and institutions.	As per left-hand column.	Leave as is.
(15) Bank lending	Regulator to audit and undertake random checks on procedure and shape of lending book focusing upon exposures to customer groups, industry types and country exposure. Also regulator to cool off excess property lending – see immediately below.	As per left-hand column.	Leave as is.

(16) Reserve asset requirements	Reintroduce reserve asset requirements such that banks have to deposit specified sums with the central bank when it appears that boom conditions are approaching.	As per left-hand column. This practice used to be part of banking system in the past and still is in some countries.	Leave system as is.
(17) Secret or prudential reserves for banks	Banks may set aside profits as secret or prudential reserves in good times to enable better survival chances in bad times.	As per left-hand column. The practice used to be part of banking in the past.	Leave system as is.
(18) Protection of depositors	Government guarantee of personal retail deposits up to very high levels. Personal depositors to be protected. Wholesale depositors also protected. Government guarantee to be funded by bank levy.	Guarantee for personal retail depositors up to high levels. Wholesale deposits protected to much lower level. Bank levy to fund guarantee.	Leave as is.
(19) Lobbying	Is it possible to stop lobbying? Probably not.	Register of members of parliamentary houses lobby encounters and interests to be declared, and audited and acted upon. No member to vote on issues where lobbying occurs.	Leave as is.
(20) Regulation	Numerous regulatory authorities with no single body at the apex of the hierarchy. This is really very risky because it would mean that regulation falls between the cracks where respective authorities' powers don't quite meet.	Although the number of regulatory bodies may increase, the ultimate responsibility (and therefore at the top of the regulatory hierarchy) must lie with one designated authority which could be the central bank – but not necessarily so.	Leave as is.

(21) Nationalisation of banks	Nationalise all banks 100 per cent.	Readers may think bank nationalisation is a joke. In advanced countries this is hardly a long-term option but in some less developed markets it is a regular route to ensuring that liquidity of a sort is available.	Leave as is.
(22) Investment banks and dealing on their account	Ban. Investment banks to deal on clients' account only. If they wish to do it, put it into separate hedge fund.	Spin off dealing arm as a separate hedge fund which would not be part of the bank. The hedge fund might have a stock market quotation.	Leave as is.
(23) The euro	Weak members of eurozone to quit the single currency. Big short-term impact in capital markets but this will subside.	Adoption of a 'soft euro' by weaker eurozone member states. It would have to devalue against the euro in its current form – the 'hard euro'. Maybe it would be a stepping stone to exit from the euro by weaker members.	Leave as is. This is risky unless austerity measures work.

indication of capitalism at work. Others might say that it appears to be an indication that the real economy is being driven by speculation in financial markets. Is company X's future a host to fortune or speculative pressure? We have stated elsewhere that the bailout of GM and Chrysler looked as if it was being partly driven by similar short-term conditions.

When insurance is available to hedge risk, and when the credit default swap was the major culprit in the financial crisis and might well be so again, we are not convinced that the case for its existence is justified. The product is a metaphorical nuclear device. We would hope that legislation would prevent ordinary individuals wandering around with nuclear weapons on board. Why is it OK for banks to have them? This is surely the most pressing issue in the whole debate on regulation to prevent a repeat of the 2007/8 débâcle. Press Cutting 17.1 reinforces this viewpoint.

Press cutting 17.1   *Financial Times*, 1 March 2010   **FT**

Time to outlaw naked credit default swaps

Wolfgang Münchau

I generally do not like to propose bans. But I cannot understand why we are still allowing the trade in credit default swaps without ownership of the underlying securities. Especially in the eurozone, currently subject to a series of speculative attacks, a generalised ban on so-called naked CDSs should be a no-brainer.

Naked CDSs are the instrument of choice for those who take large bets against European governments, most recently in Greece. Ben Bernanke, the chairman of the Federal Reserve, said last week that the Fed was investigating 'a number of questions relating to Goldman Sachs and other companies in their derivatives arrangements with Greece'. Using CDSs to destabilise a government was 'counter-productive', he said. Unfortunately, it is legal.

CDSs are over-the-counter contracts negotiated by two parties. They offer the buyer insurance on a bundle of underlying securities. A typical bundle would be €10m worth of Greek government bonds. To insure against default, the buyer of a CDS pays the seller a premium, whose value is denoted in basis points. Last Thursday, a CDS contract on five-year Greek bonds was quoted at 394 basis points. This means that it costs the buyer €394,000 per year, for five years, to insure against default. If Greece defaults, the buyer gets €10m, or some equivalent. What constitutes default is subject to a complicated legal definition.

A naked CDS purchase means that you take out insurance on bonds without actually owning them. It is a purely speculative gamble. There is not one social or economic benefit. Even hardened speculators agree on this point. Especially because naked CDSs constitute a large part of all CDS transactions, the case for banning them is about as a strong as that for banning bank robberies.

Economically, CDSs are insurance for the simple reason that they insure the buyer against the default of an underlying security. A universally accepted aspect of insurance regulation is that you can only insure what you actually own. Insurance is not meant as a gamble, but an instrument to allow the buyer to reduce incalculable risks. Not even the most libertarian extremist would accept that you could take out insurance on your neighbour's house or the life of your boss.

Technically, CDSs are not classified as insurance but as swaps, because they involve an exchange of cash flows. The CDS lobby makes much of those technical characteristics in its defence of the status quo. But this is misleading. Even a traditional insurance contract can be viewed as a swap, as it involves an exchange of cash flows. But nobody in their right mind would use the swap-like characteristics of an insurance contract as an excuse not to regulate the insurance industry. The fact that, unlike insurance, CDSs are tradeable contracts does not change the fundamental economic rationale.

The whole idea of modern financial products is to replicate the payment streams of other, more traditional instruments, while offering better conditions. Selling a CDS is like buying a bond. Buying a CDS is a way of shorting a bond – or of insuring against its default. But that does not change the fact that once you strip away the complex technical machinery, you end up with a product that offers insurance – even though it is a lot more versatile than a standard insurance contract.

Another argument I have heard from a lobbyist is that naked CDSs allow investors to hedge more effectively. This is like saying that a bank robbery brings benefits to the robber. A further stated objection to a ban is that it would be difficult to police. There is no question that a ban of a complex product, such as a CDS, involves technical complexities that commentators like myself probably underestimate. It is conceivable, for example, that the industry might quickly find a legal way round such a ban. Then again, we would not consider legalising bank robberies on the grounds that it is difficult to catch the robber.

So why are we so cautious? From conversations with regulators and lawmakers, I suspect they are not always familiar with those products, to put it kindly, and that they may be afraid of regulating something they do not understand. They understand, or think they do, what a hedge fund is. Restricting hedge funds is something they can sell to their electorates. Hedge funds were not at the centre of the crisis, but they are a politically expedient target. Banning products with ugly acronyms that nobody understands seems like unnecessarily hard work.

I do not want to exaggerate the case for a ban. This speculation is neither the underlying cause of the global financial crisis, nor of the eurozone's underlying economic tensions. But naked CDSs have played an important and direct role in destabilising the financial system. They still do. And banks, whose shareholders and employees have benefited from public rescue programmes, are now using CDSs to speculate against governments.

Where is the political response? The Germans want to bring it to the Group of 20, but they hesitate to do anything unilaterally. Christine Lagarde, the French finance minister, was recently quoted as saying: 'What we are going to take away from this crisis is certainly a second look at the validity, solidity of sovereign [credit default swaps].'

A second look? I wonder what they saw when they looked the first time.

The next major issue concerns the virtues of a reintroduction of the Glass-Steagall Act which, amongst other things, separated investment banks and commercial banks. The argument in favour of its reintroduction concerns the magnitude of risk undertaken in the investment banking arm and its ability to wipe out the commercial banking operation within the same group. This happened in the 2007/8 crisis. The argument here articulates with that under point (3) in Table 17.1. If too-big-to-fail banks are downsized, perhaps the Glass-Steagall argument carries less weight. Alternatively, the break-up could be achieved in conjunction with the split of investment banks from commercial banks.

The shadow banking system is our next big issue. Shadow banks were outside regulation in many countries in the run-up to the 2007/8 financial crisis. However, they played a large part in the collapse. The argument in favour of regulation is clear. The well-articulated advice is simple. If it looks like a bank, regulate it like a bank.

Bonuses need to be addressed. As we have pointed out earlier, the scope for excessive risk-taking and dysfunctional reward systems is evident all along Wall Street and in the City of London. In our opinion it would be as well if the banks addressed the problem themselves. If they don't, governments certainly should. Banks have had an inordinate amount of time to produce bonus systems that will not give asymmetric rewards for creating systemic risk. Given that they have failed to do so, it's about time regulators took on the role. And what formula should be used? Before mark-to-market accounting, two of the principles of accounting were the realisation principle and conservatism. What are they about? The realisation principle was concerned with profit recognition. It stated that, usually, profit would be recognised when a sale, or deal, is completed. The conservatism idea suggested that all losses, whether realised or unrealised, should be charged against profit. Profit calculation for bonus pots in banks (and elsewhere) should be via the realisation principle and via conservatism in accounting. If these methods were reinstituted in terms of calculating bonuses, such payouts would be better justified. Of course, realisation would have to be a genuine sale to a third party – not a repo type transaction. Remember repos? They cropped up in the case study on Lehman Brothers in Chapter 12. In short, for bonus purposes mark-to-market accounting should be shelved. And this should be the case not just for financial institutions but for all business. This should enable a bonus pool to be determined and allocation of the bonus between employees would follow. Senior executives know what rewards should be given according to employee input. In connection with some of the biggest paypackets, we have to say that it is pretty difficult to spend USD300 million anyway. Richard Fuld never looked happy anyway. Settle for USD30 million and enjoy it. The utility of the extra USD270 million cannot be all that great – except in terms of boasting rights.

Before leaving the question of bonuses, is there a case for an internationally co-ordinated backdated tax applied in respect of all bank bonuses paid in the three-year period to 2007? It would, perhaps, be payable on all bonuses in excess of USD 1 million per year. Of course, such a tax becomes less likely to be implemented as time elapses.

Next, the rating agencies. They made an abysmal fist of their job in the run-up to the 2007/8 financial crisis – tainted by obvious conflicts of interest. We cannot imagine that their lack of competence will be repeated. Nonetheless, there is a strong case for better supervision. Our risk-averse extreme of nationalisation is not a likely option but regular random audits of ratings logic and decision criteria are certainly justified if confidence in the system is to be recovered. A levy on the agencies and/or users could pay for such audit requirements.

A bailout levy is the next mooted possibility in the table. If banks continue to take on ever-higher risk, its case becomes stronger because it is increasingly likely to be called upon. Reference to the table shows that our next big issue concerns subprime lending. We would hope that the lessons of the recent crisis have been learned but to assume that this is so is surely an invitation for trouble. Based on the criteria in the table, some form of regulation could easily be put in place at relatively low cost.

Securitisation, especially of subprime loans and credit default swaps, played a major role in the financial crisis of 2007/8. As can be seen from Table 17.1, a course aimed to ensure that low-quality assets are kept out of the securitised mix could easily be achieved. The method would involve a requirement that originating banks keep some skin in the game – in other words, some percentage of the mix would remain with them. This might be 10 per cent to 15 per cent, meaning that only 85 to 90 per cent would be available for securitisation. But there is the stronger alternative that since the ingredients of CDOs were of such a poor quality prior to the crash with such a diverse mix of commercial mortgages, residential mortgages, credit card debt, auto loans, student loans and so on – many of them subprime – the case for banning these or at least making them more standardised and transparent (if this is possible) is advanced by some commentators – see for example, Roubini and Mihm[15].

Accounting rules were certainly not innocent in the crisis. The move to mark-to-market accounting was achieved despite worries and reservations made clear by banks and financial institutions. They had articulated their concern that mark-to-market would create wide oscillation in profits and in shareholders' funds which could mean requests to shareholders to stump up rights issue funds when markets are at their lowest levels. We suspect that mark-to-market accounting won't go away, although we continue to worry about banks' reporting. Furthermore, there must be worries when profits that are not yet realised (turned into cash or receivables) are included in income statements and thence in balance sheet values. At a more immediate level, there is a strong case for outlawing material amounts of window dressing, off-balance sheet accounting and bringing all SIVs and the like into the accounts.

In addition, the case for tightening requirements on ratio controls for all banks and institutions that look like banks – shadow banking institutions – is worth considering.

Derivatives are dangerous. They can be used to remove risk and they can be used to take on risk. The requirement for greater diligence is worth pursing if these wild creatures are to be tamed. The case for moving to a system where all derivatives (except the most simple ones) are traded according to financial futures rules and then go through an exchange where both parties contract with a clearing house in the middle and with margin requirements based on real time revaluation is worth considering.

The case for a risk monitoring agency focusing upon areas of potential systemic failure can be made, as can a procedure of regular random audits of bank lending books.

Your author qualified as a chartered accountant in the sixties (the 1960s, not the 1860s as I have had to explain to my more humorous students on more than one occasion) and can remember two features of the banking environment that prevailed then. These are numbered (16) and (17) in the table. They concern reserve asset requirements and prudential reserves (aka secret reserves) for banks. Their mechanics are summarised in the table. The former would enable governments readily to take the punch bowl away from over-indulgent banks by requesting deposits to be made at the central bank and thereby reducing their ability to lend. The latter suggestion involves banks being allowed to set aside as secret reserves some of their earnings. This enables them to keep an amount from the good times in hand for the rainy day. A form of profit smoothing? Yes. But a prudent one too.

There is little doubt that protection for retail investors should be available via government guarantees, as should wholesale depositor protection, up to a certain specified level. Most countries already have a system like this and, as we noted in the case study of Irish Banks, this may be up to 100 per cent protection.

Whilst lobbying of politicians by banks is significant, especially in the USA and especially amongst Republicans, it cannot be outlawed. Perhaps an extremely detailed register is required.

Two other items appear in the table. We feel that an overarching regulatory agency is called for if woolly control is to be avoided. Having numerous agencies with different terms of reference and no single agency responsible for overall control is an accident waiting to happen. In the UK, the various agencies are still continuing to squabble about whose fault it was that warning bells were not ringing earlier in the 2007/8 crisis. The case for overall responsibility residing with the central bank is probably the most sensible approach. They should be aware of more economic events than other agencies and they normally carry a lot of clout with the system.

In our list the nationalisation of banks is raised as an issue. This is not a joke. We see little virtue for this in the USA, Britain, France, the Netherlands, Germany and so on. But it may be a serious issue as a long-term means of obtaining a good flow of liquidity in less developed countries.

It is also worth considering a regulation that would prevent investment banks' proprietary trading, that is, for their own account, rather than for their clients. If they wish to trade on their own account, they might spin off the dealing business as a separate entity – not owned by the investment bank. It would effectively be an individual hedge fund. If it were a quoted vehicle, investors could put their money into it by buying shares. Such a business would receive no backing or lender of last resort status.

In the immediately preceding chapter we raised the issue of the eurozone and suggested various solutions to its immediate problems. We reiterate them in Table17.1.

One of the major issues to be confronted subsequently by government is their exit strategy. Having thrown money at the problem, further difficulties will have ensued, for example:

■ **Huge budget deficits**. These will have to be put right as the economy recovers.
■ **Seriously deteriorated public debt positions**. The problem here is continuing debt servicing obligations over the long term and, for some countries, potential debt management problems and, at worst, default.

- **Large amounts of outstanding government and central bank loans**. This reflects the support that has been provided to credit markets. These may be sold on elsewhere in the financial system in due course.
- **Extensive guarantees**. These may be equivalent to public debt and will have to be unwound. In the meantime these should attract realistic prices.
- **Partly nationalised banking systems**. These investments will probably be sold to investors as the markets improve.

In the shorter term, government finances will have to be augmented by tax increases, reduced subsidies, austerity measures, possible depreciation (in the worst cases) of the currency (although protectionism must be avoided), public sector cuts in spending, rephasing major infrastructure schemes, cutting quangos, implementing privatisations of government businesses and properties plus a number of other actions. Of course, by the time the reader looks at this book, some – or all – of the issues referred to in Table 17.1 may have been brought into law.

Past crises have been influential in creating changes in global power. As Harold James[16] argues, the Great Depression accelerated the decline of Britain and the rise of America. Could this crisis spur the rise of the Far East at the expense of the USA? Obviously there is not a certain answer to this question – but it is worthy of consideration.

Finally, we turn to another big question. Like the classic detective story, at the very end, the sleuth reveals who-dunnit. By now we hope you have reached your verdict. And as in the well-known Agatha Christie story (which we will not name – just in case you are currently reading it), our little grey cells have come to a conclusion. The governments did it. Personal borrowers – you and me maybe – did it. The banks did it. Subprime lenders and borrowers did it. All of those regulators, they did it. Have we missed any of the usual suspects out? And who was most culpable? Would you guess bankers and governments? Your author would. The bankers had their weapons of self-destruction – the credit default swap. And the governments around the world with their lax economic conditions created boom times and carried them on for far too long – just as the US government did immediately prior to the Wall Street Crash and the Great Depression. When will they ever learn?

Afterword

■ Introduction

Inevitably, in any book that attempts to capture events of contemporary history, the author runs the risk of being overtaken by events. This text is no exception, hence this brief Afterword. It highlights four major events which have occurred since writing the main body of the book plus an update on the eurozone. In chronological order, the four events are

- the Dodd–Frank Wall Street Reform and Consumer Protection Act in the USA (June 2010)
- European bank stress tests (July 2010)
- Basel III (September 2010)
- Ireland's banks updated (September 2010)

We look at each of these in the above order before moving on to the eurozone.

■ The Dodd–Frank Act

The law was proposed in the US House of Representatives by Barney Frank and in the Senate Banking Committee by Chris Dodd. It was signed into law by President Barack Obama on 21 July 2010.

The financial crisis sparked widespread calls for changes in the US regulatory system. In June 2009, President Obama introduced a proposal for a 'sweeping overhaul of the United States financial regulatory system, a transformation on a scale not seen since the reforms that followed the Great Depression.' Major aspects of the President's original proposal included:

- the consolidation of regulatory agencies, elimination of the national thrift charter and the introduction of a new oversight council to evaluate systemic risk.
- comprehensive regulation of financial markets, including increased transparency of derivatives (that is, bringing them onto exchanges)
- consumer protection reforms including a new consumer protection agency and uniform standards for plain vanilla products, as well as strengthened investor protection
- tools to deal with financial crises. These included structures complementing the existing FDIC, allowing for orderly winding down of bankrupt firms and a proposal that the Fed receive authorisation from the Treasury for extensions of credit in unusual circumstances
- various measures aimed at increasing international standards and cooperation. Included here were proposals related to improved accounting and tightened regulation of credit rating agencies.

President Obama added the Volcker Rule to the above proposal in January of 2010. This rule would prohibit depository banks from proprietary trading (dealing on their own behalf). Such banks were to be allowed to invest up to 3 per cent of their Tier 1 capital in private equity and hedge funds as well as to trade for hedging purposes.

The stated aim of the legislation is 'to promote the financial stability of the United States by improving accountability and transparency in the financial system, to end too-big-to-fail status, to protect the American taxpayer by ending bailouts, to protect consumers from abusive financial services practices, and for other purposes'. The Act is intended to establish rigorous standards and supervision to protect the economy and American consumers, investors and businesses, end taxpayer funded bailouts of financial institutions, provide for an advanced warning system on the stability of the economy, create rules on executive compensation and corporate governance, and eliminate loopholes that led to the financial crisis. Some new agencies of financial regulation are created. All of the new agencies and ongoing ones are required to report to Congress on a regular basis. New regulatory agencies include the Financial Stability Oversight Council, the Office of Financial Research and the Bureau of Consumer Financial Protection.

The Office of Thrift Supervision is to be wound up with its responsibilities transferred to other agencies including the FDIC and the Fed. Some non-bank financial institutions are also to be supervised by the Fed.

Most provisions of the Act become effective over the 18 months from presidential signature. This timescale reflects the need for various rules to be formally set. These include:

- **Consumer Protection.** The working of the new Bureau of Consumer Financial Protection which is required to tackle mis-selling of mortgages, credit cards and other loans.
- **Derivatives.** Derivatives that are traded in over-the-counter deals would be forced through central clearing houses and on to electronic exchanges to increase transparency. There would be exemptions for non-financial companies using derivative contracts to hedge risk. Banks to be forced to spin-off some derivatives-dealing operations into affiliates.
- **Resolution authority.** The government would be able to seize and wind up an institution if it faces impending failure and poses a risk to the broader financial system. Shareholders would be wiped out, executives fired and payments to creditors made by the government but recouped from levies on the industry.
- **Systemic risk regulation.** A Financial Stability Oversight Council of regulators, chaired by the Treasury secretary, would identify systemically significant companies and monitor markets for bubbles. Companies identified as systemically significant would face stricter capital, leverage and liquidity standards and be obliged to draw up a living will to be used in the event of failure.
- **Volcker rule.** Banks would be forced to spin off proprietary trading arms but could retain arm's-length ownership of hedge funds and private equity firms. Named after

Paul Volcker, a former Fed chairman, who observed that banks should not engage in casino activities while having government insurance over deposits.

- **Bank levy.** The US government to levy up to USD19 billion over five years on banks with more than USD50 billion in assets and hedge funds with more than USD10 billion. It would be risk-weighted so that a large mutual fund would pay less than a smaller hedge fund, because of the perceived lower risk of its operations. The levy is intended to plug a hole in budgeting for the bill. Monies raised would also be used to reduce the federal deficit.

Because of the Act's complexity with over one hundred rules to be specified on derivatives, there are areas upon which regulators have until July 2011 to work out the detail. With respect to derivatives, issues yet to be decided include:

- Who qualifies as a swap dealer? In respect of swaps, what is the position of a bank, an oil group's derivatives trading arm, a small trading firm? And how much capital is required to be held?

- What type of swap will have to be cleared? Regulators may make clearing compulsory for large, or various categories of, financial instruments or they may take a case-by-case approach. Will banks be allowed to own clearing houses?

- Will phone trading be permitted or will all be electronic? Will large trades have to be reported immediately? How much information about trades is to be made public?

- How much data will swap dealers and investors have to pass to regulators, and how quickly? Who will have access to this information?

Clearly there is a great deal of work to be done.

Interestingly, the Dodd–Frank Act contains whistleblowing incentives that could net informants multimillion dollar pay-outs. This may precipitate a surge in allegations against US-listed companies and Wall Street banks. The Securities and Exchange Commission itself is expecting an increase in tip-offs from senior employees and third parties prompted by potential seven-figure rewards.

■ European bank stress tests

In July 2010, the Committee of European Banking Supervisors (CEBS) applied stress tests to 91 European banks seeking to establish how they would fare given a double dip recession in Europe and a deviation of 3 per cent below EU forecasts – a fairly modest downside scenario. The good news was that 84 banks passed the tests. Although the stress scenario would inflict EUR566 billion of losses in 2010/2011, all of the big European banks passed. The seven that did not pass were either already failing institutions or they were weaker banks in Spain and Greece.

The CEBS tested only trading books. It did not address the European banking sector's exposure to sovereign debt. Thus the regulators assumed no European sovereign would default – brave, perhaps foolhardy, given the eurozone debt crisis.

The seven failures were required to raise new capital, or were already doing so, to bring their Tier 1 ratio to 6 per cent or above. When 19 US banks were stress tested, within the previous year, 10 failed, and were urged to raise USD75 billion in new capital.

The main aim of the European exercise was to address uncertainty about the health of the banking sector. Given the relatively undemanding assumptions, it is questionable whether the tests have revealed anything new.

■ Basel III capital requirements

Published in September 2010, the new Basel rules would require banks to hold more capital as a percentage of risk-weighted assets. The key requirements are set out in Figure A.1

In addition to the new capital requirements, the definition of core tier one capital is being tightened with previously accepted forms of top-notch capital, such as deferred tax assets, being phased out. Essentially, it is to be common stock and retained profit.

Interestingly, bank executives' worst dreams about implementation of Basel III with a deadline of 2012 were not incorporated in the new rules. Instead, banks have until 1 January 2019 before the full effect of the requirements comes into force – see Figure A.2. Their lobbying seems to have paid off again.

Hardly surprising, your author is of the opinion that the risk weighting of assets remains a flawed concept – unless securitised low-grade debt is always required to be backed 100 per cent by liquid assets.

Common equity (after various deductions) as a % of risk-weighted assets

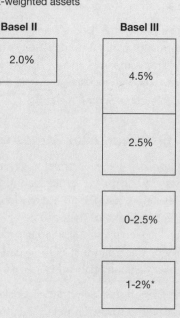

Minimum
Obligatory. Banks have to be able to meet this level of capital or they will not be able to operate.

Conservation buffer
Not required as a condition of operation. However banks with ratios below 7% will be constrained in terms of paying dividends and bonuses. Regulators expect banks to stay above this.

Countercyclical buffer
Details under discussion. To be phased in by national regulators as their markets start to boom to counter the effect of a bubble

Systemic groups' buffer
One of several proposals being considered for dealing with super-sized banks that pose global risk. If adopted this may add another 1% to 2% for the largest banks.

Figure A.1 Basel III capital requirements

Source: Financial Times, 13 September 2010, © The Financial Times Ltd

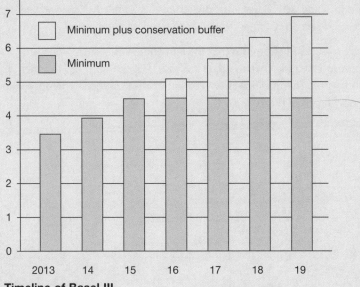

Figure A.2 **Timeline of Basel III**
Source: *Financial Times*, 13 September 2010, © The Financial Times Ltd

■ Ireland's banks updated

At the end of September 2010, Brian Lenihan, Ireland's finance minister, gave an update. It was not a happy story. Ireland pledged to inject further capital into its stricken financial sector as fears rose that the total cost to save its banks could rise as high as EUR50 billion (GBP43 billion), more than a third of Irish 2009 national income.

The Irish government promised a renewed crackdown on public spending on top of its series of austerity packages already introduced. The finance minister acknowledged horrendous costs to clear up the crash left by the country's property-fuelled boom. He said that the country had already injected about EUR32.6 billion into banks and building societies. He added that Anglo Irish Bank will receive an additional EUR6.4 billion, rising by another EUR5 billion in the event of unexpected losses, and Irish Nationwide Building Society will receive a further EUR2.7 billion. Is it the end of the story? Certainly not. Wait for an EU and/or IMF rescue package. Quitting the euro?

■ Eurozone crisis

In addition to the detail in Chapter 16, we append two figures which summarise the plight of eurozone economies. The first – Figure A.3 – focuses upon budget deficits country by country as forecast for 2010 by the European Commission. The problem for the PIGS countries is self-evident. The second – Figure A.4 – shows real effective exchange rates early in 2010. Readers will recall that this is concerned with the extent to which the currency of a country is overvalued or undervalued. This may arise because of relatively high inflation in a country which has not been compensated for by a fall in the currency.

Or vice versa. Figure A.4 tells us, for example, that if Ireland were to revert to its old domestic currency, the punt (rather than the euro), it would need a drop of 13 per cent to bring it into line with other eurozone countries. Similarly, Spain would need a drop of 11 per cent and so on. Germany, by contrast, would need a rise of 5 per cent or so.

If one were to conclude from this that the eurozone was in crisis, your author would agree. If one were to conclude that the days (or years) of the euro are numbered, your author would also agree. The question is how long has the euro got? There is fuel here to ignite a whole new financial blaze.

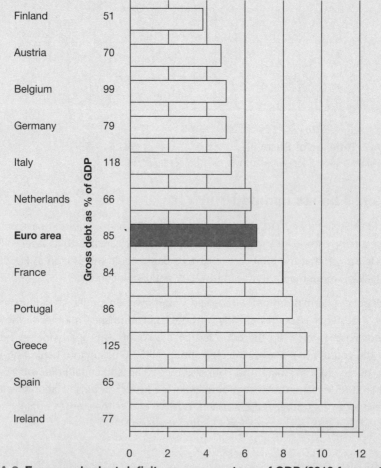

Figure A.3 Eurozone budget deficits as a percentage of GDP (2010 forecast)

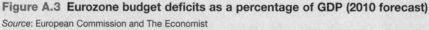

Source: European Commission and The Economist

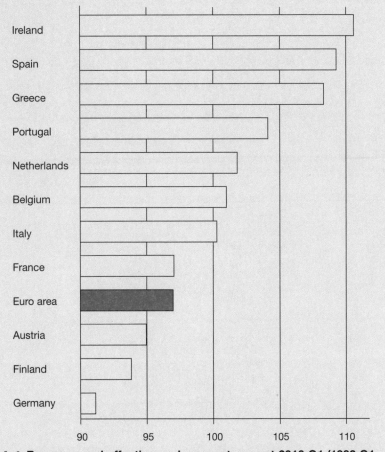

Figure A.4 Eurozone real effective exchange rates as at 2010 Q1 (1999 Q1 = 100)
Source: ECB and The Economist

■ Final words

Legislators have already put in place some changes in the wake of the financial crisis. At the time of writing, they had failed to address the most critical fuse that could set off the metaphorical bomb. It is the credit default swap. This time the smouldering relates to sovereign debt, not subprime mortgages. That should fuel the flames. A plea – act now. Act before it's too late. At the time of writing, sovereign rescue packages are being designed to avoid default which, in turn, is aimed at avoiding more bank losses on default swaps.

Notes

Chapter 1 An overview of the financial crisis 2007/8

1. Viral V. Acharya and Mathew Richardson, *Restoring Financial Stability*, John Wiley and Sons, Inc., 2009
2. Paul Mason, *Meltdown*, Verso, 2009
3. Vince Cable, *The Storm*, Atlantic Books, 2009

Chapter 2 Governments and the financial crisis

1. Thomas Hobbes, *Leviathan*, Oxford World's Classics, 2008 (first published 1651)
2. Thomas Hobbes, *Leviathan*, Oxford World's Classics, 2008 (first published 1651)
3. Jean-Jacques Rousseau, *The Social Contract*, Oxford World's Classics, 2008 (first published 1762)
4. Charles P. Kindleberger, *Manias, Panics, and Crashes*, 3rd edition, John Wiley and Sons, Inc., 1996 (5th edition by Charles P. Kindleberger and Robert Z. Aliber)
5. Carmen M. Reinhart and Kenneth S. Rogoff, *This Time is Different*, Princeton University Press, 2009
6. Simon Johnson, 'The Quiet Coup', *The Atlantic Magazine*, May 2009.
7. Simon Johnson and James Kwak, *13 Bankers*, Pantheon Books, 2010
8. Simon Johnson and James Kwak, *13 Bankers*, Pantheon Books, 2010
9. Simon Johnson, 'The Quiet Coup', *The Atlantic Magazine*, May 2009

Chapter 3 Personal finance, housing and the financial crisis

1. Raghuram G. Rajan, *Fault Lines*, Princeton University Press, 2010

Chapter 4 The business of banking

1. Philip Auger, *The Greed Merchants*, Penguin Group, 2005
2. John Kay, 'What a Carve Up', *Financial Times*, 1/2 August 2009
3. Frank Partnoy, *F.I.A.S.C.O*, Profile Books, 1997
4. Geraint Anderson, *Cityboy*, Headline Publishing Group, 2008
5. Robin L. Marris, *The Economic Theory of Managerial Capitalism*, Macmillan, 1964
6. Quoted from Robin L. Marris, 'Profitability and Growth in the Individual Firm', *Business Ratios*, Spring 1967
7. Frank Partnoy, *F.I.A.S.C.O*, Profile Books, 1997
8. Michael Lewis, *Liar's Poker*, Hodder and Stoughton, 1989
9. Geraint Anderson, *Cityboy*, Headline Publishing Group, 2008
10. Seth Freeman, *Binge Trading*, Penguin, 2009
11. Tetsuya Ishikawa, *How I Caused the Credit Crunch*, Icon Books, 2009
12. William Golding, *Lord of the Flies*, Faber and Faber, 1954
13. Satyajit Das, Traders, *Guns & Money*, Revised edition, FT Prentice Hall, 2010
14. Kevin Dowd and Martin Hutchinson, *Alchemists of Loss*, Wiley, 2010
15. Laurence J. Kotlikoff, *Jimmy Stewart is Dead*, Wiley, 2010

16. Tim Congdon, 'Central Banking in a Free Society', Institute of Economic Affairs, Monographs, Hobart Paper 166, 2009

Chapter 5 Subprime lenders and borrowers

1. Richard Bitner, *Confessions of a Subprime Lender*, John Wiley and Sons, Inc., 2008
2. Frank Partnoy, *F.I.A.S.C.O*, Profile Books, 1997

Chapter 6 Credit default swaps and toxic assets

1. John Kenneth Galbraith, *A Short History of Financial Euphoria*, Whittle Books, 1990
2. Larry McDonald, *A Colossal Failure of Common Sense*, Ebury Press, 2009
3. John C. Hull, *Risk Management and Financial Institutions*, 2nd editon, Pearson, 2007
4. Gillian Tett, *Fool's Gold*, Little Brown, 2009
5. Felix Salmon, 'Recipe for Disaster: The Formula that Killed Wall Street', *Wired Magazine*, 23 February 2009
6. David X. Li, 'On Default Correlation: A Copula Function Approach', *Journal of Fixed Income*, 9, pp 43–54, 2000
7. Simon Johnson and James Kwak, *13 Bankers*, Pantheon Books, 2010
8. Frank Partnoy, *F.I.A.S.C.O*, Profile Books, 1997
9. Benoit B. Mandelbrot, *The (Mis)Behaviour of Markets*, Profile Books, 2005
10. Nassim Nicholas Taleb, *The Black Swan*, Penguin Group, 2008
11. Pablo Triana, *Lecturing Birds on Flying*, John Wiley and Sons, Inc., 2009
12. International Monetary Fund, *Global Financial Stability Report*, IMF Publications, April 2010
13. John Cassidy, *How Markets Fail*, Penguin Group, 2009
14. Michael Lewis, *The Big Short*, Penguin Group, 2010

Chapter 7 Bank lending and control systems

1. Roger H. Hale, *Credit Analysis*, John Wiley and Sons, Inc., 1983
2. Michael Hammer and James Champy, *Reengineering the Corporation*, Harper Collins, 1993
3. Benoit B. Mandelbrot, *The (Mis)Behaviour of Markets*, Profile Books, 2005
4. Nassim Nicholas Taleb, *The Black Swan*, Penguin Group, 2008
5. Pablo Triana, *Lecturing Birds on Flying*, John Wiley and Sons, Inc., 2009
6. Yves Smith, *Econned*, Palgrave Macmillan, 2010

Chapter 8 Regulation

1. Charles P. Kindleberger, *Manias, Panics, and Crashes*, 3rd edition, John Wiley and Sons, Inc., 1996
2. Carmen M. Reinhart and Kenneth S. Rogoff, *This Time is Different*, Princeton University Press, 2009
3. Nouriel Roubini and Stephen Mihm, *Crisis Economics*, Allen Lane, 2010

Chapter 9 The business cycle, booms, busts, bubbles and frauds

1. In fact, real returns have varied. Looking at actual achieved returns from Treasury bonds and gilt edged securities, real returns in the USA and UK both achieved around 1 per cent over the last century. However, real returns pre-1980 were very low – not even 0.5 per cent – and post-1980 they were much higher (nearer 3 per cent). These data are extracted from Elroy Dimson, Paul Marsh and Mike Staunton, *Triumph of the Optimists*,

2002, Princeton University Press. Elsewhere (see Jeremy J. Siegel *Stocks for the Long Run*, 4th edition, McGraw Hill, 2008) real returns for the USA are recorded as around 1 per cent for the period from World War II to 2006, again with much higher real returns from the mid-1980s to 2006. Siegel records real returns from government fixed-interest investment from 1871 to 2006 at just above 2 per cent. If we were to look at index-linked government securities, our figure of 1 to 2 per cent is about right.

2. This accords with Irving Fisher, *The Theory of Interest*, Augustus M. Kelley, 1930
3. John Maynard Keynes, *The General Theory of Employment, Interest and Money*, Macmillan Paperback,1964 (first published in 1936)
4. D. R. Myddelton, *They Meant Well*, Institute of Economic Affairs, 2007
5. George A. Akerlof and Robert J. Shiller, *Animal Spirits*, Princeton University Press, 2009
6. John G. Matsusaka and Argia M. Sbordone, 'Consumer Confidence and Economic Fluctuations', *Economic Inquiry*, 33(2), 1995
7. Charles P. Kindleberger, *Manias, Panics, and Crashes*, 3rd edition, John Wiley and Sons, Inc., 1996
8. Hyman P. Minsky, *Stabilizing an Unstable Economy*, McGraw Hill, 2008 (first published by Yale University Press, 1986)
9. Stephen Vines, *Market Panic*, 2nd edition, John Wiley and Sons (Asia Pte) Ltd., 2009
10. John P. Calverley, *When Bubbles Burst*, Nicholas Brealey, 2009
11. Stephen Vines, *Market Panic*, 2nd edition, John Wiley and Sons (Asia Pte) Ltd., 2009
12. Stephen Vines, *Market Panic*, 2nd edition, John Wiley and Sons (Asia Pte) Ltd., 2009
13. Frederic Mishkin, 'Not all Bubbles Present a Risk to the Economy', *Financial Times*, 9 November 2009
14. Charles Mackay, *Extraordinary Popular Delusions and the Madness of Crowds*, Wordsworth Editions Limited, 1995 (first published 1841)
15. Charles P. Kindleberger, *Manias, Panics, and Crashes*, 3rd edition, John Wiley and Sons, Inc., 1996
16. Charles P. Kindleberger, *Manias, Panics, and Crashes*, 3rd edition, John Wiley and Sons, Inc., 1996
17. Bethany McLean and Peter Elkind, *The Smartest Guys in the Room*, Penguin Books, 2004
18. Mimi Swartz and Sherron Watkins, *Power Failure*, Doubleday paperback edition, 2004
19. Howard M. Schilit and Jeremy Perler, *Financial Shenanigans*, 3rd edition, McGraw Hill, 2010
20. Edward Chancellor, *Devil Take the Hindmost*, Penguin Group, 1999
21. Niall Ferguson, *The Ascent of Money*, Penguin Group, 2008
22. Harry Markopolos, *No One Would Listen*, John Wiley and Sons, Inc., 2010.
23. Erin Arvedlund, *Madoff: The Man who Stole $65 billion*, Penguin, 2009

Chapter 10 **Finance theories**

1. Niall Ferguson, *The Ascent of Money*, Penguin Group, 2008
2. Bethany McLean and Peter Elkind, *The Smartest Guys in the Room*, Penguin Books, 2004
3. Mimi Swartz and Sherron Watkins, *Power Failure*, Doubleday paperback edition, 2004
4. Howard M. Schilit and Jeremy Perler, *Financial Shenanigans*, 3rd edition, McGraw Hill, 2010
5. Eugene Fama and Kenneth French, 'The Cross-Section of Expected Stock Returns', *Journal of Finance*, 47(2), June 1992
6. Robert A. Haugen, *The New Finance*, 4th edition, Prentice Hall, 2010
7. Benjamin Graham and David L. Dodd, *Security Analysis*, McGraw Hill, 1934. More recent edition by Benjamin Graham, David L. Dodd, Sidney Cottle and Charles Tatham, McGraw Hill

8. Frank H. Knight, *Risk, Uncertainty and Profit*, (first published in 1921), Harper Torchbooks, New York 1965.
9. Nouriel Roubini and Stephen Mihm, *Crisis Economics*, Allen Lane, 2010
10. Benoit B. Mandelbrot, *The (Mis)Behaviour of Markets*, Profile Books, 2005.
11. Pablo Triana, *Lecturing Birds on Flying*, John Wiley and Sons, Inc., 2009
12. John Lanchester, *Whoops*, Penguin Group, 2010
13. Fischer Black and Myron Scholes, 'The Pricing of Options and Corporate Liabilities', *Journal of Political Economy*, 81(3), pp 637–59, 1973
14. Nassim Nicholas Taleb, *The Black Swan*, Penguin Group, 2008
15. Pablo Triana, *Lecturing Birds on Flying*, John Wiley and Sons, Inc., 2009
16. Robert Haugen and Nardin Baker, 'Commonality in the Determinants of Expected Stock Returns', *Journal of Financial Economics*, pp 401–39, 1996
17. S. Benartzi and R. Thaler, 'Myopic Loss Aversion and the Equity Premium Puzzle', *Quarterly Journal of Economics*, 110(1) pp 73–92, 1995
18. Brad M. Barber and Terrance Odean, 'The Courage of Misguided Convictions', *Financial Analysts Journal*, 55, November–December, pp 41–55, 1999
19. D. Kahneman and A. Tversky, 'On the Psychology of Prediction', *Psychological Review*, 80, pp 237–51, 1973 and D. Kahneman and A. Tversky, 'Prospect Theory: An Analysis of Decisions Under Risk', *Econometrica*, 47, pp 263–91, 1979
20. R. H. Thaler (ed.), *Advances in Behavioural Finance*, Volume II, Princeton, NJ, Russel Sage Foundation, 1993
21. Hersh Shefrin, *Beyond Greed and Fear*, Harvard Business School Press, 2000
22. Andrei Schleifer, *Inefficient Markets*, Oxford University Press Inc., 2000
23. James Montier, *Behavioural Finance*, John Wiley and Sons Ltd., 2002
24. Richard A. Posner, *A Failure of Capitalism*, Harvard University Press, 2009

Chapter 11 Other academic theories

1. John Cassidy, *How Markets Fail*, Penguin Group, 2009
2. Gillian Tett, *Fool's Gold*, Little Brown, 2009
3. John Kenneth Galbraith, *A Short History of Financial Euphoria*, Penguin Group, 1994 (first published by Whittle Books)
4. Solomon E. Asch, 'Effects of Group Pressure upon the Modification and Distortion of Judgement', in H. Guetzkow (ed) *Groups, Leadership and Men*, Pittsburgh, PA, Carnegie Press, 1951
5. Stanley Milgram, *Obedience to Authority: An Experimental View*, HarperCollins, 1974
6. Craig Haney, Curtis Banks and Philip G. Zimbardo, 'Study of Prisoners and Guards in a Simulated Prison', *Naval Research Review*, 9, pp 1–17, 1973 and Craig Haney, Curtis Banks and Philip G. Zimbardo, 'Interpersonal Dynamics in a Simulated Prison', *International Journal of Criminology and Penology*, 1, p 69–97, 1973
7. Karen Ho, *Liquidated*, Duke University Press, 2009
8. Pierre Bourdieu, *Outline of a Theory of Practice*, Cambridge University Press, 1977
9. Gillian Tett, *Fool's Gold*, Little Brown, 2009
10. Steve Fraser, *Wall Street*, Faber and Faber, 2005.
11. Michael Lewis, *Liar's Poker*, Hodder and Stoughton, 1989
12. Frank Partnoy, *F.I.A.S.C.O*, Profile Books, 1997
13. Geraint Anderson, *Cityboy*, Headline Publishing Group, 2008
14. Tetsuya Ishikawa, *How I Caused the Credit Crunch*, Icon Books, 2009

15. Alex Preston, *This Bleeding City*, Faber and Faber, 2010
16. Philip Auger, *Chasing Alpha*, The Bodley Head, 2009
17. Jonah Lehrer, *The Decisive Moment*, Canongate Books Ltd, 2005
18. Adam Smith, *The Wealth of Nations*, Chicago University Press, 1977 (originally published 1776)
19. Adolf A. Berle and Gardiner C. Means, *The Modern Corporation and Private Property*, Transaction, 1932
20. M. C. Jensen and W. H. Meckling, 'Theory of the Firm: Managerial Behaviour, Agency Costs and Ownership Structture', *Journal of Financial Economics*, 1976 (3)
21. John Cassidy, *How Markets Fail*, Penguin Group, 2009
22. George Akerlof and Paul Romer, *Looting: The Economic Underworld of Bankruptcy for Profit*, NBER Working Paper No. R1869, available at Social Science Research Network
23. John Kenneth Galbraith, *The Economics of Innocent Fraud*, Allen Lane, 2004
24. Paul Samuelson, *Foundations of Economic Analysis*, Harvard University Press, 1983 (originally published 1947)
25. Robert Lucas, quoted in Kenneth Arrow in William Breit and Barry T, Hirsch (eds) *Lives of the Laureates*, 4th edition, MIT Press, 2004
26. John Muth, 'Rational Expectations and the Theory of Price Movements', *Econometrica*, 29, 1961
27. Willem Buiter, 'The Unfortunate Uselessness of Most "State of the Art" Academic Monetary Economics', www.ft.com/buiter
28. Joseph A. Schumpeter, *Capitalism, Socialism and Democracy*, Routledge, 2010 (originally published in the UK in 1943)
29. Hyman P. Minsky, *Stabilizing an Unstable Economy*, McGraw Hill, 2008 (first published by Yale University Press, 1986)
30. Robert J. Barbera, *The Cost of Capitalism*, McGraw Hill, 2009
31. Kevin Dowd and Martin Hutchinson, *Alchemists of Loss*, Wiley, 2010

Chapter 12 Bank failures in the USA

Introduction

1. Alistair Milne, *The Fall of the House of Credit*, Cambridge University Press, 2009
2. Andrew Ross Sorkin, *Too Big to Fail*, Penguin Group, 2009
3. Henry Paulson, *On the Brink*, Headline Business Press, 2010

Case 12.1 Bear Stearns

4. William D, Cohan, *House of Cards*, Penguin Group, 2009

Case 12.2 Lehman Brothers

5. Larry McDonald, *A Colossal Failure of Common Sense*, Ebury Press, 2009
6. Allan Sloan and Roddy Boyd, 'How Lehman Brothers Veered Off Course', *Washington Post*, 3 July 2008

Case 12.3 AIG

7. Gillian Tett, *Fools Gold*, Little Brown, 2009
8. Gillian Tett, *Fools Gold*, Little Brown, 2009
9. Gillian Tett, *Fools Gold*, Little Brown, 2009
10. Iain Dey, 'London Trader Quizzed over AIG', *Sunday Times*, 27 June 2010, p B3

Chapter 13 Bank failures in the UK

Case 13.1 Northern Rock

1. Charles P. Kindleberger, *Manias, Panics, and Crashes*, 3rd edition, John Wiley and Sons, Inc., 1996 (5th edition by Charles P. Kindleberger and Robert Z. Aliber)
2. Niall Ferguson, *The Ascent of Money*, Penguin Group 2008
3. Brian Walters, *The Fall of Northern Rock*, Harriman House Ltd., 2008

Case 13.2 HBOS

4. Quoted in the *Financial Times*, 28 July 2006

Case 13.3 Royal Bank of Scotland (RBS)

5. Philip Auger, *Chasing Alpha*, The Bodley Head, 2009
6. Philip Auger, *Chasing Alpha*, The Bodley Head, 2009
7. Philip Auger, *Chasing Alpha*, The Bodley Head, 2009

Chapter 14 Bank failures in Europe

Case 14.1 Fortis
No references

Case 14.2 UBS

1. Gillian Tett, *Fool's Gold*, Little Brown, 2009

Case 14.3 Icelandic banks

2. Armann Thorvaldsson, *Frozen Assets*, John Wiley and Sons Ltd., 2009
3. Roger Boyes, *Meltdown Iceland*, Bloomsbury Publishing, 2009
4. 'Kaupthing Loan Book Details Culture of the Collapsed Bank', *Daily Telegraph*, 4 August 2009, p. B4
5. 'Bank Finance Icelandic Style', *Daily Telegraph*, 11 August 2009, p B1
6. Charles P. Kindleberger, *Manias, Panics, and Crashes*, 3rd edition, John Wiley and Sons, Inc., 1996
7. Hyman P. Minsky, *Stabilizing an Unstable Economy*, McGraw Hill, 2008 (first published by Yale University Press, 1986)

Case 14.4 Irish banks

8. Shane Ross, *The Bankers*, Penguin Group, 2009.
9. Fintan O'Toole, *Ship of Fools*, Faber and Faber, 2009
10. Fintan O'Toole, *Ship of Fools*, Faber and Faber, 2009
11. David Murphy and Martina Devlin, *Banksters*, Hatchette Books, 2009
12. Frank McDonald and Katy Sheridan, *The Builders*, Penguin Books, 2008
13. Matt Cooper, *Who Runs Ireland?* Penguin Group, 2009

Chapter 15 The Great Depression

1. Milton Friedman and Rose Friedman, *Free to Choose*, Martin Secker and Warburg, 1980
2. Liaquat Ahamed, *Lords of Finance*, William Heinemann, 2009
3. Milton Friedman and Rose Friedman, *Free to Choose*, Martin Secker and Warburg, 1980
4. John Maynard Keynes, *The General Theory of Employment, Interest and Money*, Macmillan Paperback, 1964 (first published in 1936)
5. Milton Friedman and Anna Schwartz, *The Great Contraction 1929–1933*, Princeton University Press, 2008
6. John Kenneth Galbraith, *The Great Crash 1929*, Hamish Hamilton, 1955
7. F. Scott Fitzgerald, *The Great Gatsby*, Charles Scribner and Sons, 1925

8. F. Scott Fitzgerald, *Tender is the Night*, Charles Scribner and Sons, 1934
9. Claude M. Fuess, *Calvin Coolidge: The Man from Vermont*, Little Brown, 1940
10. Robert H Ferrell, *The Presidency of Calvin Coolidge*, University Press of Kansas, 1998
11. David Greenberg, *Calvin Coolidge*, The American Presidents Series, Times Books, 2006
12. Donald R. McCoy, *Calvin Coolidge: The Quiet President*, Macmillan, 1967
13. Robert Sobel, *Coolidge: An American Enigma*, Regnery Publishing, 1998
14. David Greenberg, *Calvin Coolidge*, The American Presidents Series, Times Books, 2006
15. David Greenberg, *Calvin Coolidge*, The American Presidents Series, Times Books, 2006
16. Gordon Pepper with Michael J. Oliver, *The Liquidity Theory of Asset Prices*, John Wiley and Sons Ltd., 2006
17. John Maynard Keynes, *The General Theory of Employment, Interest and Money*, Macmillan Paperback, 1964 (first published in 1936)
18. John Steinbeck, T*he Grapes of Wrath*, Penguin, 2000 (originally published in 1939 by the Viking Press)
19. Irving Fisher, 'The Debt-Deflation Theory of Great Depressions', *Econometrica* 1(4), 1932 and Irving Fisher, *Booms and Depressions: Some First Principles*, Adelphi, 1937
20. Milton Friedman and Anna Schwartz, *The Great Contraction 1929–1933*, Princeton University Press, 2008
21. Adam Fergusson, *When Money Dies*, Old Street Publishing, 2010 (originally published in 1975 by William Kimber & Co. Ltd)
22. Robert F. Bruner and Sean D. Carr, *The Panic of 1907*, John Wiley and Sons, Inc., 2007
23. Milton Friedman and Rose Friedman, *Free to Choose*, Martin Secker and Warburg, 1980
24. Milton Friedman and Anna Schwartz, *The Great Contraction 1929–1933*, Princeton University Press, 2008

Chapter 16 Government responses to the crisis

No references

Chapter 17 Lessons and major issues

1. Charles P. Kindleberger, *Manias, Panics, and Crashes*, 3rd edition, John Wiley and Sons, Inc., 1996
2. Carmen M. Reinhart and Kenneth S. Rogoff, *This Time is Different*, Princeton University Press, 2009
3. Charles P. Kindleberger, *Manias, Panics, and Crashes*, 3rd edition, John Wiley and Sons, Inc., 1996
4. John Kenneth Galbraith, *A Short History of Financial Euphoria*, Whittle Books, 1990
5. John Maynard Keynes, *The General Theory of Employment, Interest and Money*, Macmillan Paperback, 1964 (first published in 1936)
6. John Kenneth Galbraith, *A Short History of Financial Euphoria*, Whittle Books, 1990
7. Hyman P. Minsky, *Stabilizing an Unstable Economy*, McGraw Hill, 2008 (first published by Yale University Press, 1986)
8. John Kenneth Galbraith, *A Short History of Financial Euphoria*, Whittle Books, 1990
9. Joseph Stiglitz, *Freefall*, Penguin Group, 2010
10. Robert Pozen, *Too Big To Save*, John Wiley and Sons, Inc., 2010
11. Barry Ritholz, *Bailout Nation*, John Wiley and Sons, Inc., 2009
12. Robert F Bruner and Sean D. Carr, *The Panic of 1907*, John Wiley and Sons, Inc., 2007
13. Joseph Stiglitz, *Freefall*, Penguin Group, 2010

14. Willem Buiter, 'The Unfortunate Uselessness of Most "State of the Art" Academic Monetary Economics', www.ft.com/buiter

15. Nouriel Roubini and Stephen Mihm, *Crisis Economics*, Allen Lane, 2010

16. Harold James, *The Creation and Destruction of Value*, Harvard University Press, 2009

Glossary

ABCP See Asset-backed commercial paper.

ABS See Asset-backed security.

Adjustable rate mortgage (ARM) A mortgage whose interest rate adjusts to a new rate based on prevailing market rates at the time of adjustment.

Alt-A mortgage A loan to a home buyer who may be creditworthy but does not meet the standards for a conforming mortgage. For example, the borrower may not be able to provide the required documentation.

American option An option which may be exercised on any business day within the option period. American options are traded all around the world – not just in the USA. The term American has no geographic connotation here.

APS See Asset Protection Scheme.

Arbitrage A purchase of foreign exchange, securities or commodities in one market coupled with immediate resale in another market in order to profit risklessly from price discrepancies. The effect of arbitrageurs' actions is to equate prices in all markets for the same commodity. Term now loosely used to include buying and selling almost-similar securities. This is termed risk arbitrage and it is not riskless.

ARM See Adjustable rate mortgage.

Asset-backed commercial paper (ABCP) This is similar to commercial paper, but it is issued by conduits or structured investment vehicles holding loans, structured credit securities or other credit assets. See Commercial paper.

Asset-backed security (ABS) A debt security collateralised by a pool of assets, such as mortgages, credit card debt, corporate debt or car loans.

Asset Protection Scheme (APS) Arrangement between UK government and major banks under which the government underwrote financial crisis losses beyond a certain level.

Asymmetry of Information Parties to a transaction may possess different amounts and/or different qualities of information about the transaction.

At the money An option when the value of its underlying security is equal to the option strike price.

Balance of payments A financial statement prepared for a country summarising the flow of goods, services and funds between the residents of that country and the residents of the rest of the world during a particular period.

Basel Accords A set of international agreements adopted by the Basel Committee on Bank Supervision providing guidelines on capital and asset levels in banks.

Basis point One basis point equals one hundredth of one percentage point – that is, 1 basis point = 0.01 per cent.

Beta A measure of the sensitivity of an asset to changes in the market. A beta of 0.5 means that on average a 1 per cent change in the market implies a 0.5 per cent change in the value of the asset. See also Systematic risk.

Big Mac Index An index of foreign exchange rates based upon the prices of Big Mac burgers around the world. Published and updated regularly in *The Economist* magazine. There is also an iPod index. See Purchasing power parity.

Billion One thousand million.

Bistro Also called BISTRO. Broad Index Secured Trust Offering. The term initially used by J. P. Morgan bankers in their redevelopment of the credit default swap.

Black and Scholes model A model that provides a means by which to value option contracts. It involves using information on the underlying asset, the strike price, volatility, time to expiry and the interest rate.

Bond A promise under seal to pay money. The term is generally used in relation to the promise made by a corporation, either public or private, or a government to pay money, and it generally applies to such instruments with an initial maturity of one year or more.

Bond rating A grade given to a bond by a credit-rating agency based on an evaluation of the bond issuer's ability to pay the bond's interest and repay capital on time.

Bonus issue An issue of shares to existing shareholders, usually in some set proportion to their holding, but requiring no payment. This has the effect of increasing the company's issued capital and is normally made possible by the capitalisation of reserves. Sometimes known as a scrip or capitalisation issue.

BPR See Business process re-engineering

Business process re-engineering (BPR) The analysis and design of workflows and processes within an organisation.

Bullet A straight debt issue with repayment in one go at maturity.

Callable bond A bond with a call provision giving the issuer the right to redeem the bonds under specified terms prior to the normal maturity date.

Call option A contract giving the holder the right, but not the obligation, to buy a specified security at a specified price on or within a specified time.

CAPM See Capital asset pricing model.

Capital adequacy The minimum amount of capital that bank, non-bank financial intermediaries and other financial market operators must maintain in proportion to the risks that they assume.

Capital asset pricing model (CAPM) Model in which expected returns increase linearly with an asset's beta.

Capital requirements The amount of capital a bank is required to hold, relative to its average assets, to meet its obligations and absorb unanticipated losses.

Capital structure The distribution of a company's issued capital as between bonds, debentures, preferred and ordinary shares, earned surplus and retained income.

CAPM See Capital asset pricing model.

CBO See Collateralised bond obligation.

CDO See Collateralised debt obligation.

CDO squared A CDO containing other CDOs.

CDS See Credit default swap.

Central bank The entity responsible for overseeing the monetary system of a nation or group of nations. Central banks generally influence the money supply and interest rates and act as a bank of the government, managing gold and foreign exchange reserves and act as a lender of last resort.

Chapter 7 bankruptcy The section of the US bankruptcy code applied when a company is liquidated and all of its assets are sold to repay its debtors.

Chapter 11 bankruptcy protection The section of the US bankruptcy code that allows an indebted firm to obtain protection from its creditors while being reorganised.

Chapter 15 bankruptcy The section of the US bankruptcy code applicable when an insolvency involves debtors and assets in more than one country. Used in the case of Bear Stearns funds because their bankruptcy proceedings involved assets in the Cayman Islands, where the funds were registered. Chapter 15 prevented debtors pursuing these assets simultaneously through the US courts.

Clearinghouse An entity responsible for settling and clearing trades, collecting and maintaining margin and reporting data on trading.

CLO See Collateralised loan obligation.

Collateral Security placed with a lender to assure the performance of an obligation. Assuming that the obligation is satisfied, the collateral is returned by the lender.

Collateralised bond obligation (CBO) A tranched security backed by a portfolio of corporate bonds.

Collateralised debt obligation (CDO) A type of asset backed security that is backed by diversified securities such as loans and credit default swaps and it derives its cash flow from these sources. The asset backing is often split into tranches with different rights in terms of interest receipt and redemption.

Collateralised loan obligation (CLO) A credit structure using tranched securities of different seniorities and involving a portfolio of loans.

Commercial bank A bank which takes deposits from customers and lends to customers.

Commercial paper (CP) Basically an IOU from a company. Short-term paper, of maturity up to one year, issued by a company. The issue of commercial paper usually requires an underwriting facility from a commercial bank standing ready to purchase the paper, if necessary. Without such underwriting to guarantee the ability to refinance the commercial paper, then it can be difficult to get investors to hold commercial paper.

Commodity Futures Trading Commission (CFTC) CFTC is an independent agency with the mandate to regulate commodity futures and option markets in the USA.

Common stock A US term meaning ordinary share.

Community Reinvestment Act US Federal law designed to encourage commercial banks and savings associations to meet the borrowing needs of all segments of the community, including low-income areas.

Conduit An off-balance sheet vehicle established by a bank, often in a tax haven, to hold and/or have passed through it asset-backed and mortgage-backed securities. Their losses are theoretically borne by the bank setting them up.

Conforming loan A mortgage that does not exceed the amount of the maximum loan limits and meets the requirements set by Fannie Mae and Freddie Mac.

Conservatorship A US term for an arrangement whereby an entity or person is appointed by a court to make legal decisions for a company or for a financial institution.

Contingent obligation An obligation that a bank or company may have to fulfil depending on future events, for example a guarantee – perhaps in the event of credit losses.

Copula A way of formulating a distribution with many variables such that relationships can be represented – a multivariate distribution.

Correlation A standardised statistical measure of the dependence of two variables.

Cost of capital The rate of return expected by a party providing finance.

Counterparty risk In a contract, the risk to each party that the other party, the counterparty, may not honour its contracted obligation.

Country risk Corporate goals of multinationals and the national aspirations of host countries may not be congruent. The essential element in country risk is the possibility of some form of government action preventing the fulfilment of a contract or the endangering of an asset held overseas. Covers political as well as economic risk.

Coupon The regular payment made to an investor in a bond or similar security.

Covered bonds Bonds backed by mortgages or cash flows from other assets.

CRA See Credit rating agency.

CRA See Community Reinvestment Act.

Credit crunch A situation where banks become so fearful that they stop lending. Used in the financial crisis of 2007/8 when banks became so suspicious of the creditworthiness of other banks that they ceased lending to one another.

Credit default swap (CDS) A contract that entitles the protection buyer to a payment if there is a default on a bond or other type of debt obligation. To enable the contract to continue, the protection buyer pays an annual premium to the seller. Rather similar to insurance but there are differences. Both parties to a credit default swap may sell on their rights and obligations in a secondary market. Credit default swaps normally have a finite life. To be technically 100 per cent correct, the definition could be as follows. A credit default swap is an instrument which gives the holder the right to sell a bond for its face value in the event of a default by the issuer.

Credit rating agency An entity that analyses and rates the creditworthiness of debt and bonds issued by companies or countries as well as similar financial products. The main ones are Moody's, Fitch and Standard and Poor's.

Credit score A quantified estimate of a potential borrower's creditworthiness (see FICO).

Credit spread The difference between the market rate of interest paid on a safe and widely traded bond, such as those issued by the US Treasury or the UK or German governments, and the relatively higher rate of interest paid on a riskier bond of the same maturity. Riskier bonds offering high-credit spread include corporate bonds.

Current account As used in the balance of payments, it is that section that records the trade in goods, services, interest and dividends among countries. Also refers to a bank account where amounts are withdrawn on demand.

Current account balance (surplus or deficit) The amount of a country's total exports of goods and services plus interest and dividend payments exceeds or falls short of its total imports of goods and services plus interest and dividends.

Debenture In the UK, a fixed interest secured loan which can be for a fixed maturity or irredeemable. There are two main types: mortgage debentures, which are secured against a specific asset of the issuer; and floating debentures, which are secured against the entire asset base of the issuer.

Debt capacity The total amount that a company is capable of borrowing.

Debt security A security, such as a bond or note, representing an obligation of the security's issuer to make payments as specified in the debt contract.

Debt-to-income Usually, the ratio of a mortgage loan divided by the borrower's annual income

Default The failure to make on-time contractual payments of principal and/or interest or the failure to meet other obligations as specified in the debt contract. In other words the act of breaching a covenant or warranty in a loan agreement.

Default risk The chance that a borrower will not pay in full on the contractual due date interest or principal on a loan.

Deflation A general decline in prices.

Deleveraging Repayment of debts with the purpose of reducing the proportion of debt in a capital structure.

Department of Housing and Urban development (HUD) A cabinet-level agency in the USA whose mission is to increase homeownership, support community development and increase access to affordable housing.

Deregulation The removal or relaxation of the barriers or rules that have previously restricted the scope of securities trading and the nature of the operations undertaken by financial institutions.

Derivatives Financial instruments, such as options, whose price is dependent upon, or derived from, the price of one or more other securities or assets.

Devaluation A decline in a currency exchange rate. With a fixed exchange rate system, it is effected in one go by government decree.

DCF See Discounted cash flow

Discounted cash flow A quantification exercise in which expected cash flows in different time periods are converted to value now by applying a process based upon expected interest rates, inflation and risk.

Dividend A distribution of a portion of a company's earnings to shareholders. It is determined by the company's board of directors.

ECB See European Central Bank.

Efficient Market Hypothesis (EMH) Theory that security prices reflect publicly available information, although there are different grades of efficient market.

EMH See Efficient markets hypothesis.

Equity Ownership interest after debts are subtracted.

Equity Risk Premium The excess of the required rate of return on equities over that required on a risk-free security.

Escrow account Monies held in a separate specified account to pay obligations or potential obligations but not to be used for any other purpose.

Euro The currency unit of 16 European Union nations – see Eurozone.

European Central Bank (ECB) The European Central Bank determines monetary policy for the participating member states in the eurozone.

European option An option that can be exercised on the specified expiration date of the option only. Such options may be traded in the USA and elsewhere. The term European has no geographical connotation in this case.

Eurozone The area covered by the 16 European Union countries which use the euro as their currency, namely Austria, Belgium, Spain, Finland, France, Germany, Greece, Ireland, Italy, Luxembourg, Malta, the Netherlands, Portugal, Slovakia, Slovenia and Spain.

Exercise To carry out a transaction, usually applied to the options market.

Exercise price The price at which an option may be exercised (aka Strike price).

Exploding ARM A form of adjustable rate mortgage widely offered to subprime borrowers in which the interest rate is set at an adjustable rate for the first two or three years of the mortgage and then switches to a relatively high fixed rate.

Face value The money value of a security as stated by the issuer. Not to be confused with market value. Interest and dividends are usually payable as a percentage of face value (aka Nominal value).

Fair market value (FMV) An estimate of the amount that would be received if an asset were sold.

Fair Value Accounting (FVA) The use of a market price to establish the balance sheet amount of some assets and liabilities.

Fannie Mae See Federal National Mortgage Association (FNMA).

Fat tail distribution A distribution in which the tail events are much more likely to occur than those of a normal distribution curve.

Fed See Federal Reserve System.

Federal Deposit Insurance Corporation (FDIC) An agency in the USA that insures US banks and thrifts. It is the regulator of all state-chartered banks that are not members of the Federal Reserve System.

Federal funds rate The interest rate charged by a bank when lending its balances at the Federal Reserve to another bank.

Federal Home Loan Mortgage Corporation (Freddie Mac) Freddie Mac is a publicly chartered corporation in the USA with a mission to provide liquidity, stability and affordability in housing backed lending. It was set up and privatised in 1968 to provide competition for Fannie Mae.

Federal National Mortgage Association (Fannie Mae) A US-government agency set up in 1938 and privatised in 1968 with the same mission as Freddie Mac.

Federal Reserve discount window A facility of the Fed to allow banks and other eligible financial institutions to obtain short-term loans.

Federal Reserve System (Fed) As the central bank of the USA, the Fed conducts the nation's monetary policy, supervises both state-chartered banks that are Fed members and all bank holding companies, maintains the stability of the financial system, and provides financial services.

Federal Trade Commission (FTC) Enforces certain consumer protection laws and tries to prevent anticompetitive business practices in the USA.

FICO Fair Isaac Corporation. Provider of credit worthiness rating scores for individuals.

Financial Accounting Standards Board (FASB) The organisation responsible for setting accounting standards for company financial statements in the US.

Financial bubble A prolonged increase in prices of stocks and shares, real estate, or other assets, which is reckoned to be unsustainable since it is not well founded on fundamental factors or fundamental analysis.

Financial Industry Regulatory Authority (FINRA) FINRA is the self-regulatory organisation for securities firms doing business in the USA. It was created from the National Association of Securities Dealers and the regulatory unit of the New York Stock Exchange.

Fiscal policy Government spending and tax policies.

Fitch A credit rating agency.

Fixed-rate mortgage A mortgage whose interest rate does not change during its life.

Fixed-income security An investment that offers a return in the form of payments and it involves the same amount as interest in all years.

Freddie Mac See The Federal Home Mortgage Corporation (FHMC).

FT-SE100 A real-time weighted arithmetic average of the equity market capitalisations of the 100 largest UK companies on the London Stock Exchange.

Fundamental analysis A branch of security analysis based upon attempts to value securities in accordance with estimated future profits and cash outturns.

FVA See Fair Value Accounting.

G8 See Group of Eight.

G10 See Group of Ten.

G20 See Group of Twenty.

GAAP See Generally accepted accounting principles.

GDP See Gross domestic product.

Generally accepted accounting principles US GAAP are the rules for company accounting statements applicable to US companies.

Ginnie Mae See Government National Mortgage Association.

Glass-Steagall Act A USA statute, enacted in 1933 and repealed in 1999, that prohibited commercial banks from engaging in investment banking activities and setting certain other regulations.

Gold standard A monetary agreement under which national currencies are backed by gold and gold is utilised for international payments.

Goodwill The intangible value of an ongoing business over and above the value of its tangible net assets.

Government National Mortgage Association (Ginnie Mae) Ginnie Mae is a US government-backed corporation that guarantees to investors the timely payment of principal and interest on securities of federally insured or guaranteed loans.

Government sponsored enterprises (GSEs) Shareholder-owned corporations, like Fannie Mae and Freddie Mac, or government agencies like Ginnie Mae, chartered by the US Congress to promote stability, liquidity, and affordability.

Gramm-Leach-Bliley Act The US act of 1999 that repealed the Glass-Steagall Act.

Greenspan Put The monetary policy pursued by the US Federal Reserve Bank under Alan Greenspan's Chairmanship from 1987 to 2006. When confronted with financial crises, the Fed came to the rescue by lowering the Fed Funds rate, often producing negative real yields. The Fed put liquidity into the market to prevent further financial deterioration. This was done repeatedly, for example after the October 1987 stockmarket drop, the Gulf War, the Asian Crisis, the LTCM problem, the bursting of the dot.com bubble and the 9/11 attacks.

Gross domestic product (GDP) The market value of goods and services created or provided within a country for a specified period of time – usually 12 months.

Group of Eight (G8) Eight major industrial nations whose ministers meet on a periodic basis to discuss and agree on economic and political issues. It comprises Germany, France, Italy, the United Kingdom, Canada, Russia, Japan and the United States.

Group of Ten (G10) Ten major industrial countries – Germany, France, Belgium, the Netherlands, Italy, the United Kingdom, Sweden, Canada, Japan and the United States – that agreed in 1962 to stand ready to lend their currencies to the IMF. The Group of Ten has taken the lead in subsequent changes in the international monetary system.

Group of Twenty (G20) The G20 is a group of 20 finance ministers and central bank governors from 20 countries who meet periodically to discuss key issues in the international financial system.

Haircut The difference between the amount of money lent in a repo contract and the true market value of the security sold and then repurchased. This represents the amount of protection offered to the lender of the money. A haircut of 10 per cent means that the lender is safe from financial loss, should the security not be repurchased, as long as the value of the security falls by not more than 10 per cent.

Hedging An investment strategy designed to reduce or eliminate certain specified risks.

Hedge fund An investment fund attracting high net worth investors and pension funds where investors hope to make money from the returns, including capital gains, on the fund's high-risk investments. Hedge funds charge their investors fees and use leverage, market knowledge, trading skills, mathematical models, near-arbitrage (called risk arbitrage) and other techniques to achieve their returns.

Historic cost accounting The method of accounting by which assets are valued at their original purchase price less depreciation or a permanent impairment to value.

Hubris Pride or arrogance. In Greek tragedy, an excess of ambition or pride ultimately causing the transgressor's ruin.

IASB See International Accounting Standards Board.

IFRS See International Financial Reporting Standards.

Illiquid A security or a market that is lacking activity.

Illiquid market A market in which active trading is absent or barely present and hence market prices may be out-of-date, unreliable or unavailable.

Inflation A general increase in the prices of goods and services in an economy.

Inflation target A policy aiming to keep inflation around a specified level. It usually involves the central bank in raising interest rates if core inflation exceeds a specified percentage over a specified period of time.

Initial Public Offering (IPO) When shares in a company are first sold on the stock market.

Instrument A generic term for securities, ranging from debt to negotiable deposits and bonds.

Insurable interest In insurance, the requirement that the insured must possess an insurable interest. This means that the insured would suffer a loss if the event that is being insured were to occur.

Inter-bank rate The rate at which banks offer and bid for funds between each other.

Interest rate Annualised rate of compensation for borrowing or lending money for a time period. It comprises three parts, namely a real requirement, an inflation premium and a risk premium to compensate for the perceived risk that the borrower may default. Interest rates may be fixed rates or floating rates. With the latter, the rate alters, maybe daily, maybe weekly, maybe monthly.

Interest rate risk Broadly, the risk that the value of a fixed-income asset will fall in value due to a rise in interest rates.

Intermediary company A vehicle company used as a conduit for the transfer of funds between fellow affiliate companies.

Internal risk models In-house mathematical models used by financial institutions to determine the riskiness of their investments.

International Accounting Standards Board (IASB) The IASB is an independent standard-setting board whose mission is to develop a set of high quality and understandable financial reporting standards for companies in all countries.

International Financial Reporting Standards (IFRS) A set of accounting standards for financial statements that is now used in over 100 countries.

International Monetary Fund (IMF) The IMF is an organisation of over 180 countries, working to foster monetary co-operation, financial stability, international trade, economic growth and reduced poverty around the world.

In the money A call option when its strike price is less than the value of the underlying security price. Also a put option when the strike price is higher than the current price of the underlying security.

Intrinsic value The difference between the strike price of an option and the current market price of the underlying security where the option has value.

Investment bank An institution that acts as an underwriter for companies and others, advises on issuing securities, making acquisitions and divestments, offers investment advice and may deal in securities on its own account.

Investment grade A bond rated BAA or above by Moody's or BBB or above by Standard and Poor's and BBB or above by Fitch.

Investment grade bond Bond rated at least BAA by Moody's or BBB by Standard and Poor's or Fitch.

IPO See Initial Public Offering.

Junk bond Debt that is rated below investment grade. Usually it carries a relatively high interest rate and yield.

Lender of last resort A concession given to a select number of financial institutions whereby their central bank agrees to provide them with funds if they should get into difficulties.

Leverage Borrowing, financial gearing, either by individuals, households or by corporations. The leverage ratio represents the proportion of debt in a company's mix of debt and equity. Financial leverage is measured by the ratio of debt to the sum of debt and equity.

LIBOR See London inter-bank offered rate.

Liar loan A loan, based on deliberately or negligently incorrect information, supplied by the borrower or mortgage broker and accepted by lenders in mortgage lending. Usually occurs in the subprime area.

Liquidity risk The risk that a security or other asset cannot be readily traded hence making meaningful market prices difficult to obtain.

Listed security A security that is quoted and traded on a major stock exchange.

Loan loss reserve Monies set aside by a financial institution to cover projected losses on loans.

Loan-to-value ratio (LTV) The ratio of the amount of a mortgage to the value of the home securing the mortgage loan.

London inter-bank offered rate (LIBOR) The interest rate at which prime banks offer deposits to other prime banks in London. This rate is often used as the basis for pricing loans where the lender and the borrower agree to a mark-up over LIBOR. The total of LIBOR plus the mark-up is the effective interest rate for the loan.

Long position The ownership of an asset usually with the expectation that the asset value will rise.

Long term In bond markets, bonds with initial maturities of more than seven years. In terms of company balance sheets, debts with a maturity of more than one year.

LTV See Loan-to-value ratio.

Margin call In futures contracts and in other similar situations, a requirement to provide more margin (that is, more money).

Market capitalisation Market value of a company's outstanding shares. Price per ordinary share (or common stock unit) multiplied by the number of such shares in issue.

Mark-to-market (MTM) Under fair market value accounting, assets are valued on the basis of their current fair market price or other market indicators. Mark-to-market is this process of valuation.

Mark-to-model The valuation of an asset based on internal assumptions or estimates based on a financial model rather than current market prices.

Market risk (systemic risk) Risk that cannot be diversified away.

Maturity The date on which the principal of a bond must be repaid according to the bond contract.

Maturity structure The expression used to describe the borrower's repayment obligation. The term may be used either in relation to a specific loan or to describe the composite repayment obligation arising from a company's total portfolio of obligations.

MBS See Mortgage-backed securities.

Medium term In bond markets, bonds with initial maturities of between three and seven years. In money markets, maturities of more than one year.

Merchant bank An old-fashioned UK term for an investment bank.

Million One thousand thousand.

Monetary policy The actions of a government or central bank or other authority to influence the money supply and interest rates.

Money markets The different markets where money is borrowed and loaned short term, for periods of up to one year.

Monoline An insurance company that specialises in insuring financial securities, such as municipal bonds or structured credits.

Moody's A credit rating agency.

Moral hazard The situation that arises when a person or institution is totally insulated from risk and, consequently, has no incentive to prevent such a risk.

Moral obligation A strong obligation, though not legally binding, such as the moral obligation of the US government to rescue Fannie Mae and Freddie Mac.

Mortgage Loan secured on property.

Mortgage-backed securities (MBS) Securities supported by the cash flows from pools of mortgages.

Mortgage prepayment Making payments on a mortgage before they are due.

Mortgagee The mortgage lender. That is the party that holds the mortgaged property as security for the mortgage loan.

Mortgagor The mortgage borrower. That is the party that mortgages the property to secure a mortgage loan.

MTM See Mark-to-market.

Mutual fund A pooled vehicle, run by investment managers, that invests collected funds from savers in securities such as stocks, bonds, or money market instruments.

Nationalisation When a national government buys out or otherwise eliminates all shareholders of a company and assumes total ownership.

Negative amortization loan A loan whose monthly payments do not cover the interest due on the loan. The interest shortfall is added to the loan's principal.

Negative equity Where the amount owed under a mortgage or other loan outstanding exceeds the current market value of the property forming the security.

Nemesis In Greek mythology, the goddess of retribution and vengeance. Without a capital letter, any agency of retribution and vengeance.

Net position The overall position given by subtracting short positions (liabilities) from long positions (assets).

NIMBY Not in my back yard.

NINJA See NINJA loan.

NINJA loan A mortgage where the borrower is someone with No Income, No Job, No Assets.

Nominal value   See Face value.

Nonagency mortgage-backed security Mortgage-backed security underwritten or guaranteed by financial institutions other than government sponsored enterprises.

Nonbank lenders Providers of credit that are not banks, for example, some credit card companies, some mortgage lenders and so on.

Non-performing loan A bank loan where the borrower has stopped paying interest and is therefore in default.

Non-recourse loan Loan under which the borrower has no personal liability for unpaid amounts. So, if the loan defaults, the borrower's loss is limited to the equity in the relevant asset, for example a house.

Normal distribution curve A curve in which the first standard deviation includes 68.2 per cent of its area and the first two standard deviations include 95.4 per cent of its area and it has a bell shape (aka bell curve).

OECD See Organisation for Economic Co-operation and Development.

Off-balance sheet Assets and liabilities held by firm X via a separate legal vehicle whose assets and liabilities do not appear on the balance sheet of firm X.

Office of the Comptroller of the Currency (OCC) Charters, regulates and examines all national banks in the USA.

Office of Federal Housing Enterprise (OFHEO) The Federal housing finance agency of the USA. It was the regulator of Fannie Mae and Freddie Mac.

Office of Thrift Supervision (OTS) The OTS charters, regulates and examines thrift organisations in the USA.

Official reserves Holdings of gold and foreign currencies by the official monetary institutions of a country.

Open Market Operations Process by which central bank buys or sells government securities from or to others (usually banks or financial institutions) in order to affect money supply.

Opportunity cost The rate of return on the best alternative investment available, or the highest return that will be foregone if funds are invested in a particular project or security.

Option A contract providing the holder with the right but not the obligation either to buy from or sell to the counterparty a given number of securities at a specified price at or over a specified time.

Option premium The price paid to the seller of an option contract for the rights involved. The price is usually paid up-front.

Organisation for Economic Co-operation and Development (OECD) An organisation that provides inter-governmental discussion in the fields of economic and social policy. It collects and publishes data and makes short-term economic forecasts about its member countries.

Originate To issue a mortgage or other type of loan.

Originate-to-distribute Issuing or making a mortgage or loan with the intent of selling it on to another party (aka originate to sell).

Originate-to-hold Issuing or making a mortgage or loan with the intent of holding it to maturity.

Originate-to-sell See Originate-to-distribute.

OTC See Over-the-counter derivatives.

Out-of-the-money A call option when its strike price is greater than the current price of the underlying security. It also applies to a put option when its strike price is less than the current price of the underlying security. In other words, the option has no intrinsic value.

Over-the-counter derivatives (OTC) Derivatives whose terms are privately negotiated, or made to measure, rather than standardised. OTC derivatives do not trade on established exchanges.

Parity The official rate of exchange between two currencies.

Permanent impairment A permanent reduction in the fair market value of an asset.

Plain vanilla An issue of securities that lacks any special features. It is just the basics.

Policy rate The target for short-term interest rates set by a country's government or central bank.

Ponzi Scheme Fraudulent investment scheme, where apparent returns to early investors are financed, partly or wholly, by new monies subscribed by later investors. Named after US swindler Carlo Ponzi.

PPP See Purchasing power parity.

Preferred stock A form of capital that pays a fixed dividend each year, as opposed to common (or ordinary) shares for which the directors use discretion about whether to pay dividends and at what rate.

President's Working Group on Financial Markets (PWG) The PWG co-ordinates USA policies in the financial area. Headed by the Treasury Secretary, its members include the Chairman of the Fed, Chairman of the SEC, and the Chairman of the CFTC.

Prime loan Loan to high-quality borrower. In mortgage market this, broadly, means a borrower with a FICO score above 620 or 640.

Prime mortgage A high-quality mortgage that meets the credit, documentation, and other standards set by Fannie Mae and Freddie Mac.

Prime rate A US banking term to indicate the rate at which banks are prepared to lend to borrowers of the highest standing.

Private equity fund A pooled investment vehicle that buys control, or substantial amounts, of companies in an effort to increase their value and sell them on at a higher price.

Protectionism Policy of tariffs or other protection against import of goods from abroad.

Purchasing power parity (PPP) The hypothesis that, over time, the difference between the inflation rates in two countries tends to equal exchange rate changes between the currencies of the countries concerned. Does not work in the short term. Tends to be a long-run phenomenon. It is used to estimate equilibrium exchange rates.

Put option A contract giving the holder the right, but not the obligation, to sell a specified amount of an underlying asset at a specified price within a specified time. If the writer of the put option is not hedged, the writer can lose the whole amount of the option.

QE See Quantitative easing.

Quantitative easing (QE) An open market operation in which a central bank buys securities from or loans money to banks. The aim is to increase money supply and stimulate lending and spending in the economy. Expression coined in Britain following the financial crisis of 2007/8.

Random walk A term implying that there is no discernible pattern of travel. The last step, or even all the previous steps, cannot be used to predict either the size or the direction of the next step.

Rational expectations A concept implying that the market forms expectations in a way that is consistent with the actual economics and structure of the market. The prices that result in the market place represent an average of all investors' expectations.

Real effective exchange rate A rate calculated by adjusting the home country's actual nominal effective exchange rate by an index of the ratio of average foreign prices to home prices. If purchasing power parity is holding, the real effective exchange rate would remain constant.

Real exchange rate The value of a currency in terms of real purchasing power. It is calculated by comparing the price of a hypothetical market basket of goods in two different countries, translated into the same currency at the prevailing exchange rate. It is useful in measuring the price competitiveness of domestic goods in international markets.

Real return The rate of return of an asset after adjusting for inflation.

Recapitalisation A change in the mixture of a company's debt and/or equity with the intent of making the company stronger and more stable.

Receivership A type of company bankruptcy in which a third party, the receiver, is appointed by a court or by creditors to run the company and reorganise it for the benefit of creditors.

Recession A fall in real gross domestic product for two successive quarters.

Repo See Repurchase agreement.

Repurchase agreement (repo) A form of short-term borrowing in which institutions sell securities to investors or to one another and buy them back, usually the following day, at predetermined prices basically reflecting prevailing interest rates.

Reserve requirements or reserve asset ratio The amount, usually expressed as a percentage, of different types of deposit or eligible asset which banks must hold with their central bank.

Resolution Trust Corporation (RTC) The RTC was a USA government-owned asset management company for liquidating assets of insolvent savings and loan associations (S&Ls).

Revaluation An increase in the spot value of a currency (UK parlance). A change – either an increase or a decrease – in the spot value of a currency (US parlance).

Rights issue A new issue of shares in a company to existing shareholders and to be subscribed, in cash, to raise equity capital. Shareholders who do not wish to take up their rights to subscribe cash for the new shares can sell the right to them in the market. If the shareholder neither takes up the rights nor sells them in the market, the company will do this on the shareholder's behalf and give the proceeds to the shareholder.

Risk Chance of possible loss where future outcomes can be estimated. Contrast with uncertainty.

Risk premium Expected additional return for making a risky investment rather than a safe one.

Risk-weighted assets (RWA) A bank's assets weighted according to perceived credit risk. Thus, corporate loans would have a higher risk rating than government securities.

Run on the bank A large number of bank depositors withdraw their funds simultaneously and the bank's resources cannot cover the withdrawals.

RWA See Risk-weighted assets

S&P 500 See Standard and Poor's 500 Index.

Sarbanes-Oxley Act of 2002 (SOX) A statute passed after the Enron and Worldcom failures, which increases standards of corporate governance, in such areas as internal controls and financial statements.

Savings and Loan Association (S&L) A depository institution, also called a thrift, which specialises in taking deposits, making mortgages and real estate loans in the USA.

SEC 10-K The 10-K report is an annual report which the SEC requires from companies issuing securities in the USA.

Secondary market Market for securities in which investors can deal securities on a 'second-hand basis'.

Securitisation The process under which cash flows from assets are packaged into securities and sold on to investors. Packaging assets and liabilities such that they can be sold and traded in markets allows the financial institution that originates a loan – a mortgage, an auto loan, etc. – to sell it on to other investors, thus freeing its capital for alternative uses.

Securities and Exchange Commission (SEC) An agency in the USA responsible for enforcing the federal law on securities, regulating the securities industry and protecting investors.

Short A UK government bond with a maturity of less than five years.

Short position Selling shares, borrowed rather than owned, with the expectation that the share price will fall and the borrower of shares will be able to buy them back and make a profit. The sale of non-owned shares creates the short position.

Short selling Borrowing shares and selling them now with the expectation of a fall in price enabling them to be bought back at a lower price to create a profit.

Short term In bond markets, bonds with initial maturities of less than two years. In company balance sheets, debt with a remaining maturity of less than a year.

Sight deposits Current accounts, overnight deposits and money at call. Deposits with longer maturities are term deposits.

SIV See Structured investment vehicle.

S&L See Savings and Loan Association.

Solvency ratio The ratio of a bank's assets to its liabilities, used to assess its ability to meet its obligations. The higher the ratio, the sounder the bank.

Sovereign debt The loans outstanding in respect of individual countries, usually negotiated by their governments.

Sovereign risk The risk of government default on a loan made or guaranteed by it.

SOX See Sarbanes-Oxley Act of 2002.

Special purpose entity (SPE) A separate legal and accounting entity from the bank or company sponsoring it, usually created for a particular investment purpose, but which is moved off the balance sheet of the bank or company sponsoring it.

Special-Purpose Vehicle (SPV) A legal entity set up as a device to acquire and hold assets off its balance sheet, usually prior to selling them to third parties. Putting the assets into the SPV takes them off the balance sheet of the selling entity. Used to window-dress the accounts – especially by investment banks prior to and during the crisis. Also widely used by Enron.

Specific risk Another name for unsystemic risk.

Spread The difference between two prices or rates, such as the bid and offer prices of a security (aka bid-ask spread). It is also used to refer to the yields of two bonds of differing credit quality when the term credit spread is used.

SPV See Special purpose vehicle.

Standard and Poor's A credit rating agency.

Standard and Poor's 500 Index (S&P 500) An index of 500 US stocks. Its movement reflects the general level of stock prices of large publicly traded US companies.

Standard deviation The positive square root of the variance. This is the standard statistical measure of the spread of a sample.

Stock warrants Right to purchase a specified number of shares at a specific price within a specified time frame.

Strike price The price at which an option may be exercised (aka exercise price).

Structured finance A method used to transfer risk through the use of complex techniques, structures and separate entities. Embraces the securitisation of mortgages and credit card debt.

Structured investment vehicle (SIV) An off balance sheet vehicle usually established by a bank, often in a tax haven, to hold and/or have passed through it asset-backed and mortgage-backed securities. Their losses would technically not be borne by the banks setting them up – but in practice, in the crisis, they were for the banks' account.

Subordinated debt Corporate debt that ranks below all other debt with regard to claims on company earnings and claims on assets in bankruptcy.

Subprime mortgage A mortgage made to a borrower who does not qualify as being sufficiently credit-worthy enough to qualify for a prime mortgage and who, consequently, pays a higher interest rate.

Systemic risk Risk posed to the entire financial system by the possible collapse of an interconnected financial institution, or a particular financial product, for example credit default swaps.

Systematic risk The volatility of rates of return on stocks or portfolios in relation to changes in rates of return on the whole market. Also known as market risk, it stems from such non-diversifiable factors as war, inflation, recessions and high interest rates. These factors affect all firms simultaneously; hence this type of risk cannot be eliminated by diversification. See also Beta.

TAF See Term auction facility (USA).

TARP See Troubled Asset Relief Programme (USA).

Tariffs Taxes imposed by a country on goods imported into it.

Tax haven A country or state that imposes little or no tax on companies or individuals residing there or doing business there.

Teaser rates Low initial rate of interest on a loan, which lasts for a short period, maybe two years, then rises sharply.

Term auction facility (TAF) A USA term for the Fed's auction of term funds to depository institutions with the intention of addressing elevated pressures in short-term funding markets.

Term deposits Deposits, including certificates of deposit, for terms longer than sight deposits. See sight deposits.

Term loan or credit A bank advance that is for a specified period of time.

Term structure An explanation of the framework for establishing money-market interest rates based upon cash flows and maturity or holding periods.

Tier 1 Capital Ratio Requirement for capital adequacy under the Basel Accords. The ratio between a bank's capital and its risk-adjusted assets.

Thin A market with low trading volumes and poor liquidity.

Thrift A depository institution, also called a savings and loan association, which specialises in taking deposits, offering home mortgages or other real-estate loans.

Time value The value of an option taken as the difference between the premium and the intrinsic value. Time value decreases as the expiry date comes nearer.

Toxic asset The term is best illustrated by an example using a credit default swap. With no default or only a low probability of default, a CDS might have a positive value of, say, 100 based on the expected income stream from insurance-like premiums. But with defaults looming, the worth of the CDS could alter and acquire a negative value as the probability of having to pay out under the CDS exceeds the probability of receiving inflows (the insurance premiums). The asset, previously worth 100 in this example, may become a liability worth minus 500. The description toxic asset, also known as toxic debt, is truly justified.

Toxic debt See toxic asset.

Traded option An option that is itself tradable on a securities market.

Tranche One of several levels to a security with different risk/reward characteristics for each level.

Treasury bill or T-bill A UK or US government short-term debt instrument normally issued at a discount.

Treasury bond A long-term government bond.

Treasury note A US government coupon security with a maturity of not less than one year and not more than ten years.

Trillion One thousand billion.

Troubled Asset Relief Program (TARP) A US government programme to purchase assets and equity from distressed financial institutions in order to strengthen the financial firm concerned.

Umbrella regulator A regulator in charge of an entire sector of the economy, or comprising all regulators of that sector.

Uncertainty Lack of knowledge about the future such that probabilities cannot rationally be estimated. Differs from risk where probabilities can be estimated.

Underlying asset The asset on which an option or warrant is based.

Undervalued A security (also a market) whose price is considered to be lower than that indicated by fundamental analysis.

Underwater mortgage A mortgage in which the outstanding mortgage balance due exceeds the current market value of the property securing the mortgage.

Underwrite Undertake to buy unsubscribed securities on a given date at a particular price, thus guaranteeing the full proceeds to the borrower.

Unique risk (residual risk, specific risk, unsystematic risk) Risk that cannot be eliminated by diversification.

Unsecured bond Bond that entitles the holder to no recourse to specific assets in the case of default.

Unsystematic risk That part of a security's risk associated with random events which do not affect the economy as a whole. Also known as specific risk, this refers to such things as strikes, successful and unsuccessful marketing programmes, fire and other events that are unique to a particular firm. Such unsystematic events can be eliminated by portfolio diversification.

Value at risk (VAR) A single number estimate of how much a bank, financial institution or company can lose due to the price volatility of the assets it holds, for example, a fixed rate bond or an unhedged currency payable/receivable. More precisely, it defines the likelihood of potential loss not exceeding a particular level, given certain assumptions.

VAR See value at risk.

Variance of the probability distribution The expected value of the squared deviation from the expected return.

Volatility The variability of movements in a security's price.

Window A time during which certain deals can occur because of particular market conditions. For example, it may be possible to issue certain types of security **because** of ruling investor sentiment that is not expected to last.

Window dressing An accounting device used to make financial ratios look better. For example assume a firm with assets of 100, debt of 60 and equity of 40. Its debt to equity ratio is 60 to 40, that is, 1.5. If, just before the year-end, the firm uses some assets temporarily to repay debt but to reverse the transaction immediately following the year end, its debt to equity ratio at the year-end falls. Assume the amounts involved in the window dressing are 30 of assets and 30 of debt, then the year-end figures are assets amounting to 70 financed by debt of 30 and equity of 40. The debt to equity ratio has now fallen and is 30 to 40, that is, 0.75. The ratio has been cut in half. An apparently much more respectable ratio – but really just smoke and mirrors.

World Trade Organisation (WTO) The WTO is an international organisation that sets and enforces rules designed to facilitate cross-border transactions in goods and services.

Yield The amount of interest payments as a percentage of the amount lent or borrowed.

Zero-sum game A game, or market, in which the sum of the gains made by winning players is equal to the sum of the losses of losing players.

Index